The Dominica Story
A HISTORY OF THE ISLAND

Lennox Honychurch

All maps and drawings by the author

© Copyright text Lennox Honychurch 1995
© Copyright illustrations Lenox Honychurch 1995

All rights reserved. No reproduction, copy or transmission of this publication may be made without written permission

No paragraph of this publication may be reproduced, copied or transmitted save with written permission or in accordance with the provisions of the Copyright, Designs and Patents Act 1988, or under the terms of any licence permitting limited copying issued by the Copyright Licensing Agency,
90 Tottenham Court Road, London W1P 9HE.

Any person who does any unauthorised act in relation to this publication may be liable to criminal prosecution and civil claims for damages.

First edition 1975
Reprinted once
This edition 1995
Published by
MACMILLAN EDUCATION LTD
London and Basingstoke
Associated companies and representatives in Accra, Banjul, Cairo, Dar es Salaam, Delhi, Freetown, Gaborone, Harare,Hong Kong, Johannesburg, Kampala, Lagos, Lahore, Lusaka, Mexico City, Nairobi, São Paulo, Tokyo

ISBN 0–333–62776–8

10	9	8	7	6	5	4	3	2	
05	04	03	02	01	00	99	98	97	96

Printed in Hong Kong

A catalogue record for this book is available from the British Library.

Cover illustration courtesy of the National Maritime Museum, London

Other publications by the author:

GREEN TRIANGLES – Poetry – 1979

THE CARIBBEAN PEOPLE – Three volume history
Published by Thomas Nelson Ltd, England, 1979, 1980, 1981

OUR ISLAND CULTURE
Published by the National Cultural Council, 1982
Revised 1988

THE CABRITS AND PRINCE RUPERT'S BAY
Published by Dominica Conservation Association, 1982
Republished by The Dominica Institute, 1983

CARIBBEAN LANDMARKS
Published by Thomas Nelson Ltd, England, 1986

DOMINICA: ISLE OF ADVENTURE
Published by The Macmillan Press, 1991
Revised 1995

Contents

	Foreword	iv
	Acknowledgements	vii
	Introduction	ix
	Map of Dominica	x
1	An Island of Fire	1
2	The First Settlers	11
3	The Kalinago – The 'Island Carib'	20
4	Columbus and Spain	30
5	Land of Two Nations	40
6	France Moves in	49
7	The British in Dominica	61
8	The Plantation	72
9	The French Return	83
10	The Fighting Maroons	91
11	Revolution and Ransom	100
12	The Last Maroon War	116
13	Peace and Freedom	122
14	The Years of Change	127
15	An Unsettled Society	135
16	New Men, New Energy	145
17	Between Two Wars	156
18	The Church	173
19	Development and Welfare	185
20	After God, The Land	206
21	Statehood	226
22	Towards Independence	253
23	A Stormy Path	261
24	Inventing a Nation	286
	Bibliography	307
	Index	315

Foreword

This book is for all Dominicans. It comes at a time which demands firm questioning and self examination, a time when we must know, understand and come to terms with our history. There are many people in our midst who urge us away from contemplating on our past experiences. But we cannot create a new society unless we know where we have come from. It is ironic that at such a stage in our development few Dominicans have had the chance to grasp even the general outline of their history. And it is probably this scarcity of material which has led to the generalisations and misunderstandings which are spread by politicians and educators, and which has in turn created misconceptions, a lack of concern and even a lack of pride among our island people.

Dominica is unique, not only for its towering mountains and physical rarities but historically as well. Although it may follow the basic pattern of West Indian history there are important features which have always made the island stand apart from the others in the Caribbean chain.

This work was first presented as a dramatised radio series tracing the origin and development of the island up to the attainment of Associated Statehood in 1967. The reader will find history interwoven with geography, flora, fauna, folklore and social habits. The original radio script has been rewritten and the episodes have been grouped into chapters while many of the excerpts and quotes from the radio version have been included.

In this new edition there is additional information and more illustrations in some of the later chapters. The most difficult task perhaps was working on the period of the 1970s and 80s, turbulent years so close that at times I had to imagine myself catapulted fifty years forward so as to look back in an attempt to assess the period as dispassionately as possible.

Simplification of historical fact is always a precarious business and I have gathered my material from wherever possible: primary, secondary and oral sources, and I trust that the historical part of it at least will stand up to critical scrutiny. This work, it is true, is a result of my own observation and research but I am indebted to a number of persons for their interest and assistance who are individually acknowledged in a special section at the end of this section.

I have been deeply touched by the kindness and encouragement which I have received from fellow Dominicans of all walks of life and from all parts of the island who have helped to produce a book which I hope is not unworthy of the spirit of this complex little island.

LEH

In Memory of
my grandmother
Elma Napier
whose life shall forever
be an inspiration to me.

'Love for an island is the sternest passion
pulsing beyond the blood through roots and loam
it overflows the boundary of bedrooms
and courses past the fragile walls of home.'

Phyllis Shand Allfrey

Acknowledgements

The first edition
When originally preparing this work in the years before its first publication in 1975, I received assistance and guidance from a number of persons. Among them were my mother and father; Rita Riviere and her staff at the Roseau Public Library; Rev Fr Raymond Proesmans, CSsR, whose extensive work on the 17th and 18th centuries gave a firm background to my research; Robert and Phyllis Allfrey whose kindness and historical and literary criticism helped immensely; Havis Shillingford, EC Loblack, Eugenia Nicholls, Sylvester Joseph, Randall Lockhart and Marie Davis-Pierre. The staff of DAWU, and CSA also assisted on various topics. Gloria Bardouille, Penny Honychurch, Carol Bunting and 'Mena' Boyd gave invaluable assistance preparing the manuscript; Curtis Henry and Peter Green helped with the photographs. I also owe a debt of gratitude to Barnet Defoe and the staff of Radio Dominica for their help with the original broadcasts back in 1974.

The second edition
In Barbados I am grateful for the support and encouragement of Susan Walcott, my aunt Ellice Collymore, Jill Sheppard of CCA and Alissandra Cummins of the Barbados Museum. Thanks also to John Shearn of Letchworth Press for his advice and personal interest; Sonya Lawrence and Jean Morgan of Secretarial Services Ltd for their combination of advice and typing services; Dr and Mrs Renee Charles, Mark Hunte.

In England I am grateful for the continued assistance of the staff of the Royal Commonwealth Society Library and the Public Records Office at Kew. As always, I am grateful to David Hamilton, 'Pepper' and Mark Varvill, Michael and Josette Napier, the Gordon-Cummings at Oxford and Freya Watkinson. I have been very much influenced by Desmond Nicholson of Antigua. Clinton Black of the Jamaica Archives sent useful material.

In Dominica I am grateful to: Cornelia Williams and the staff of the Roseau Library for their ever-ready assistance; Dorothy Griffin; Daniel Green for the use of his Library, old photo negatives and donation of books; Clem Dupigny for his old newspapers; John Gallagher for all he found in Paris; Fred Joslyn of the Dominica Social Security; John Archbold for use of the soldier's diary; M Eugenia Charles for the use of her personal files and documents; Alwyn Bully and the staff of the Cultural Division; The GIS staff; Lennox Linton, Solange Bellot and the staff of the New Chronicle; the Agars; Phyllis Garraway for her very varied contributions; my mother Patricia and sister Sara for so many things and to all those hundreds of people who in their homes, gardens, rumshops, on the seashore, along roadways and at village feastdays, continue to open their hearts and minds with a flow of knowledge which has spread itself across the pages of this book.

The third edition
In this edition I have completely revised the chapters on pre-Columbian Dominica. This is as a result of new material and recent theoretical revisions in Caribbean archaeology as well as new insights on the subject which I gained during research at Oxford. For this I am indebted to my supervisor Dr Donald Tayler and my other tutors in the Department of Anthropology and Geography at Oxford University. I am also grateful to Polly Pattullo for her assistance with my research on the new final chapter. At Macmillans, I wish to thank Bill Lennox and Michael Bourne for their interest and support for this project.

Photographic Acknowledgements
My picture research for the increase of illustrations was made possible by the assistance of the following institutions and persons in providing the prints, photographs, negatives, copies, postcards and documents reproduced herein: Photo One; Depex Ltd; the Government Information Service; The Bajan Magazine; The New Chronicle; Public Records Office, Kew; National Maritime Museum, Greenwich; Roseau Public Library; Dominica Trade Union; Michael Wright, World Wildlife Fund; M Eugenia Charles; Gerry Aird; Penny Hynam; J Bernard Yankey; The Allfreys; Daniel Green; J Ralph Casimir; Desmond Nicholson; Michael Napier; Patricia Honychurch; John Gallagher; Dr David Clyde; Phyllis Garraway; Elliot Anthony; Emmanuel Joseph. Cover photograph courtesy of National Maritime Museum, London.

Introduction

Dominica is the most mountainous island in the Caribbean. Twenty-nine miles long and sixteen miles wide, it lies between the French islands of Martinique to the south and Guadeloupe to the north. The island rises in places sheer out of the sea, towering in a series of jumbled peaks to a height of almost 5,000 feet. This rugged landscape of blue-green slopes, rushing streams and cloud drenched mountain peaks has given the island a legendary beauty, a fatal gift some call it, which has created both major problems and great advantages for those who have lived here. More than most islands, the environment has guided the course of Dominica's history.

The steep mountains, rising above many of the other peaks which make up the chain of the Antilles, brought rain and with it thickly forested slopes and well watered valleys. This environment gave the early Caribs a natural fortress against the European settlers and kept Dominica uncolonised for a longer period than other islands. It prevented the development of very large estates and cut down on the profits of sugar and coffee. The forests gave the Maroons protection from slavery and later provided the freed slaves with land to begin a peasant society. Well into the twentieth century, the terrain made communications difficult and hindered development: Dominica's story is not only of battles between men, but even more so, the battle between man and the island itself.

1
An Island of Fire

Dominica lies almost in the centre of the arc of islands known as the Lesser Antilles. This arc extends from the Trinidad-Grenada Passage in the south up to the Anegada Passage between the Virgin Islands and Anguilla. These islands of the Lesser Antilles are of volcanic origin. They have rugged mountains in the central areas and narrow coastal shelves and valleys. On the more mountainous islands, south of Montserrat, numerous streams flow from the rain-drenched central highlands. The formation of these islands began millions of years ago along a section of the sea bed where two of the several tectonic plates which make up the crust of the planet collide. There were no islands as we know them today and the land mass of South America extended much further north than at present and included all of the island of Trinidad.

During the Miocene period, 26 million years ago, Dominica and her sister islands were beginning to take shape. The sea bed in this area was already covered in thick layers of sediment which had been washed down by the rivers of South America from the lands which now make up the Guianas, Venezuela and Colombia. Beneath this sediment, pressure was building up in the earth's crust as the thick tectonic plates pushed and ground against each other, moving like heavy rafts upon the hot soft mantle heated by the fiery core at the centre of the earth.

Our planet's solid surface is a restless jigsaw of these abutting, diverging and colliding slabs called tectonic plates. Two of these plates meet along the curved line where our islands now stand. To the eastern side is the Atlantic or South American Plate beneath the Atlantic Ocean which is being pushed westward. Our islands sit on the edge of the Caribbean Plate which is being pushed eastward. As these two plates collide into each other from opposite directions, the Atlantic Plate has been forced under the edge of the Caribbean Plate. We are therefore sitting on top of what geologists and geophysicists call a subduction zone.

As the subducted ocean crust of the Atlantic Plate descends beneath the Caribbean Plate, its load of low density sediment spread on the sea bed is largely scraped off and deformed. The subducted plate is pushing its relatively cool crust material into the hot mantle rock beneath. The friction of its passage generates earthquakes.

The deeper it sinks, the hotter the melting plate becomes until it is completely broken up. Being less dense than the surrounding mantle, the molten matter from the subducted remnants of the Atlantic Plate shoots upwards. It has now become hot molten volcanic rock, melting holes through the weak edge of the Caribbean Plate which lies above, erupting with volcanic force out onto the surface. Together with the scraped-off sediments this process builds island arcs: rows of volcanic islands occurring in a curve.

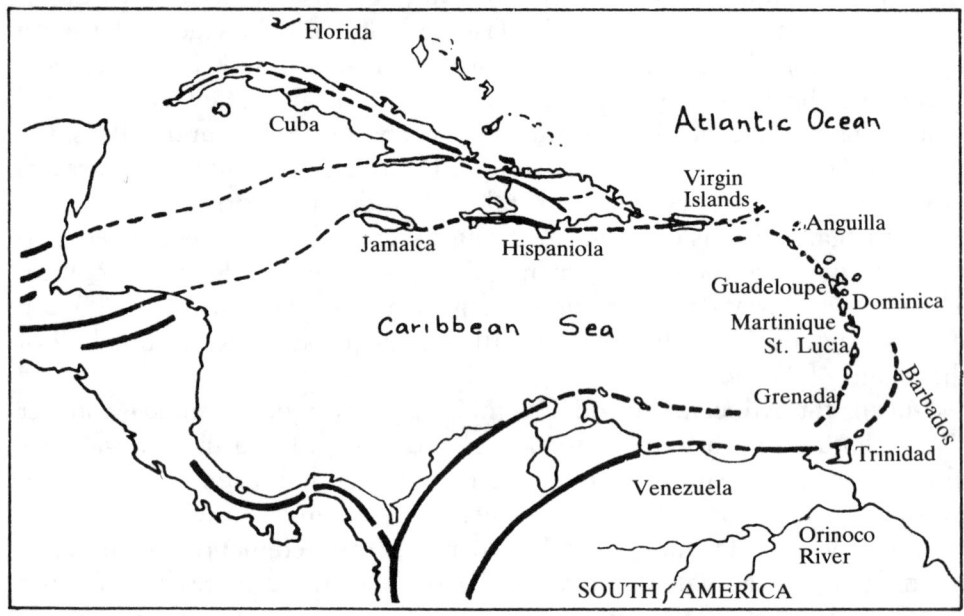

Mountain ranges of the Caribbean.

The Lesser Antilles is really made up of two arcs lying almost parallel to one another. The outer arc is older. The inner arc, of which Dominica is a part, is younger, ie of more recent formation. Being older, the outer arc of islands has had more time to be eroded and worn down. They are also flatter and drier. Erosion has made the surrounding water more shallow. Coral reefs developed and created white sand beaches. These older islands of the outer arc are: Anguilla, St Martin, St Barts, Barbuda, Antigua, the eastern wing of Guadeloupe and the island of Mariegalante. Geological evidence of the outer arc also appears in the southern tip of Martinique, the northern coast and southern tip of St Lucia, the Grenadines and the southern tip of Grenada. Dominica, by contrast is totally part of the younger inner arc. The evidence of its recent origin can be seen in its dormant volcanoes, peaceful crater lakes, fumeroles at the Valley of Desolation, the Boiling Lake, Wotton Waven, Soufriere and the many hot water springs dotted around the island. Similar examples of continued activity can be found in St Vincent, St Lucia, Martinique, Basse Terre – Guadeloupe and Montserrat. The more placid islands of the inner arc are Redonda, Nevis, St Kitts, St Eustatius and Saba.

But even within Dominica, certain parts of the island are older than others. The mountain range along the east coast from Atkinson to Rosalie, for instance, is much older than the more recent eruptions in the Morne Micotrin area and at Morne Patate at Soufriere. The shape of the island was constantly changing as the volcanic peaks rose above the surface of the ocean and their steep rocky cones were eroded by wind, rain and the action of the sea. At the same time there was a continual piling up of ash and lava from later volcanoes. This action created noticeable layers of rock of different colours and consistency which are known as strata. These can be clearly seen along the face of cliffs or where roads have been cut into mountainsides. The stony aggregate which we call 'tarrish' and which is used as a foundation for our roads is actually the remains of debris which was ejected from erupting volcanoes.

For a time, millions of years ago, the west coast of Dominica was tilted sideways beneath the surface of the sea and was then shifted into its present

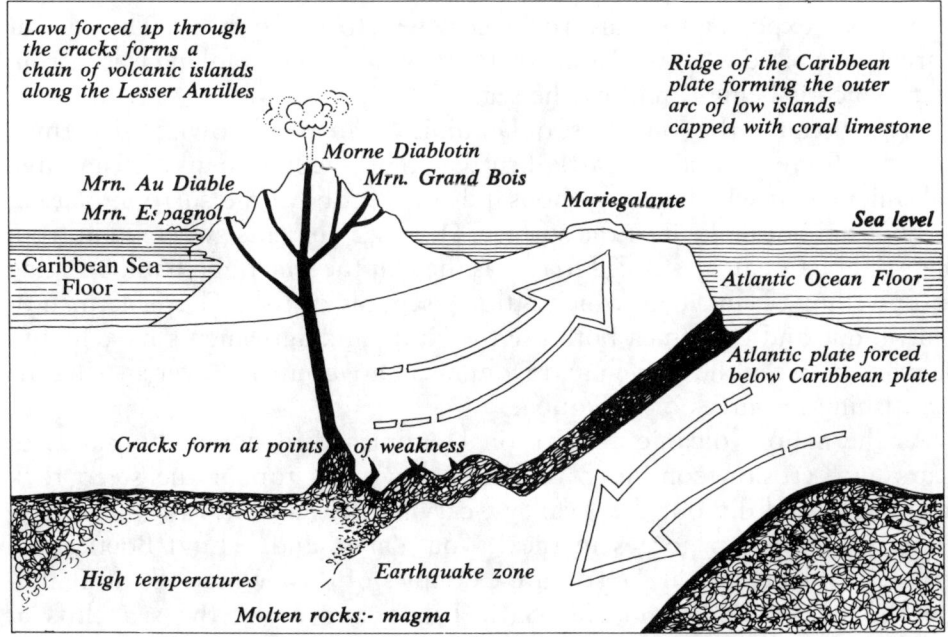

A simplified diagram showing the formation of the northern section of Dominica in relation to the movement of the Caribbean and Atlantic Plates of the earth's crust below the Lesser Antilles.

position so that today areas of coral, sea shells, gravel and limestone can be seen along the cliffs at Canefield, Tarreau, Guel Lion and near Colihaut where sizeable deposits of compacted coral limestone can be found in the area of Bouleau. This was deposited on top of the volcanic cliffs at a time when they lay beneath the surface of the sea.

The central backbone of Dominica is made up of rounded peaks of dormant volcanoes which follow the same line as the arc of the island chain, lined up upon the edge of that tectonic plate. Looking at the island from south to north we see several volcanic centres, the more recent piled up against those that are far more ancient: Perdu Temps, Morne Watt, Micotrin, Trois Pitons (4,672 ft), Diablotin (4,747 ft), the highest of them all, and Morne Aux Diables at the extreme north. Although these areas have been quiet for some 10,000 years, recent studies have shown that at least four of them can still become violently active. As recently as 1974 tremors originating from beneath Morne Micotrin and brief surface activity at Soufriere in 1994 gave cause for concern.

On the sea bed near to the island some submarine eruptions did not last long enough to break the surface of the ocean. They remain today as submerged volcanic pinnacles covered in coral growth and the more accessible of them, such as one near Scotts Head, is visited by scuba-divers. Scotts Head itself is an example of a small volcano which barely made it above the surface and then stopped erupting. The sea ate around three sides of the cone exposing the hard rocky core which we see today. The ancient Caribs recognised what was going on for they called the headland Cashacrou: 'that which is being eaten' by the sea.

In the ocean to the south-east of Dominica is an area known to fishermen from Soufriere around to Castle Bruce as the Macouba bank. It is a large volcanic massif which stands thousands of feet above the surrounding sea bed but did not make it to the surface. Deep sea currents sweeping in from the Atlantic Ocean are forced to rise as they hit the Macouba bank bringing an upwelling of nutrients which attracts schools of fish. The fishermen of Martinique and Dominica both use the bank, and agreements have had to be made between the French and Dominican governments over sharing the rich fishing resources of Macouba.

As the major volcanic activity on Dominica died down thousands of years ago, erosion continued to break down the top of the steep rock formations and dig out deep valleys, carving the land into the shapes we know today. Sharp gorges in the Layou Valley and behind Boetica, La Plaine, Dublanc, and at Ti Tou are examples of this. Waterfalls at Trafalgar, Victoria, Middleham, Sari-Sari, Taberi and along the sea cliffs at Boetica are just some of the sites where we can witness the continuous carving away of thick volcanic layers of rock. Landslides scar the mountains after heavy rains and raging floods tear away river banks and

Hikers peer over the edge of the crater into the steaming cauldron of the Boiling Lake. It last erupted in 1880.

pulverise rocks. We see it all in action today as it was in the beginning.

The loose earth which was formed settled in the bottom of the valleys along the coast creating the richest areas of soil, later to be occupied by the big plantations. Thinner layers clung to the tops of ridges and along mountainsides where the early peasantry was to establish itself. The rivers brought down alluvial deposits and worn boulders which formed flat fan-shaped ledges and coastal shelves where narrow valleys opened out onto the sea shore. Here future Dominicans would place their towns and villages. Powdered black volcanic sand ground from rocks by the action of waves and rivers created the majority of our beaches. Coral sand was only able to form along a small section of the north coast where conditions were right for wide bands of coral reefs to grow. The gently sloping shoreline was shallow enough and the small streams in the area between Woodford Hill and Calibishie did not bring down much sediment or fresh water and therefore allowed coral growth to prosper. Today, however, increased erosion from banana fields and the effects of agricultural chemicals are killing the reefs. New elements of geophysical change are making their mark.

Life

Even before the violent volcanic activity was over, plants were taking root in the rough soil. The charred remains of these early plants have been found embedded in layers of volcanic ash and some of them have proved to be over 45,000 years old. There are many theories on the way in which plants and animals came to Dominica and the islands of the Caribbean, but it is generally accepted that most of the early plant life originated from South America.

Dominica, lying roughly 15.5 degrees north of the Equator, is in the path of the south equatorial current. This flows from West Africa to South America where a branch of it mingles with the Orinoco River and then flows into the Caribbean waters.

Fruit and seeds which had remained fertile in spite of long ocean journeys were brought by the south equatorial current to the shores of the Antilles. It carried plants and even animals from the Guianas in South America. The seeds found floating in this ocean drift came from plants growing on beaches, in mangrove swamps and also from plants further inland which grew on the banks of the Orinoco and its tributaries. Around most seeds there is a dry husk which enables them to stay afloat for long periods. Even

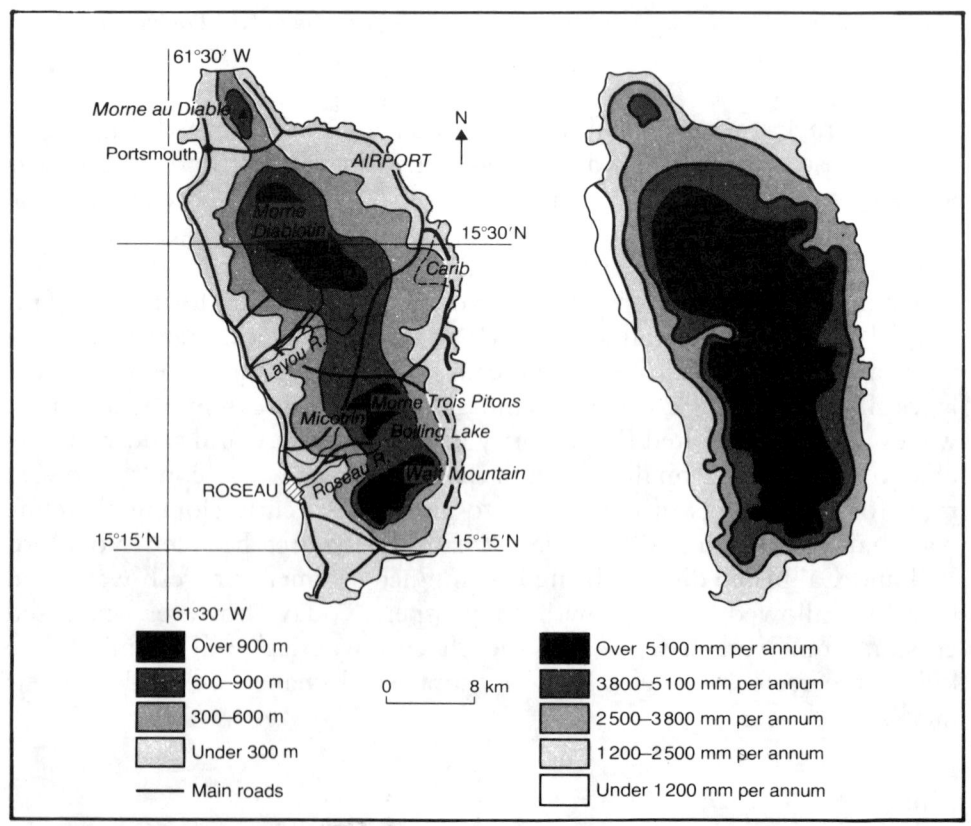

The relief and rainfall of Dominica.

An Island of Fire

after many months in the sea they are still able to germinate when washed up on fertile ground. Debris and driftwood are also capable of transporting the germs of plants along with them and once a plant has taken root on the seashore the seeds it produces are easily dispersed further inland. Birds also

Morne Micotrin (also known as Morne Macaque). An example of volcanic formation.

1 *Eruption creates a crater 1½ miles wide.*

2 *Development of a cone within the old crater.*

3 *A diagram of the mountain today with Dominica's two lakes caught in the bowl of the older crater.*

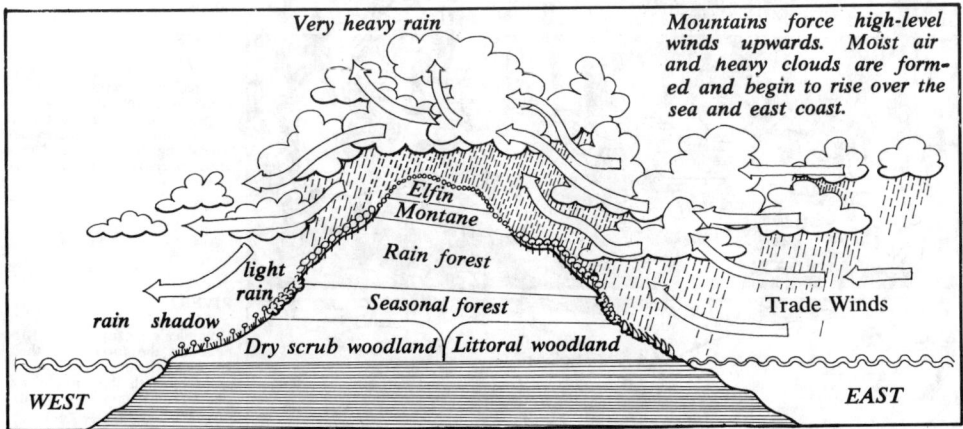

Diagram showing cross-section of the island and location of forest types in relation to altitude, rainfall, and wind patterns. The mountainous central range forces high level winds to rise long before they reach the land. Showers fall over the sea and windward coast as well as on the mountains themselves. On reaching the west or leeward coast the air has lost most of its moisture, resulting in a dry 'rain shadow' coastline.

EMERGENT LAYER

Lofty crowns of the tallest trees rise above the canopy, taking the most light, rain and wind. These giant trees such as the Gommier, provide flowers, fruit and safety for bees, parrots and smaller birds, notably the humming bird and Siffleur Montange.

CANOPY

Rain and sunlight filters through this cover some 100 feet above the forest floor. The top sides of the wettest branches are hanging gardens of orchids, bromeliads, ferns and other plants whose roots never touch the soil. Floor-based lianas climb to the canopy to get sunlight.

UNDERSTORY

Palms, tree ferns and thin trees stretch upwards in search of scarce sunlight. This is the most active layer for moths and thousands of other species of insects.

FLOOR

The dark humid forest floor is covered with seedlings starting their long journey upwards. Termites, fungus and bacteria feed on the layer of leaves decomposing on the ground creating nutrients for the trees above.

RIVER

Dominica's many rivers depend on the forests for their survival. Clean filtered water seeps beneath the forest floor into streams supporting a variety of fish and crustacea.

The tropical rain forest is the most varied and complex eco-system on Earth. With a delicately balanced micro-climate of its own, the rain forest of Dominica supports thousands of plant and insect species. It is among the last oceanic or island-based rain forests in the world.

carry seeds to the islands. Many varieties of birds migrated north and south along the Caribbean chain from the mainland continents. In their stomachs they carried seeds for great distances and eventually dropped them in the territories where they alighted or settled permanently.

Another strange example of seed dispersal occurred in recent times. Today there is a vine which grows all over Dominica and is called in patois 'volcan'. It was given this name because it had never been seen on the island before 1902 and it is believed that its seeds or roots were among the ashes which landed on Dominica during the 1902 eruption of the Mount Pelee volcano in Martinique. Many of the common fruit trees of the Caribbean did not arrive until men had settled on the islands. The mango, breadfruit and coconut, for instance, did not exist in the region before the coming of Columbus.

The introduction of animals is also a much debated topic. As we have seen, the movement of birds along the islands was easy, but for Dominica's other forms of wild life we turn once more to the system of currents and floating drift. It brought varied insect and reptile life including the five species of non-poisonous snakes, the largest of which is known locally as 'tete chien'. Though the two small mammals, the Agouti and Manicou, which inhabit Dominica's forest, originally came from the mainland, it is believed that they were brought later by man.

Dominica is 29 miles long and 16 miles at its widest point. Its land area is just under 300 square miles or 751 km^2. The high backbone of mountains which runs along the centre of Dominica from north to south, cuts straight across the path of the north-east trade winds sweeping in from the Atlantic Ocean. The average height of the mountainous central range is about 3,000 feet with three major massifs being much higher. This forces the high level winds to rise long before they reach the island. Moist air and heavy clouds are formed by this action over the sea and east coast, and rain showers fall along the windward side and most heavily on the central mountain peaks. By the time the air reaches the west or leeward coast it has lost most of its moisture, resulting in a dry 'rain shadow' coastline.

Sharp variations of temperature caused by altitude, also create different micro climates which, linked to the rainfall pattern, determine which species of plants will grow in which area. Rainfall figures in Dominica range from an average of 50 inches per annum, along the driest west coast stretch, to 300 inches in the central range. Although fair amounts of rain occur throughout the year, recent averages show February and March as the driest months and July as the wettest. The hottest month is June: 23°–32°C and the coolest is January: 20°–29°C.

All of these factors have combined to give us roughly six different types of forest. Along the east and north coasts we find the *windward littoral woodland*, including the *swamp forest*; on the west coast, the *dry scrub woodland*; going higher, we find the *seasonal or deciduous forest*; then between 500 and 2,000 feet on the east side and 1,000 and 2,000 feet on the west side we get into the *tropical rain forest*; higher still is the *cloud forest* which is made up of *montane forest* and around the peaks of the highest mountains the *elfin woodland*.

Six thousand years ago no human being had yet discovered Dominica. Forests grew luxuriantly down to the water's edge. The rivers abounded in fish and eels, and across the silent valleys flew birds of many kinds. After millions of years of formation the island was at peace but its recorded history had not yet begun. From the coast of South America that had brought the island its wildlife and vegetation, there was to come a new creature: Man, the first Dominican.

2
The First Settlers

The first human beings to set foot on the shores of Dominica came by the sea along the island chain from the region of the Orinoco River delta on the coast of South America. Recent research indicates that they set out on their journey 5,000 years before the birth of Christ. There is proof that people were living on neighbouring islands in 3,100 BC and others may have been here even earlier. But who they were, what they called themselves and exactly how they lived we will probably never know.

Up until quite recently there was a simple theory given to explain the groups of people who lived on these islands before the Europeans arrived in 1493. First came the Ciboney or 'stone people', then came the 'peaceful Arawaks' who were followed and killed off by the 'warlike Caribs'. Because there was no other general information on the matter, this was the theory we were taught and which was repeated well up to the end of the twentieth century.

To understand how these indigenous people lived, we depended on the accounts printed by European explorers and missionaries dating from the sixteenth and seventeenth centuries. Their opinions were republished by others verbatim over the last three hundred years and were used as the basis for educational material up to the present time.

The original texts were often biased and had to be carefully assessed for obvious inaccuracies. But apart from some general archaeological information, there were few other sources for historians to work with when locally produced Caribbean text books began to be published in the 1960s. However, detailed research carried out in more recent years, particularly since the 1970s, has shown that the story is far more complex. To understand how it has been pieced together we need to consider how the different branches of research have contributed to the improvement of our knowledge on the origin and culture of the indigenous people of our island and how this work enables us to take a fresh look at the new evidence which has now emerged.

The study of human origins falls within the academic discipline of anthropology. Under this heading are five groups of specialists who have become organised into separate sub-disciplines because each of them base their conclusions on different kinds of evidence.

Archaeologists working in the Caribbean have been the major contributors to our improved knowledge of the prehistory of our islands. By unearthing different layers of human habitation in the soil they seek to understand and explain not only the physical remains which they find, such as clay bowls, stone axes and post holes of houses, but use these artefacts to interpret the social and cultural traditions of the people who created them. The archaeologists adopt a systematic view of past populations. They consider how they adapted to the environment and the process of their cultural change and development or decline. New scientific techniques such as radio carbon 14 dating, mathematical models and computer simulated projections, now enable the prehistoric archaeologist to construct a far more accurate picture of past ways of life than was possible for their predecessors to accomplish in the twentieth century.

The physical or biological archaelogist studies the biological remains of the people being studied. By testing bones, checking for evidence of injury or disease, looking at the state of the teeth, the position in which the skeletons are found and analysing preserved remains of food, seeds, and animals nearby, the physical archaeologist can piece together information on how the people lived before recorded history.

Ethnohistorians study the written accounts of ships' captains, missionaries, explorers, soldiers, settlers, government officials and general travellers who had met with and made observations on the indigenous people during the first years of European exploration, conquest and colonisation. But such documents have to be carefully judged before coming to conclusions. Questions have to be asked and satisfactorily settled. Who wrote them? Whose side were they on? Did the authors have some ulterior motive for writing what they did? How accurate were their observations? How do the reports compare with the known physical geography of the islands and places they describe? How do they compare with the reports of others describing the same group of people? How does it compare with the evidence unearthed by the archaeologists? Because of the very nature of Caribbean history, based as it is on colonisation and the exploitation of groups along racial lines, these questions are crucial in the historian's attempt at reaching an accurate conclusion.

Linguists contribute to our knowledge by studying the language patterns of the first islanders, researching the reports on language written down by the early European settlers. They combine this with fieldwork among the indigenous groups still living in the Orinoco region of South America whose ancestors emigrated to the Caribbean islands thousands of years ago. By sorting out and tracing the origins of the language groups, they have been able to explain the link between the island tribes, the zones which they occupied, and their connection to the mainland.

Ethnologists study the pattern of culture and society as it exists today by doing fieldwork while living among the people who are the subject of their study. They compare one group to another, note examples of social, political and cultural change and record historical factors which influence the present state of the community. Since the 1930s, the Caribs of Dominica have become accustomed to being the centre of fieldwork for increasing numbers of anthropologists from Europe and North America. Interest surrounds the fact that, except for a diffused population in St Vincent, the Caribs of Dominica are the last surviving descendants of the people who occupied these islands at the time of the arrival of Columbus. The combined contributions of archaeologists, biological archaeologists, ethnohistorians, linguists and ethnologists have provided us with a much improved picture of our past than that which was previously available. And their work and revelations continue.

The Ecological Setting

The geological formation of the Lesser Antilles determined that the islands lie like a row of stepping-stones or beads of a necklace from south to north. Except for the 65-mile gap between Tobago and Grenada, the distance between each island is seldom more than 20 or 30 miles and in some cases it is much less. The first groups of people who set out from the shores of the mainland near the mouth of the Orinoco River in about 5,000 BC saw before them the island we know today as Trinidad. They moved northwards in search of new food supplies of shellfish, wild roots and fruit and were probably also being edged out by other tribal groups from land along the delta. Tobago was not too far off, and from the top of its highest mountains on a clear day they could see the clouds piled over Grenada beyond the horizon. The strong Orinoco current, at a point where the South Equatorial Current shifts northward into the Caribbean current, helped them on their way. Taking into account the means of their navigation in roughly hewn canoes dug out from long straight trunks of rain forest trees, they landed on each island as they progressed, sometimes settling for a number of years before moving on. The sea was their highway. Like all Orinoco River tribes, they were expert canoeists, as confident and at ease on water as on land. Unlike today there were no borders or restrictions to their movement and they could settle on any island they pleased. The concept of man owning land was as alien to them as man owing parts of the sea or sky. The natural resources available determined their points of settlement.

Certain parts of Dominica offered a combination of resources which were more attractive than others. Looking at the island through the eyes of hunter-gatherers, fishermen and early cultivators, particular zones stand out. The best reefs are located along the north-east coast from La Soye Point to Anse Soldat, around Scotts Head and at Toucari. The best canoe beaching areas would be along the sandy sheltered bays of the west coast and along the north-east. River estuaries such as Roseau, Canefield, Belfast, Layou, Batalie and the Indian River could even harbour canoes and rafts. The widest valleys would provide easy access into the rain forest and gently sloping land for slash and burn agriculture. The oldest geological areas along the east coast provide the hardest igneous volcanic rock for making axe-heads. Deposits of jasper, flint and pottery clay are available. Prime sea-bird nesting sites along the north, south-east and western cliffs would have been a source of eggs. These are just some of the considerations for settlement. Being acutely attuned to the ecology around them for their means of survival, they chose their sites carefully. Most of the 34 prehistoric sites found on Dominica up to 1994 show certain distinct preferences. They exist near the mouths of rivers or by springs in sheltered bays, on ground above flood level during heavy rains. A few sites are further inland but usually close to rivers. Some sites, believed to be of later settlements (perhaps even after European arrival in the region), are situated at high points overlooking the sea channels to the north and south of the island. These indicate positions chosen because of their panoramic views for advance warning of impending raids. Other favourable locations were near coral and rocky headlands where shellfish, lobster, octopus, white sea eggs and a wide selection of fish could be caught by hand, speared or shot with bow and arrow. Easy access up the larger river valleys into the rain forest is another important factor, for these 'high woods' were the source of liana rope, materials for shelter, canoe building, rafts, basketry, medicine, narcotics, wild yams (*wa wa*) and other foods including grubs and hearts of mountain palm. It was here that most of the hunting was done. The larger rivers teemed with fish, crayfish and the edible snail (*vio*). Out in the open sea there were the large pelagic species such as tuna, king fish, sword fish and dorado among others. On the sandy beaches at night turtles were easily caught, although some tribes were recorded as refusing to eat turtle. Migrating ducks were hunted in the swampy wetland areas such as the Cabrits and Indian River. Iguanas were found in the drier coastal zone.

The indigenous people would have made seasonal movements to various parts of the island, aware of the best sources and most bountiful periods for certain types of food, materials and species of wildlife. The location of special clays for pottery and types of rock best suited for making into particular tools such as mortars and axe heads were known. Flakes of jasper, for instance, were vital in the making of graters for shredding cassava tubers and the location of jasper deposits was crucial. By making a geological and biological assessment of the island in terms of the requirements of these people we can see how well-suited Dominica was to their survival.

But we must not limit our assessment to Dominica alone. We must shed our modern insular concept of space and appreciate their freedom of movement and access to resources on other islands. People on the north coast would think nothing of making trips to the superior reefs of eastern Guadeloupe or to collect oysters in the extensive mangrove swamps of Grand Terre. Cassava gardens were planted in Mariegalante by groups who lived permanently in northern Dominica. Similarly there is evidence of goods being traded along the islands from as far as South America and northwards to Puerto Rico. This uninhibited movement was to confound the Europeans during the period of indigenous resistance in the sixteenth and seventeenth centuries.

The Ortoiroid Peoples

Given this background of ecology and geography we can now look at the arrival of successive groups of people into this environment. Very little is known about the earliest groups to arrive. The most ancient evidence of the archaic peoples in our part of the Lesser Antilles is from a carbon date taken from remains at Little Deep at Mill Reef on Antigua, which gave a date of about 3,100 BC. We do not know what these people called themselves but from examples of their stonework we can trace their origin back down the islands to sites on the coasts of Venezuela at the Orinoco delta which give a date of about 5,000 BC. Evidence of the first step in their movement northwards has been found at Ortoire in Trinidad. To identify these people, the archaeologists call them the Ortoiroid. They gradually moved through the Lesser Antilles and by 1,000 BC they had reached Puerto Rico and established a frontier with another ancient group who had entered the Caribbean by way of the Yucatan peninsular and Cuba in 4,000 BC. The most recent sites containing Ortoiroid artefacts in these islands are dated 400 BC. It can be said therefore that, until more detailed study is done in Dominica itself, we can assume that the Ortoiroid occupied Dominica roughly from 3,000 BC to 400 BC. These people became extinct very long ago. Up to now, in Dominica and elsewhere in the Caribbean, we have been calling them the Ciboney, but that people was, in fact, of another age living in Cuba. This name should therefore be dropped from our island's history.

The Ortoiroid people were basic hunter-gatherers. They did not make pottery or cultivate plants. They lived close to the sea shore and their simple settlements were transient and intermittent. They depended on shell fish and wild plants for food. The remaining artefacts which have been found are basic stone tools, battered or ground through use, such as hammer grinders, manos and metates, consisting of a hand held stone and underlying stone slab used to grind vegetable foods. Other artefacts, crudely shaped through chipping, include net sinkers used for fishing.

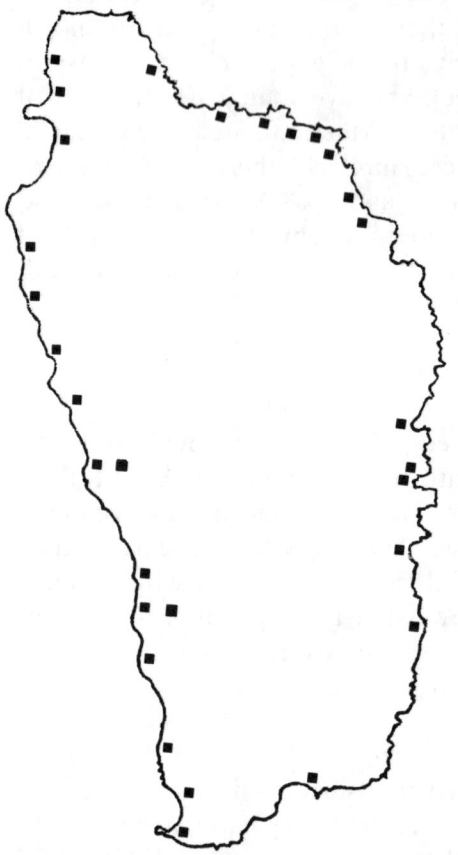

The clay adorno above was used as a handle for a food bowl. It was found along with other shards at a village site at Woodford Hill Bay. The map left, shows other archaeological sites where evidence of pre-Columbian settlements have been found.

The Arawakan Speakers

Arawakan is a family of languages widely distributed throughout the Amazon River Basin, the Guianas, the Orinoco Valley and, in Columbus's time, throughout the Caribbean as well. Many different tribal groups spoke Arawakan, depending on where they lived. Many people in the West Indies speak English but they would not call themselves Englishmen. The people of Puerto Rico speak Spanish and are Hispanic but they are not Spaniards. Reflecting on this may help us understand that although the various ethnic groups in the Caribbean when Columbus arrived spoke Arawakan based languages they cannot all be called Arawaks.

Groups of Arawakan-speaking people began to colonise the Lesser

Antilles from the Orinoco region from about 400 BC. Eventually they were to occupy the entire region as far as the Bahamas and Cuba. But specific groups dominated different zones. These Arawakan-speaking people made a great change on the islands for they introduced slash and burn agriculture and ceramics (the making of pottery) into the Caribbean. The archaic Ortoiroid non-agricultural people disappeared as they were either displaced or assimilated by the new arrivals.

By AD 1,000 zones of tribal influence had become defined in set areas of the region. As time passed each group developed on its own and lost all connections with their origins in South America. Again an analogy can be made with the situation in the modern Caribbean, where distinct communities have developed among descendants of people who arrived here a couple of hundred years ago from other parts of the world. Rather the same thing happened one thousand years ago. We find the Greater Antilles dominated by a people called the Tainos who had developed out of the early Arawakan-speaking settlers. The region was divided among three groups of Taino, Central Cuba, Jamaica and the Bahamas were controlled by the Western Taino, Hispaniola and Puerto Rico by the Classic Taino while the islands between the Virgin Islands and Antigua were occupied by the Eastern Taino. The Windward Islands, from Guadeloupe to Grenada was occupied by the Igneri. There was much interaction between these Igneri and the Eastern Taino because of joint use of resources as well as trading and raiding. The Western Tainos were the first people who Columbus met when he arrived in the Bahamas. The most advanced were the Classic Taino who had plazas and ball courts in their villages and possessed highly artistic skills. The larger size of the islands they inhabited provided more extensive resources which appears to have aided their expansion, population growth and marked development.

The Igneri

In about AD 400 a group of Arawakan-speaking people called the Igneri settled in Dominica and the other Windward Islands. These are the people who up to now we have been calling the Arawaks. They were not as advanced as the Classic Taino, but even so they were well adapted to their environment and took full advantage of the resources available. They were skilled potters and weavers of cotton, they made excellent canoes, processed cassava and built good strong houses out of the material of the forest. They had a system of leadership and set religious beliefs. All the designs painted and etched onto their pottery were representations of these beliefs symbolising their mythological spirit world of animals and nature. By comparing changes in these ceramic styles and design archaeologists have shown how the period of Igneri occupation of the Windward Islands went through marked phases of development. Each phase is signified by a change in the style of pottery depending on shape, colour and technique. Each of these phases has been given a name based on the type of pottery which has been found. They also signify a cultural change in the people who made them. Based on detailed studies carried out in Martinique, the Igneri of our islands underwent three phases, defined by the archaeologists as: Saladoid between AD 400 and AD 600 which evolved into the Troumassoid AD 600 to around AD 1,000 and finally the Suazoid from AD 1,000 until it died out about the time of European arrival.

An important Saladoid site was found behind the modern-day village of Soufriere in 1977. There were fine ceramics with a great variety of decoration – broken bowls with handles modelled in the shape of turtles, parrots, bats and symbolic designs representing frogs, pieces of incense burners as well as griddles for baking cassava bread from manioc which was their most important food. Many artefacts of perishable materials – wood, fibres and reeds – have not been preserved, but even so, a combination of ethnohistory and archaeology enables us to have some idea of their way of life in Dominica over one thousand years ago.

In reviewing the Igneri culture, their bond with the sea and land runs through all aspects of their life. They exploited sea and shore resources with great skill. Their most important artefact was the canoe. The value of canoes to these people cannot be overemphasised. They were dependent on canoes for migration, trade, fishing and hunting along coasts and for inter-island visits. They had numerous dugouts, some estimated to have carried over forty passengers. They were also farmers, cultivating maize, beans, sweet potatoes, peppers, pineapples and fruit trees such as the paw-paw, kashima and kowosol, but the most important was the bitter manioc. Useful non-edibles were calabash gourds, cotton and plants like the annatto (roucou) from which body paint was obtained. Year round provision of food was achieved by putting different kinds of plants in garden plots. Wooden digging sticks were used for planting.

Their houses were of wooden framework with sharply sloping thatch roofs to let the rain run off quickly. The huts were enclosed with walls of woven reed and the roofs had wide overhangs to let in the breeze but not the rain. Like all the other tribes on the islands and the mainland, the Igneri slept in hammocks slung from the main posts of the houses. They lived in small communities with a chief who guided the group, usually by general consensus. They wove cotton cloth in narrow strips, made amulets of stone, bone and shell and the ceramics already described. There were musical instruments: shell trumpets, wooden trumpets and drums, bone whistles and flutes, maracas or shack-shacks and rattles. The men hunted with spears and arrows tipped with sharpened bone and shark's teeth. They wore little more than strings of beads and on occasion narrow cotton apron loin cloths. They painted their bodies, and as on pottery, this decoration was a means of fixing their beliefs and myths.

Like the other Arawakan-speaking people of the region the Igneri worshipped the spirits of nature represented by the *zemi*. The *zemis* could be many things: gods, idols or symbols of gods, remains of the dead and the powers of sky, sun, moon, wind and earth. They were gods of an agricultural people. The representations of these gods took various forms, often carved with great skill and sophistication. A *zemi* in the form of a three-cornered, triangle-shaped idol of stone or conch shell was common to these islands.

One of the most remarkable of these 'three-pointer' *zemis* was found in a cave at Soufriere at the end of the nineteenth century by the parish priest of the village who later sent it to France. It is carved from stone in the shape of a volcanic peak on the back of a crouching figure. Each of the three sides measures some 21 cm. It is now displayed at the Musée de L'Homme in Paris. It apparently represents the god who was the giver of manioc. Since plants were often thought to come from earth deities, and earth deities were often thought to live in mountains and volcanoes, it would be logical to depict a mountain with a face. Another theory is that it represents the whole island and all it provides. Offerings of manioc were placed on the *zemi* and such idols were used in a ritual in which the shaman took narcotics and conversed with the *zemi* to find out weather and crop predictions. The *zemi* was not only an image of a god, but an oracle, an intermediary between men and gods.

From about 1400 this Igneri pattern of life, balanced between the natural cycle of the land and the animistic religion of nature spirits was to undergo a significant change. A new band of people were setting off from the Orinoco region in the south. These new immigrants were similar in many ways to the Igneri. They spoke a branch of the same Arawakan language. But they were making forays into settlements along the chain of the Windward Islands, gradually imposing themselves on the Igneri people and their language and culture.

3
The Kalinago – The 'Island Carib'

It was the Europeans who called these people the Caribs, for that is not what they called themselves. While Christopher Columbus was still on his first voyage he picked up the word, or something like it, from the Tainos of the Greater Antilles.

The earliest mention of the Caribs is that made by Columbus in his journal on 26 November 1492: 'All the people that he has found up to today, he says, are very frightened of those of *caniba* or *canima*.' Note that it is mentioned as a place where people live rather than the name of the people themselves. In other statements the Tainos may have been using the term to refer not to a specific ethnic group but to any hostile band who attacked their villages, particularly those who came from the small islands to the east of where they were in Hispaniola. Again on 13 January 1493, the journal notes: 'The admiral also says that on the islands he passed they were greatly fearful of *Carib* or on some they call it *Caniba*, but on Española, *Carib*.' This was modified in later Spanish writing to *canibal* and in other texts to *caribi* or *caribe*. Once the word hit the printing presses of Europe and became common parlance, the name 'Carib', like 'Indian' and 'West Indies', even if based on a mistake, was to remain for ever more.

One hundred and fifty years later in Dominica, the French priest Fr Raymond Breton who lived among the 'Caribs' recorded the people's own name for themselves as *Calliponam* in the women's speech, and *Callinago* in that of the men. Another ancient Arawakan language term for them was probably *kaniriphuna*, or *kallipina*, origin of the term *garifuna* which is what the 'Black Caribs' of Belize call themselves. Because the mainland immigrants who entered the Windward Islands in about 1400 were essentially a male-dominated band, who took brides and fathered a new group within the islands, it would be accurate to use their name in the men's language: *Callinago*.

In Fr Breton's day, the letter 'k' did not exist in the French language so the printers of his 'Carib Dictionary' used 'c' throughout. The word is however better represented phonetically as *Kalinago*.

But things were to get even more confusing. In the twentieth century, anthropologists needed to differentiate between the 'Caribs' on the islands and their supposed ancestral people on the mainland. To do so they coined a new term: 'Island Carib' when referring to those of the Lesser Antilles and maintained 'Carib' when referring to those on mainland South America. To simplify and indeed to try to correct matters, I shall be referring to this distinct group of people, who emerged on the Windward Islands and Guadeloupe, by the name which they called themselves: the Kalinago.

The Kalinago control of the Windward Islands lasted from about 1400 to 1700, with the last of them holding on to Dominica and St Vincent for another twenty or thirty years before finally retreating to the most inaccessible parts of those islands in the face of English and French colonisation. In St Vincent they mixed with escaped African slaves and held out against the British until 1796, when some 5,000 were deported to the island of Ruatan off Honduras and moved to the area of what today is southern Belize. In Dominica they concentrated themselves on the isolated parts of the north-east coast where they were eventually granted 3,700 acres of land by the British in 1903. They were the last of the Amerindians to enter the region and they were the last to survive.

Our knowledge of the Kalinago is based almost entirely on the written reports of European observers. The Kalinago had arrived in the islands from South America less than a hundred years before the Spanish arrived from across the Atlantic. The first encounter of the two groups was on 4 November 1493 on Guadeloupe, the day after Columbus had sighted Dominica on his second voyage.

Unlike the Tainos, the Kalinago had arrived in the islands recently enough to have retained traditions of their mainland origin. They were accustomed to making trips back and forth between the mainland and the Windward Islands. They explained this to European missionaries and told them that they had conquered an ethnic group named Igneri or Eyeri. Their raids were aimed at bride capture. The capture of women of an enemy group was a feature of raiding and warfare among tribes who were traditionally in conflict with each other. Such inter-tribal raiding was common to several South American forest tribes. A well-known example would be the Yanomamo of Amazonia. According to theories of primitive marriage in all races, the earliest form of marriage was bride-capture, when shortage of females obliged early man to seek his mate in war.

By the time Columbus arrived, the Kalinago were raiding Taino villages on Puerto Rico to obtain additional wives. The admiral found over twenty Taino women when he visited Kalinago villages on Guadeloupe during his second voyage, and returned them to their homes on the Greater Antilles. This taking of captives by one Amerindian tribe from another was a method of avoiding inter-marriage among the small communities. The Kalinagos, like other tribes on the mainland, integrated their captives as wives or, in the case of males, as *poitos* (sons-in-law) into their kinship network.

Taino and Igneri men were killed in these bride-capture raids and often a limb was severed from the body of the bravest warrior, both to strike fear among his people, and to take back home as a trophy and proof of victory. The Kalinago, like the Taino, also preserved the bones of their ancestors within their houses in the belief that the ancestral spirits were watching over them and protecting them.

When Columbus's men entered the Kalinago villages in Guadeloupe they reported 'we found great numbers of human bones and skulls hanging in the houses as vessels to hold things. Very few men appeared and the reason was as we learned from the women that ten canoes had gone to raid other islands.' From that day onwards the Kalinago and their descendants stood accused of being cannibals.

The vast majority of early chroniclers did not explore alternative interpretations of the circumstantial evidence of finding bones and limbs. They did not consider the alternative possibility – that the pieces might have been intended for use in rituals.

Some later visitors, however, such as John Scott in his *History of Grenada*, contended that if there was cannibalism at all it was a ritual. 'They rather eat out of Mallice, chewing only one Mouthful and spitting it out againe, and animating one another thereby to be fierce and cruell to their Enemies . . . and it hath been a great mistake in those that have reported the Southerne Indians eat one another as food.'

Columbus's verdict had been influenced by the Tainos who told him on his first voyage that those of 'Caniba' 'travel through all these islands and eat the people they can take.' From 'Caniba' a new European word was created: cannibal.

But no eyewitness account exists of cannibalism actually taking place among the Kalinago. Significantly, six men from Columbus's fleet were lost wandering in the jungles of Guadeloupe for four days but returned unharmed and uneaten. A detailed study on the subject done by American anthropologist Robert Myers concludes: 'Available data do not allow an absolute conclusion, but all the evidence is weak, circumstantial, and largely second-hand. If the Caribs were on trial for cannibalism, they would be acquitted.'

The subject of warfare and cannibalism has so dominated historical writing about the Kalinago that the positive aspects of their society has been largely overlooked. Yet on that first meeting, Dr Chanca, the surgeon of Columbus's fleet, admitted that he was impressed.

'The people seem to us more civilised than those elsewhere. All have straw houses, but these people build them much better, and have larger stocks of provisions, and show more signs of industry practised by both men and women. They have much cotton, spun and ready for spinning, and much cotton cloth so well woven that it is no way inferior to the cloth of our own country.'

The Kalinago were, like the other Amazonoid tribes from South America, handsome, graceful people with a light brown complexion and long, straight black hair which they oiled, combed and decorated with ornamental bands and feathers. They wore no clothes but like the Igneri and Tainos sometimes tied a strip of narrow cotton like an apron to hang from their waists, usually on festive occasions. Each day they would bathe and rub each others' bodies with bright red 'roucou' or annatto and use white, black and ochre colours to draw patterns on their skins. Dr Chanca and others reported that they stained around their eyes and brows 'which I think They do for show. It makes them look more terrifying.' They also pierced their ears and lips in which to place ornaments of shell and bone. The *caracoli*, a crescent-shaped ornament of hammered gold or copper was a mark of distinction among the men. The women wore tightly woven cotton bands around their lower legs. 'One below the knee and one at the ankle. In this way they make their calves large and constrict the knee and ankle. They seem to regard this as attractive, and by this feature we distinguished the Caribs from the others,' noted Dr Chanca. The mothers continued the Igneri custom of flattening the foreheads of their infants while their skulls were soft. It was thought that this formation was more handsome and made the skull stronger.

The Kalinago religion was a simple adaptation of the Igneri ancestor and nature worship through *zemis*. They believed in the evil spirit *mabouya* who they had to placate to avoid harm. The chief function of their shamans or *boyez* was to heal the sick with herbs and cast spells or *piai*, a term still used in Dominican spiritualism. Kalinago youth had to undergo strict and painful initiation rites to test their resilience and bravery.

The invading Kalinagos appear to have imposed the masculine aspects of their ancestral culture on the domestic life of the preceding Igneri culture. The males of each village lived together in the large central men's house, from which they visited their wives in surrounding family huts. The Kalinago chief was headman of the district around his village. French visitors in the mid seventeenth century noted that Dominica was roughly divided into different zones of control and under chiefs such as Kalamiena of Itassi (Vielle Case) and Ukale of Sairi (Roseau). The chief might gain his position through right of birth, but more often he was chosen by his peers for his bravery. He led their raids and could be changed depending on his performance. Their judicial system was very simple, those who were wronged righted their wrongs by taking revenge.

They continued to practise the Igneri form of agriculture, raised the same crops and gathered wild fruit and vegetables. As the Kalinago came from the rain forest areas of the Guianas they appear to have favoured the moist, mountainous, larger Windward Islands which had the kind of environment and forest resources they had utilised in their homeland. As in the Guianas, the men burnt the trees and prepared the land and the women dug the holes and planted.

Hunting with bow and arrow was a sport as well as a necessity. For this they used non-poisonous arrows made from the *roseau* reed and tipped with sharp wooden heads. For war they made arrow heads of sharp fish bone and smeared the tips with poison from the machineel tree. Sometimes they fixed blunt plugs on the arrows to stun birds wanted alive. They captured parrots and tamed them as pets. They ate agouti, iguana, birds and fish.

The Karifuna group, performing above, was formed in 1980 by young people in the Carib Territory to try to trace and recreate Carib cultural patterns.

The last stages of digging out a gommier tree trunk for a canoe. Stones, fire and water will then be used to broaden out the canoe before adding a lee-board or 'bordage.'

But more important to the Kalinago than hunting and agriculture was fishing and the sea. Here they excelled. They knew the location of islands by heart and had their own concept of the constellations of stars in the night sky which they used for navigating in the open sea. Today we still use the type of canoes in which the Kalinago crossed these waters hundreds of years ago. Carved out of whole tree trunks they were of two kinds. The smaller, called *couliana* was at most twenty feet long and pointed at both ends. This type was only used for offshore fishing and short trips and could hold few people. The bigger craft was called *canoua*, the word we still use today, and the more significant of these were said to be up to 50 feet long and could carry 30 to 40 people. These vessels were dug out of the solid trunks of gommier trees (*Dacryodes excelsa*), using fire and stone gouges. They were stretched open by a combination of water and stones on the inside and fire on the outside, after which the hulls were kept in position with wooden ribs.

The complete equipment of the early Kalinago canoe included paddles shaped like narrow shovels, a long pole for navigating over reefs, rope made from *maho* bark, a stone anchor and a calabash for bailing out water. It was in the large canoes that the Caribs went to attack other islands and made long trading voyages and fishing and gathering trips. They also constructed rafts out of Bois Canon (*Cecropia peltata*) called *pwi pwi*, which are still popular today.

The Kalinago had a great variety of fishing techniques and their fishing grounds extended well into the Leeward Islands: to the reefs of Guadeloupe, Antigua and Barbuda for shellfish, lobster and conch; to Mariegalante for crabs. In the rivers of Dominica they knew how to poison the rocky pools with pounded leaves of *kunami* or *nivwage* and other plants which stunned the freshwater fish. Using bows and arrows they shot fish close to the surface. Using baskets they scooped up millions of tiny *titiwee* on their seasonal run up-river from the sea.

While the men were fishing and hunting the women planted, prepared food, spun thread, wove hammocks and made earthenware vessels for holding food and liquid. Baskets were woven from the dried outer bark of the *larouma* reed. Communal meals were eaten as the need arose, the men simply dropping their catch at the entrance of the house for the women to clean and prepare. The usually sober Kalinago got very drunk on *ouiku*, a manioc beer which was prepared by the women chewing and spitting out the manioc into large earthenware jars. Enzymes in their saliva began the process of fermentation and the *ouiku* was ready after a few days. This was consumed at festivals and pre-raiding feasts and on such occasions their principal amusement was dancing, telling mythical stories and recalling the injustices of their enemies and the righteousness of their revenge.

Language and names

The Kalinago or 'Island-Carib' language was originally assigned to the Cariban family of languages, but linguists have found that it, like Taino, is a member of the Arawakan language. The Taino, the Igneri and the

Kalinago languages therefore all originate from a branch of the type of Arawakan which was spoken on the mainland areas from where they came. Variations of these languages were different in different parts of the Greater and Lesser Antilles but they all came from the same source. To use an example in today's context: raw, basic Barbadian dialect is different from Jamaican dialect, but both of these dialects are descended from a branch of the English language which was introduced over 300 years ago. Yet a Bajan would not like to be classed as a Jamaican and vice versa.

In the case of the Kalinago, they had been too few in number and had not been in the islands for long enough to change the language and culture of the Igneri completely. They were immigrants into the Windward Islands, gradually assimilating themselves into the Igneri population. The Kalinago succeeded in changing the name of the Igneri to their own and in modifying certain aspects of their language and culture. The men used their own pidgin language among themselves and as a 'trading language' throughout the islands. The women continued to use their Igneri-Arawakan language and their descendants used a mixture of the two. But after initiation the males preserved their 'men's language' when they were together as a sign of adult Kalinago manhood. By the time the Europeans began to record the Kalinago language things had changed again as the language was further modified by Taino refugees who retreated into the Windward Islands, fleeing the horrors of the Spaniards in the Greater Antilles. The language which was recorded is called 'Island-Carib' by modern linguists.

This confusing language pattern may be the cause for the mix-up over the original name of Dominica. The day after Columbus named Dominica, his men reported that 'One of these Indians told us that . . . one of these islands, called Ceyre, . . . is the first we saw but did not visit . . .' What the Spaniards did not realise is that the Arawakan word for 'island' is *kairi*. In the Taino language it was *caya* or *cayo* and in Island-Carib it was *acaera*.

When Fr Raymond Breton lived among the Kalinago in the 1640s he found out that their name for Dominica was actually *Wai'toucoubouli*, meaning 'tall is her body'. The people who inhabited the island were called *Wai'toucoubouliri*. The names they gave to their settlements, although changed a bit by French influence, are still in use today: Kalibishie, Koliho, Makusari, Mero, Kulibistri, Layou, Taro, Batali, Bataka, Bwetika, Sari-Sari and Ouanari are just a few. There were other place names which have since gone out of use. Vieille Case was Itassi, Portsmouth was Uyuhao, Roseau was Sairi, La Plaine was Kulirou and Salisbury was Baoui. The original two languages became fused over the years and were eventually replaced among the descendants of the Kalinago by the mainly French-influenced Creole. But in terms of our names for plants, wildlife and places, modern Dominicans are still the largest users of Island-Carib words. One of the last more fluent speakers of the ancient language died in 1920, but luckily, some of

The Kalinago – The 'Island Carib'

it and a number of old Kalinago legends have been preserved for us by Douglas Taylor, a British anthropologist who spent his lifetime studying the Kalinago/Island-Carib culture.

Tales and legends

For the early Kalinago the moon was a man with a dirty face. The story is that once a Kalinago girl was visited during the night by an unknown man and became pregnant. Her mother therefore found someone to keep watch

An old print showing a Carib flute dance.

A Carib with a pegall, known in Creole as a 'conta'. When the base of the basket is complete it will be used for carrying goods on the back.

on her daughter and that night the guard lay waiting for the lover to return. But because it was very dark the guard decided to take the juice of the genipa fruit (*Genipa americana*) and smear it on the lover's face so that he could be recognised the next day.

In the morning they found out that the girl's lover was her own brother and people mocked him so much that for shame he withdrew to the sky. There he is seen as the moon, his face still dirty with genipa stains.

The child who was born of this union was called Hiali and it was believed that he was the founder of the Kalinago nation. When Hiali was still a baby, a humming bird was chosen to take him to the sky so that his father might see him. As a reward for this service the humming bird was given his beautiful feathers and the little cap he wears on the top of his head.

Ebetimu

This Kalinago legend tells of the stars known as Orion's Belt and the Seven Sisters in the constellation of Taurus.

Once, Ebetimu loved the daughter of an old woman called Bihi. But Bihi hated the boy very much and would wait until he was asleep in his hammock and then put her behind near Ebetimu's face. Soon Ebetimu fell ill and went to the old fortune teller Uanhui to ask for advice.

'You have grown so pale that you will surely die unless you take good care and do what I tell you,' Uanhui said. 'Go and lie down in your hammock, sharpen your knife, and pretend to be asleep. When your mother-in-law comes near you, slash her with your knife.'

Ebetimu did as he was told and after slashing the old lady he and his loved one ran away. They tried to escape as fast as possible but old Bihi was not to be defeated. She sharpened her own axe and came after them. Little by little she caught up, and seeing her so close behind, the couple took the road to the sky. But it was too late. Just as they left the earth, Bihi managed to cut off one of Ebetimu's legs. They were all three swept up and became parts of the constellation of Taurus which glitters every evening above the Caribbean Sea.

The Charm Makers

Maruka and Simanari were brothers who lived at Salybia long ago and were famous for the charms they made. It was said that these two men would climb to the Maison Tete Chien, a cave above Salybia, and there they would burn tobacco before the master snake on the blade of a canoe paddle. The Tete Chien would vomit arrowroot, known as 'toulamon', and then he would vanish. In his place a naked man appeared and would ask

Maruka and Simanari what charms they wanted. When they had told him he would explain how to make them out of the toulamon.

The two charm makers did not die at Salybia. When they were getting old they returned to the continent of South America, dived into the Orinoco and became two young lads once more. The story also related that, when all the earth was soft, the Master Tete Chien of the cave made the 'L'escallier Tete Chien' or snake's staircase, which is at Sineku on the windward coast.

Another landmark of the Kalinago legends is the Pagua rock. This gigantic outcrop of stone stands atop a cliff overlooking the Pagua River near Hatton Garden Estate. According to an old legend all types of charms grew on the summit of the rock. There was a sweet smelling white flower which was very difficult to obtain, but if anyone was able to scale the rock, find the flower and bathe with its petals, that person could command whosoever he wished. Old Kalinago stories relate the adventures of those who tried to use the flower. Interwoven into other legends are references to the rocky islet which stands about 100 metres off Londonderry beach on the north coast. It was believed that the rock turned into a large canoe during the night and would take the spirits of ancient Kalinago out to the sea.

What little remains of the old legends and stories shows that the Kalinago culture was rich in myth and folklore. But it was not to last forever; like all the Indian cultures in the Americas, the Kalinago settlements of the Antilles were to undergo great changes as a new wave of conquerors swept across the Atlantic.

4
Columbus and Spain

It was 25 September 1493. Seventeen ships carrying 1,500 men including soldiers, priests, government officials, farmers and workmen were leaving the important Spanish seaport of Cadiz for the New World. The breeze was light and the sailing ships, or caravels, as they were called, made their way swiftly out of the harbour into the open sea. Their bright painted sails had been hoisted and the gorgeous royal standards of Castile were displayed from their main masts. So many other colours fluttered from the ropes and mastheads that they became entangled in the rigging. Cannons roared, trumpets brayed and music echoed from ship to ship as the armada led by Don Christobal Colon, Admiral of the Ocean Sea, sailed westward into the Atlantic.

Almost one year before, sailing in three small ships, the *Nina*, *Pinta* and *Santa Maria*, Christopher Columbus had sighted the Antilles for the first time. Believing the islands to be off the mainland of Asia, he called them the West Indies, and this mistaken identity gave the region its name. Unaware of his mistake, Spain welcomed him back from his first voyage with heroic honours and speedily prepared for a second voyage. Adventurers, eager for

Sighting Dominica.

Columbus and Spain 31

gold and quick fortune flocked to join Columbus. Horses, cattle and pigs – animals unknown to the 'Indians' – along with seeds and farming equipment were packed aboard the 17 caravels which left Cadiz that September of 1493.

This time Columbus sailed further south than on his first voyage. The weather was perfect and the journey was uneventful. On 1 November, All Saints Day, the admiral was so sure he would sight land within three days that he issued an extra allowance of water to the men on his flagship. At sundown on 2 November, he was certain that land was near from the look of the sea, the flight of the birds and an unmistakable piling up of clouds on the horizon which seemed to indicate a mountainous island. As it got dark he ordered his ships to shorten sail. This would ensure that the vessels moved more slowly and would not pass any islands during the night.

At about five o'clock the following morning, 3 November, in the faint light of early dawn, a seaman saw a black mass on the horizon ahead.

'Abricas que tenemos tierra! Tierra! Tierra! Tierra!' 'Land! We have sighted land!' The call spread from ship to ship. As soon as the Admiral was

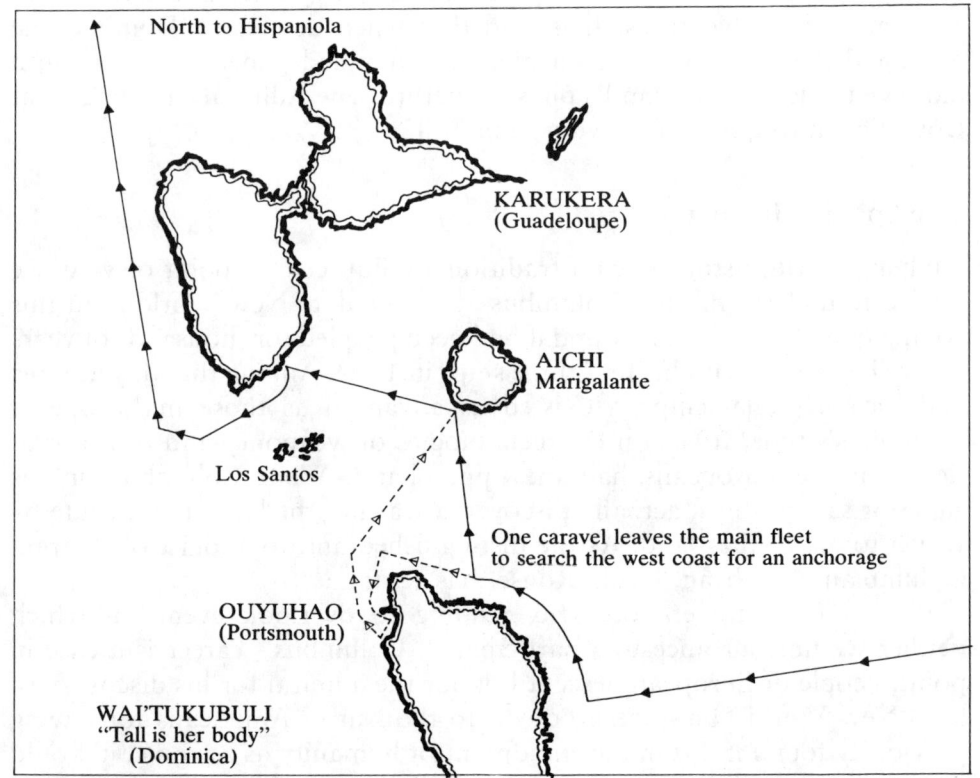

The passage of Columbus' fleet on 3 and 4 November 1493; with the original Carib names of the main islands.

certain that it was land indeed he called 'all hands to sing *Salve* and other prayers and hymns very devoutly rendering thanks to Our Lord' for so short and safe a voyage. Columbus named the island Dominica, the day being a Sunday.

The fleet came closer to the island looking for a harbour in which to anchor, but Dominica's jagged windward coast offered no safe anchorage, and the fleet moved northwards to the islands of Marie Galante and Guadeloupe which had also been sighted that day. One fully manned caravel was ordered to continue searching the coast of Dominica for a suitable harbour and it was only after rounding the northernmost point of the island that shelter was found. The caravel entered a large bay but no one landed. On returning to the sixteen other ships at Marie Galante the captain told Columbus of his findings and reported that they had seen dwellings and people. The fleet had made its landfall at one of the loveliest islands of the new world. Nicolo Syllacio, a translator of accounts of the voyage, recorded: 'Dominica is remarkable for the beauty of its mountains and the amenity of its verdure and must be seen to be believed.'

When Columbus returned to Spain after his second voyage he made his customary appearance before King Ferdinand and Queen Isabella to give an account of his adventures. It is said that when describing Dominica he presented the sovereigns with a piece of crumpled paper to give them a more vivid idea of the island's physical nature. The Admiral called again at Dominica during his fourth voyage in 1502.

The Spanish Impact

Studying world history from a traditionally Eurocentric point of view we are led to understand that Columbus 'discovered' a 'New World'. But this continent and the islands around it had been peopled for thousands of years before he arrived with his first three ships in 1492. Among the Maya, Aztec and Inca, regional empires existed as advanced as those in Europe at Columbus's time. It was in the technologies of weaponry and transportation that the Europeans had the upper hand. What Columbus, in his superior sailing ships, actually discovered was not the land, but a route by which to get to that land. As the distinguished anthropologist of the pre-Columbian Caribbean, Irving Rouse, has written:

'We humans are ethnocentric, tending to overlook events in which neither we nor our ancestors participated. Columbus's career is a case in point. People of European descent honour the admiral for his discovery of the "New World" but give no credit to the Native Americans for having previously found it. From the standpoint of humanity as a whole, it would be more accurate to say that Columbus discovered a new route from Europe to the Americas.

'Two other routes between the hemispheres had been found before Columbus's time. The ancestors of the American Indians had moved from Siberia into Alaska and the rest of the New World toward the end of the Ice ages, and the Norse had travelled from Iceland to Greenland and Newfoundland in tenth century AD.'

Columbus and his men arrived here at a time when Europe was emerging from a century of bloody conflict and violent disputes over boundaries and expansion of territorial control. A growing mercantile system needed gold for currency. Their Christian religion was backed by a crusading militarism in the belief that God would bless those who spread the faith by any means necessary, however brutal. And even if one did not believe, the faith itself was used as an excuse to attack and plunder 'the pagans and the infidels' especially if they had gold and one wanted their lands. This was the mental baggage which the Spaniards, and later others, carried with them as they entered their New World.

The impact of the Spanish conquest on Hispaniola, Cuba and Puerto Rico, the effects of European diseases and the systematic genocide of the Taino people throughout the Greater Antilles is one of the most horrific cases of inhumanity in the history of the world. Every conceivable form of brutality is recorded over the thirty or so years it took the Spanish to eradicate an entire ethnic group from the face of the earth. Taino refugees, fleeing Spanish persecution filtered southwards into the Leeward Islands. As news was spread into Kalinago territory of the destruction and enslavement of the Tainos to the north, the Kalinagos were resolved not to let the same thing happen on their own soil. All along the islands, both the remnants of the Eastern Tainos and the refugee Classic Tainos as well as the Kalinagos, took up arms in defence of their islands. This further confused European accounts of the inhabitants of the Lesser Antilles at the time, for whoever took up arms to defend themselves south of Puerto Rico was identified as 'a warlike Carib' whether or not they were Taino or Kalinago.

The Spaniards compensated for the decline of Taino labour on their haciendas by increasing the importation of Indian slaves from other parts of the Caribbean area including slave raids on the smaller islands of the Lesser Antilles. Slaves were transported directly from Africa, beginning in 1518. Spanish royal edicts dated 7 November 1508 and 3 July 1512 authorised settlers to capture and enslave Kalinagos on 'the islands of Los Barbados, Dominica, Matinino, Santa Lucia, San Vincente, la Asuncion (Grenada) and Taraco (Tobago)', because of their 'resistance to Christians.' These edicts, giving permission to wage war upon, enslave and sell duty-free any Kalinagos on these islands between Dominica and Trinidad were aimed not only at providing slaves but at the same time clearing the islands of dangerous neighbours. Later attempts to revise these laws made no change in the relationship and efforts to placate the Kalinago with Christianity failed utterly. The Spanish missionaries were massacred or held captive.

Apart from keeping the Kalinagos at bay, the Spanish did not favour these islands for settlement. The rugged terrain of Dominica in particular did not tempt settlers and the fighting skills of the Kalinago became known and feared throughout the Spanish Main. The early colonists of the Americas preferred the more accessible islands of the Greater Antilles where the indigenous people had been subdued and which offered more extensive land which was easier to colonise.

On 3 June 1514 Pedro Arias de Avila called at Dominica with a fleet of nineteen vessels and 1,500 men, arriving at the large bay on the north-west shore, now called Prince Rupert Bay. He landed with troops but those who entered the forests were immediately showered with poisoned arrows. Despite the danger of sudden attacks, the fleet stayed anchored offshore for four days taking on wood and fresh water from the rivers flowing into the bay. During the visit the first Roman Catholic Mass at Dominica was celebrated aboard the assembled fleet.

Arias continued across the Caribbean sea to the isthmus of Panama where, the year before, Vasco Nunez de Balboa had seen the Pacific Ocean for the first time. He wrote to the Council of the Indies, the body which controlled all Spanish dominions in America and the West Indies, and strongly urged that Dominica be colonised. He argued that this would enable ships from Spain to obtain wood and water in safety and would provide a depot for Spanish exploits in the Main. The Royal and Supreme Council assured Arias that this would be done, and took a first step by adding Dominica and 20 other islands to the Bishopric of Puerto Rico in 1519.

The following year, Antonio Serrano, a councilman of Hispaniola, was chosen to colonise Guadeloupe and then move across to develop Dominica and the surrounding islands. Kalinago attacks on Puerto Rico were making the conquest of that island a long drawn out affair for the Spaniards. It was hoped that by sending Serrano to Guadeloupe this would draw off the Kalinago raids on Puerto Rico and would create an all out war with them. If the Kalinago were defeated Dominica and the Lesser Antilles would be free for Spanish settlement. But the plan did not work. When Serrano attempted to colonise Guadeloupe in 1525 he was soundly beaten by the Kalinago.

Although Europeans made no major impact on Dominica for the next two centuries, the island was subject to short visits from time to time. As the Spanish Empire in the Americas expanded, the island gained importance as a point for collecting wood and fresh water and for cleaning out ships and refreshing crews after the long transatlantic voyage. The course which Columbus had taken from the Canary Islands on his second voyage was so good that it was used for 300 years until steam replaced sail in the middle of the nineteenth century. The ocean currents and the flow of the northeast trade winds were important for sailing vessels, and for a westbound European ship the natural course was to make for the Dominica passage between Dominica and Guadeloupe as the gateway into the Caribbean.

An increasing number of Spanish ships bearing the treasures of Peru and Central America were criss-crossing the Caribbean Sea and as the threat of piracy increased the Spanish Council of the Indies organised a convoy system to protect their merchant shipping from attack. Large fleets of merchant vessels sailed together on an appointed date with warships for protection. These convoys of flotas and galleons would sail twice a year. From 1535, Prince Rupert Bay on Dominica was decreed as one of the refreshment points for these convoys after the crossing. At Dominica they would divide into two; one half sailing to Mexico via Puerto Rico and Hispaniola, the other to Cartegena and on to Nombre de Dios and Porto Bello on the isthmus of Panama to collect the plunder from Peru.

Mariners who landed at Dominica had to be well-armed, for their reception by the Kalinago, hidden in the surrounding forests, was unpredictable. Some reports talk of spirited attacks with showers of arrows from the Kalinago while sailors were drawing barrels of water from the rivers; others indicate no action at all. British accounts later in the century give reports of peaceful trading taking place with the Kalinago.

Spanish ships wrecked on Dominica's shores were at the mercy of the Kalinagos who stripped the vessels of nails, iron and survivors. Wrecks, loaded with vast quantities of gold, silver, pearls and other precious goods were reported to have been plundered by the Kalinago and the treasure hidden in large caves one or two leagues from the sea. The most remarkable account of such an event was told by a black woman, Luisa de Navarette, who was captured by the Kalinago during an attack on Puerto Rico in 1576 and who lived as their captive on Dominica for four years. She managed to escape and recounted her experiences to the Bishop of Puerto Rico in 1580. She gave details of her life with the Kalinago and how she learned their language and customs. In October 1588, Luisa was once again questioned, and in a sworn statement before the Governor of Puerto Rico, she recalled that ' . . . she saw lots of silver bars in the manner of bricks. That questioning . . . the Indians about where they had come from, they responded from a navio that had struck the coast of that island . . . and that some of the people that came in the said ship drowned and others were killed by the Caribs and seven or eight men were held captive . . . and since the Indians have suspicions that the Christians will fall upon them, they have hidden this treasure in a watering spot or cave that is a league from the sea and inland in other parts . . . and this is why she has seen lots of gold.'

Another witness before the Governor at the same time reported that: '... being there he saw lots of silver that he recognised as being from New Spain and from Tierra Firme marked silver bars ... in the same manner he saw lots of silver and gold made into eagles ... guinea pigs and other figures ...'

Documents from investigations into Spanish prisoners on Dominica dated 1587 add more details: '... there is a cave full of silver bricks and much reales of 4 and of 8 and other merchandise and that the silver pile is so high that a man on a horse could not be seen from the other side ...'

Research published in 1983 claims that ships lost in 1567 were part of the New Spain Fleet commanded by Juan Valasco de Barrio, who, upon hearing that two fleets of English pirates were in the waters at the usual exit route off Cuba, took his division eastwards to exit into the Atlantic through the Dominica Passage. However at that point the fleet was struck by a violent hurricane which drove six ships against the north coast of Dominica. They were carrying a reported three million pesos of treasure. Each ship was between 120 and 150 tons and apart from two unidentified naos, their names were recorded as the *San Juan, Santa Barbola, San Felipe* and *El Espiritu Santo*. Apparently the Spanish began to attempt salvage in 1568. Kalinagos were captured but despite being tortured never revealed where the bulk of the treasure lay.

For years during the Spanish settlement of Puerto Rico the Kalinagos harassed the east and south coast of that island in order to prevent further expansion southwards into the Virgin Islands. Documents in the archives of Santo Domingo record: '... each year they go to steal by the months of June, July and August, to the Island of Puerto Rico and other parts. In this manner they have captured many Negro slaves and some Spaniards in some haciendas by which fear many lands have been depopulated and two mills that make sugar.' In the process they plundered plantations, fired buildings, sacked churches, slayed livestock and took away treasure, guns and clothing as well as captives. They even fell on loaded vessels in mid-ocean. The warfare they practised was swift and fierce and most efforts to control the Kalinago assaults proved useless. On returning to Dominica they hid themselves easily in the mountainous jungles. By the end of the sixteenth century Spanish ships were seldom calling at Dominica. Not only had they given up any idea of taking the island, but their power in the region was dwindling as other European nations joined in the mad grab for the riches of the New World.

Captives and Trade

An intriguing collection of different nationalities was to be found in Kalinago villages on Dominica during the late sixteenth and early seventeenth centuries. They were Africans and various Europeans who had either been captured by the Kalinago from neighbouring islands and passing ships, or who had escaped from slavery or indenture on plantations in Puerto Rico. Others were survivors of shipwrecks or deserters in hiding.

One example of this comes from neighbouring Guadeloupe in 1625 where a mulatto called Lewis had escaped from a ship while it was visiting the island 'resolved rather to die among the Indians . . . than ever more to live in slavery under Spaniards.' However he was well accepted and 'in twelve years that he had thus continued amongst them he had learned their language, was married to an Indian, by whom he had three children living.'

Others who had been held captive returned to European settlements with bitter stories of their sojourn on Dominica. They were compelled to adopt the Kalinago customs and go naked with only a covering of *roucou* to protect them from mosquitoes. They slept on the ground and, according to one escaped captive lived on raw mice, snake, fish and crab. They had to work for the Kalinago in the provision grounds and row canoes on fishing trips as well as chew manioc for the provision of *ouikou* beer. In 1569 it was estimated that there were more than 30 Spanish and 40 Africans living among the Kalinago.

During this period an increasing number of French, English and Dutch ships were beginning to call at Dominica, particularly at Prince Rupert Bay. Gradually the Kalinago took to trading with these ships that anchored to refresh their crews. As their old ways were dying out due to depopulation and to the pressures of defending themselves, there was less time or inclination to fabricate the tools necessary for their traditional way of life. Their dependence on European trade goods became greater. Loading their canoes with produce of the island they would row out to visiting ships to exchange plantains, tobacco, cassava bread and pineapples for knives, cutlasses, axe heads and cloth if the trade was good or for coloured beads, glass and other trinkets if it was not. But it was an unstable relationship, each side never sure what the reactions would be from one visit to the next. Among the well-known adventurers of the age who called at Dominica during that period were Sir John Hawkins, Sir Francis Drake, George Clifford Earl of Cumberland, Sir Richard Grenville and in 1652 Prince Rupert of the Rhine whose name was given to the bay. In 1564 the French captain René Laudonnière recalls: 'As soon as we cast anker, two Indians (inhabitants of that place) sayled towards us in two canoes full of a fruite of great excellencie which they call Ananas' (pineapple). After capturing one of the Kalinago to question him, Laudonnière 'suffered him to depart after I had given him a shirte, and certaine small trifles.' Drake, calling in 1585 received assistance from the Kalinago in 'carrying on their bare shoulders fresh water from the river to our ship's boats' and fetching from their houses tobacco and cassava in return for which 'we bestowed liberall rewards of glasse, coloured beads and other things.'

Robert Davie gives another similar account of a visit in 1595 when the Kalinagos brought them 'plantains, pinos and potatoes and trucked with us, for hatchets, knives and small bead-stones.' Drake, calling again that same year gave trading gifts of 'a yellow waistcoate flanell and an hankerchief.' The Earl of Cumberland calling in 1598 and Anthony Sherley in 1596 both landed with sick crews who benefited from soaking in the hot springs near the Picard River. Clifford notes that the Kalinago spoke some Spanish words. Two of his captains rowed up the Indian River to the Kalinago village of some twenty houses, where they were entertained by the chief and danced with his two daughters after the meal was finished.

In March 1607 an English group in three ships led by John Smith and Christopher Newport, captain of the *Godspeed*, landed for two days to refresh themselves before continuing on to Virginia in North America. There at Jamestown, they established the first permanent English settlement in the Americas. These accounts give another perspective of the Kalinago/European relationship but we must see this period as just a lull in hostilities: the Spanish threat had subsided, Europeans had not yet taken physical control of any of the Kalinago-held islands. But by 1625 that would change and the temporary peace would be swept aside as the Kalinago faced the fiercest challenge to their control of these islands.

Meanwhile in Europe a new wave of writers were printing books and pamphlets recounting ever more gory stories about the 'cannibal' Kalinago. The seventeenth century, which was just beginning, would see some of the most exaggerated accounts, several based only on hearsay by people who had never even visited the islands. Some were presented as travel books, others as ships' log books and as early studies in ethnology. These reports were read by playwrights, novelists and poets and the Carib/Kalinago character was further altered in fiction which caught the public imagination and remained in print and performance for centuries. The most famous are Caliban in William Shakespeare's play *The Tempest* and Man Friday in Daniel Defoe's *Robinson Crusoe*. Less famous now than it was two centuries ago is the legend of Inkle and Yarico, the story of a Carib maiden betrayed and sold into slavery by the Englishman who she thought was in love with her.

In Dominica, from 1625, military resistance appeared to be the only option as the Kalinago began a defensive war against French, English and Dutch encroachment. But force of numbers, superior weaponry, and European diseases would slowly take their toll as one island after another fell from their grasp and the final retreat to the forested citadel of Dominica was complete.

In 1627 the English Earl of Carlisle, with the backing of a clique of rich merchants obtained from the King letters of patent granting him rights over the 'Caribee Islands' lying between 10° and 20° north latitude. Dominica was almost in the centre of this group, to be known as Carlisle province or Carliola, but the name was never used. Then the French declared it a possession of the 'Compagnie des Isles d'Amerique'. In spite of these competing claims the island was left untouched for the time being. Neither nation was anxious to tackle the steep, heavily forested land which seemed to offer few possibilities for profit.

5
Land of Two Nations

To the north and south of Dominica English and French settlers were rapidly founding new colonies. The English, under Sir Thomas Warner, had occupied St Kitts in 1624 and were later joined by the French led by Pierre d'Esnambuc. The two nations agreed to combine against external foes, Kalinago or Spanish, and thanks in part to this pact, the Europeans were able to stay in St Kitts and later extend their colonising activities. The French moved into Guadeloupe and Martinique where, after an initial struggle with the Kalinagos, they established flourishing colonies. By the 1650s the Kalinagos had been driven out of the Leewards but this did not cease the daily invasions made on the settlements by Kalinagos from Dominica. When later in the 1660s the French and English scrapped their arrangement for peaceful partnership, the Kalinagos assumed a new role and sided with one against the other, more often than not, with the French against the English. This situation was further confused when at times the Kalinagos of the windward and leeward coasts would each support an opposing European power. Although both powers appeared to have little interest in the place they made very sure that the other would not have the upper hand among the natives and the rivals actively wooed Indian friendship.

At the same time during that period the Kalinago continued to fight a rearguard action concentrating on French and English settlements which were being established closest to Dominica in a range that included Antigua, Barbuda, Nevis, Montserrat and Guadeloupe. In 1635 French settlers under Captain Du Mé began colonising Mariegalante. This was an important farming and gathering ground for the north coast Kalinago of Dominica and they saw Du Mé's settlement as a direct threat to their stronghold on the island. One night in 1635 they raised a raiding party and paddled across the 18-mile wide channel to Mariegalante, attacking the village, burning houses and killing some Frenchmen. Soon afterwards Du Mé retaliated, swooping down upon a Kalinago village in the north, likewise burning and massacring its inhabitants. French cartographers put his name on the site and it is still called Anse Du Mé, (usually spelt Anse Du Mai).

The Missionaries

It was during one of the periods of French-Kalinago cordiality that the first opportunity was taken to send Roman Catholic Missionaries to Dominica. Père du Tertre was the superior of the Dominican fathers stationed in Guadeloupe, a religious order which generally spoke and acted in favour of the aboriginal inhabitants of the West Indies.

Father Raymond Breton, accompanied by Brother Charles of St Raymond, was sent to Dominica by du Tertre in 1642. They landed at the carbet of Chief Ukale on the reed river, later the site of Roseau, the island's capital. It was a large village dominated by the impressive carbet or hall of Chief Ukale who was regarded as the main chief of the leeward coast. The huts were crowded along the banks of a lagoon near the mouth of the river. This feature has since disappeared but the area of Roseau where it existed is still known as Lagon.

Fr Breton, then aged 33, had been teaching himself the Kalinago language before coming to Dominica and, despite some mistakes on his first introduction to Ukale, he was able to make himself understood amongst them. The Chief welcomed the two priests and made them guests of his large community house. They had brought no food or provisions and were determined to trust themselves to the Kalinagos, and to God for shelter. As a result, they were accepted as friends by all and could move in and out of the settlements or wherever they cared to go, speaking as much as their knowledge of the language allowed while observing the Indians' customs and life styles.

On the first day of his arrival, Fr Breton had met the Chief of Uyuhao (known today as Portsmouth). Later he had been introduced to Chief Kalamiena of Itassie, today's Vielle Case, and was invited to go to the Chief's carbet. As they sailed northwards along the leeward side of the island, Fr Breton received his first lessons in Dominican history and geography. Kalamiena – naked and dignified, twice Breton's age or more – was proud to instruct these two French priests, dressed always in their long soutanes. At Itassie they became great friends, and yet Fr Breton was not prepared to try to explain the secrets of his Christian faith. He felt that the Kalinagos would not understand the rites and sacraments he practised and therefore would be offended, even angered by this religion that was new to them. In the early morning, before the Kalinagos were up, the priest would secretly administer Holy Communion to himself and his companion.

Eventually, when he felt the mood was right, he began translating the most common prayers and made the first major step of his mission by instructing the children of Itassie. Though he had been granted permission to instruct only children, adults would gather around also, listening to stories about the strange god and spirit of Christianity.

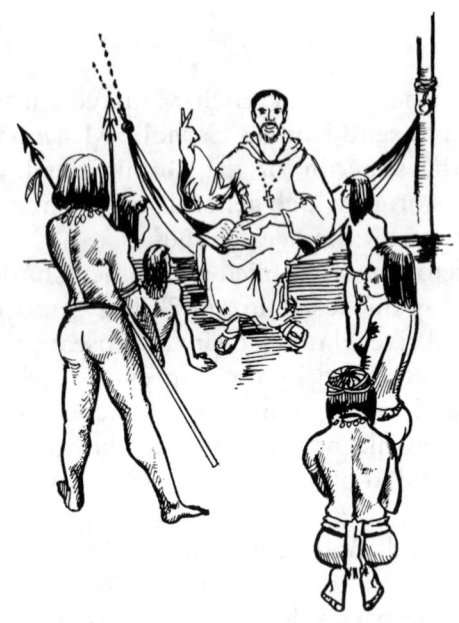

Fr Breton teaching the Kalinagos.

At the same time, Fr Breton enquired into everything going on around him, and the information he compiled became part of his 'Dictionnaire Caribe – Français'. This amazing book does not limit itself to Kalinago words and meanings but gives a detailed description of Kalinago life in the mid-seventeenth century. For instance ' . . . no religion, no prayers, no altars, no temples among the Caribs. They have an idea of divinity, and male and female gods, some beneficent, others evil. The latter they call mabuya, and to protect themselves from their vexations they practise some superstitious rites in their honour: offerings of wiku with the first cassava bread.

' . . . at an eclipse of the sun or moon they dance and howl without interruption and dare not stop before light has returned.

'They believe in the immortality of the soul and they are three of them in each individual. One in the head, one in the arm and a third in the heart. The one in the heart is supposed to go happy to heaven; those of the arm and the head turn into mabuyas – those are the bad spirits.'

These deeply rooted Kalinago beliefs clashed with the new religion which the missionaries taught and soon Kalamiena had to advise Breton to leave Itassie; his teachings were being dangerously misunderstood by the inhabitants. Their friendship remained intact, however, and Kalamiena provided his canoe and men for the trip back to Guadeloupe. On reaching Basseterre, Breton and Br Charles learned of the death of du Tertre and that Fr Breton would be taking his place in Guadeloupe.

After four years, Fr Breton crossed the channel again and returned to Itassie. The Kalinago greeted him as an old friend and presented a welcome ceremony of chants and gifts of food. Despite their kindness, Baba Raymond, as the Kalinagos called him, remained cautious. No attempts were made to baptise them but he saw to it that dying children within his reach received the sacrament. Months later, he was joined by Fr Alexis of Auxerre, priest of the Capuchin order, who had brought all that was necessary to celebrate the Roman Catholic Mass. That year, 1646, the first Christian mass was celebrated in Dominica in the 'long house' of Itassie. Fr Alexis did not stay many weeks and soon Breton was continuing his daily catechism lessons alone. After periodic visits to Guadeloupe he settled at Kolihao in 1650 and erected a chapel of reeds and thatch. By now he spoke their language as fluently as any native and because of his knowledge of languages he understood the grammatical construction better than any of them.

'God granted me that I endeared myself to them and that they had become confident enough never to undertake any serious business without asking me for advice. Whenever a new matter, or only a rumour of one cropped up, they sent some of theirs to meet me and I was always able to set them there and then at their ease. . . . '

The missionary method of Fr Breton can be summarised simply: Except for a short period during his first visit he did not baptise adult Kalinagos in good health; nor did he organise rushed instructions just for the sake of baptising as many as possible; he wanted them to understand the true meaning of the Christian faith. But he was fighting a battle doomed to failure; the Kalinagos had little use for the religion he preached and soon after he left Dominica, only the memory of his presence remained.

Fr Raymond Breton died at a monastery of the Dominican fathers at Caen in France on 8 January 1679. His superior praised him as one of the best and bravest missionaries in the history of the province. But his greatest contribution was his information on the Kalinagos, yet basically, he had failed, as he was bound to fail, in his religious mission among the natives of Dominica.

It was Father Phillipe de Beaumont who noted this failure. When he came to live in Dominica in about 1655, the Kalinagos still spoke fondly of Baba Raymond but could not remember a word of catechism. Beaumont was sympathetic and understood the Indians' panic at being chased from island to island by European settlers. 'What is to become of the poor Carib' one of them had asked him, 'must he go and live in the sea with the fish?'

Beaumont urged the French Governor of the islands, De Poincy, to make a treaty with the Kalinagos assuring them that Dominica and St Vincent would remain uncolonised. Just before De Poincy died in 1660 one of his last acts was to sign this important treaty with the Kalinagos. The two islands were reserved to them on condition that they made no claim on the other territories. But within three years the treaty was seen to be useless and the British were beginning to use 'half-breed' Indian Warner as a deputy ruler of Dominica.

Indian Warner

In 1630, twelve years before Fr Breton began his mission, a son was born to the English Governor of St Kitts by a Kalinago slave woman from Dominica. The French priest, du Tertre, knew the boy and recorded his observations.

'General Warner, a contemporary of General De Poincy, had a son by a Carib slave woman of Dominica. He recognised him as his own, he saw to it that he carried his name and saw to his education in his own house, together with his other children . . . As was to be expected, his hair was jet black . . . his height was below average but there was a fine proportion among all his limbs. He had an oval face and a large forehead with aquiline nose and his eyes shining and bright – not slit. There was gravity on his face that bespoke the temper of his daring character . . . '

During his boyhood Indian Warner, as he was generally known, lived among the English of St Kitts enjoying the privileges of his father's household. But after Sir Thomas Warner's death, the youth was persecuted by his English step-mother, and though his half-brother Phillip defended and helped him, Indian Warner fled to Dominica.

The Windward coast was at that time inhabited by Kalinagos more friendly to the French and Warner took refuge among his mother's people on the leeward side of the island. Here he adopted the traditional way of life and was soon raised by the Kalinagos to be their chief. He maintained contact with the English, especially Lord Francis Willoughby, then governor of the 'British Possessions in the Caribbee', stationed in Barbados. In 1664, Indian Warner led 600 Kalinagos with 17 canoes to assist the English attack on the French settlement in St Lucia. They landed with over 1,000 Englishmen from Barbados and the small French garrison of 14 surrendered without resistance. In the hope of getting control of Dominica, Lord Willoughby made Indian Warner Deputy Governor in the same year. Two years later, Warner was captured by the French and treated harshly in Guadeloupe and St Kitts, but was released in 1668 when a peace was signed.

During those years, there was a great difference of opinion between Barbados, the Windward Islands and the Leeward Islands about the value of the Kalinagos as allies against the French. While many planters were eager to wipe the Kalinagos out once and for all, Governor Willoughby was trying, through Indian Warner, to come to a more diplomatic arrangement and also win over the French-influenced Kalinagos of the windward coast.

Sir William Stapleton who became Governor of the Leeward Islands in 1672 was one of those who wanted the Indians driven from the area and when the Kalinagos of Dominica raided Antigua in December 1674, he decided that a harsh counter-attack should be made. A militia of 'six small companies of foot' was raised from Antigua and St Kitts with Colonel Phillip Warner in command. They sailed to Dominica to 'put down' the Kalinagos and 'be revenged on those heathens for their bloody and perfidious villanies'. It is said that no prior approval for this expedition was obtained from the new governor of Barbados, Sir Jonathon Atkins. Sir Jonathon viewed the situation differently, believing that any such conflict with the Kalinagos would make peaceful settlement impossible.

French historians have it that Phillip Warner treacherously went among his half-brother's tribe, plied them with brandy at a feast and then massacred them; the signal for the massacre was supposed to have been given by Phillip stabbing his own half-brother. This story was repeated by a captain of one of the raiding sloops, though other reports claim that Indian Warner had helped in a successful action against the French-allied Kalinagos of the windward coast and that on their return to the Layou River anchorage he joined the English in a celebration feast. At the height of the party, Indian Warner was killed in a drunken brawl which incited the Kalinagos to take revenge – a move which resulted in the massacre of their tribe. The site of Warner's village is traditionally believed to have been in the area of Checkhall Estate. Reports indicate that on leaving the Layou anchorage, the sloops swept southwards towards the settlement and even William Stapleton admits that eighty Kalinagos were killed and some taken prisoner, their provisions destroyed while their canoes were carried away. From early French times the village in that area has been known as Massacre.

The incident caused quite a fuss in other colonies. Sir Jonathon Atkins had Phillip Warner arrested. He was confined to the Tower of London for 18 months and was eventually brought back out to Barbados where he was tried and acquitted in 1676. Nevertheless, the King ordered that he should be removed from the post of Deputy Governor of Antigua 'and any other employment of trust in His Majesty's Service'. But the Antiguans were strong supporters of Phillip Warner's case and when he lost his official position, they elected him Speaker of the Antigua House of Assembly.

The whole truth of the matter will now never be known, but the violent expedition had no lasting effect on the courage of the Kalinagos; in 1676 they murdered many colonists in Antigua and Montserrat, and again in 1681–82 it was reported that Kalinagos from Dominica and St Vincent had raided Barbuda and Montserrat, killing, burning and carrying off a few negroes.

Dominica Declared a Neutral Territory

For the last 20 years of the seventeenth century the Kalinagos continued to be a thorn in the flesh for both French and English planters in the Caribbean. Both nations talked among themselves of the conquest of St Vincent and Dominica. Letters were sent to King Louis XIV from Martinique calling for the total annihilation of the Kalinagos.

' . . . The Caribs are savages. At first opportunity and whenever it suits them, they are ready to break any peace agreement made with them – commit hostile acts and kidnap and harbour among them runaway slaves that are too lazy to work and thus ruin the King's subjects. But we cannot wage war against them for lack of troops and of men . . . If it were His Majesty's pleasure to rid the inhabitants of these unpleasant and ruinous neighbours, I think it would be necessary to wipe them out altogether or at least drive them off the nearby islands. To this effect we would need six more companies and sufficient provisions for all that a real campaign would be launched, and an arduous campaign it would be. For it is no easy matter to pursue the Caribs into their impenetrable woods over dangerous precipices . . . '

Meanwhile, the English were writing in the same vein to their own court at Whitehall:

> 'I beg your Lordship pardon if I am tedious and do pray your Honours to represent to His Majesty the necessity of destroying those Caribie Indians and that he would be graciously pleased to order the Governor of Barbados to destroy them heathens, which is so easy a thing for that Governor to execute in regard to its nearness to the islands of St Vincent and Dominica – or put me in a capacity to perform that good piece of service, whilst we are in amity with the French who have them in subjection or at least wise, that it may not be disliked if I take all opportunities to make them fly to the Main, if I cannot compass their total destruction . . . I once more crave for the prolixity of your lordship's most humble and obedient servant.
> William Stapleton'

The King gave permission to Stapleton's request and in June 1683 he went 'Indian hunting' as he described it. He felt satisfied with his raid on St Vincent, though in Dominica he was only successful in killing 11 Kalinagos and burning 11 canoes. He burned 'upwards of 300 houses, but pitiful little ones, except their day-houses, that is their war and carousing houses. I measured one, 100 feet long and 30 broad'. He further stated that the French had supplied the Kalinagos with firearms, powder and bullets. 'They buy the plunder and negroes taken from the English islands'.

Hostilities between the French and English continued to rise and fall throughout the period with the Kalinagos torn between two forces always getting the worst of every bargain and the brunt of every attack. On 7 February 1686, French and English officials in America signed a Treaty which included an agreement that Dominica would be a neutral island belonging only to the Kalinagos.

Article Ten stated:

'The island of Dominica shall remain in the state in which it now is and shall be inhabited by the savages to who it has been left, so that neither of the two nations may place her under possession.'

But rather than being a neutral territory, Dominica became a no-man's land of battle. The whole spiral of 'French' Kalinagos on the windward coast and 'English' Kalinagos on the leeward coast continued to turn. By 1699 the English had set up a small wooden fort and mounted several small cannons near Roseau, claiming they had only come to cut timber and that the guns on the fort were for saluting the Kalinagos! Within months French pirates had carried off everything including their tools.

When the adventurous Père Labat called in January 1700 on a 17-day visit, the Kalinagos were still in total control of the island. On arriving at Roseau, he met the mother of Indian Warner, known among the Kalinagos as Madame Ouvernarde (Warner).

She had been sent back to Dominica after Sir Thomas Warner's death and was well over a century old in 1700. With gifts of rum and cloth Labat made a visit to the windward coast, observing the Kalinago settlements and making a rough estimate of their numbers. While the European conflict continued the Kalinago population was declining. The long years of attack and massacre had taken its toll. In 1647 they had numbered 5,000, and as the century ended they were down to about 2,000. Illness and travel back to South America reduced them to an estimated 500 in 1713, and in 1730 they were a mere 400. As their numbers diminished, their legendary courage and bravery declined and the sad fate of these noble warriors was certain. Permanent settlers now began to move into their last island stronghold, gradually pushing them off their ancestral grounds.

But it was not only the effects of French and English military action, occupation and disease which heralded the fatal impact on the Kalinago. It was the possession and destruction of the delicate environment on which the indigenous people depended which robbed them of the very source of their survival. Their free movement had been restricted. Their access to traditional fishing and gathering grounds on various islands had been cut off. The reefs, swamps, inlets, springs, forest sources of ethnobotanical material and rock sites for the production of tools had been taken from them. The freedom to use the land in the manner learned over thousands of years by the previous ancestral tribes was gone within a few decades. The initial European vision of a land of plenty as described by Columbus and Dr Chanca was gradually replaced over centuries of colonisation by an awareness of the geographic and ecological fragility of the area. In our own time it explains how the exploitative industrial and agricultural systems of the colonial and modern Caribbean have not adjusted to the demands of the environment and has resulted in the ecological degradation we see today.

As for the Kalinago, they lost even their own name. Soon their islands were being called the Caribbees and by the late nineteenth century the whole area from the western tip of Cuba down the islands to Trinidad and all along the coast of central America between these points, became known as the Caribbean. By the eighteenth century they had heard themselves being called 'Caribs' for so long, that even their own identity with the name 'Kalinago' died away. In 1492 the Bishop of Avila told Queen Isabella of Castile 'Language is the perfect instrument of Empire.' When that had been taken away from one and replaced by the language of the victor, the conquest is complete. So the Kalinago called themselves Caribs, the name they had been given, and in keeping with the cycles of history, so shall this book, as the first permanent French settlers began to arrive on Dominica at the dawn of the cataclysmic eighteenth century.

6
France Moves in

From the 1690s French lumbermen had made settlements for cutting and shipping lumber and a few families had even started to cultivate small holdings. Because of the neutrality agreement in 1686, King Louis XIV was against any permanent French settlement in Dominica. There was concern that the Caribs would join the other Indians and runaway slaves in St Vincent to threaten French commerce once more. But neither his royal will nor the demands of the Caribs prevented wood-cutters from coming, and by 1727 there were fifty to sixty French families in Dominica along with a few Spaniards, Portuguese and English Catholics.

While most set about cutting wood for export, others cleared provision gardens and planted small fields of cotton and tobacco. These early settlers were a rough, hardy group and little organised rule or justice prevailed. They informed and assisted pirates, sold them goods and stored their stolen goods. It was a society in which only the toughest survived. Their houses were of roughly sawn timber with thatched roofs of roseau and palm

Fr La Vallette supervises work at Grand Bay.

Early French settlers.

branches and one or two rooms. Settlements were strung along the coast in the isolated bays and flat coastal areas of Colihaut, Pointe Michel, Soufriere and Grande Bay. Roseau, a sandy delta of long river reeds, was dotted with patches of cultivation. The main group of huts was clustered near the sea close to a gently rising point of land on which stood a small fort of rough wooden palisades. In the areas where Pottersville, Goodwill, Newtown and Kingshill now exist, there were small clearings and light forest.

By this time the French inhabitants were giving names to places on the island and most of them are still in use. For years, the large bay in the north of the island had been called Grand Anse. Moving south there were the major landmarks of Morne Espangnol, Le Grand Savanne, Le Roseau, Morne Anglais, La Soufriere, La Grande Baie and Petite Savanne, while the unsettled windward coast was simply called Au Vent. For centuries the people living on that coast were referred to generally as 'gens au vent'. As the settlers increased and spread over the island new names were constantly replacing or being added to the original Carib ones.

There were danger signs in this growing community and the spirit of independence among the settlers was worrying the Governor of Martinique. Although he had orders to leave Dominica and St Vincent alone he also felt he should guard French interests in Dominica. In 1727 he selected a man of Martinique family already residing there and a year later appointed him commander of the island. This officer, M. Le Grand, had landed in Dominica in December 1727 and settled his household and several negro slaves on property given him by a Carib chief. Because of his personality and fair mindedness he won the respect of the fifty-odd families on the island who willingly accepted him as their leader and agreed to submit to his judgement. Pirates vanished from the bays of Dominica, the English-Carib relationship was successfully broken and after testing his strength, the Caribs accepted, or rather were forced to accept, the idea of French occupation. Assured that France had the upper hand, and that law and order existed, the number of settlers increased rapidly, buying Carib lands with rum, cloth, trinkets and tools. Most of them were by no means rich; some had lost their land on the other islands owing to the increase of large estates as the sugar industry developed. Debtors and criminals came in hope of safety while coloured people left the restricted societies of the sugar islands to establish their own estates and social groups. The population of the West Indies was still unsettled and there was much movement from one island to another. In the confusion, Dominica provided a new frontier for poorer whites and freed slaves. By 1750 the Caribs had been forced to withdraw from the leeward side of the island and settle in small groups on the rough and rocky north-east quarter. Soon they were seldom seen except when they came to trade for rum or made fishing trips along the coast.

Most of the small farmers in Dominica before 1740 did not need and could not afford many extra labourers. Their holdings were worked by family and friends paid in kind. Apart from limited supplies of coffee, cotton, cocoa and tobacco, their main cash crop was ground provisions for feeding slaves in the larger French islands of Martinique and Guadeloupe. These islands also provided Dominica with a trade in timber needed for building ships, carts, gun carriages, mills and houses. By 1731 suitable wood near the shore was so scarce that carts and animals were being used to haul lumber to the coast.

From the 1720s the cultivation of sugar cane and production of sugar in Dominica was discouraged by the authorities in Martinique. Large investments were needed to work sugar estates and since the legal ownership of the island was in doubt, people were not prepared to risk the considerable amounts of money that were necessary. Commander Le Grand had asked that one or two estates in each district be allowed to grow sugar cane, if only for local needs, but officials in Martinique did not approve the idea. Even without sugar, however, the small holdings were expanding and, as more prosperous settlers arrived the demand for labour increased. For over 200 years the other colonies of the Indies had been importing forced labour from Africa and by the time Dominica joined the trade in the eighteenth century, it had become a major business of the western world.

Africa and Slavery

In 1518 a Spanish ship had carried the first cargo of African slaves directly from the Guinea coast to the Americas. With this there opened a regular slaving system which was to endure for three and a half centuries and convey across the ocean some tens of millions of Africans. This peculiar form of trade, very valuable to western Europe, became increasingly disastrous for Western Africa. Yet, slavery had existed there long before the Europeans began their Atlantic trade. Its roots lay in the social systems of Africa. For centuries men, women and children had become slaves through conquest, capture in war, or punishment for crime.

More often they were peasants, very similar to those of feudal Europe, used for household or military services, to provide crops and food or handmade goods, and they could be used as gifts or for trading. There was important slave trading between the kingdoms of Guinea and western Sudan to the north spreading southwards to the forest regions under the Alafins of Oyo and the powerful kings of Asante. Chiefs raised slave armies to protect and expand their kingdoms and wealth. Even in Africa, household slaves had been regarded as superior, living with their masters often as members of the family and able to work themselves free. An old Asante proverb runs: 'A slave who knows how to serve, succeeds to his master's property.'

When the Europeans came in the sixteenth century they were new

A settler's house in the Roseau valley painted by the Italian artist Agostino Brunias who lived and painted in Dominica during the eighteenth century. The main house is surrounded by an outside kitchen and slave huts. Women beat their clothes by the river while others carry water. Plantains ripen on a frame while balizier, castor oil, logwood and cocoa plants flower along the river banks.

customers to an old trade. But there was the major difference that the slaves were sold for transport oversea instead of transport overland and the harsh treatment and numbers soon exceeded anything that had previously been known on the slave coast. For a time, the trade remained small, but by 1650 it was well into its stride and although some kings expressed concern at the vast numbers being exported, most coastal chieftains willingly met European demands and organised slave-raiding parties far into the interior. Slaves were traded for guns, cloth, iron and other goods; and if one local chief or 'prime merchant' should refuse, his rival or neighbour would undoubtedly comply. From the trading stations and forts, slaves were packed into ships to make the dreaded Middle Passage to the Caribbean. Few slaves came directly from Africa to Dominica before the 1760s; the prosperous sugar islands of Barbados, Antigua, St Kitts, Guadeloupe and Martinique were far more attractive to the slave merchants. Slaves brought to Dominica in the early days were usually transhipped from these larger trading centres and many who came to the island were already West Indian born.

The French custom of slavery followed usual set patterns. As a French Island, Dominica possessed a general code of slave law, Louis XIV's 'Code Noir' of 1685. This celebrated and detailed code was often disregarded. Yet it made clear the legal status of slaves, whose ownership and sale was to be regulated. It limited the punishment of slaves and laid down minimum conditions for feeding and housing. It assured the slave's right to legal trial and granted them a number of civil rights, especially in the matter of marriage. The new slaves would be entrusted to a more experienced worker who directed them in the estate's duty and usually prepared them for

baptism. This custom of introducing the slaves into Christianity was one of the major differences between Catholic and Protestant owners and even an English writer at the end of the eighteenth century admitted: 'In the good management of slaves the French planters, I think it is generally allowed, are superior to the English.'

As on all plantations in the West Indies, the slaves were provided with basic clothes, food and their small roughly thatched and walled houses. Since so much extra land was available in Dominica slaves made their own provision gardens to cultivate small crops and raise pigs and chickens. These they sold at the Sunday markets after which they would dress in all the finery they could afford and attend mass and evening vespers. The slave could rise out of his slavery. He could occasionally, with money earned by selling ground provisions, buy his freedom or be manumitted by his master. In small French colonies such as Dominica, the negroes were generally well treated and good relations existed between masters and slaves, but any attempt of a slave to overstep that line was sternly repressed. The fact the Dominica had a coloured plantocracy made no difference in the treatment of slaves. The minutes of court cases against planters for mismanagement and maltreatment of slaves indicate that coloured 'mulatre' masters could be just as, and sometimes even more harsh, than their white colleagues. These free coloured inhabitants, known as 'Afranchis' as well as 'mulatre', owned large portions of the cultivated land, but some professions and trades were closed to them and they were compelled to serve in the militia in lower ranks than the whites. Ironically, the free coloured would have nothing to do with the free blacks. Dominica's economy was also responsible for the closer relationship between slave and master, whites and coloured. This island with its small estates of mixed crops, differed greatly from the vast thousand-acre estates in Barbados, Jamaica or Martinique, which were rolling in sugar cane and had been reaping the cream of the European market for almost a hundred years. It was after the 1760s during the expansion of British estates that slavery in Dominica developed rapidly in line with other sugar islands.

This does not mean that Dominica was not bringing money into the French Treasury. Besides supplying the French islands with food, cassava flour, wood and animals, the planters were paying export taxes on their coffee, cocoa, cotton and tobacco and import duties on iron, farm equipment and other goods. They were also paying the required tax on slaves and, because Dominica was technically a neutral island, all this revenue had not cost the French Government one sou!

Government

By 1745, the population had grown to 3,032 well over half of whom were slaves. These numbers were posing problems on control and Dominica was being described as a place 'without faith, without religion', where 'an honest man lived in peril'. The Governor of Martinique realised that since the days of Le Grand, law and order had deteriorated and a stronger system of government had to be imposed. In 1742 a new Commander was sent to Dominica, a prison was built and obedience was won through strict order. Other officials placed in Dominica included a judge, a notary and five assistant military officers. The defence militia of local residents was expanded and reorganised. The island was divided into eight districts for civil and military purposes and each district militia was led by officers under orders from the Commander in Roseau. Smuggling of slaves and illegal goods was checked and the coast was watched for English pirates and war vessels attempting to hide or land in bays and inlets. A customs officer collected payments from Dutch and English traders as well as export and import duties. Taverns were taxed and, to prevent the destruction of wildlife that had occurred in other islands, a restricted hunting season from July to December was put into force. The civil and military officers of the island were also planters, some having come directly from France, while others had been born in Martinique and Guadeloupe. The origin of most local surnames can be traced back to France; names like François, Jean Baptiste, Laronde, Latouche, Laroche and Sorhaindo appear in the very early records of the island.

Religious life during this period left much to be desired. Priests were scarce in the French West Indies and the continuous wars between the European powers and the hardships of colonisation distracted attention from religious matters. In 1730 Father Guillaume Martel landed at Roseau and, appalled at the crime and vice which flourished in the community, as yet without judges or laws, he set to work organising the religious administration of the island. He founded the parish of Roseau under the title of 'Notre Dame du Bon Port' and built a church capable of holding 600 persons. This was on the site of the present cathedral, and its main door looked straight down Church Street to the harbour. He built two other chapels along the coast at Grande Savanne and Malalia (now Douglas Bay) and visited them by boat four times a year keeping the first registers of baptisms, marriages and burials. He worked on the island for ten years and was eventually followed by Capuchin fathers from Guadeloupe who set up missions in the north and the Jesuit fathers from Martinique who settled in the south. These areas became known as Land of the Capuchins and Land of the Jesuits. This strong French influence however, did not prevent Dominica from being preserved as a 'neutral island' when the Treaty of Aix-La-Chapelle, between England and France, was signed in 1748.

Grand Bay and the Jesuit Fathers

Overlooking the Grand Bay cemetery is a large cross, 10 ft high, 6 ft wide, 15 × 11" thick, carved from solid stone. This oldest remain of early European settlement began the history of Grand Bay and Geneva estate.

Jeannot Rolle, a coloured settler from Martinique arrived in 1691 with two slaves to cut wood for boat-building. He had known the Caribs when they came to trade on Martinique and was able to speak their language. On his arrival at La Grande Baye, he was welcomed by the Caribs under their chief, and in exchange for rum and other goods they helped Rolle construct boats which he would sell across the channel. Using the same method of exchange he purchased a well wooded property from the Caribs and brought in a few more slaves to start working the place. His first years as a planter were not peaceful. As a devout Catholic, he insisted on erecting a wooden cross in the middle of his property but the Caribs took an extreme dislike to this edifice and went on the warpath, uprooted the cross, pitched it into the sea and burned everything Rolle had left behind. The planter made peace with the Caribs, but any attempt to put up another cross was met with hostility. Finally, he decided to erect a cross of stone and got his slaves to chisel it from a huge rock, ordering cattle from Martinique to drag the finished work. A minor guerilla war broke out but soon the Caribs retreated and Rolle appropriated additional property.

He appealed to the Jesuits in Martinique to come over and bless the 'Belle Croix' as it became known and offered them part of his estate to start a mission. In 1747 Fr Antoine La Vallette arrived and said the dedication mass, surrounded by Rolle's entire household. When Rolle died many years later he was buried at the foot of his cross.

On his first visit in 1747, Fr La Vallette noted the opportunities open to him in Dominica. Every available acre in Martinique was being planted in cane and coffee and these forested acres on the south shores of Dominica offered great scope. He bought the estate of a settler who wanted to sell out and return to France and added it to the other land purchased from Rolle and neighbouring colonists. To get slaves at a lower cost, La Vallette disguised himself as a buccaneer and went to the cheaper English slave port of Bridgetown in Barbados where he bought over 200 slaves. In 1749, they were landed at Grande Bay, also known then as Les Jesuits, and were put to work clearing land, planting tea, indigo, coffee and cocoa. Soon the estate was producing impressively with coffee well in the lead. La Vallette installed Brother Jean Nichola La Vasseur as overseer and keeper of accounts and erected a small chapel putting Abbé Catherine as its priest. Huge buildings were constructed for the storage of crops, preparation of cassava and the milling and manufacture of coffee. By 1753 many ships were loading cargoes at Les Jesuits to be sold to French merchants for money and merchandise.

Fr La Vallette remained based in Martinique but as he has written, he frequently visited Dominica to check on the work of Brother La Vasseur: 'Every month I made a voyage to Dominica to see what had been done and to give orders for what was to be done . . . How many times have I crossed the Dominica channel in a pirogue! For the first two years I made the crossing and often in such weather that the biggest vessels did not dare set out to sea. But I did and reached according to schedule.'

La Vallette extended himself in speculative activities, borrowed money on short and long terms and prolonged payment at high interest rates. Besides shipping produce to Europe he supplied the French forces with timber for cannon mounting and building. With the money, he bought more slaves and set them to work along with some whites increasing production at Grand Bay.

In 1753 he was named Superior General of the Martinique Mission and Apostolic Prefect, but despite his prosperity and apparent spiritual success he had earned many enemies and complaints had reached France about his exploits in foreign commerce. He was ordered back to France to explain himself to the Minister of Marine but skilfully cleared himself of all charges, proving that he had not engaged in foreign trade. The estate in Dominica, he declared, was bought as part of his missionary activities, to make it easier for him to convert the Caribs to Christianity. Fr La Vallette was allowed to return to the Antilles, but on his arrival in Martinique he found affairs in a mess. Hurricanes had damaged both crops and buildings on the estates in Martinique and Dominica which required reconstruction and reactivation. But luck had now turned against him. English pirates captured ships laden with valuable produce from Les Jesuits at Grand Bay and an epidemic killed off many slaves, bringing work virtually to a halt. Faced with these problems and then a fall in the price of provisions, La Vallette tried to save himself by renewing loans and buying and selling products through agents in Roseau and St Eustatius where he was able to get his goods to Holland at a profit.

Criticism was increasing once more and finally the Jesuits urged an enquiry into the West Indian Mission. In 1762 Father De la March reached the West Indies and island by island began to collect evidence. For a second time La Vallette was recalled to France and this time admitted his guilt and was removed. The rest of the drama took place in Europe; the head of the Jesuits in Rome refused to pay the debts, and in France, where the Jesuits were already unpopular, the order was suppressed in 1764 and three years later was expelled from the country. In its condemnation, the French parliament permitted the creditors to sell the Jesuit properties in the neutral islands of the West Indies and in Dominica and Canada. The estate at Grand Bay with its numerous buildings, 194 slaves and valuable coffee was sold to English creditors.

The La Vallette scandal crippled Jesuit influence in Dominica and Martinique, La Vallette returned to Europe and the Jesuits left both islands. Only Fr La Vasseur and Abbé Catherine, who himself was not a Jesuit, remained in Dominica, the latter until his death. Other religious orders along with a few independent missionaries lingered on the island. In 1753 the Franciscans had sent their first representative, Fr Jochim Massey to Roseau where he was to play an important role during the British capture of Dominica.

War and Conquest

Between 1756 and 1763 Dominica was caught up in what was known as the Seven Years War. Developing from a dispute over military and naval bases, this war was not limited to the West Indies alone and the French and British forces had confrontations on their home grounds and in Canada and India on land and sea. Great expeditions were sent out on both sides, and their commanders had orders to take the enemy's colonies, not merely to destroy them. Both nations therefore set about capturing islands which would serve as ransoms so that they could bargain for possessions in North America and Europe.

Early in the war incidents occurred on the coast of Dominica between English and French ships. The French colonists were harbouring their country's vessels which later attacked enemy ships and caused the English to retaliate with raids on settlements at Grand Anse, Colihaut and Roseau. By October 1759 Commodore John Moore had written to his Prime Minister William Pitt stating:

> 'Dominica is absolutely under the direction of the Governor of Martinique and is developing into an island of consequence . . . Dominica is troublesome to the British and since the French in Dominica are not neutral I would advise that the island be treated as it deserves.'

In 1761 Pitt wanted Dominica seized before the hurricane season and on 3 May, 2,000 experienced men under Lord Andrew Rollo sailed from North America to Guadeloupe. The most recent information had been gained about the state of Dominica's defences and the inhabitants of the island had been ordered to declare whether they were enemies of the British or neutral. The French settlers diplomatically answered that they were neutral, but this did not save them. In Guadeloupe, Lord Rollo and his men met other ships under Sir James Douglas and their large fleet of four war vessels carrying 10 cannons along with four transport ships packed with men, sailed towards Roseau.

Rollo sent two officers ashore with a letter calling for the surrender of the island. French Commander Longpre stoutly refused, and hastily manned the defences with members of the local militia. But in the face of the vast British force they were powerless. At 4 o'clock that afternoon, 6 June, Rollo landed his troops and took the town. The French report of the collapse reads:

'Sieur Longpre resisted for a few minutes at the head of 80 men. His resistance was the cause of the destruction of Roseau and the surroundings. Guards had been stationed by Admiral Rollo at the church presbytery, but this did not prevent these from being looted . . . De Longpre, Du Parquet and Latouche were captured arms-in-hand and made prisoners.'

One of the best records of this brief battle is an old print made from a drawing done on the spot. It is also one of the earliest views of Roseau, showing the first church and gives an idea of the size of the town. The harbour is crowded with ships and flat bottomed boats are ferrying troops ashore. Troops already landed are moving along the shore towards the rough defences where Fort Young now stands. Others are engaged with French militia men on the slopes above the town where the defenders shoot desperately from trenches and wooden palisade batteries. Roseau appears to be deserted, the inhabitants having moved to safety.

At noon the following day, the plunder of Roseau was ended by official order. The inhabitants were directed to surrender and take an oath of submission which the parish priest of Roseau, Fr Massey, persuaded most of the leading planters and officers of the militia to agree to. This surrender greatly angered the French Governor in Martinique who had hoped that the colonists would have let Roseau burn and continue to harass the British from the steep mountains around Roseau. He was most annoyed however by Fr Massey's role of peace diplomat and ordered the priest never to communicate with him again.

The British attack on Roseau in 1761.

By December 1761, Lord Rollo was confident that the islanders were going to remain at peace and he left the island in charge of a British commander. Lord Rollo and Lord Douglas gave the island two new place-names: Douglas Bay, formerly Malalia; and Rollo's Head, known to the French as Pointe Ronde. The following year the British captured Martinique, St Lucia, St Vincent and Grenada. In Dominica there was little the French inhabitants could do but settle down peacefully under the new British military rule. At the Peace of Paris in 1763, when Britain and France bargained for Canada, Dominica was officially ceded to Britain. But France had made a permanent mark on Dominica, and despite British political power, the French language, customs, religion and place-names would remain forever strong in the island's history.

7
The British in Dominica

The Treaty of Paris had transferred to the British the islands of Dominica, Tobago, St Vincent, Grenada and the Grenadines. In 1764 Brigadier-General Robert Melville was appointed Captain General and Governor-in-Chief of this group, which was described as the Southern Caribee Islands. The headquarters of the group were at Grenada and Lieutenant-Governors were appointed to the other islands. This arrangement continued until 1770 when Dominica was given a separate government under the administration of Sir William Young, who was succeeded in 1774 by Thomas Shirley. The French in Dominica noted with concern that the treaty gave them no guarantees; but there was no question of them having to leave, for the British were interested in keeping the agricultural production and trade of the island operating. Since the French planters owned well-established estates there was no point in disrupting production by sending them off their lands. The export duties and taxes were needed to finance British development, and the French coffee from Dominica swelled the West Indian exports to Britain.

With British occupation, the number of settlers in Dominica increased rapidly and though they were able to live altogether in relative peace, there were noticeable divisions between the two European groups on the island. Everyone serving as an official had to take several oaths which were aimed at eroding the political and religious rights of the French. The first simply declared allegiance to the British Sovereign; this was followed by the Oath of Supremacy, swearing that no other power or religious authority within Britain or her Dominions were superior to the King; and the third, the Oath of Abjurations, declared King George III the rightful King of Britain. The last oath, a declaration against transubstantiation, shook the very foundations of the doctrines of the Roman Catholic faith:

'I . . . do solemnly and sincerely profess in the presence of Almighty God, testify and declare that in the sacrament of the Lord's supper there is not any Transubstantiation of the Elements of Bread and Wine into the Body and Blood of Christ, at or after consecration thereof by any Person whatsoever. And that the Invocation or Adoration of the Virgin Mary or any other Saint and the sacrifice of the Mass as they are used in the church of Rome are supersticious and idolatrous . . .'

The people were allowed the 'free Exercise of the Roman Catholic Religion as far as the Laws of England permit.' But as the Law required each member of the Legislature to take all the oaths, the French Catholics were excluded from participating in the government of the island. Many Frenchmen signed these declarations to avoid trouble and though British planters filled the Legislative Assembly it had little effect on religion, and Catholicism continued to flourish.

Under Britain, Dominica was officially Protestant but the numbers were small. The minister was appointed through the government, worshipping for the government, controlled by the government, and its buildings were repaired with government funds. The first Anglican church was built in 1766. It was a large wooden building which stood in the centre of the 'Church Savannah' now known as Newtown Savannah. Behind the church was the cemetery, still used today, which contains some of the oldest tombs in the island. The British planters were a very irreligious lot and soon the church was in disrepair and services were being held in the Court House; it was not until the following century that a permanent Anglican Church was built.

The Division of Land

This is a subject of capital importance in the history of every country and likewise it has determined Dominica's economic and political history. When Britain took over the island one of the main tasks which occupied attention was the redistribution, sale and setting aside of land. Surveyors and commissioners came out to make maps of the island and to organise the division of Dominica into lots. The chief surveyor was John Byres and the map which he produced laid the guidelines for map making of the island until the aerial photographs and electronic equipment of the twentieth century improved on his work. His large master-map gives the numbers of lots and the areas that were divided. These sections covered most of Dominica except for the extremely mountainous areas in the centre of the island. Even so, very little regard was given to the lie of the land and many of the lots were on the sides of precipitous slopes and deep valleys. Most were almost impossible to get to on foot, let alone establish estates and transport goods.

The commissioners were directed to sell the land by public auction to British subjects; an individual could not buy more than 100 acres if the land had been cleared or 300 acres if the land was forested. Auctions were held throughout Britain and it must be remembered that these people were bidding for land of which they knew nothing except for the marks on the map which Byres and his team of surveyors had produced. A map, which though accurate in outline, only sketched in five or six taller peaks and gave no clue of what the rest of the island was like. This added to the general confusion of land distribution. Many buyers were only speculators – they were not interested in cultivating the land but used their deeds to borrow money in Britain and hopefully sell the land at a profit. Others were rich proprietors who had no intention of coming out but would send or appoint attorneys to cultivate and run their estates. Those who did decide to settle had to invest vast sums building roads even before they began spending money on mills, estate buildings, canals and slaves. Years later, planters in the Assembly stated that, had they been told what was in store for them in Dominica, not one of them would have bought a single acre of land on the island! But they had received some warning. A little handbook on Britain's new colonies printed in 1764, gives this interesting comment.

'These islands are not the promised land, flowing with milk and honey . . . of those who adventure, many fall untimely. Of those who survive, many will fall before enjoyment; and to the happy few that providentially succeed, may peace and plenty without envy be their lot, and crown them with felicity.'

The French settlers already on the island were not allowed to sell or dispose of their lands without the permission of the Governor and had to

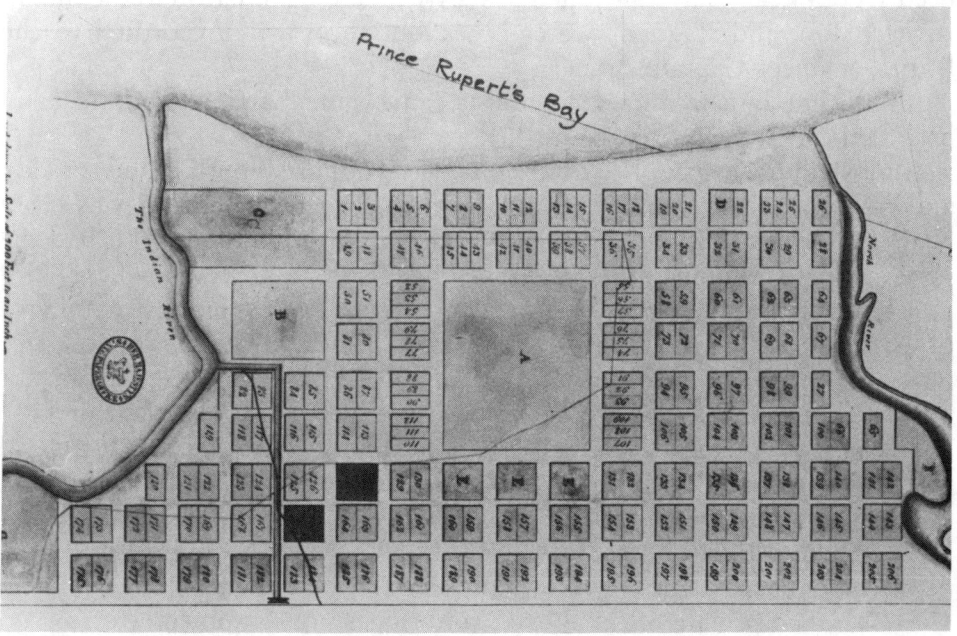

The 1765 town plan of Portsmouth laying it out as the capital of Dominica. Letters indicate A: Public Square. B: Market Place. C: Bleaching place and Careenage. D: Customs House. E: House of Assembly, Court House, Public Offices. F: Jail. G: Land for Governor.

pay an annual rent on every acre they owned. The commissioners were also empowered to make grants of land of up to 30 acres to certain British subjects but much of the land was never sold and most of what was sold was never cultivated. In all this activity the Caribs were ignored and only a 232 acre plot was set aside for them in the centre of what is now the Carib 'reserve'. The surveyors also outlined a strip of land three chains wide along the entire coast of the island. This was known as the 'King's Three Chains' or 'King's Fifty Paces' because it was set aside for the government to construct any necessary building or fortifications.

Dominica was valued at £313,666. 19s. $2\frac{1}{4}$d. and the money from these sales of land went to the British Crown. It is said that George III stated 'the money from the sale of Dominica could make up for lack of a dowry from Queen Charlotte', thus establishing the legend that this happened! It is probably because of this that many Caribs have believed that Queen Charlotte was instrumental in setting aside for them their original portion of land.

Towns and Names

Portsmouth was intended to be the seat of government of the island and this was a natural choice, for Prince Rupert Bay is an excellent harbour and land surrounding the bay is flat. But it never became the capital for it had been set out near a large swamp and partly in it; the land around the Indian River is low and stagnant water lay about the town. According to the British engineer Captain Bruce:

'In this hot climate the water soon becomes putrid and exhalations from it taint the air to the leeward of it.'

Almost all of the people who tried to settle at Portsmouth found it sickly and were forced to abandon it and go to Roseau where the air was more healthy. Portsmouth made little progress as a town and in 1770 it had the appearance of a ruined and deserted village. Roseau however, where shipping and anchoring places were much inferior was rapidly becoming a flourishing town. One reason was that in 1766 it had been declared a free port along with Portsmouth, under the British Free Ports Act. This meant that foreign ships and merchants could use the port as a place to purchase and export slaves or any British goods legally imported except for naval stores and tobacco. They might pay for these purchases either in coin or in their own colonial produce.

This interesting account of the arrival of slaves in Dominica forms part of the memoirs of James Aytoun who served for three years in Dominica, 1788–91, as a private of the 30th (Cambridgeshire) Regiment:

'Dominica was, I believe, a free port. There were frequently two or three slave ships or more at anchor, almost always about a quarter of a mile from the shore. The shipmasters had to have the slaves on deck at certain times during the day and it was said, obliged them to sing a yo-yo-yo but whether by compulsion or voluntary I know not, but it is certain they yo-yo'd in concert, so that we could hear them more than a mile and on certain days in the week the slaves were landed outside of Roseau and walked easily in what we call Indian file, that is two ranks side by side following one another like geese. The women were clothed with a short petticoat that reached to the middle of the thigh. The men had a square piece of coarse clothing and an apron about fourteen inches each way. It was a custom with those who purchased a slave to clothe the men with a pair of Osnaburgh trousers and a round hat. When a woman was purchased she was clothed in a better and decenter petticoat.

'They are all on an allowance of provisions: man, woman and child. Perhaps they live on deaf nuts. The planters generally supply them with salted fish, either from Newfoundland or United States, of an inferior quality, but the saltings of the fish is corrected by the continual use of roots, fruit or vegetables of a great many sorts. I never saw any beggars in Dominica except an English sailor sometimes who happened to be left on shore accidentally or from bad behaviour.

'It was on Sunday that the principal market was held. The slaves have Saturday afternoon and Sunday to themselves. Some of our wiseacres suppose that the negroes are ignorant. They are so in respect of religion but they are shrewd and acute and are capable of conducting themselves as well if not better than a great many of the white slaves in the British Isles. I may return to this subject again.'

In Dominica the object of this Free Port Act was trade with the French islands. Sugar, coffee and the rest were allowed to be imported where they could be sold to English merchants, and they sold in England as foreign produce. The small quantity of sugar produced in Dominica itself was sold as British grown. But this cumbersome system proved unworkable; there were opportunities for swindling, bribes and smuggling. For a short while however Roseau boomed. There were taverns, gambling houses and so-called 'hotels' run by brightly dressed free coloured women – Les Matadores. Sailors of many nations came on shore to enjoy a spot of rowdy living and visit the tippling houses where the new rum was very cheap. 'This,' commented Captain Bruce, 'occasions the loss of more men than all other bad effects of the climate.'

One of the more amusing developments of the period was the changing of names on the island. It was rather like a war with words between the English and French. The French seemed more willing to adapt to their new surroundings and gave names which suggested the natural features of the island: La Grande Bay, Le Grand Savanne, Pointe Ronde, Anse Noir and Soufriere are examples. There were other places of peculiar interest: Gueule du Lion near Colihaut, because the point resembled the mouth of a lion;

Detail of an oil painting by Agostino Brunias c. 1780s showing a vendor's stall (left) and an impression of Fort Young in the distance. (Courtesy Mark Gilbey)

Roseau, because of the tall river reeds which covered the area; Capucin, after the religious order which had missionaries in the district and Massacre, after the massacre of the Caribs at Indian Warner's settlement.

Early in the English period however the map makers and the government officials swept most of the French names off the map and put British place-names and those of British colonial personalities instead. La Grande Bay became Colebroke, but that did not last. La Soye Bay became St Andrews Bay and later Woodford Hill. Grand Anse was named after the gay cavalier Prince Rupert and officially this name remains, although people of the north coast still say in patois: 'Mwe ka alle Gwand Anse.'

The old Carib name Cashacrou was replaced by Scotts Head, named after the first British Lieutenant-Governor, Captain George Scott, and as has been mentioned, Bay de Mallalia became Douglas Bay. These are just a few examples and a study of the maps will show others. One of the biggest failures was in trying to call the Layou River the Thames and to rename Roseau Charlotteville after the wife of George III. The British had hoped to move the town further south thereby creating a new town. The plan never materialised but the area is still known as Newtown. Other names were added throughout the course of history, especially estate names; those such as Blenheim, Stewart Hall, Hodges, Melville Hall, Hatton Garden and Castle Bruce were called after their owners or notable places in Britain.

The Island Fortress

To keep Dominica under her rule, Britain had to defend the island. Besides the surveyors and commissioners who came out to plan and organise the sale of land, engineers were commissioned to produce plans for the defence of the colony. Captain Bruce, Royal Engineer, was head of that particular project in Dominica and in March 1770 he dispatched a report to London giving his suggestions, maps and designs for fortifications needed on Dominica. The leeward coast from Scotts Head to Capucin, then known as Cape Melville, had excellent anchorages along its shore. They were protected from strong winds and had few dangerous rocks or reefs about them.

It was decided that this coast needed to be well defended, while the windward coast with its rough and dangerous shoreline would offer little temptation to an enemy. However, Captain Bruce made provision in his plans for mounting a couple of guns in each of the major bays on that coast which were used by the planters for shipping produce. These harbours are known today as: Grand Bay, Woodford Hill, Marigot, San Sauveur, Hodges, Batibou near Calibishie and Anse du Mé. The main fortifications were centred around the principal towns.

The courtyard of the Roseau Town Council buildings were once used as slave-trading baracoons.

Remains of the iron crane which lowered estate produce into boats from the cliff-top at Rosalie on the rough windward coast.

Portsmouth and Prince Rupert Bay were considered to be the first and most important object to be secured by fortifications in the island. This was because of the spaciousness of the bay, the good anchorage and the general safety of the area. Ships could lie at anchor even in the hurricane season and they were assured of fresh water from the rivers running into the bay. Douglas Bay was also a very good anchorage and Toucari, just further north, was constantly visited by coasting vessels. Bruce noted that during a war it would be the first bay to be visited by ships coming from the north in need of protection.

His plans for the Cabrits were very detailed. He thought it was an excellent position and planned a fort with barracks to hold 500 men and a company of artillery with officers, a powder magazine to contain 1250 barrels of gunpowder with a storehouse, hospital, cisterns and other necessary buildings. Guardhouses were also to be constructed at different positions on the hilltops and small batteries and outposts were to be positioned along the south side of Prince Rupert Bay.

In Roseau, Bruce planned small forts or batteries to protect the town and the bays to the north and south. He reorganised Melville's Battery overlooking Newtown; expanded Fort Young to contain 17 cannons; designed defences for Morne Desmoulins, Loubiere, and Woodbridge Bay. Extensive plans were made for the fortification of Guys Hill, later to be known as Morne Bruce after the engineer himself. This fort was one of Bruce's main interests. The cliffs and steep slopes which surrounded it on three sides made it a natural post for the defence of Roseau.

To get messages up and down the coast he organised a line of signal stations. It was said that a message could get from Scotts Head to the Cabrits in less than half an hour by this method. If, for instance, there was a fleet of French ships approaching Dominica from the south, Scotts Head station would signal to Fort Young; the gun and flag signals went on to Morne Daniel, Layou, Grand Savannah, Pt Crabier, Pt Ronde, Cabrits and finally to Cape Melville.

Work on the defences for Portsmouth and Roseau began in 1771 but not all of Bruce's plans were carried out. Yet well over £100,000 were spent on defences. Slaves and skilled craftsmen were rented by the government from planters to cut stone from quarries on Grand Savannah, carry boulders, haul cannon and clear land. When Britain had completed the project 235 cannons of varying types and sizes were pointing seawards from the coast of Dominica waiting for the enemy.

Government

When Dominica became a separate colony of Britain in 1770, the island inherited the complex colonial representation system which was already causing trouble in other British colonies. Dominica had been the first to break away from the government of Grenada, formed in 1763, but largely because of planter pressure, within twelve years all the other islands of the group had separate Assemblies also. The government of the colony was placed by the English Crown in the hands of a Governor, Council and Assembly.

The governor was appointed in England by the Crown and was made responsible for the peace and safety of the island. His salary, however, and all the money for the running of the colony was voted by the Assembly. Apparently West Indian governors were supposed to be superhuman, for besides being responsible for the defence of the colony and the upkeep of forts, his was the final word in difficult law cases; he was in charge of the financial matters of the Anglican church, and most difficult of all, he was expected to be on good terms with the Assembly. The governor appointed the Council, and this body was usually on good terms with the governor because obviously he would not nominate people with whom he found it difficult to work. Its members were planters and merchants, but it was especially difficult to get suitable people in Dominica as so many of the British residents were roughly educated attorneys taking care of estates for absentee landlords. It was the Assembly which attracted these types most and it was this body which caused the governors most trouble. Governors often called the members arrogant and difficult. This they may have been, but their position did not encourage them to be anything else. One of the most sensible rules for making an institution run smoothly is to make the people in power also responsible for good order and efficiency. In the eighteenth century, the governors and lieutenant-governors had the responsibility but the Assemblies had a great deal of power. They had power to criticise the governor and deny him money for his schemes, but the constitution did not allow them to do the job themselves. In addition, since the governor was appointed by the government in England, he always had instructions from that government as to what he was to do. In many cases these instructions did not meet with the approval of the Assemblies. There was constant friction over how much money should be spent on defence; whether the church and rector should receive funds; which roads were most important and what laws should be passed. In the latter case especially, the plantocracy, via the Assembly and the Council, could impose its views on the governor and stand in the way. This was most evident with regards to laws for improving the conditions of slavery. Towards the end of the eighteenth century the Dominica Assembly was even writing to the British crown demanding that their governor be removed.

From 1770 to 1972, meetings of the Assembly were held at the Court House in Roseau. In this building, all court cases were tried and all business of the colony was transacted. The Court House of 1770, of wood construc-

The mace, given to the Dominica House of Assembly in 1771, is one of the oldest in the West Indies.

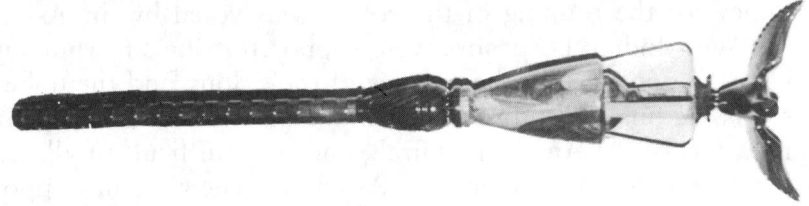

The new wooden mace, topped by a sisserou parrot in flight was carved from local wood by craftsman Martin Allen for Independence in 1978.

tion, was replaced in 1810 by a handsome stone building on the same site. This was in constant use until arsonists set fire to it on 16 June 1979. The building stood in ruins until 1993 when it was restored and was used as the House of Assembly once more. In 1771 the governor presented the Assembly with an ornate silver mace – the ceremonial staff representing authority and symbol of the monarch during sessions of the House. This two-hundred-year-old mace was used up to 1978 when a replacement, carved from Dominican woods was adopted by the House of Assembly on the night of the island's independence from Britain.

With the establishment of a government under the British there came the first printing press. The first English printer on the island was William Smith, who established *The Dominica Gazette* at Charlotte Town (Roseau) in July 1765.

To protect the island, and to protect the white and free coloured inhabitants from possible slave rebellion, a local militia system was instituted. The Militia Act of 1772 directed that every able-bodied free man between 16 and 50 was to serve on the Militia in their district. The companies of the Militia held exercises in their Parish on an appointed Saturday once every month and once together in Roseau and in Portsmouth. There were different uniforms for the southern and northern troops and the flashy display gave those who wished to play the dandy a good opportunity twice a month. Besides this Militia, there were the 'Regulars' – troops of British regiments stationed in the garrisons at Morne Bruce and the Cabrits.

Much is said about the conditions of slavery in the Caribbean and its effects on the slave populations but less is heard of the brutal treatment meted out to the soldiers stationed in the garrisons and barracks of the islands.

The letters, diaries and reports which have been found written by men stationed at the Cabrits and Morne Bruce reflect the miserable existence of British privates at these and other stations in the Caribbean. James Aytoun of the 30th (Cambridgeshire) Regiment based at Morne Bruce for three years from 1788 notes that the officers were ill trained and took little interest in the men. Rations of food and clothing were irregular. There was corruption at lower levels also and brutality was so rife that 'No wonder that so many of our men deserted to the enemy.' The harshness of military life blunted whatever sympathy he may have otherwise had for the slaves. 'The negroes have a good deal more liberty than soldiers,' he noted bitterly.

A large percentage of the money spent by Britain on Dominica was devoted to defence; the colonial society lived in constant fear of slave risings and the threat of maroons who had escaped to freedom in the hills. A show of force was always necessary for internal order while at the same time a close watch had to be kept for French activity across the channels to the north and south. Although the planter Assembly was constantly bickering with the governor about the amounts spent on defence, they knew only too well that military presence was vital for their survival.

8
The Plantation

Coffee

It was the French planters who introduced coffee to the island after 1725 and their estates became the most flourishing. South of Roseau, especially in the area of Soufriere, there were the main groups of French coffee estates as well as in the north around Colihaut and Capucin. When the British came, they also developed coffee estates at the same time establishing sugar cane. Work in the coffee field was less laborious than on a sugar estate but nevertheless there was much to be done.

The forest had to be cut and burnt and the land prepared for planting coffee seedlings. Fields were marked out in even rows with plants an equal distance from each other. On steep slopes the land was levelled with terraces – both for the convenience of working and to prevent soil from being washed away by rain. On old French estates, especially in the most southern and northern areas of the island, dry-stone terraces can still be seen along the hillsides. It was on the earth between these terraces that the coffee was planted. Well trimmed wind-breaks of *Poixdoux* trees protected

Bois Cotlette near Soufriere, pictured here in 1905, is one of the oldest and last surviving estate houses in Dominica.

the plants from strong winds and the fields were constantly kept weeded and tidy to ensure good yields. Ground provisions were planted between the young trees and on French plantations, cassava was a favourite cash crop, providing an income for the estate until the coffee trees had matured.

By the end of August and beginning of September the coffee was ready for harvesting. From early morning the slaves went out to pick the berries. There was a break at midday and then work continued until late afternoon. At the end of the morning and afternoon sessions the negro slave driver would check how much each worker had brought in and those who failed to show full baskets would be punished. The driver was usually allowed to give up to six lashes on such occasions.

When the coffee berries were brought in from the field they were put through a mill to take off the skin and would then be washed in a cistern of water. The coffee was next spread out on a drying platform, known to the French as the *glacis*. From here the beans were stored in a granary or *beaucan*, after which the old or sick slaves and children would sit and clean the coffee, storing the good beans and throwing away the bad. Each estate was more or less a factory, growing and processing its own product. Like any modern factory the buildings and the labour force were organised on the most economical lines and before the finished product left the estate it was packed and ready for the coffee shops of Europe.

Sugar

In comparison to the other islands of the West Indies, the cultivation of sugar cane came to Dominica very late. The early French settlers had not grown it on a large scale and it was only after the British firmly took hold of the island that any major sugar estates were planted. The larger British plantations developed in the broad river valleys along the coast. To the north there was Hampstead, Hodges, Blenheim, Woodford Hill, Londonderry, Melville Hall and Hatton Garden, while the plantations of Castle Bruce, Grand Marigot, Rosalie and Tabery dominated the Windward coast.

Like the coffee estates, specific buildings were required for the processing of sugar. On some estates there were hospitals for the treatment of the sick, as well as a *cachot* or small cell for the imprisonment of slaves. The most important buildings were the boiling and curing houses, the distillery, workshops and mill. In Dominica there were three types of mills. Estates with rivers nearby had canals and huge water wheels to drive the iron rollers which crushed the cane. The water mill was the best type, the most reliable, though the most expensive and we only see these on the larger plantations. On most coffee estates and sugar estates where rivers were difficult to tap, mills were driven by wind and animal power.

In the cattle mill, iron rollers stood upright in a circular shed and mules

An old water-driven mill on Geneva Estate.

or oxen attached to a long beam moved round and round the mill. Relays of fresh cattle kept constantly coming in. There were never more than five or six windmills on Dominica and only the ruins of two remain standing. These mills were driven by large wood and canvas sails facing the prevailing wind but were far more effective on the flatter islands of the Leewards and in Barbados.

The plantation was a community working solely for the production of sugar or coffee, and, in Dominica, many plantations grew both. Throughout the eighteenth and nineteenth centuries coffee was periodically affected by disease and during those years sugar would outstrip coffee production and estates would change crops.

In the cane fields two types of cane were planted; plant cane and ratoons. For plant canes, the land was cleared of trees and bush and burnt by 'great gangs' composed of the strongest men and women under a driver. Then trenches were dug for 'holing'. The slaves worked in a straight line, placing cane shoots into the holes. In the ratoon method, a fresh crop was grown from the new shoots which sprang from the previous crops. This method involved less labour, but if continued for too long, less sugar was produced and it became uneconomical. As the canes grew they were cleared and tended by a 'second gang', made up of the old and infirm slaves and older children. Field work was laborious and, as on coffee estates, the slaves were roused by bell or conch shell at early dawn. No labour-saving devices such as the plough were used and agriculture was primitive. When the canes were ripe they were cut with cutlasses or cane bills and were bundled and carted to the mills without delay, for sugar is highly perishable.

Crop time was a time of bustling activity and harder work. Continuously from January or February to May or June the estate ran feverishly. Only in the fields did work cease at night. The canes were stripped of their leaves and fed into the mills; the juice was channelled from the rollers along gutters into siphons, where it was clarified by heating with a little lime. From the siphons it passed into copper boilers hanging over fires fed with wood and cane trash, and was continuously stirred. In the third, the *teche*, the smallest and hottest of the boilers, the boiling was completed and the juice became a thick syrup.

From the *teche* the syrup was led into shallow troughs to cool, then put into 'hogsheads', large barrels for storing syrup in the curing house. Through holes in the bottom of these casks or sugar moulds molasses fell into cisterns to be reboiled. What remained in the casks was muscovado, or crude brown sugar. From the factory the sealed hogsheads were exported. The estates also made rum, and for this the juice was heated, distilled, and stored in casks.

Because there were no roads, schooners travelled round the coast of the island carrying mail, food and merchandise for the isolated settlements. These schooners, also known as droghers, landed at various bays off-loading supplies for estates and taking on sugar and coffee.

Plantation Society

The plantation society was rigidly divided into set groups. Most British estates in Dominica were run by managers or attorneys while the actual owner remained in England or resided in another more prosperous colony. The attorneys in charge wrote long detailed letters to their proprietors and from these we get a good idea of the problems and methods of running an estate in eighteenth century Dominica. Many complained of the climate, bad communications, and seemed to dislike living on their isolated estates. One distraught attorney living on the windward coast in 1780 was constantly asking the owner for a transfer to a more favourable post in St Kitts!

Some managers came out to Dominica with their wives, but many were bachelors who had mistresses from among the slaves or free coloured women. A coffee planter in the parish of St Paul, wrote that it was better to have a wife than a mistress, 'who, with the whole of her family and connexions, must be pampered and indulged, and thus spread jealousies, murmurs, and discontent, throughout all the other negroes of the Plantation.' Yet he admits in the same chapter that few attorneys in Dominica

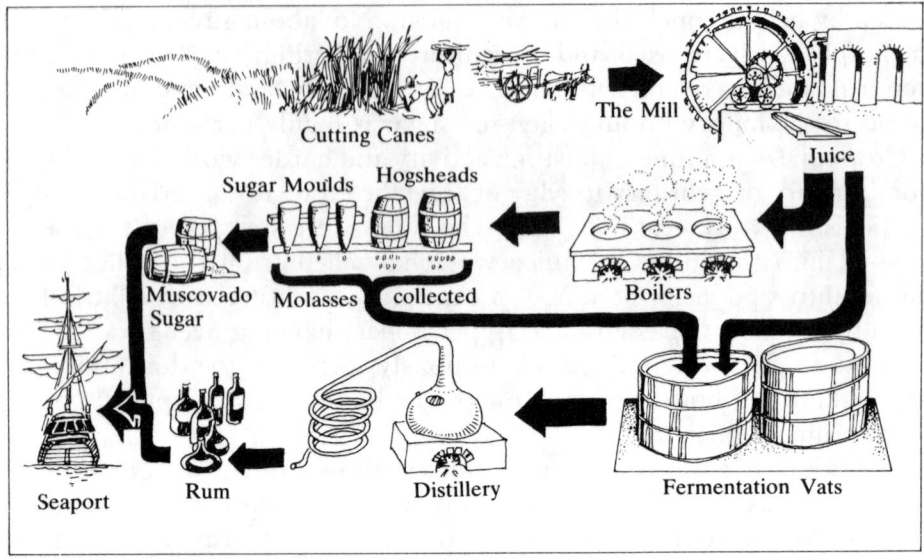

The manufacture of sugar and rum from the sugar cane fields to export.

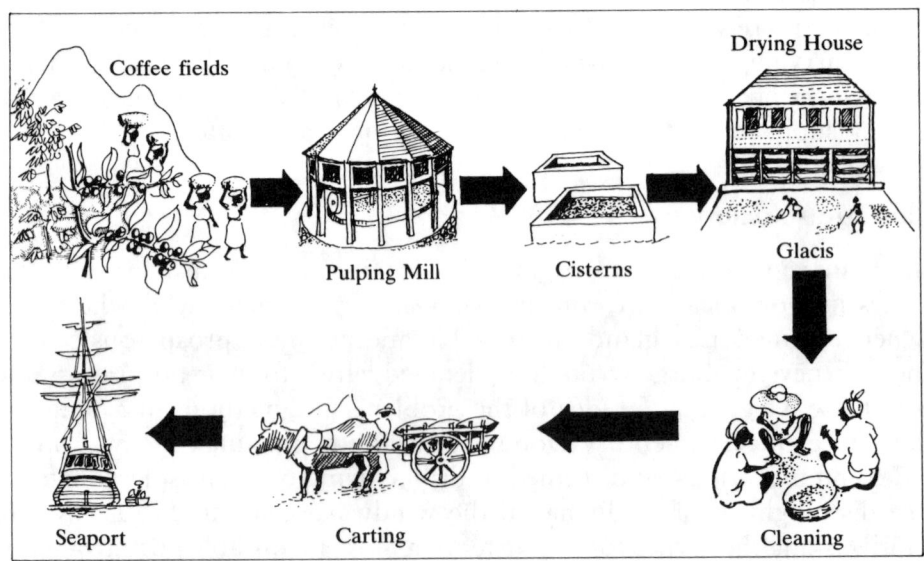

The stages of coffee processing and export.

could be called gentlemen. 'When we look round and see the many drunken, ignorant, illiterate, dissolute, unprincipled Characters, to whom the charge of Property is confided . . . it is no wonder the Estate goes to ruin and destruction.'

Along with a manager, the larger estates had overseers, also called bookkeepers, for besides keeping books it was their duty to see to odd jobs, be responsible to the manager, oversee the slave driver and check on field work. They were poorer white men hoping to better themselves, but they usually remained among the lowest dregs of the European society in the islands.

Next on the scale was the driver. He was taken from among the slaves but was an officer of importance and had to be respected. His duty was to preserve order among the slaves; to discover and expose any plots or secret plans among them and to direct them at work. Two, three or more drivers were necessary on big estates.

Then there were the other slaves. On the larger estates, such as Castle Bruce, there were between two to three hundred and sometimes more. They lived in wood and thatch houses some yards from the sugar works and had their provision grounds in the hills above the estates. There were two main groups; field slaves and skilled slaves. As the name implies, the first group worked in the field, planting, weeding and reaping the crop. The skilled slaves were the masons and carpenters; coopers, who made barrels; and wheel-wrights who produced the ox-carts and wheels. The planters hired out these skilled slaves to the government for building fortifications and general public work. Slaves skilled in the production of sugar and syrup were very important figures in the mills and boiling houses. White artisans, masons and carpenters, were also employed on the estates.

In the plantation houses there were house slaves, cooks and chambermaids who often considered themselves to be superior to the rest. This main house, in which the planter or manager and his family lived was the 'great house', though in French-influenced Dominica, it was more often called 'La cou'; the yard. On some estates La cou referred to the mill yard itself, while the 'great house' was called the 'chateau'. But in Dominica, few of the planter's houses were grand. The landowners did not reside here and saw no need to spend money on elaborate houses for their managers. Therefore, the island has no fine plantation mansions characteristic of the rich sugar islands. Only a few old stone residences of the French proprietors remain to give us an idea of these estate dwellings, and these have an air of quiet charm rather than richness. Most of the old estate buildings have gone to ruin; destroyed by hurricane, fire and time, but with a little imagination one can still have an idea of the rush and bustle that went on among these ruins over two centuries ago.

78 The Dominica Story

Dominican dancers in the eighteenth century.

A fascinating comparison can be made of these two pictures (above). One was drawn in the 1780s by Agostino Brunias, the other is a photograph of 1910. Inspite of being 130 years apart they show an identical scene of Bellaire dancing.

A New Culture is Born

There is an old patois saying: 'En temps esclavage negre teyka dansé Kalanday en glacis.' The *glacis*, we know, was the wide stone platform for drying coffee. On Sundays and holidays it was here that the slaves would gather to play music and dance. An old eighteenth century print of Dominica gives us an idea of these occasions:

A brightly dressed group is dancing and singing to the beat of a goat skin or 'la peau cabrit' drum. One of the women, probably the 'chanteulle', claps her hands and sings the 'lavway' while a man provides accompaniment on a 'tambou'. A couple in the centre dance what could be the 'bele'. Others, dressed in their best finery, sporting silk foulards and gay umbrellas, look on at the action. Dancing usually took place, as in Africa, in the centre of a ring of spectator participants. During the eighteenth and nineteenth centuries the slaves developed and adapted many of the dance forms that have come down to us today. In all cases, the African rhythm and tempo were added to the dances of European origin – dances such as the Flirtations, Mazook, Lancers and the Quadrille.

From the French estate houses they adapted the Mazook – known in Europe as the Mazurka. Also from France there came the delicate steps of the 'schottische': partners faced each other and exchanged sides, touching the other's hands as they passed. The Quadrille was introduced in the early nineteenth century and the intricate movements of this dance were soon quickened and enriched. Among the different types of Quadrille are the 'Sharp', 'Slow', 'French' and 'Irish' Quadrilles, each having their own detailed 'sets' and 'pieces'.

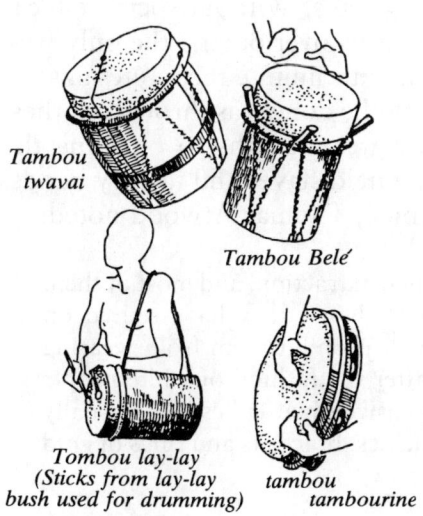
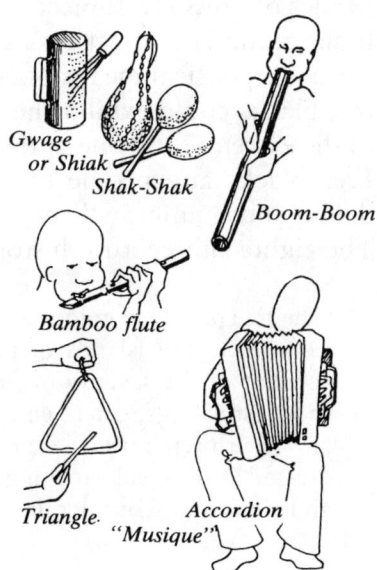

Folk music instruments.

Probably the earliest dance, the root, and the one that seems to have survived stronger than the rest is the 'Bele'. The African influence appears to be untouched by other dance or music forms and there are many types of 'Bele': Bele Rickety, Bele Contredanse, Bele Juba, Bele Priority and Bele Sauté.

The drums they used were purely of African origin. Hand drums and stick drums of varying shapes and sizes were carved from wood and stretched with goat skin, though later, the estate cask replaced the carved hollow. From the *bois canot* and the bamboo, the *boom-boom* was fashioned. There was the triangle and the *tambal* or large tambourine of goat skin while the fiddle and much later the accordion were added to the traditional instruments.

There were also sports and games, many of which have since died out. An old print shows a 'cudgelling match' though the men themselves may have known it as 'Bwa', there were wrestlers and 'stick men' who danced on stilts and can be remembered on the streets of Roseau as late as the 1950s. There were children's games and play songs, songs for wakes, work-songs, songs of sadness and songs of joy, religion and celebration. Some are remembered but many more have been forgotten and are lost to us forever. The story of these developments was studied and recorded by the local folklorist Mabel 'Cissie' Caudeiron, and her various articles on these old customs make very interesting reading.

Clothes

Modes of dress is a subject of importance and much debate among all West Indians and is a direct result of historical systems. Without social, educational or political means of showing their status over others, the only way free blacks could exhibit their superiority was to imitate the white masters to the extreme, and one of the ways this could be done was through clothes. Free blacks and people of colour went to great lengths to outshine the denim and chambray 'livery' or 'livre' of the field slaves and factory hands. The eighteenth century historian of Dominica, Thomas Atwood noted:

> 'The free people of colour are chiefly of French extraction, and most of them came from the islands of that nation from whence they have retired on account of the severity of French laws which prohibit them from wearing shoes, stockings, ornaments of any dress after the fashion of white people . . . Their preparations are usually very expensive; their ladies being usually dressed in silks, silk stockings and shoes; buckles, bracelets and rings of gold and silver to a considerable value . . . '

The colours and turbans of Africa were added to European dress and from these fashions the traditional island costumes developed; the 'jupe' and the beautiful 'robe douiette', along with the use of family treasures such as the extravagant 'graise d'or' and the 'zanneau chenille'.

Free Dominicans in the 1770s. The artist Agostino Brunias lived and painted in Dominica for a long period during the eighteenth century.

An interesting comment on dress and free black enterprise comes from a soldier stationed at Morne Bruce in 1788:

'The women who came to market took pride in sporting five or six printed petticoats above their haunches and as many large printed handkerchiefs tied round their heads to make a cotton cone, fourteen or more inches in height. I should have observed that the planters or managers of estates or plantations send their fruits and roots not to the market but to a trusty negro wench who is kept in Roseau permanently to act as huxter or retailer of such fruits and roots as she receives and when working negroes cannot sell what they have brought to the market, they are constrained to bargain with the black resident woman who, as huxter, makes a respectable living and appearance by buying cheap and selling dear.'

In observing the dress of the men, the soldier continues:

'The men slaves are generally allowed yearly a round hat, bound with blue tape and a pair of Osnaberg trousers. The hat and trousers are worth about three shillings but blackey manages, by selling his spare provisions, to add a shirt to his wardrobe. The men slaves never wear the shirt at work but when they go to market or on an errand they pull a clean shirt out of the crown of their hat and put it on.'

This concern for standards of dress is not altogether over and as ideas changed in the twentieth century the House of Assembly even passed an Act in July 1971 to make special provision for a national dress and an order was issued laying down the details and colours of 'shirt-jacks' and footwear to be worn on official and formal occasions.

9
The French Return

The American War of Independence

Traders from North America supplied Dominica with lumber, shingles, wood hoops, flour, rice, salt fish, livestock and other produce which the local planters badly needed. These articles were essential for running the estates: food for the slaves and management, lumber for buildings and barrels, as well as horses and cattle for breeding and rearing. In return for these goods, the islanders traded rum, molasses and other produce of the estates. Besides this, Roseau was a free port, visited by merchant ships of all nations operating in the Caribbean and the town had become quite a business centre. An even more notable free port was the small Dutch island of St Eustatius through which Dominican merchants and planters were doing a big trade in sugar and coffee. But these established trade patterns were soon shattered by the American War of Independence.

During the eighteenth century the desire of the thirteen British colonies in America to assert their rights to independent government steadily increased. The majority of English politicians and indeed King George III, did not agree with the American claims, and the result of divided interest and misunderstandings was that England and her American colonies went to war in 1775.

The Americans knew that people in the West Indies also felt their interests were not those of the mother country. Many of the planter Assemblies agreed that England was anxious to receive West Indian sugar but she was not anxious to allow her colonies to act as they thought fit.

On the other hand, the West Indians realised that their island position made them easy targets for other European powers, and knew that they depended for their existence on the good offices of the British navy. To this end naval bases had been set up at Port Royal in Jamaica and English Harbour in Antigua for the upkeep of the British fleet in the Caribbean. The West Indians therefore refrained from declaring themselves independent when the Americans did so in 1776. West Indian sympathies, however, were with their fellow colonists.

As things turned out, Dominica, along with the rest of the West Indies, suffered materially from the war. The food supplies she had been getting from North America were cut off as the Americans became occupied with fighting or their traders were halted by British naval blockade. The people who felt the shortage most were the slaves of Barbados whose rations of salt fish, flour and biscuits were sadly depleted. In Dominica, however, extra land was planted in provisions and the forests provided the estates with wood and thick vines for making the important hogshead barrels. All the same, there was still suffering and inconvenience as a result.

The Capture

In 1778 France entered the war for American independence against Great Britain. The French had had their eyes on Dominica since 1761 and took the earliest opportunity to launch an attack. Spies had been sent from Martinique to check on the island's defences and note the condition of the militia and troops. Many French inhabitants had been informed of the impending attack and even Maroons in the hills had pledged their support to the French cause.

Their offensive began between three and four o'clock on the morning of Monday 7 September 1778. They had chosen the hurricane season and a night of the full moon in the belief that the English would not expect an attack during that period. The fleet of four frigates, ten armed sloops and schooners, and about twenty troop transports carrying almost 3,000 men crossed the channel from Martinique. Besides the regular troops this number included over a thousand renegade whites, negroes and mulattos.

The French capture of Scotts Head.

Their first obstacle was the fort at Cashacrou or Scotts Head. But this was easily taken, for it had been well planned. The night before, French inhabitants had visited the fort and entertained the British soldiers until they were properly drunk; then they spiked the cannons with sand. When the French stormed the fort the following morning, the troops were taken by surprise. At the capture, a celebration signal was fired and this was the first notice the British in Roseau had of the attack.

The rest of the action that day was swift. The men of Roseau were called to arms while women and children were guided into the hills by their slaves. The French members of the militia did not assist in the defence of the town and the number of active men was less than a hundred. The guns on forts and batteries surrounding Roseau were in bad repair, especially those on Melville's battery where the gun carriages were so rotten that they were soon broken to pieces and the guns had to be rested along the wall for shooting.

Nevertheless, the French did not march on Roseau easily. By midday all the troops had landed and were pushing towards the town from Pointe Michel. After three unsuccessful attempts they took Loubiere and headed on for Roseau. Later that afternoon the French gained possession of the heights above the town and it appeared to the British governor, Stuart, that the enemy were waiting for darkness to make their final attack. Realising his force was small he therefore decided to surrender the island to the French.

The victors were then led triumphantly into Roseau by their general, the Marquis DeBouille. They had put flowers in their caps as a sign of victory and with their drums beating a slow march they passed the small British company and entered Fort Young.

The commanders of both forces met at Government House to sign the 27 Articles of Capitulation which laid down the terms of the surrender. The following day Prince Rupert Bay surrendered and the British troops, led by Governor Stuart, left Dominica. For several days afterwards, British inhabitants from all parts of the island came to sign the articles. As soon as a new form of government had been settled, the Marquis DeBouille appointed the Marquis Duchilleau to be governor of the island and returned to Martinique. Dominica would be under French rule for the next five years.

French Occupation

The instructions Duchilleau received were to promote general contentment, agriculture and commerce. But most important he was to make Dominica a strong bastion and communication link between Martinique and Guadeloupe. Fortifications had to be improved, a strong garrison had to

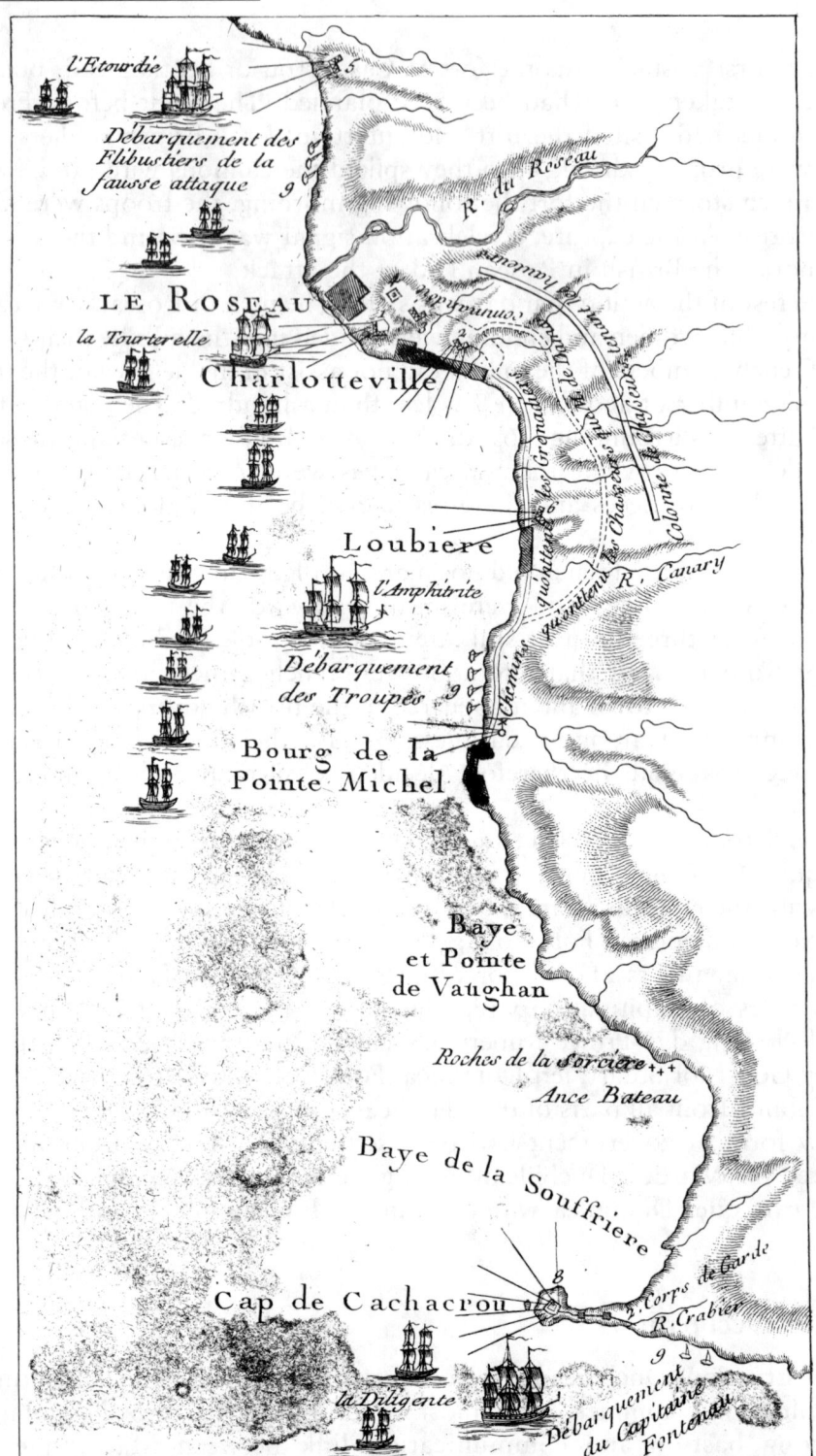

The French plan of their landing and attack on the south-west coast on 7 September 1778.

established, and a French militia formed, while at the same time the British population and slaves had to be controlled. At that time the island's population consisted of 1,574 whites, most of them French; 574 free mullatos and blacks, and 14,309 slaves.

The British resented Duchilleau and all he stood for, and were increasingly angered by his high-handed manner of government. Fearful of plots, he ordered that no more than two Englishmen could assemble in any place and that no lights should be seen in English houses after 9:00 pm. Other strict orders on British assembly and movement were instituted, including the opening of private letters. Violators could be shot, jailed or exiled. Throughout his period of government the British inhabitants were constantly protesting that many of the agreements or articles signed on the surrender had been broken by Duchilleau.

Nevertheless, the dictatorial commander continued apace. Disregarding French pleas for economy he drove ahead with plans for forts and roads. He employed engineers, pressed slaves into service, and called in all heavy arms and ammunition. The strong stone roads he built remained for many years the best in the island and patches of the French 'pave' still exist.

To man the forts and organise labour the troops were increased, and to feed them, Duchilleau ordered the planters, via the Assembly, to provide meat. The Assembly protested, for with the large number of troops stationed on the island, one horned beast was required daily. Cattle diminished at an alarming rate, a fate that was to be repeated during the Second World War. By July 1779, work for the defence of Dominica had been completed and Duchilleau was commanding an army of heavy eaters that totalled 1,519 strong.

Under the general pressure, commerce and production dropped. Trading was difficult and there were problems with shipping even to St Eustatius. With little importing or exporting, times were hard. Slaves could not be provided with imported salt meat or fish and were encouraged to rely more on local resources. Coffee prices dropped and every Englishman who could leave the island began to do so. Even the French planters were complaining about shipping and taxes but their petitions were unsuccessful.

The bitter years of French occupation were marked by three major disasters. In 1779, a terrible hurricane hit the island, followed by another in 1780. Both were disastrous to buildings, crops and livestock. In April 1781, Roseau was destroyed by fire, resulting in property losses amounting to £200,000. This third catastrophe in three years was more than the colony could take, and the ruined English residents strongly suspected that Duchilleau had organised the destruction of the capital. But even the formidable Duchilleau was broken and in August he asked to resign the governorship and return to France.

For the next months of French occupation governor De Beaupre was in charge. But the planters felt little improvement. By this time, the Maroons were becoming a serious threat to estates as they swept down from their fortified mountain camps, and a new confrontation was beginning.

As a result of the hurricane damage, a fund was launched in London to raise money for the destitute in Dominica. It was organised by English proprietors with interests in the island and donations amounting to £1,500 were recovered. The destitute did not see a penny of the fund, however, for the committee in charge had other ideas.

'... Taking afterwards into consideration that a public gaol was much wanting in the island ... and being convinced that the distribution of so small a sum as £1,500 amongst many sufferers would tend very little to alleviate their losses, (the committee) were of the opinion that the best manner of disposing of the said sum would be towards the building of a convenient and sufficient island gaol at Roseau, in ease of the Colony expenses.' And so it was thanks to a hurricane that Dominica received her first proper jail!

The Battle of the Saintes

For a brief period in 1778, the French held Guadeloupe, Dominica, Martinique and St Lucia. These four islands set in a direct line between the two large groups of British colonies to the north and south, were valuable to France. They provided her with a position of naval superiority which was vital in the eighteenth century. Moreover, in Martinique and St Lucia, were the two best harbours in the eastern Caribbean. But the situation changed in December 1778 when the British captured St Lucia and took over the useful base from which to launch attacks on the French possessions.

In February 1782, Admiral Sir George Rodney stationed his fleet in the north of St Lucia so as to keep watch on Port Royal in Martinique. There, the French Admiral DeGrasse had collected a huge fleet comprising ships of war, a convoy of transport and store ships, along with 10,000 men. This build-up was in preparation for an attack on Jamaica, and on the morning of 8 April, Rodney was informed by British signal ships that DeGrasse was leaving Martinique.

Within two hours, Rodney's fleet was underway. Sir Samuel Hood led the front section or vanguard, while Admiral Drake commanded the rear; using all available sail, the fleet swept northwards in hot pursuit of the enemy.

The following morning the French were sighted off the north coast of Dominica. The vanguard of the British fleet were within cannon-shot of the enemy's rear division, but most of the British ships had been becalmed off Dominica's leeward coast. This was an area unpopular with seamen, for the

The French Return

The lines of French and British ships meet in the Battle of the Saintes. The British are in the foreground of the picture.

high mountains of the island block the trade winds from aiding sailing ships. The delay meant that only Hood's section was able to get into action and there was a brief exchange of fire.

For two more days the French and British fleets manoeuvred off Dominica with Rodney trying to get into a position where he could compel the enemy to fight. De Grasse had been directed to get the French convoy to Jamaica without action on the way but besides the British menace, two or his ships were now damaged and he decided to go to their rescue. As a result of this decision battle could no longer be avoided and on the morning of 12 April, between the islands of Les Saintes and Dominica, the two long lines of ships engaged.

The British had the wind in their favour. During the battle, Rodney's flagship, the *Formidable*, broke through the French line. This was soon repeated at another point and the string of French ships was divided into three scattered squadrons, with the centre suffering badly from British bombardment.

By nightfall, DeGrasse had surrendered in his great flagship the *Ville de Paris*. Four other ships were taken, while the rest of the French fleet took flight. But the entire store of heavy artillery intended for the attack of Jamaica was aboard the captured ships and that important British colony was saved; Britannia became the unquestioned ruler of the waves; and in spite of his gambling, debts and malpractices, Rodney became an unchallenged British hero. Although he helped restore Dominica to Britain, the local planters were not exactly overflowing with praise for early in 1781 Rodney had sacked St Eustatius, the Dutch free port with which they had been doing much trade in coffee and sugar.

One fascinating account of the conflict comes from John Mair who owned a 150-acre estate north of Toucari and thus had a ringside seat at the battle. 'On 12 April I saw directly opposite my home (where had assembled several friends) the famous action between Rodney and Degrasse. I was breakfasting in my portico when the English fleet began the engagement, bearing down from the north on the French fleet which hugged the land and stretched from north on to south in a very regular line . . . one o'clock . . . we perceived that the English had broken the French line and were doubling on them.

'About half past two o'clock, the ships now being pell mell, we saw a French ship strike her colours . . . At about eight o'clock as I was looking at the moving lights a large flame appeared which I immediately knew to be a ship on fire . . . and with my glasses the whole scene of distress on board was clearly seen.'

Peace negotiations began soon after the Battle of the Saints and, at the formal Treaty of Versailles in September 1783, Dominica was handed back to the British. The French would have liked to retain the island and offered Tobago to Britain instead. But the British knew only too well, that although Dominica tended to be an economic liability, the island stood between two French strongholds and would be a strategic post for British forces.

British troops landed at Pointe Michel and camped there until the French government and soldiers had left the island. They then marched into Roseau and, almost tearing down the flagpole, the British inhabitants jubilantly assisted in hoisting the Union Jack over Fort Young once more.

10
The Fighting Maroons

Governor Orde and the Assembly

Immediately after the French forces got aboard their vessels at Roseau harbour in January 1784, the new British governor, John Orde, was welcomed ashore. Amidst shouts of 'Long live King George', he was escorted by the inhabitants to the Court House where he took the usual oaths of a new governor.

But when the celebrations had died down, and the reorganised English and Protestant legislature got back to work, Orde found out how short-lived the hospitality had been. He learned how difficult the men who had to vote money for his schemes could be and from the very start he did not have much luck with his secretaries; they were too free with his secrets, too deeply involved in local feuds – and there were many of these. Within months of taking office Orde became unpopular, both with the Assembly and the public.

Beside this political bickering and the problems of reviving trade and production, the government of the colony was faced with two major burdens: Americans, loyal to the British crown, had fled from the newly declared United States of America and ventured to establish new settlements in Jamaica, the Bahamas, Dominica and St Vincent. Those who came to Dominica required land and funds to get started and the Assembly, eager to increase the depleted white population, was willing to grant favours. At the same time however, the Assembly had to finance expeditions against the Maroons and these escaped slaves were by now a well-armed force.

The American Loyalists

Britain was concerned about what should be done with the British loyalists from America who could stay there after independence of the States had been recognised. Other islands had received some of these refugees and the planters of Dominica offered their services even before the French troops had left. They urged the British government to grant Crown lands in Dominica to the settlers and recommended that their possessions be transported free of cost, that they be given food supplies for at least nine months, and that they be free of taxation for 15 years.

The Home government willingly agreed to these petitions and by July 1784 a party of loyalists had arrived at Roseau and were asking Governor Orde for the promised supplies and land. According to Orde, this was the first information he had about the project.

But with the agreement of the Assembly, he issued provisions sufficient for thirty days; allowed the Americans to erect temporary houses; asked the residents to be generous to the settlers, and wrote to England for instructions. Meanwhile, the Assembly granted them tools and building materials and urged the establishment of a relief fund. Rations were distributed at the colony's expense until the Lords of the Treasury sent out supplies early in 1785. This included vast quantities of salt pork and flour, but even so, pressures were increased as more groups arrived. By August there were almost 600 refugees, many without a house or shed to cover them. Every dwelling place was full and Orde was having difficulties with the British government over the granting of lands. There was soon resentment among the Americans and conditions were made even more wretched by a destructive hurricane in 1787.

The refugees were, however, hard workers, and it was felt that this had a healthy influence on the planter society. Some attempted to establish

A cudgelling match between French and English slaves in Dominica.

cotton and according to the historian Southey, the growing of rice was introduced to Dominica by them.

The Early Maroons

Even before the European occupation of the island, Negro slaves had escaped to Dominica or been captured by the Caribs from settlements on other islands. When the French arrived, there were already a few Maroons living in Carib villages or in their own settlements in the forest. Later, the French slaves took advantage of the change of power in the 1760s and during this period the first large numbers escaped from the French estates. In the case of Grand Bay and the Jesuit confusion, a good opportunity was provided to get away.

In the safety of the mountains they built huts, planted gardens and even raised small livestock such as chickens. They had not yet taken to attacking settlements and using weapons, for these were not easy to obtain and the few estates which existed did not yet pose a threat to their freedom. But the British expansion; the building of forts, increase of troops and the importation of slaves on a larger scale, meant that Maroon activity took a new turn.

With the development of estates all over the island, the labour force constituted an overwhelming majority of the island's population. The European minority lived in constant fear of revolt and to secure their safety they maintained a rigorous discipline. Servile disobedience was, by modern standards severely punished. Flogging was common. This was an age in which people accepted the brutality of life in the British Navy, the wretchedness of workers in European factories and the hundreds of starving paupers who died daily in London, the capital of the empire itself. In the West Indies, the slaves showed their resentment in deliberate idleness or carelessness at work, and by suicide or running away in the hope of freedom. The planters called those who escaped 'runaways', as they had run away from their system. In Dominican patois they were 'Negres Marron', better known elsewhere as Maroons.

When talking of the Maroons, one must make a close study of the geography of Dominica. Modern aerial photographs of the central mountains vividly show the complex formations which aided the escaped slaves. The terrain of deep valleys and puzzling ridges was an excellent hideout for any force. The Caribs had used it to their advantage for over two hundred years and once again the luxuriant forests were offering protection.

During the first British period a number of 'runaways' were captured and brought to jail in Roseau. Conditions in the jail were appalling, and the lists of captured Maroons show that many died in prison soon after their arrival.

By the time of the second French occupation, the groups of Maroons had greatly expanded and were by now well-armed. Duchilleau had engaged some of them to help defend the island and for this purpose they had been given muskets and ammunition. When the governor received complaints from the English planters he suggested an amnesty between the two groups:

'Gentlemen of Council,
The reiterated complaints which I receive concerning the runaways, invite me to propose to you a grant of general pardon to those who will return to their masters, directing them to receive their said slaves without inflicting any punishment on them.

I submit, Gentlemen, to your opinion and your knowledge of the country, the advantages or inconveniences which might result from this measure and I will with eagerness subscribe to whatever you think proper to be done, to bring them to their duty again, to lessen their number and to prevent the continuance of their depredations . . . '

The French council tackled the problem for some time but came up with no concrete agreement. Complaints continued to pour in from planters throughout the island reporting the robbing of ground provisions, plantains, bananas, and small stock.

Eventually the Maroons began to kill and carry away cattle and plunder and set fire to the buildings on the estates. In 1781 a planter was murdered in his house and English inhabitants asked for the return of their arms to defend themselves. DeBouille, in Martinique, gave his permission for this and directed that parties should be sent into the woods to deal with the Maroons. But by then they were attacking travellers on main roads near Roseau, even at midday, and as raids on estates increased some planters found it necessary to abandon their properties.

The First Maroon War

When Governor John Orde took up office in Dominica, he faced planters who had just come through several disasters and, burdened with the American loyalists, they now also had to concentrate on the serious Maroon threat. In the Assembly, they faced the fact that they would have to organise their own little army.

By 1785, a string of Maroon camps had developed in the centre of the island. Each was led by a chief and at this time there were thirteen major figures. In the southern camps there were Congo Ray, Balla, Zombie, Jupiter, Juba, Cicero and Hall. Above Grand Fond was the camp of Mabouya and in the higher reaches of the Layou valley there was Jacko, Goreé Greg and Sandy; above Colihaut was Pharcelle. These camps were also inhabited by women and children – women such as Charlotte,

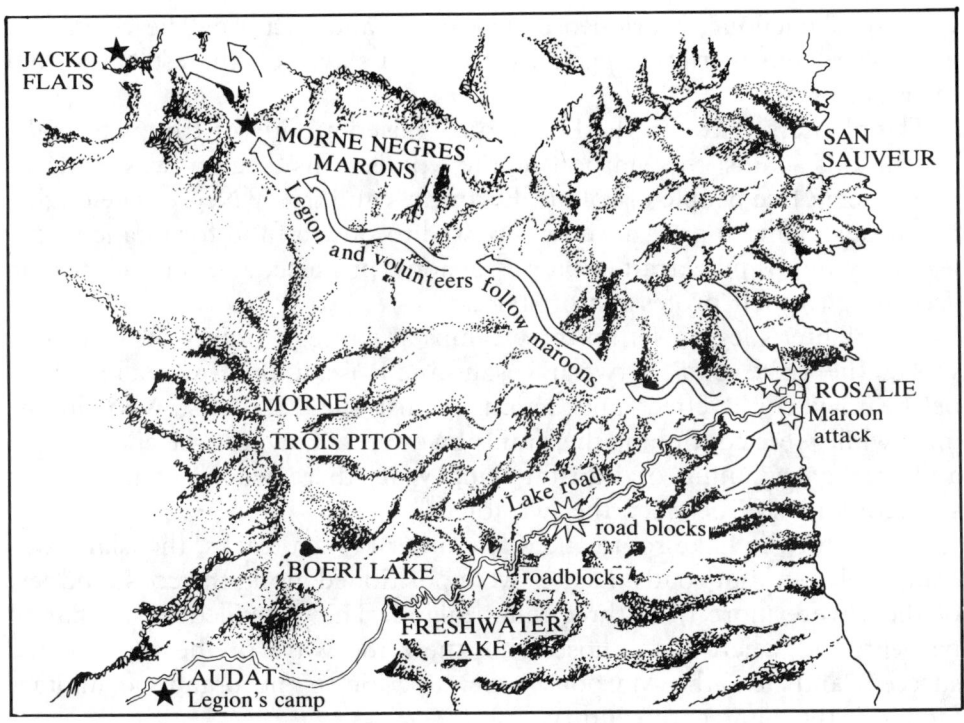

A map of Rosalie and the mountains behind showing the movements of Legionaries and Maroons during the events of 1785–86.

Morne Negres Marron, also known as Morne Laurent, rises above the rain forest in the central mountain range. Jacko Flats is away to the left of the picture.

Calypso, Angelique, Marie-Rose, Tranquille and Victorie. The chiefs had gunbearers and recruiting agents who urged slaves on the estates to join their camps.

The planters, through the Legislature, raised a body of troops to make expeditions against the Maroons in the woods. This 'Legion' was made up of 500 men: free people of colour, Europeans and trusty Negroes belonging to various plantations. An Act was passed to raise a fund for financing the legion by imposing extra tax on possessions, produce, and on each person according to their profession or status.

The planter's legion set up three camps at strategic points. A major one was on the 'Lake road', between Rosalie and Roseau. But it was a long time before they could effect any action against the Maroons, who, in the meanwhile were continuing their raids on estates. Towards the end of 1785 and at the beginning of the following year, there was a major test of strength and skill between the two forces.

Except for the Lake route and a few other French tracks, the island was completely without roads. Estates were positioned along the coast and few of them were more than three miles inland. This provided an uncharted battleground where only those who knew the ways of the forest could succeed, and here the Maroons were superior to the organised military tactics of the eighteenth century.

Their major attack on the windward coast estate of Rosalie is an example of their well-laid plans. The Maroons of Balla's camp had blocked the Lake road with large trees and guards had been set to warn them of the legion's movements. Sweeping down from the hills in the dark they plundered the sugar estate, murdering and burning the manager, the two overseers, a carpenter, and the chief Negro driver. For two days they ate, drank and revelled at the estate, most of which they had burnt. And the news of this reached Roseau before the legionaries at Laudat knew a thing about it.

This matter caused the legion to be greatly blamed for slackness and it was only with the assistance of some private persons that any counter-attacks were successful. Among these helpers was an English carpenter employed to rebuild the works at Rosalie. Leading a group of Legionaries he made an expedition across the difficult terrain towards the encampment of Balla. They must have roughly followed the course of the modern Rosalie-Pont Casse road and then swerved north to the mountain where Balla had his camp. But their main object failed, for the Maroon warriors fled from the camp during the surprise attack, leaving only women and children to be captured. These prisoners were taken to Roseau where they appeared in court in early February 1786.

The women gave away valuable information at their trial. One of them, Rosay, gave a rough census of the Maroons in Sandy's camp while others added facts concerning the position and size of certain other major camps. In the same month the chief, Cicero, was captured at Fond Boeri, near the Boeri Lake, by a free Negro, Augustine. The chief had been betrayed by a fellow slave called Petite Jacques, who appeared before the court, and on his evidence, Cicero was condemned to death. 'He shall be carried back to the common gaol of this island, there to remain until Saturday fourth March 1786, and from thence be carried to Woodbridge Bay beyond the French houses on the Kings 50 paces and there be jibbeted alive.'

The scene of Cicero's execution was Fond Cole, and there he was left exposed on the gallows as a lesson to others. The following day was the main market day, and all persons going into Roseau to sell their produce would have seen the body. The man who had helped to capture him was paid a reward of £33.

The following month three more chiefs were taken: Balla, Goreé Greg and Sandy. Balla was betrayed by a slave of Belfast Estate and was shot and injured by a party of Legionaries who brought him into Roseau. Orde, writing to the Secretary of State Viscount Sydney on 16 April, gave his account of Balla's last defiant stand. It is just one example of the hundreds of detailed reports on the Maroons which were sent to London by the governors of Dominica during the thirty years of Maroon resistance:

' . . . good fortune has given us possession of the principal Runaway Chief, Balla, many of his followers are killed and taken, many have surrendered and the rest are greatly dispersed and distressed . . . Balla . . . would not suffer himself to be taken until so wounded that he could not fly. The behaviour of this deluded wretch at his death, proved him as hardened as previous conduct had done – he refused answering almost any questions that were put to him, though perfectly in his senses – he called upon his captors repeatedly to cut off his head, telling them that they might do so, but that Balla would not die – his Obeah or charm and his child were the only things that he expressed much anxiety about. The former he wished to bury, the latter, a boy of about 5 years old he bid to remember, the Beckeys or White Man had killed his father.'

Balla, like Cicero, was taken out and exposed on the iron frame of a gibbet and took a week to die. The slaves sang a mournful Creole lament 'Balla mort, bwa gatay': Balla is dead, the woods are spoilt.

One landmark associated with the militia attack on Balla's forces still exists on the cliffs of the upper Layou gorges near Belles. These are steps cut out of solid rock called the Jacko steps after another Maroon chief. Scaling these heights was a severe test for the Legionaries as Thomas Attwood recounts:

'... having travelled all night through the woods, wading through rapid rivers, crossing over steep mountains, and encountering many rivers in their way, by noon next day they came to the mountain whereon was the encampment of Balla. This they ascended with great difficulty, it being cut into steps of a great height above each other, which had been done by the runaways for their own convenience, as being the only possible way to ascend the mountain.'

Elsewhere in the forest between Belles and Morne Diablotin, present-day hunters have reported finding china and cutlery among tree roots at the site of another Maroon camp, considered to be loot raided from plantations during the Maroon era.

Meanwhile, rangers were on the look-out for Pharcelle, one of the main chiefs in the Morne Diablotin area above Colihaut. One slave accused of supplying these Maroons with food was sentenced to death, and despite his master's efforts to save him, he was brought back to Colihaut where he worked and was burned at the stake. This came towards the end of the first roundup or Maroon war and at last, satisfied that their objective had been successful, Governor Orde wrote to the Assembly:

'Gentlemen,
I have the pleasure to inform you that in consequence of the capture and surrender of the Runaway chiefs: Balla, Goreé Greg and Sandy and the destruction and dispersion of so great a part of their followers as has lately taken place, the council and myself have determined that keeping up so large a Force as was hitherto employed against them, will no longer be necessary.

'I have therefore with their advice directed it to be reduced ... and so to be continued until Farcelle (sic) and his followers (who are still formidable) shall be broken up – until the Legislature shall determine upon some permanent establishment better suited to the present circumstances ... '

In the same letter, Governor Orde urged that the slave laws should be revised and made more humanitarian in order that slaves might not be so tempted to escape. He also called for the completion of roads, especially between Rosalie and Pagua, which would allow for better communication between estates.

The appalling state of these tracks was one of the greatest hazards to the security of the colony. A soldier of the 30th Regiment which was called over to the Windward Coast to combat some sporadic outbreaks of continued Maroon activity in 1791 recalls:

'We crossed the island, being provided with a pound of flour and a gill of rum for our day's provisions. No horse, bullock, ass or mule could go on that road ... covered with the finest natural timber I ever saw.' A section of his party was ambushed, 'three killed by stones that a party of runaway Negroes rolled down on them.'

'When on our trip around the island we came to a plantation called Castle Bruce. Our deputy governor's name was Bruce . . . he had a considerable number of slaves armed with pikes . . . He had some small cannon mounted and cared not for the runaways.'

In spite of Orde's statement, nothing seems to have been done to these tracks, for another soldier writing in 1795 comments 'The Roads are traces, not more than four and often less than two feet wide, and seldom repaired, cut thro' Woods, over Mountains, Precipices and rocky steeps, from whence the descent is made into the Ravines . . . and you have thus to ascend and descend the same face of Country, in any journey through this Island.' These were conditions which remained the same until the middle of the twentieth century.

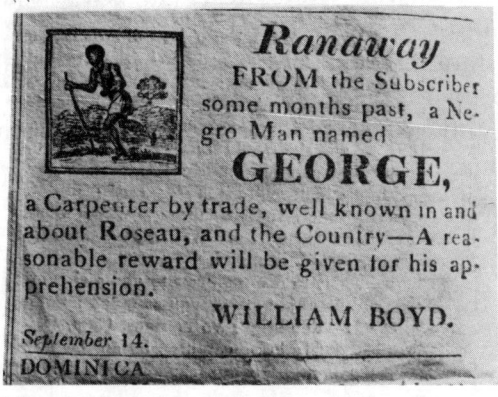

One of the many notices in the local press at that time advertising rewards for the return of Maroons.

11
Revolution and Ransom

One of the most misleading statistics quoted in outlines of Dominican history is the respective dates of French and British occupation of the island. Judged simply on that basis, Dominica should be among the more Anglophile of the West Indian islands, having had only five years of French control since it was ceded to Britain in 1763. But the island's position between two of the most important and valuable colonies of the French Empire created a constant imbalance between British occupation and French influence. The majority of the European population on Dominica was French and by cultural transfusion, so were their slaves. The movement of people and the business and family connections which were maintained between the islands defied the state of war, peace, or treaties between the colonial powers. The culture of the French families on their scattered estates triumphed over that of the British officials huddled in Roseau, or of the attorneys on the dwindling number of British estates.

As far as the British were concerned, Dominica had suffered most severely of all their islands during the war of American Independence and the related war with France. The French occupation 1778–1784 during which trade ceased and Roseau had been burned, had blasted the hopes of those engaged in developing the colony. The decade after the American Revolution found them deeply involved, unable to secure further credit, and with sizable payments still due to the British Crown for the land which had been purchased twenty years before. The intensive and long drawn out activity of the Maroons further complicated the situation. In despair, the British planters petitioned for 'a remission of the balances still due on their estates and for such other relief as would seem fair.' By about 1790 only fifty plantations were in operation while some thirty had been abandoned.

The Mulatto Connection

As the British sold off parts of their ruined estates the mulattos or free coloured tradesmen from Martinique and Guadeloupe bought and developed them. Dominica offered opportunities to these people which were restricted on their own islands. The French of all colours here took advant-

Free 'people of colour' promenade on the outskirts of Roseau during the 1780s. By 1813 there were 3,111 free coloured people in Dominica and only 1,261 whites. These mainly French families were the ancestors of the influential merchants and planters of the twentieth century. From an oil painting by Agostino Brunias. (Courtesy Mark Gilbey.)

age of the loopholes available in the colony of another nation. They were considered to be notorious smugglers through whom sugar of French origin entered England thus evading the strict trading and navigation laws currently in force.

'Mulattos', a term originally used to identify the first shade on the broad spectrum between black and white, was by now applied loosely to all 'high coloured' people. They had other more personal reasons for investing in Dominica during the late eighteenth century. The Code Noir of 1685 had given the mulattos all the rights of free men, but that came to an end in 1766 when the French colonial planter councils persuaded the government to pass laws restricting their rights. These new regulations were an irritant to men who regarded themselves as being more French than African.

Already they were denied any political rights although many of them were well off, educated owners of slaves and property. Now they could no longer be officers in the militia or hold legal posts. Even the wearing of certain clothes was banned. Mulatto men were forbidden to carry swords, in a period when the wearing of a sword was the sign of a gentleman. In 1787, the French colonies were granted assemblies, but the mulattos were barred from membership.

In British Dominica there was greater latitude regarding personal affairs and although political activity was also restricted, special mulatto militias existed. This did not mean that the mulattos were any less patriotic to France. They were pragmatists who balanced their state of virtual dual nationality to their own advantage whenever possible. As far as the British were concerned, their presence was of economic advantage in a colony which needed every penny of taxes, export duty and private enterprise it could muster, regardless of the colour of the entrepreneurs.

Laws, however, could not control subversive political and military activity and it was this weapon, a three pronged weapon linking mulattos, Maroons and France, which tormented the British in Dominica for over twenty years. While Governor John Orde addressed the House of Assembly in 1786 on his satisfaction at the surrender of the Maroon chiefs 'and the destruction and dispersion of so great a part of their followers', little did he know that a spark was then being lit in the streets of Paris, the flames of which would rage through France and across the Atlantic to the broad plains of Haiti, the towns and villages of Guadeloupe, and from there scorch the tenuous British hold on Dominica. The early effects of this holocaust were to make the last years of John Orde in Dominica the most miserable of his life.

Agents of the Revolution

Between 1789 and 1799, France was torn by revolution. Inspired by the writings of French philosophers and fused with a variety of financial, social and historical causes, the revolution broke out. The fall of the Bastille in Paris sparked off revolts throughout France. King Louis XVI and his queen Marie Antoinette were executed, and the Reign of Terror began; aristocrats were guillotined and a dictatorship set up. This period of rapid change and political intrigue led to much confusion and bewilderment among the French inhabitants of the West Indies and to restlessness among the free coloured people and slaves. There were disturbances in all French colonies; in Haiti it had its most violent and long-lasting effects.

French Royalists who came to Dominica for safety were armed to assist the British in the defence of the island. But Republicans, Frenchmen sympathetic to the Revolution, were also entering the island and added to this, there was the large French population already in Dominica who were quietly taking sides. Secretly printed pamphlets were being circulated. 'L'ami de la Liberté – l'enemi de la licence' they proclaimed; the friend of liberty – the enemy of the law.

This paper was of grave concern to the Assembly for its Minutes of 25 January 1791 notes: 'Encouragement is given to slaves and opinions promulgated in their favour so dangerous to lives and properties of their

Masters . . . it appears that (the publication) is one of the principal causes to which the present disaffection amongst the Negroes may be attributed.'

Already disturbances at estates in the south were causing tension. That same day, Orde informed the House that strong detachments of 30th and 15th Regiments 'have forced the post occupied by the revolters without loss, have taken some of the insurgents in arms . . . Great numbers of negroes . . . have surrendered.'

This outbreak at Grand Bay in the parish of St Patrick was the first of a new form of revolt, inspired not merely by the yearning for freedom but fed also by the philosophy of French revolutionary ideas. The leader among these agents operating in the south was a Martiniquan mulatto called Jean Louis Polinaire. His attempt to mobilise and control the southern parishes was part of a plan to effectively take over the whole island by starting from the windward areas.

The uprising was unique in the history of West Indian slave revolts. What the slaves under Polinaire's influence were demanding was freedom to work for themselves for more days in the week, as well as the customary one and a half days on weekends. When this demand was refused the slaves virtually went on strike 'without going off the estates or attempting any acts of violence'. Governor Orde even visited the affected estates to see the situation for himself and to tell the slaves that there was no truth in the rumour that he had returned from a visit to England with orders for the planters to allow their slaves three days in each week for work in their own gardens. But at 10.00 pm on 20 January the slaves rose up in revolt.

At about noon on 1 February 1791 a Carib came to James Bruce on his estate at Castle Bruce and informed him that he knew where Polinaire was hiding. Bruce offered him '5 Joes', in the currency of the day, if he would take him to the place, and the Carib accepted. Bruce immediately sent into the cane fields for slaves. 'I had twelve of my best people armed with every firelock that could fire.' They found Polinaire and brought him captive to Castle Bruce at about 7.00 pm and put him in chains. During the night he tried to persuade one of the Rangers guarding him to obtain poison but was refused. He was put on the next coastal sloop bound for Roseau to await trial.

Polinaire was tried by a jury made up of French and English residents. He was found guilty and sentenced to one of the most horrific executions recorded in the local Minutes of the King's Bench. On 7 March, Polinaire was taken from the common jail to the Newtown Savannah and hanged; his body was cut down while still alive, his bowels removed before his face and his body cut into four quarters 'to be disposed of at the King's pleasure'.

The landing of free mulattos on Dominica's shores and their movements along the bridle paths and countryside was by now a matter of grave concern to the Governor and Assembly. The 1786 action against the

Maroons had only achieved a brief respite, for now their numbers and movement in the mountains were intensifying once more.

All this activity was going on against a background of personality conflicts within the British hierarchy of the colony. At a period when their unity was vital for their security, the forced co-operation between Governor Orde and the Assembly was swept aside. Feuds and personal ill-feelings were rampant, disagreement over the handling of the Republican threat raised tensions, and finally in a dispute over funds, the Assembly sent a petition to the Crown asking for Orde to be removed. In 1793 he was recalled to London to answer various accusations made against him by the inhabitants, but was honourably cleared of all these charges which were dismissed as frivolous. His replacement in Dominica, George Hamilton, was a spirited leader who gained the colonists' confidence and guided them ably through difficult years.

At this time a name which we have heard of before, emerges again and again upon the pages of the Assembly Minutes, the letters of the governors, reports of regimental commanders, and in the press, and this is: Pharcelle. The same Pharcelle who was of concern to Orde in 1786. A man whose life and activities is still shrouded by the dusty papers of the archives.

What we know of this Maroon chief is full of contradictions. He seems to have aided the French in their conquest of 1778. In the 1780s messages are being exchanged between himself and the British Assembly. In 1791 Orde offers 'a considerable additional reward to those who take the Rebel Pharcelle.' In 1795 he is involved in French revolutionary activity in the heights of Colihaut. In 1798 he surrenders slaves to the governor. In 1799 he is guiding parties of British black rangers. He serves time in jail. It is recommended that he be banished from the colony. (Why banished and not executed like the other chiefs we may ask.) Then in the church records that same year we find: 'Pharcelle born on the Guinea Coast' is baptised a Roman Catholic in Roseau. In 1800 the Assembly seeks to introduce a Bill 'to deliberate on the case of Pharcelle'. And from then the records are silent.

What we can grasp of his life from 1786 reflects some of the turbulent events occuring in the island at the time. World affairs were also shifting at a considerable pace. In February 1793, the French Convention declared war against Britain and Holland.

When the news reached Dominica on 19 March the tension of the past years turned to desperation. It 'induced many Merchants, Tradesmen and Manufacturers with Clerks, Servants and vessels employed in their affairs, to abandon this Country, by which, a very considerable body of land and seamen were withdrawn from it strength.'

Those who remained could only muster a militia force of 400 men scattered among the several parish companies. Military engineers with their bands of rented slaves, worked feverishly on the improvement of local forts, especially on the Cabrits. In the same year, 1793, British forces captured Guadeloupe, Martinique and St Lucia, but the occupation of these islands did not remain unchallenged for long.

With their colonies in the Caribbean threatened, the French Jacobins who dominated the National Assembly in Paris sent out commissioners to spread the revolution to the Caribbean and ensure that their colonies were kept as part of the French Republic. The commissioners came out with troops to restore order and to defeat those planters loyal to the monarchy. Commissioner Sonthonax was sent to St Domingue, soon to be renamed Haiti, while Victor Hugues sailed south to Guadeloupe. He was formerly a trader on that island and returned now with a guillotine sharpened in readiness for the Royalists of the colony. He landed and retook the island in June 1794. He declared the abolition of slavery, mobilised the entire population of whatever racial origin to man the powerful coastal batteries and to commence offensives against the British-held colonies.

Royalist planters, most notably in Martinique, turned to the British for help. To defeat them Hugues encouraged the slaves to revolt. He sent agents among the Maroons of St Lucia, Dominica and the Black Caribs of St Vincent. In Grenada, French whites, mulattos and their slaves under the leadership of Fedon, a mulatto agent of the Republic, joined together to fight the British.

With Guadeloupe in the hands of Hugues, the situation in Dominica became more strained. The new governor, George Hamilton, called on the Assembly to provide parties of black rangers to search the heights and suspected parts of the island. He urged that ships patrol the Dominica-Guadeloupe channel and that 100 extra slaves be granted to work at the Cabrits. Martial law was declared in Roseau in March 1795 and the French inhabitants were directed to sign a declaration of loyalty to the British Crown. In spite of this the Assembly was still insecure.

'And people of colour are seen daily in the highroads of the island with arms . . . and numbers of slaves are secreted among them. As if carefully timed a party of armed people of colour . . . landed with arms at an outbay, and proceeded to the woods with intent to join the Runaways. So that a Proclamation had to be issued that magistrates, militiamen and every citizen was supposed to do his duty in this emergency.'

As French refugees continued to arrive, the British in Dominica were at a loss to know who to trust. 'The far greater part of these' notes soldier Robert Browne in his diary, 'were Republicans professing themselves to be Royalists, many unquestionably Spies; a few, very few indeed, in whom confidence could be placed.'

While the British were trying to make sense of all these unnerving events, sorting out the wild rumours from facts, a plan was being hatched by Hugues for the invasion of Dominica with the co-operation of Republican sympathisers gathered around the west coast village of Colihaut. Here was the centre for the French coffee planters of the leeward valleys, a vibrant community with church, shops and a surprising number of billiard tables and taverns.

The message circulating Dublanc, Bioche, Coulibistrie and Colihaut was that a force from Guadeloupe would land on the north-east coast in June of 1795. Hugues issued a proclamation calling on all true Frenchmen in Dominica to join the invading forces and many planned to do so. Hugues had added that those who did not assist would be punished by death along with their families.

Maroon tracks existed, as hunters' paths still do, from the Colihaut valley up and across the foothills of Morne Diablotin, branching out north into the Melville Hall Valley or, keeping east, into the Concorde Valley and so to Pagua Bay. Guided by the Maroons, notably Pharcelle, this was the planned route of the invaders and local rebels.

The Invasion

The events of June 1795 were concentrated in three areas of the island: the north-eastern district, Colihaut and Roseau. Each point of that triangle was so cut off from the others by mountains and inaccessible coastline that communication between them was almost impossible; a problem which further confused the whole episode. Both parties, government and rebels, found themselves making grievous mistakes because they did not know, or were misinformed about, the state of their forces at the other ends of the island. Slave messengers moving across the forests with dispatches for their respective commanders were either ambushed or events changed by the time their messages arrived. Under these circumstances rumour and misjudgment was rife. Although the events unfolded simultaneously in each area it makes it easier to record the whole action in one place at a time.

The north-eastern coast of Dominica from Pagua to Anse Soldat is lined with sandy coves and jagged windswept headlands pointing towards the flat French coral island of Mariegalante. Most of these coves are inaccessible from the sea, but about six of them can be entered by small sailing boats with captains experienced in dodging the several reefs and outcrops of volcanic rock which dot their entrances. At the time these bays were used for shipping estate produce and most of them are still popular with fishermen today. The Atlantic breakers coupled with the difficulty of landing made this a low priority area for coastal defence, and so only a few guns were mounted at Marigot, La Soye now known as Woodford Hill Bay and Batibou now Hampstead. The population in that area was sparse and the district militias very small. It was for all of these reasons that the agents of Victor Hugues selected that coast for landing their invasion forces.

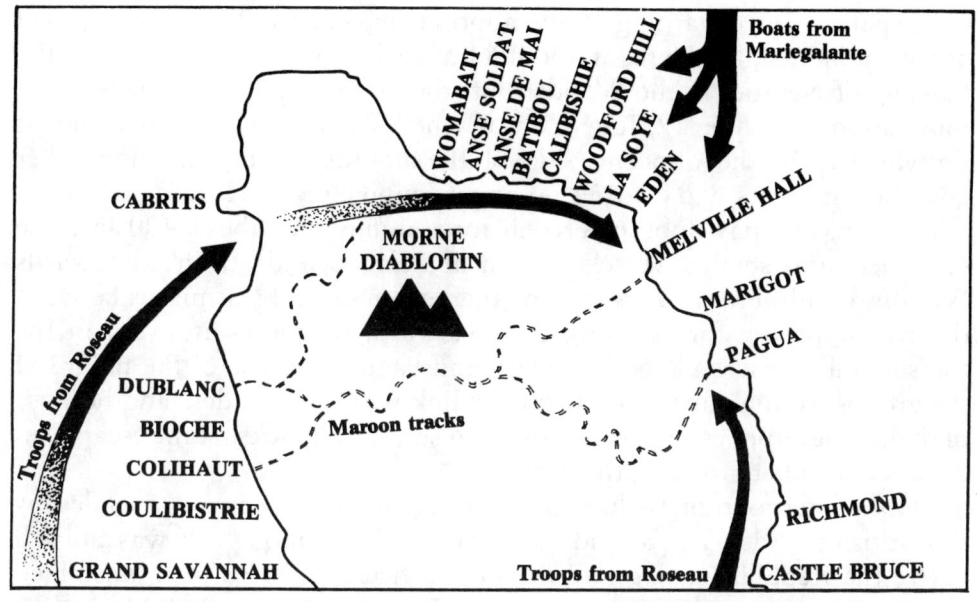

A map of the northern half of Dominica showing movements during the French Republican invasion.

On the evening of 4 June, five boats containing about fifty men in all, attempted to land at Woodford Hill but were repulsed by militiamen manning the post. Four sailed west and landed at Anse de Mai but soon returned to Mariegalante. One report states that 800 men landed at Pagua that day but other more reliable accounts indicate that they landed in groups over the next four days at various points along the coast.

On 6 June the invaders were back, landing at Hampstead with 200 men and moving cross-country to Pagua with no opposition. Here they took control of Hatton Garden house and sugar works, set up tents and established it as their main camp. News of the first attempt at landing had by now reached Roseau, where, in spite of the weak state of the British troops, Governor Hamilton was able to muster about 200 militiamen making up the St Georges Regiment, the Point Michel Regiment, the Coloured Fuzilliers, the Coloured Artillery Company, the Black Rangers and members of the Light Infantry Company and Grenadiers. The St Mark's and St Patrick's militias were reserved as reinforcements. The combined force divided into two groups with orders to proceed around the island in opposite directions until they had the enemy between them.

One detachment went up the west coast by sea to Prince Rupert Bay and was joined by 60 'regulars' from the Cabrits garrison as well as detachments of the St John's and St Andrew's militias. The other group left for Rosalie via the Lake Road and then up the coast through the Carib Quarter. Slaves loyal to these government forces combed the woods ahead of the party to give warning of any approaching enemy. They over-nighted at Richmond Estate. 'Here, at about 11 at night, they were alarmed by the bawling of Negroes in the Woods (but) the alarm appeared to be without foundation.' On the 12 June they reached Pagua and set up camp at Entwhistle. On the opposite side of the bay at North End, the other government forces had also set up an encampment.

On the same day another French force numbering about 400 in three schooners and smaller vessels landed at Batibou and advanced towards Woodford Hill. From 12 to 17 June there were several skirmishes between the two opposing forces along the roadways, on the estates and in the forested hills between Woodford Hill and Pagua. Because of the failure of the groups from Colihaut to effectively link with the invaders and because of dwindling supplies the French suffered serious setbacks. Some escaped in canoes and others took to the hills.

On the afternoon of 16 June the main French group was surrounded by the British at Eden Estate and surrendered. The Union Jack was hoisted above the Republican flag and the nine officers and 192 men assembled there were taken as prisoners of war. Two others, Norbert Motard of Colihaut and Marie Petit of Pointe Michel, were seized as Rebel British Subjects. During the following days the militiamen combed the surrounding countryside for rebels; capturing some, killing others and repulsing various schooners and canoes from Mariegalante which arrived to rescue the remaining invaders still on the run. Prisoners taken during this action totalled over 300 and were imprisoned at the Cabrits.

The Colihaut Revolt

One parish militia was conspicuously absent in the action against the Republican invaders. The St Peter's Militia of some 100 men with its base at Colihaut did not respond to Governor Hamilton's call for a volunteer force. Along with others they planned to use the government arms to assist the invaders. Reports of suspicious conduct among them caused the governor to order troops to disarm the militia and burn every small boat and canoe on that part of the coast.

Colihaut had always been an area under suspicion for it was a channel through which the French had supplied arms and ammunition to the Maroons for years and it had been Pharcelle's link to support and information from outside. From 14 June agents in the area were circulating false news that the British were being defeated at Pagua, ships were fleeing from Roseau and that the French inhabitants of Couliaboun (Giraudel), Pointe Michel and Grand Bay had taken up arms for the Republic and were in possession of the town.

This propaganda had the desired effect in most hamlets along the coast, spurring the people on to support their cause. On 16 June, the Coulibistrie division of the St Peter's militia took up arms against their British officer in charge and seized the keys of the arms and powder magazine. According to one officer's account, 'The Rebels marched off the ground huzzaing, Vive la Republique! Marchons! Marchons! They proceeded to join the Dublanc Company who were waiting for them, and with these they advanced to Colihaut, where the Company of that place, joining, they formed a body of 150 men and commanded by three commissioned officers of the St Peter's Militia and JB Meltz.'

The band immediately set off through the forest to the north but because of the turn of events at Woodford Hill and Eden their departure was too late to be of any use. By the morning of 18 June when still on the foothills of Morne Diablotin overlooking Picard Estate, they learned of the defeat and surrender at Eden. They had been planning to go around the north to Pagua, instead of taking what they thought was the more dangerous route as planned, but now they moved back to the paths above Dublanc and Colihaut. By 22 June they realised that the whole plan had been a failure. While about sixteen of the ringleaders made their escape by sea, others were forced to surrender. Over the next three days, 108 surrendered. Those others who could not escape by sea took refuge in the mountains.

While all this was going on rumour was going wild in Roseau. On 18 June news was that the British had been overrun and the French were moving steadily for the capital. 'Before dark, the bay was thronged with Ladies, Children, Female Domestics, Chests and Bedding, Chests of Linen, Books, China, Cash, Plate and other valuables of the generality, and the Boatmen attending to put them on board' ships in the harbour. The scene was reversed twelve hours later, when the correct information arrived in town.

Now, with hostilities over, punishment and revenge fell heavy upon the captured rebels. Speedy trials in late June and early July sentenced 110 to be sent to England as prisoners of war. Others were banished from the island for life to places determined by the Crown while another group was simply sent away with orders never to return.

Norbert Motard and Marie Petit were sentenced: 'to be hanged in the Market Place till dead and afterwards their bodies to be exposed in Chains, the first at the River's Mouth, Petit at Pointe Michel.' Motard, a white man, was executed on 25 June while Petit, a mulatto, was executed two days later. Another two were hanged on 7 July. Two others were also sentenced to hang but had their sentences commuted to banishment almost as the ropes went around their necks. One agent was sentenced to be hanged but was also banished instead. Three 'received 200 lashes each on their bare backs in the manner used in His Majesty's Armies'.

By then the activities of Victor Hugues in the Antilles was even causing concern in Paris as he moved Guadeloupe towards virtual independence from France. By 1801, Napoleon Bonaparte, the new First Consul of the Republic, had reimposed slavery in the French colonies. But Admiral Lacrosse whom he sent out as the new Governor of Guadeloupe found things so hot there that amazingly he made arrangements with the British whereby he could govern Guadeloupe from Dominica. He administered from here for a number of months until he felt it was safe enough to re-instal himself at Basseterre.

The Black Regiments

The profits being derived from sugar and trade began to fall towards the end of the eighteenth century. The military forces required in the area were not only causing a strain on the revenue of the islands, but disease and other ill effects of the climate caused the loss of many members of the resident British regular troops. The garrison at the Cabrits, close to the swamps surrounding Prince Rupert Bay, was notorious for its malaria and yellow fever.

Britain was keenly aware of this drain on her revenue and man-power and could no longer stand idle while her forces in the West Indies dwindled. In some colonies the death rate was at times as high as a dozen a day. Already the colony was reinforcing its militia system by recruiting trusted slaves into various corps of Black Rangers and Black Shots whose main task was to assist in combat against the guerila warfare of the Maroons and with coastal defence in case of invasion. During the French Republican uprising the Roseau batteries were reinforced by the arrival from St Lucia of forty members of the Carolina Regiment, a regiment made up of black soldiers which was the first of its kind in these colonies. Blacks with arms training were also attached to certain regiments as Pioneers, men responsible for setting up camps, heaving cannon, erecting palisades and other military preparations.

The crisis of European troop losses and manpower for defence was met by the colonial government with a plan to raise twelve West India Regiments entirely made up of African and Creole slave soldiers who would better survive this climate. Needless to say, the legislatures in the islands protested, considering it highly dangerous to have armed and trained black forces stationed to guard the planter interests, but the Colonial Office was insistent.

These 'slaves in redcoats' were to be under the command of white officers and although still technically slaves pressed into service, they would receive the same allowances and be under similar regulations as other British troops. This peculiar arrangement was to be the source of strained relations between the black troops and the regular European soldiers as well as with the plantation slaves, particularly those living around the respective garrisons on the islands. Eventually in 1807 all members of the West India Regiments were declared to be free men and this in turn encouraged other free black civilians to volunteer for regimental service.

In 1797, 29-year-old Andrew James Cochrane Johnstone was appointed governor of Dominica. Though he had assumed the title of Johnstone, his real name, and the name by which he was best known in Dominica, was Cochrane. He bought Hope estate in the parish of St Paul, and as was the custom, the estate was popularly named after its master. This was the origin of the present-day village of Cochrane.

As governor, one of his main tasks was to organise the formation of the local company of the West India Regiment, known unofficially as the Black Regiment. From 1795 men had been recruited and trained for their military duties. The year after Johnstone's arrival, recruitment was intensified. He bought a shipload of 200 Africans in one of the neighbouring islands and lodged them in Roseau in preparation for their training. The Anglican rector, Rev Charles Peters, visited the men often and noted that things were not going smoothly among their ranks.

'They were lodged and fed in a spacious building not far from the Government House. And at one of their meals I remember witnessing a scene which at first excited in our mind very serious apprehensions. Their provisions had scarcely been set before them when we perceived throughout the whole room the strongest indication of discontent and anger. The countenances of many became quite infuriated, and violent agitation of their minds expressed in their looks and gestures, seems to forebode some sudden and general commotion.'

According to the attendants, this was because the men had been put together without any distinction as to their tribal origins and feelings; either of enmity or friendship which they bore to each other. However, when these men were trained and became members of Dominica's 8th West India Regiment, they distinguished themselves in action, notably at the capture of St Martin in 1801. The British General, in his report on the fighting wrote:

> 'I have particular satisfaction in being enabled to add that in the 8th West India Regiment, formed within the last three years, and composed almost entirely of new negroes, who never had before seen an enemy, engaged with a degree of gallantry, and behaved in a manner that would do honour to any troops.'

The Revolt of the 8th West India Regiment

In 1802, the 8th West India Regiment was stationed at the Cabrits. There were some 500 men at the garrison with Major John Gordon in command and Captains Carr, Cummins, Casson, Cameron and Arbuthnot at the head of 100 men each. Cochrane Johnstone was Colonel of the Regiment; while he was running the colony from Roseau his men were permanently stationed at the Cabrits although they had previously been at Morne Bruce. The Governor's treatment of his men was causing discontent. He was accused of setting the men to work for his private use. They were put to dig fields, repair walls around Government House and work on his estate. Food and clothing supplies were irregular and because of Cochrane's swindling they failed to get the regular soldier's allowance due to them.

They were insulted when put to clear bush and open up drains in the Cabrits swamp. The talk of the Portsmouth market place and taverns was that the cane bills which they used were to be replaced by hoes and that the soldiers would be pressed into field slavery. Other rumours coupled with their earlier dissatisfactions raised their suspicions to the point of revolt.

On 9 April 1802, a frigate of the Royal Navy, HMS *Magnificent*, anchored off Fort Shirley with a detachment of the 68th Regiment aboard. The arrival of the 68th, to be stationed at the garrison, decided the men of the 8th West India Regiment that it was the time for action. That night, under the code words 'Black Man,' they took control of Fort Shirley and

A private in the 'Black Regiment'. As they found it difficult to march in boots they wore slippers.

Fort Young in the early days, looking towards Scotts Head.

the fortified hills on either side. As the first shots rang out officers momentarily believed it was an attack by the French, but soon, with three of their number dead and all others imprisoned, they were shocked into the realisation that a revolt was in full swing. On the following day, the *Magnificent* and the troops and marines aboard were joined by the St John's militia in an attempt to combat the mutineers, but stiff firing was returned from the batteries.

On 12 April Colonel Cochrane Johnstone arrived from Roseau and marched into the fort with the Royal Scotch Regiment and the 68th. The rebel troops were drawn up in formation with three of their officers as prisoners and presented arms to the troops. When the Governor ordered them to shoulder, order and ground their arms, they obeyed. But on being commanded to step three paces forward the cry was 'No!' and they resumed their arms and fired a volley. This was returned and followed by a charge of bayonets which broke their ranks and a wild gun battle ensued at close range. Mutineers who tried to escape over the ramparts and precipice in front of the fort were exposed to a fire of grapeshot and canister from the *Magnificent*. Those few who made it across the bay or through the swamp fled towards the foothills of Diablotin. Like one deserter we know called Hypolite, they joined the Maroons and with their military training added a new element to the camps.

A cannon on the Inner Cabrit points over Prince Rupert Bay where squadrons of the Royal Navy anchored to refresh their ships.

The court-martial which followed sentenced 34 rebels to hang. The 8th was disbanded and some men who were cleared were absorbed by the remaining West India Regiments. An investigation into the conduct of Cochrane Johnstone began; it was said that his rule was marked by 'tyranny, extortion and vice,' that he drove a brisk and profitable trade in slaves, and kept a harem at Hope Estate. In respect of the revolt, he tried to shift the blame to his subordinate John Gordon, but after hearing the evidence, the court acquitted Gordon and indicted the Governor himself. In March 1804, Cochrane faced four charges before another court-martial, this time in London. To the disgust of George III, who was following the developments, the prosecution failed. The King however ensured that Cochrane was never promoted and was made to resign his commission.

The revolt at the Cabrits raised serious questions for the British Army regarding the operation of non-European troops within its forces. Significant changes, including the liberty of black soldiers, were made as a result. It was the basis of new guidelines for 'native troops' in Africa, India and the Far East at a time when the British Empire was expanding its interests in those parts of the world.

La Grange and the Ransom of Roseau

With the rise of Napoleon, France was once more concerned with regaining and controlling her French West Indian colonies. Early in 1805 it became known that a French fleet was cruising the Caribbean, making raids on British possessions and crippling British West Indian trade. The forts and defences in Dominica were hurriedly put in order, the militia alerted, and a close watch was kept for the French squadron.

At dawn on 20 February, the storm broke. Strange armed vessels flying the Union Jack were sighted from the signal station on Scotts Head. An alarm was fired and the news quickly spread through Roseau; soon Fort Young was crowded with militiamen and a small body of regulars. The ships swept towards the town and when the harbour master boarded the foremost vessel he was immediately taken prisoner. The British flag on the ship was lowered and the French tricolour hoisted in its place – it was indeed the enemy.

The guns of the fort rang out and a steady fire was exchanged. Then from the leeward came more ships, including *The Majesteux*, several frigates amounting to 120 guns and nineteen barges full of troops. These were rowed ashore under cover of guns of two armed cruisers and seven other ships carrying cannonades. The commander of this French attack was General LaGrange, and for years the invasion was spoken of in Dominica simply as 'La Grange'.

Preparations were made to prevent the French from landing but one section got ashore at Pointe Michel only to be strongly resisted beneath the cliffs near Loubiere. Meanwhile another division had successfully landed at Woodbridge Bay and entered Roseau from the north. At one period in the fighting, 200 British were holding off 2000 of the enemy. Then the town was accidentally set on fire. Flaming cotton wads from the British cannon were blown onto the houses by the wind. This sealed the fate of Roseau, and with the Governor's permission, the Council surrendered the town.

The capital had fallen, but Governor George Prevost was determined to save the island for Britain. He ordered his troops, the 46th Regiment and the 1st West India Regiment, to make forced marches across the island to Rosalie and join him at Prince Rupert Bay. Then with a few of his staff, he made a dash for the Cabrits. With the help of some Caribs he cut across the island to the north-east coast, arriving at Portsmouth within twenty-four hours. The rest of the troops followed, making their difficult march in four days.

At the Cabrits, Prevost hastily put the fort in order. Cattle were driven in and the cisterns were filled with water from North River. On 25 February, he received a letter from La Grange summoning the garrison to surrender. In it, he reminded the English governor of the fate of Roseau and urged him to accept the honourable conditions of surrender. Prevost replied simply: 'My duty to my King and Country is so superior to every other consideration that I have only to thank you for the observations you have been pleased to make on the often inevitable consequences of war.'

Noting the formidable appearance of the garrison, La Grange returned to Roseau. There he demanded a ransom of £20,000 and threatened that if this was not paid he would carry the members of the Legislature as prisoners to Guadeloupe. This sum was not forthcoming and eventually he settled for less than half the amount. After seizing everything of value he could lay his hands on – including a large number of slaves – he withdrew his forces from Dominica. For some days he hovered off the island but, deterred by the strength of the Cabrits, he soon sped off for St Kitts and the last French attack on Dominica was over.

General George Prevost and the 46th Regiment (known later as the Duke of Cornwall's Light Infantry) received many honours for the defence of the island. Besides being voted money to buy a sword of honour and a service of silver plate by the Assembly, the Patriotic Fund and the West India Committee, Prevost was also awarded a baronetcy.

Until some years ago, the tattered colours of the St George's Regiment hung in the Court House in Roseau. They had been presented by Queen Charlotte, and emblazoned on their folds were the words 'Woodbridge Bay' and 'Pointe Michele' – the two main areas of action in 1805. In 1905, the centenary of 'La Grange' was celebrated, and in 1955 there were also parades and festivities observing 150 years of uninterrupted British rule.

12
The Last Maroon War

The last period of Maroon activity began roughly in 1802 and climaxed with a guerilla war between 1812 and 1815. As the nineteenth century began, confrontation between the Maroons and authorities cropped up once more. A party of armed slaves attacked a camp and succeeded in killing the chief and taking six prisoners and in 1809 the Legislature was requesting the governor to take measures to break up encampments. Again in 1810 the Legislature noted Maroons increasing in the parishes of St Joseph and St Peter. In St Patrick a large camp of 20 huts was attacked but was burnt by the escaping Maroons.

As the tension mounted, the Lieutenant-Governor, Colonel Barnes, decided to make use of the Regular troops stationed in Dominica, as part of the offensive against the Maroons. The Regional Commander in Barbados objected, on the grounds that it was against universal practice to use such Regulars to quell internal disturbances. When the matter was referred to London, the authorities were astonished that the system of internal security which worked elsewhere seemed to have failed in Dominica. Despite the colony's anxiety, they declined to give any immediate permission for the Regulars to be used.

The next surprise came in July 1812 when over 75 slaves of Castle Bruce packed what little they had, and took to the woods. The number of Maroons at this time was estimated to be 800 strong and camps had been established in the woods behind Woodford Hill, Hampstead, Rosalie, Pointe Mulatre, River Claire, Morne Anglais and in the upper Layou area as well as the other earlier established sites behind Colihaut and Dublanc. Negres Marron leaders at this period were Elephant, Soleil, Battre Bois, Hill, Nicholas, Diano, Noel, Robin, Quashie, Apollo, Jean Zombi, Lewis, Moco, Nico and Jacko. This latter had been in the forest for over 40 years.

By now, new developments had added to the complexity of the situation. Apart from the French Revolutionary ideas with which some slaves had come in contact, many were becoming aware that slavery was now regarded with disfavour in Britain. In 1804, William Wilberforce and his supporters in the Humanitarian Movement in England had stepped up their demands for abolition of the slave trade. Finally the Abolition Act was passed in the British Parliament in 1807 and from the 1 January 1808 all trading in African slaves was 'utterly abolished, prohibited and declared to be unlawful.' Scattered among the Maroons were deserters from the 'Black Regiment'; men well-trained in British warfare. In 1810 rewards were

'Pacification of Maroon Negroes' by Agostino Brunias. This scene depicts treaty negotiations in St Vincent, but Brunias lived in Dominica during the most active Maroon period and also used local Maroon events in his paintings. No such formal meeting occurred in Dominica, but it gives us an accurate impression of the two opposing forces.

granted to parties capturing Maroons; in 1811 Elephant was captured.

In 1812, George Robert Ainslie was appointed governor and was immediately faced with the problem of the Maroons' increased ferocity and boldness. He issued proclamations offering a free pardon to those who would surrender. But this was in vain, for no Maroon would dare take the risk of being tricked by an amnesty. He then sent messengers to offer terms to the Maroons, but, still suspicious of treaties, they murdered the couriers. Soon it seemed that the successes of the Negres Marrons were encouraging the slaves to consider revolt.

In these circumstances, Ainslie gave orders for the ruthless extermination of their forces. He sent out local Rangers, principally in three directions: to the Windward from Rosalie and Tabery to Pointe Mulatre; in the centre of the island above the Layou Valley; and in the heights of Colihaut. In the same year, 1813, Dominica was hit by two severe hurricanes in July and August which totally destroyed Government House, the Court House, and other major buildings. It affected the life of the whole community, including the Maroons and added to this, the wide-spread action against their members intensified in 1814. In April, a chief called Clemence was brought in from the Colihaut area; in May, Hill from Woodford Hill and Robin from Hampstead. Fifteen Maroons were brought to Roseau by sloop from Rosalie. They had not bargained for traitors, and it was the Rangers – fellow negroes who knew the forests as well as the Maroons – who were the main cause for the downfall of the Negres Marrons.

In June, at the height of the action, Governor Ainslie was called back to England to answer for the severe measures he had taken. Before leaving he received addresses from the inhabitants, both coloured and white, thanking him for saving them from the 'Maroon menace'. Although he had been recalled, Ainslie's plans were still followed and the most decisive blows on the Maroons fell after his departure. The war reached its climax in July and August. Ageing Jacko was shot on 12 July after a desperate resistance and later five men from his camp surrendered. On 16 August, 16 were brought in from the camp of Quashie who had himself surrendered with 11 of his followers a few days earlier; and two soldiers of the army were shot after court-martial for aiding Maroons.

The lists giving the final account of the climax of the Maroon conflict between February and November 1814, make chilling reading:

Maroons killed in the forest: 15 men and 3 women. Those captured in the forest and jailed: 109 men, 11 women and 68 children. Maroons who surrendered: 6 men and 1 woman. Slaves taken and jailed for 'loitering off the plantations to which they belong without passes': 100 men, 48 women, 5 children. Those who surrendered and were pardoned and returned to their owners: 75 men, 31 women, 5 children. Slaves who surrendered direct to their owners: 100. The total directly involved: 577.

Of the above number, 11 were hanged and had their heads cut off and exposed on poles at various places around the island. Two others were sentenced to hang but died in jail. Fourteen received lashes ranging from 100 to 30 strokes each. Of these, one died following his punishment. Several others were sentenced to work in chains for three months. The Maroon forces never recovered from the events of mid-1814. Their camps had been broken and their respected leaders were dead. But the tide was turning, the slave trade had been abolished and whether the planters liked it or not, emancipation seemed not too far off.

Problems on the Estates

Towards the end of 1812, America declared war against Britain, supplies from the United States became more scanty every week and soon ceased completely. The problems that had been faced during the War for American Independence cropped up once more. Besides the intense Maroon activity, estates were devastated by the hurricanes of 1813. One attorney, writing to a friend, described the damage on the estate he managed.

'The shingles were stripped off the east of the dwelling house and part of the east end of the boiling house roof fell in. The hospital, horse stable, wood and timber house blown down as well as several of the Negro houses. Others were unroofed and otherwise injured. Canes twisted and twirled about and most of them laid flat. And an almost entire destruction of the provision grounds . . . At present the island is destitute of rice, flour, biscuits, corn meal or, in fact, any sort of eatables. We shall be obliged to feed the Negroes three or four months, regardless of the expense or inconvenience as they may be driven to use improper food which might bring

An English coffee estate in the parish of St Paul in 1801.

disease or other serious ills . . . I have never witnessed such havoc and destruction in so small a compass and how to convey the sad intelligence I am really at a loss.'

Even when Britain and America signed a peace treaty in December 1814, it was some time before trading was back to normal. Not a single hogshead of saltfish or pickled pork was for sale, nor lumber of any description, and in desperation, planters and merchants made a few unsuccessful attempts to establish a trade link with Canada. By 1817, supplies were trickling in but prices were very high and the discontented Legislature was pressing the British Crown to remove trade restrictions. Another hurricane struck that year, but Britain rejected the Legislature's plea for relief aid and this added to the mass of ill-feeling already evident in the planter-merchant community.

Those who could emigrate were moving to the new and promising British colonies of Trinidad and Demarara. When Henry Nelson Coleridge visited Dominica early in 1825 he found the capital of the island virtually abandoned. 'All was silent, and soft and lifeless like a city in the Arabian Nights. Roseau is now in a most singular state of existence . . . the dirty row of storehouses gave me an impression of want and depopulation . . . the grass grows lush and verdantly between the stones . . . But I am afraid, the spirit which should undertake . . . obvious and easy improvements is at present something drowsy in Dominica; there is no public voice to call forth or public encouragement to support the exertion of individual virtue and talent; the community is first divided by language, then by religion, and the inconsiderable residue, which is supposed to represent the whole, is so torn to pieces by squabbles as bitter as contemptible, that the mere routine of government was at a dead stand while I was on the island.'

1825 Hurricane

The colony was now struggling through a period of grievous depression. Debts were high, credit was non-existent, supplies were short and British import duties paid on sugar rose sharply between 1810 and 1820. To top it off another severe hurricane hit the island at the end of July 1825. We turn to the Roseau Chronicle of 3 August of that year for a report.

'We have received distressing accounts from the northern parts of this Island particularly in and about Prince Rupert and La Soye. Mills, works and dwellings are destroyed, canes lodged or torn up, Coffee Estates almost deprived both of their old and young plants, some pieces completely washed away, and their buildings blown down, are among the heavy calamities, occasioned by this afflicting visitation of Providence. Negro houses and grounds laid waste, plantain walks ruined, fruit and other trees destroyed, and the Country round those parts looking as if a fire had gone through and blasted it, makes a finale of this devastating gale.

'Indeed we may also add that there is not an Estate in the whole Island but what has had their Plantain trees blown down.

'The Garrison at Prince Rupert is in a deplorable state from the quarters and King's Store Houses being unroofed.' Many ships at anchor were also wrecked and the paper comments that 'Some idea may be formed of the destructive violence of the Wind, when it is said the Ship and Brig's masts were actually blown out of them.'

It adds, 'The noted fine large Tamarind Tree, under whose shady boughs the Market has been held for years, having been planted, according to tradition, a century or two back, was torn up by the roots.'

Again in 1834 a hurricane wrecked the island. Battered both naturally and economically, Dominica virtually resigned herself to poverty during the mid-nineteenth century.

13
Peace and Freedom

Following the French attack under La Grange and the suppression of the Maroons in 1814, Dominica was entering a long period of peace. In 1815 Napoleon was finally overthrown and the threat of French attack on Dominica was over for good. For almost a hundred years the inhabitants had lived in constant fear of invasion and yet, now they were faced with problems no less important than war. The most insistent was slavery.

After about a quarter of a century of agitation the English humanitarian movement had secured the passing of the Act for the Abolition of the Slave Trade. In the West Indies this caused considerable discontent among the planters, and in the Assemblies they at once voiced their dissatisfaction. Parliament, they claimed, had no power to make laws concerning local affairs.

A special provision of the law allowed an owner going from one British colony to another to take with him four slaves as personal attendants. The Dominica and Grenada planters, especially, abused this section in order to supply slaves to Trinidad and other colonies which were prepared to pay high prices for them. In 1815, the Imperial Government urged the Assemblies to promote the physical, religious and moral improvement of the labour force. A few minor changes in the slave codes were made but generally they were most unsatisfactory. In Dominica, emotions were running high. When the Governor, Charles Maxwell, made efforts to protect the slaves from oppression and ensure that the wishes of the British Government were carried out, the local Grand Jury censured the Governor for his action. This was followed in 1823 by a circular from the Assembly protesting against the move towards full emancipation.

'Sir:
The House of Assembly of this Island appalled at the Enormity of the proposition lately introduced into the House of Commons relative to the Emancipation of the Slave Population of these colonies, have seized the earliest opportunity . . . to bring the same under their most serious consideration, fully aware from sad Experience that even the slightest discussion on that fatal project places in Jeopardy the Lives and fortunes of all the

White Population of these Colonies, and that should such a Measure be carried into Effect it will sweep the whole of us into a Vortex of indiscriminate Ruin such as has overwhelmed the unfortunate island of St Domingo some Years ago, from precisely the same cause . . . '

The letter also called on the other Assemblies to join efforts to condemn the action being taken by the Anti-Slavery Society, the Methodists and other bodies striving for abolition. During this period the planters were even talking recklessly of declaring the island independent.

In 1830 the Assembly was again petitioned to change their slave codes. In 1831 all legal discrimination on the grounds of colour was abolished in Dominica. The 'Brown Privilege Bill' allowed equal political and social rights to free non-whites and it was obvious that Britain was determined to liberate the slaves in spite of West Indian opposition. On the 29 August 1833 the Abolition of Slavery Act received the Royal assent and became law. It would take effect on the 1 August the following year.

When the sun set on the 31 July 1834, there were some 668,000 slaves in the British West Indies – in Dominica there were 14,175 – and at midnight they were free from slavery. The drunkenness and disorder which the planters had expected did not take place, many going to Mass in thanksgiving. Under the Act, the owners were to be compensated for the loss of their slaves while the labourers had to serve a period of apprenticeship. Compensation was given according to the age and status of each slave and the planters of Dominica received £275,547. Slavery had ended, but the problem of labour and the creation of a new society had just begun.

Apprenticeship

This new method of labour was intended to safeguard the estates and in fact was part of the compensation granted to the planters. Field labourers were to be apprenticed for six years while artisans and skilled workers would remain on the estates for four years. Some claimed that this method would help introduce the ex-slaves gradually into total freedom and self-sufficiency. Children under six however, were free of apprenticeship.

The masters were to provide their apprentices, as they did before, with shelter, clothing, medical attention and food, or instead of food with land and time for the apprentices to make their own gardens. Apprentices had to work no more than forty hours a week, and for eleven hours they had to be paid cash. Apprentices could buy their freedom, whether their masters were in favour or not. Many did so by banding together in groups to work their plots of land and used the profits of their sales to buy their certificates of manumission.

Stipendiary magistrates paid by the British Government, were appointed to supervise the working of the new system. They saw to it that ex-slaves were not taken advantage of by their former masters. These magistrates were one of the successes of the system for they did their job well and used their wide powers to enforce the Act. Obviously, they received strong opposition from many planters. One stipendiary magistrate in Dominica, a coloured man named William Lynch, noted that little was being done to prepare the labourers for the change to total freedom expected in 1840.

'My official intercourse with the labouring classes enables me to discover their ignorance of letters and too general disregard for the Sabbath; as well as the other moral obligations of civil and religious society. I fear there are not eight of them to be found in my district who can read any book. The pastoral visits of ministers of religion are exceedingly infrequent, and instruction of any kind, rarely within their reach.'

The Methodists and Quakers were two religious groups who had been striving for the abolition of slavery and the rights of Negro people in the West Indies for some time. In December 1836, Joseph Sturge, himself a Quaker, visited Dominica along with three colleagues to examine the working of the apprenticeship system on the spot. They visited estates, talked to planters, magistrates and members of the Assembly, both coloured and white. They noted that nearly the entire population was Roman Catholic and were told by the Anglican rector that the desire for education was so great, that he would be able to fill eight to ten schools if the means were supplied to build them and to pay teachers.

On their visits to estates, they noted the difference between French and English methods. As the owners of most English estates were absentee landlords, their attorneys made little effort to care for the labourers. On these estates the decrease of numbers by death during slavery had been astounding. On Castle Bruce estate for instance, deaths between 1817 and 1834 had amounted to 224. On French estates, where owners were resident, the relationship between planters and labourers were far better. On some of them, planters were actually teaching the labourers themselves.

Joseph Sturge and his group left Dominica feeling that the ex-slaves had gained nothing by the exchange of slavery for apprenticeship. This also seemed to be the opinion of the British government, who felt that serious difficulties would arise when domestic and skilled slaves were freed first. Therefore they cut short the period of apprenticeship and scrapped the entire system so that from 1 August 1838, the labourers were completely free of obligations to anyone.

Land and Villages

When apprenticeship was suddenly swept away, the estates were faced with a labour crisis. Once freed, the ex-slave was not eager to continue to work

A very early photo of a family outside their thatched cottage at Portsmouth. The walls of the hut are made of woven 'gaulettes'.

on the estate, even for wages. To meet this need the larger colonies were already working on a system of immigration, whereby labourers, mainly from India, would work as indentured servants for a fixed period, usually five years. This system was termed 'industrial apprenticeship' and accounts for the large Asian population in Trinidad, Guyana and Jamaica. In Dominica there was also talk of immigration. A planter, writing in *The Colonist* newspaper in 1842 suggested that 'immigration and immigration alone . . . is the only way in which you can meet this growing evil, and save the colony from eventual ruin.' Some estimated that the island needed an annual supply of at least 300 to 400 labourers for many years, in order that the estates could carry on a reasonable standard of production. But the plans for immigration were never carried out, no Indians or Chinese, and only a few Portuguese came to Dominica, where the labour force on local estates had declined with amazing rapidity.

Here, there was land in abundance, and the free citizens preferred to set up their own small holdings; the beginning of Dominica's independent peasant society. In other islands where all land was occupied by large plantations, this was not possible, and most labourers could do nothing but work on their former plantations for a living.

As was to be expected, the situation in Dominica caused a drop in production and ruined many planters. Already coffee had suffered badly because of blight and planters realised they would have to encourage labourers to work for them. Land was offered on easy terms and many purchased small properties. Others were allowed to occupy their former houses and grounds, giving the estate part of their produce as rent. Many ex-slaves, especially on the leeward side, had set up houses along the coast. Carrying posts and boards from their estate dwellings, they erected new homes on the strip of coastland known as 'The Queen's Three Chains'. As was explained earlier, the land had been set aside in the eighteenth century as Crown property. Owners of estates which bordered this Crown land, complained to the magistrates and wanted the squatters ejected. But because of the conditions under which the 'Three Chains' had been set aside, it was a difficult problem to solve and the question of title to these lands occupied the attention of the British and local government for some time. This was to result in serious disturbances among the population in future years.

Those who lived on the coast would also squat on Crown lands in the interior and walk daily from their homes to their 'gardens'. They practised shifting cultivation. They cleared land in the forest, used it for one growing period and then moved on to a fresh spot. Not until 1946, did the government take strong action to stop this practice.

During those early years new villages grew up and old ones were expanded. In this new society the feeling of independence was strong; their land provided them with what they needed and they were responsible to no one; perhaps this is in part the reason for our fiery independence and all that is stolid and unyielding in the Dominican character.

French Slave Refugees

As a result of emancipation, Dominica once again found herself influencing events in the French islands on either side of her. Slavery was not abolished in the colonies of Martinique and Guadeloupe until 1848 and for fourteen years the freedom of Dominica's shores drew French slaves across the turbulent sea channels. John Gurney, an American visitor to Dominica in 1840 described the exodus in letters to a friend in New York.

'Several hundreds of the slaves, since the British act of emancipation, have made their escape to Dominica – chiefly, I believe, from Guadeloupe. The poor creatures run prodigious risks in their attempts to cross the water, in small open boats; and we are informed that at least one third of them perish before they reach the land. One hardy fellow arrived on the shore of Dominica, after extreme peril, on the remains of a small raft which he had constructed of the pithy stems of the great aloe, or century plant. When at Dominica, we heard excellent accounts of the behaviour and industry of these runaway slaves.'

14
The Years of Change

The second half of the nineteenth century was a period of social and political re-organisation. By today's standards the changes were small and took a long time, but the former systems still dominated the government and society and the old order could not be swept aside overnight.

Since the beginning of Dominica's colonisation, 'people of colour' or mulattos, had been an important part of the society. They owned estates and businesses, and slaves, and were members of the local militia. They had participated in everything except the government of the island. In most of the West Indies, the white population had entirely dominated the social life of the colonies, but in Dominica there had existed side-by-side two high societies: the mainly French mulatto families and the white attorneys and government officials. These two divisions of the 'gros bourgs' continued to dominate business and government well into the twentieth century.

In 1832, the year after the 'Brown Privilege' bill was passed, three coloured members were elected to the House of Assembly and by 1838 there was a coloured majority. These members immediately began to press for legislation promoting the welfare of the newly liberated citizens of the island. This rapid turn, heightened political pressures and created two unofficial parties on the island: the white attorneys on one hand and the 'Mulatto Ascendancy' on the other. Caught between these two factions was the Governor. Although he usually sided with the more conservative section of the House and Council, he was at the same time being directed by the Home Government, to improve the education and general welfare of the population as a whole. The two groups supported rival newspapers, *The Colonist*, conservative, and *The Dominican*, liberal. And these journals were the springboards for vicious personal attacks between the two forces. But the insults were not confined to print, they were common during deliberations of the Assembly and by 1858, the island had become a notorious hotbed of political ferment as the *Antigua Weekly Register* commented that year.

'The political disputes, engendering social discord and strife of our neighbours in Dominica, have for so long a period been a reproach to the legislation and government of that island, as to cease to attract even

Falconer speaking in the House of Assembly.

ordinary attention. Charges of gross official and legislative corruption on one side and violent abuse on the other form nearly the sum total of the political intelligence that is from time to time recorded in the journals of the colony. These have been so common for years past that no one appears to expect anything else.'

But such comments came from islands that were still firmly under the power of white planters and businessmen. Dominica was the only island in the British West Indies where white rule was successfully challenged. The group of coloured families, the Mulatto Ascendancy, kept control of the legislature for two generations until they were finally defeated by the introduction of Crown Colony rule.

Chief among these early Dominican politicians was Charles Gordon Falconer who kept up a constant tirade against the established order. He was an ex-schoolteacher and was the sharp-minded and sharp-tongued editor of *The Dominican* newspaper. He had gained his seat by defeating the then Sugar King of the island – Charles Leatham – at the polls. Mr Leatham owned most of the estates in the northern district including Londonderry, Woodford Hill, Eden, Hampstead and Blenheim Estates as well as land in other parts of the island. He represented Roseau in the House of Assembly and his defeat was a severe blow to the then privileged class. There was also Joseph Fadelle, who was known even in England for his fearless exposure of misconduct among certain colonial officials in Dominica.

On a more moderate level was James Garraway, a coloured merchant who was raised from the Assembly to the Council in 1840 and on a number of occasions administered the government as President and senior Council member. In the words of *The Dominican:* 'The first man of African blood who ever reached this high honour in any of the former slave holding dependencies of the British Crown.'

But this political action was still centred around the tiny liberal and conservative groups of the Roseau elite. The mass of the people were as yet inactive in this field and in most cases turned to the Roman Catholic priests for guidance and leadership rather than to the British or coloured Dominican leaders.

Towards Crown Colony Rule

For the rest of the nineteenth century the British Crown tried several ways to deal with the problems of governing Dominica. In 1833 Dominica was included with Antigua and other Leeward Islands in a semi-federal arrangement under a Governor-in-Chief residing in Antigua. Locally other changes were afoot.

The pressures created in the Assembly by the liberal factions had annoyed the executives and conservative English merchants and attorneys for some time. As early as 1853 some of these persons had discussed the possibility of abolishing the representative system. They wanted Crown Colony Rule operating with a single chamber government of carefully chosen nominated members and officials. It appeared that whereas they had been willing to accept the misconduct of the old planters in the Assembly, they did not feel that the new mulatto order should take the same liberties. By 1857 this conservative group had formed the Dominica Association for the Reform of Abuses in the Administration of Public Affairs, and single chamber government was their leading goal.

Emancipation had not given political rights to the freed, and the educational facilities were too meagre to train them for effective citizenship. In 1850 the population of Dominica was about 25,000 and less than 5,000 could read or write.

In this year a bill was introduced to increase the numbers of voters and candidates for office. But the British government did not assent to it, stating that the method of proving a person's qualification to vote was too flimsy and could be abused. Many members of the Assembly knew only too well that this was true, for it was common for people to fake or exchange title deeds to prove that they could vote. Therefore when the Governor pressed for a proper registration of voters' qualifications, the electives took strong offence. There was so much controversy over the matter that Lieutenant-Governor Thomas Price dissolved the House and called a new election. The conservative faction took over the majority, and Price lost no time in presenting the bill on voter registration. That same year, 1862, a bill was also introduced to sweep away the old two-House system and create a single chamber. Despite Charles Falconer's strong opposition to this bill, it was passed both in the Assembly and Executive Council the following year. It was known as 'The Single Chamber Act', by which the Council and the House of Assembly became one chamber of 28 members who elected their own Speaker.

The new body of 1863 was made up of nine members appointed by the Crown and nineteen representatives. But this overcrowded single chamber Assembly failed. The name-calling and accusations made any organised business impossible. It was soon realised that for single chamber government to work, the number of members would have to be sharply reduced.

Falconer's house on Hanover Street, Roseau was the meeting place for the liberal politicians and thinkers of the day.

The officer who took over from Thomas Price was a coloured gentleman from Montserrat called Cleaver Robinson. Finding the state of affairs confused, he attempted to form a Legislative Council composed of a limited number of members all nominated by the Crown. On 8 March 1865, the bill to make Dominica a Crown Colony was introduced into the Assembly and was supported by a large majority.

The Falconer group had lost popularity and in a desperate effort to keep some sort of representative system they tried to make another suggestion. They called for an Assembly which would have an equal number of elected and nominated members. Public meetings were held, petitions and deputations appeared before Robinson and rumours of every sort soon spread. As a result the Crown Colony bill was withdrawn and the other measure – providing for an equally divided legislature – was introduced and passed. This act reduced the numbers of the Legislature to 14, of whom seven were elected by the people and seven nominated by the Governor. He also replaced the elected Speaker as presiding officer.

At this meeting marines from the warship HMS *Aurora* had been stationed at Fort Young while a contingent surrounded the Court House with loaded guns and fixed bayonets. At later meetings crowds booed and hissed at the men who opposed Falconer. Window bars sailed through the air landing on the large table around which the members sat and an estate overseered by one nominated attorney was set on fire and damaged. This only made things worse for Falconer among the conservative faction.

Attempts were made to still Falconer's voice in the Assembly and on one occasion whilst addressing the House he was interrupted by the Speaker, Mr Doyle, and asked to sit. He refused and was promptly marched to the common jail. There was a great uproar and his wife Mary went to prison and served the short term with him. On his release, Falconer brought an action for damages against the Speaker of the House. Judge Thomas Sholto Pemberton found in favour with the plaintiff and awarded £700 damages. The government, not being satisfied, took the case on appeal to the Privy Council who confirmed the judgement of Mr Pemberton and increased the damages of £1,000.

An Act was passed to tighten up certain rules of the House and increase the property requirements for electors and electives. There was further protest from Falconer and his group and a three-man delegation made up of Lewis Bellot, George Garrway and Falconer himself, sailed for England to present their grievances to the Secretary of State for the Colonies. But their protests against the new measures were in vain. They were told that the island was too small to have a large body of representatives and that changes had to be made. Soon after the delegation returned to Dominica elections were held and in a show of support the electorate firmly placed them back into the new Legislature.

The government could not then afford to pay the whole amount and arranged for the payment of this amount by annual instalments. Falconer died 29 March 1872, aged 53 years. Mrs Falconer drew these amounts until about the time of her death in 1917.

In November 1865 the Legislature settled down under its new constitution – seven elected members and seven nominees. The public mood became calmer and under the guidance of Falconer the electives were more restrained in their opposition. Yet the system did not run as had been hoped. The nominated members who were expected to vote in favour of the Governor's actions seldom did so. They were often either halfhearted or uninterested and had to stand up to the electives, who acted as one party, opposing measures and blocking changes, especially concerning the spending of the colony's funds. Outside the Legislature the local newspapers carried on the battle, and those nineteenth century newspapers were fine examples of sharp, strong and witty political argument. One governor was of the opinion that the bickering and divisions in Dominica made the Legislature 'a perfect farce'.

In 1871 Dominica was made a unit of the federal colony under the Leeward Island Federation. The seat of government was transferred to Antigua and local affairs were administered by a 'President' later styled a 'Commissioner' carrying out the duties assigned to him by the Governor in Antigua. The President worked with a small nominated Council and Dominica elected two members to send to the central Legislature in Antigua. Until 1898 Dominica was the only Presidency of the Federation which sent representatives duly elected by the people to the Federal Legislature. Federation was not popular with Dominicans; they did not feel that they were well governed from Antigua and were shocked when some Antiguans arrived to sit as nominated members in the local Council. But the Colonial Office found this system a much more convenient way of running her possessions in the area and therefore Dominica's position in the grouping was never a happy one.

Soon resolutions were being passed in Dominica demanding that the island be withdrawn from the group and the elected members continued to make repeated calls for a fully responsible elected government as had existed before 1863. But this was not to be. Britain was already finding that elsewhere in the Caribbean the 'strong government – Crown Colony government – was the easiest way to run the islands. There would be no elected members to block action or oppose schemes and, as the political ferment in Dominica continued the representatives were made to appear worthless and dishonourable in the eyes of the people and it gave Britain a greater excuse to make the change.

In 1896 financial help was promised on condition that we gave up our constitution. The people, through their representatives replied that the

The weekly Saturday market, when hucksters and peasant farmers came into town from the countryside, was the spot for political meetings during the nineteenth century.

difficult financial position was not due to the constitution nor the inability of the representatives to govern but due entirely to Britain's economic policy. The Imperial Government was adamant and a telegram was sent to the Governor of the Leeward Islands saying that Crown Colony Government must be made law in Dominica at all costs. In spite of protests, the Bill was introduced in the Legislature but was thrown out by the unanimous votes of the elected members together with the vote of LA Giraud, a nominated member and grandfather of Dominica's first native born Governor Sir Louis Cools-Lartigue.

The government would not accept defeat and immediately dissolved the Legislative Assembly and issued writs for a new election. This time they would not rely on their own strength but sought the help of the church. Father Branchereau of the Catholic Church and Reverend Jones of the Methodist Church were entrusted with the task of converting the people of Vielle Case and Wesley to Crown Colony. For his part in the matter Reverend Jones was asked by the Methodists to leave the colony. With the help of these gentlemen Mr J Colin Macintyre defeated Mr DO Riviere at the polls. It is interesting that on account of the qualifications being so high at the time there were only 27 voters in that large district, 18 voted for Mr Macintyre and nine for Mr Riviere. At the first meeting of the Assembly after this election Mr Colin Macintyre introduced the Crown Colony Bill which was passed by a vote of eight to six.

In that fight it may be well to mention the names of some of the men who took a leading and active part. The leader of the people was William Davies who was then owner of Bath Estate. Mr Davies with the help of his confreres, notably Alex Ramsey Lockhart, DO Riviere, Jabez Bellot and Henry Hamilton fought strongly against Crown Colony rule but the constitution was lost through the single vote of an elected member, Colin Macintyre, added to that of the nominated members.

That Crown Colony Bill of 1898 created a Legislative Council of six officials and six nominated members. Elected government in Dominica had been dealt a final blow and the Imperial Government took full control and responsibility for the affairs of the island. Most natives of Dominica immediately withdrew from every government board in protest and the veteran local politicians left the arena. Many retired to concentrate on their land or businesses while some continued to express their ideas in the newspapers. Few of them lived to see the day when there would be elected members in the Council once more.

15
An Unsettled Society

During the 1840s there were still many suspicions and misunderstandings among the population regarding the running of the colony's affairs and the ex-slaves were distrustful of any laws which concerned their activities. Six years after full emancipation, the Legislature passed an Act to authorise the taking of a census. The peasants were already in a state of irritation owing to the unsettled question of squatters and added to this, certain persons spread the false rumour that the object of the census was the collection of names to re-establish slavery.

On 3 June 1844, enumerators preparing to take the census in several country districts found that houses had been abandoned and the people had armed themselves with sticks and cutlasses. They were assembled in large crowds threatening death to anyone who tried to take their names. Disturbances took place in areas south of Roseau and in the Colihaut and Canefield districts. Officers were threatened, and at Pointe Michel and Canefield they were beaten and wounded.

The following day, the Privy Council recorded the alarmed and excited state of the peasant population and noted that the mood was spreading rapidly. Martial law was proclaimed, and regular troops, police, and militiamen were sent to the troubled areas. A proclamation was issued advising the misguided and ill-advised persons that the census was solely to get the number, sex and age of the inhabitants and it added that once emancipated by law they could no longer be made slaves.

In putting down the rebellion, several people at Canefield, Colihaut and Grand Bay were killed and at Grand Bay, the most active area in the uprising, one man committed suicide when he was surrounded by militiamen. At the close of the action another man threatened the militia and was shot down; his head was later stuck on a pole along the road to that village, as a warning to others. Some days afterwards, a warship, with the Governor of the Leeward Islands aboard called at Roseau. His Excellency issued a proclamation offering pardon to those taking part in the revolt, except for the ringleaders, who were to be tried for their offences.

In the course of the week, the island's garrison was reinforced with 200 soldiers. Most of the prisoners taken were sent back to their homes and the ringleaders were tried in July by the Chief Justice and 18 unpaid justices. One of the rebels was publicly hanged at Pointe Michel while another five, also condemned to death, were pardoned. Towards the end of the month the justices were becoming tired of the endless cases and on 31 July, the remaining number of accused were dismissed. For years this revolt was known as 'La guerre negre'.

Religious Riots

Early in 1847, Roman Catholics were calling for their church to be granted funds by the colony. They argued that as Catholics formed the bulk of the population their church was more entitled to state aid than the Anglican church, which was then provided for with money from the local treasury. Several petitions were presented to the Legislature on the subject and there was much argument.

On 4 May, a staunch Catholic member of the House of Assembly, TF Lockhart, introduced a bill to provide incomes for the Roman Catholic clergy. Mr Lockhart's emotional address in the House caused much agitation among Catholics and this was heightened by the strong opposition of Charles Falconer, a fiery Methodist. He objected to any religious denomination receiving money from the government, especially in a poor island such as Dominica. Because of this, Falconer and his fellow Methodists became the targets of insult. The newspapers of the time claim that Methodists were mocked at and jeered in the streets, and accused important members of the community of encouraging these acts. Catholic priests were also publicly accused of being the cause of this ill-feeling.

During this feud, the Roman Catholic cathedral was being enlarged, and on moonlight nights churchgoers would volunteer to carry stones from the Roseau River to the building site. They were summoned by the ringing of a bell and the gang usually exceeded a hundred persons. The discontent between the churches could be strongly felt during these occasions, and according to one observer: 'They went about their work with cries and insults against the Methodists and night after night the ringing of the church bell was the signal for disgraceful scenes of disorder.'

On the evening of 18 October, 1847, the Methodist Society held an anniversary meeting in their chapel next to the cathedral. The stone carriers had earlier threatened to disrupt the meeting and soon after the Methodists had assembled, the carriers gathered in front of the building causing such a commotion that police had to be called. They then began to stone the building and as friends of both parties ran to take sides a general riot ensued; the numbers were estimated at 3,000 with even members of the Assembly involved. Woundings occurred, and over the next few days tension was running high in Roseau. The troops on the island were alerted

Cocoa production became important at the end of the nineteenth century. This scene from a Victorian Stereoscope plate shows cocoa drying on the glacee at Soufriere estate.

and though some minor incidents were reported this put an end to the disturbances.

Batalie and the Queen's Chains

The owners of Batalie estate on the leeward coast, had been able to prove their title to that part of the 'Queen's Three Chains' which bordered their property. They unsuccessfully tried to evict the squatters who had set up houses on the sea-shore and therefore called in a magistrate to settle the dispute. The squatters were offered leases on the land they occupied on condition they paid a small rent, otherwise they would be given notice.

The elected members of the Assembly, led by Charles Falconer, objected to this and called on squatters throughout the island to stick to the land on which they had settled and resist any move to eject them. The people of Batalie followed these instructions, as they had been told by the elected members that with continued resistance they would eventually get possession of the land.

On 21 January, 1856, the Crown Surveyor and three policemen arrived at Batalie to eject the squatters, but were soon forced to hurry away without completing their mission. The next day Lieutenant-Governor

Blackhall went down, accompanied by a stipendiary magistrate, eight armed policemen and four sailors who had been sworn in as special constables. It was thought that a show of force would deter the crowd and after Blackhall had made an unsuccessful speech on the shore, the policemen began to take possession of the huts. This signalled a strong attack from the squatters and once more the forces returned to Roseau leaving the villagers triumphant.

The Governor then sent for assistance from Antigua and detachments of the 2nd West India and 67th Regiments immediately sailed to Dominica. Warrants were issued against the rioters and the Provost Marshall prepared to lead the regiments to Batalie. But the boat-men of Roseau refused to take him down the coast, and the Governor finally had to ask the ships in the harbour to provide boats for the journey. This delayed the Marshal for many days, and when he did eventually reach Batalie he was only successful in arresting three women.

It was decided that the affair could only be settled with force and this time the Lieutenant-Governor sailed to Batalie with the magistrate, 24 soldiers, 10 officers, the Inspector of Police and eight constables. When their schooner appeared the ringleaders fled to the hills and those who remained were forced to come to terms. The police broke one hut and formal possession was taken of the other buildings in order to get the squatters to agree to the conditions of rental and ownership.

The Bretons and Italians

Another minor disturbance occured in Roseau between two factions of Roman Catholics in the town. This absurd episode began in 1869 when an Italian priest named Sebastiani arrived in the island and speedily became very popular with a large number of the Roseau congregation. Possibly for this reason, Sebastiani became unpopular among his fellow priests especially Pere Ardois, the Vicar General who was administering the diocese while the Bishop, Monsignior Poirier was in Rome. Eventually Pere Sebastiani was threatened with interdiction and because he would not bend to the wishes of this superior, he was soon deprived of the right of performing divine service. This caused the congregation to divide into factions, those supporting Sebastiani calling themselves the 'Italians' and those faithful to Pere Ardois banding together as the 'Bretons'. This name was used, as many of the French priests were natives of Britanny. Each party had their 'King' and 'Queen' and the street quarrels created much disturbance in Roseau.

It was thought that the return of Bishop Poirier in November 1869 would bring an end to the trouble, but by early the following month there were even unpleasant scenes in the Cathedral. On the first Sunday in December the Bishop stood in the pulpit and spoke on the affair. In the words of *The Dominican* newspaper: 'He commenced to use language of a very insulting and abusive nature against Sebastiani and his party.' The service was immediately followed by a minor riot in and around the Cathedral during which the Bishop 'was loudly threatened with death' and had to be escorted by police from the altar to this residence. The Lieutenant-Governor called together the Council and it was decided to swear in special constables at once, as there was evidence that the Italian group were planning to wreck the Bishop's house during the night. When the mob marched to the presbytery they found the area surrounded and eventually dispersed.

After a picnic at Fond Cole on Boxing Day that year, a crowd of 300 'Italians' gathered to attack the house of the 'King' and 'Queen' of the 'Bretons'. There were minor injuries and many arrests were made. The trial lasted two days, but the jury, mainly 'Italians' returned a verdict of not guilty. The Chief Justice was shocked at the jury's decision: 'Gentlemen, I record your verdict but I never expected it.'

Patois songs were made up on the topic and it was only towards the end of 1872 that ill-feelings were forgotten. Sebastiani remained in Dominica for a few years. His supporters had bought and furnished a house for him and provided a small income. For this he ministered to them privately and eventually returned to Italy.

Peasants and Capital

The traditional theory of economic development was directed at maintaining the viability of large plantations by ensuring a constant supply of cheap labour and through protected markets, securing high incomes for exported goods. With slavery over, other pressures would have to be used to influence the labour force to continue working on the estates. In Dominica where more land was available for squatting and peasant agriculture than anywhere else in the Eastern Caribbean, the temptation for the people to set up on their own was great indeed. As we have seen at Batalie, land holding laws and eviction by force was used to deal with squatters. But it was soon realised that the pressure of taxation could be used to deal with those who legally held small portions of land. By demanding taxes from the subsistence farmer his family would be forced to go to work on the estates to earn wages so that he could pay the taxes on his land. This economic pressure on the smallholder was seen as a means not just of raising money, but of securing labour for the estates.

No large external market existed for the produce of small farmers and the sale of small quantities of cocoa, cassava farine or coffee to Roseau merchants was not regular enough to provide a secure income. But the official view was that the peasant proprietors were lazy and that measures

Lime production quickly gained prominence at this time also. In the foreground a woman on Canefield estate presses lime oil using an ecuelle while an oxcart passes along the road behind.

should be instituted to maintain a dependence of the small farmers on the estates. The estates however were in serious economic difficulties during the latter part of the nineteenth century. The Sugar Duties Act passed in Britain in 1846 had removed the protected status of West Indian sugar on the British market. A gradual lowering of duties on foreign sugar meant that the inferior quality British West Indian cane sugar now had to compete with a superior product from other countries including beet sugar from Europe. Dominica's product was the lowest grade of all. A report of 1869 stated, 'The Dominican sugar planters contend that the reduction in duty had hurt their low quality sugar. But [this colony] was notoriously backward, even as muscovado producers . . . If not sufficiently tempered, the juice refused to crystallise, or formed a doughy, moist sugar with a small grain – common in Dominica.'

By the end of the century, an enquiry into the sugar industry in the West Indies considered that there was no point in attempting to resuscitate sugar in Dominica but rather an alternative was advised in the form of agricultural education and land settlement for peasants. But that was the view in 1897. As we shall see, several events, some of them violent, had to occur before that was to be seen as the accepted solution for Dominica's development. In the meantime, self sufficiency among the 'labouring classes' was not seen to be acceptable. In 1882 the Acting President of the island, John Spencer Churchill declared: 'Peasant proprietorship is, no doubt, rather to be deprecated than encouraged in the case of the Negroes, who are apt in that state, to lapse into barbarous idleness.'

A report by a similar official thirty years earlier, commenting on the wages of field labour at six pence a day was of the view that it was 'adequate remuneration in a colony where ground provisions are so easily cultivated and to be obtained at a very reasonable rate, an advantage not possessed by the labouring population of most of the other West India islands.'

James Anthony Froude who visited with Churchill in 1887 observed that 'Such industry as is now to be found is, as elsewhere in general, the industry of the black peasantry . . . Skill and capital and labour have only to be brought together and the land might be a Garden of Eden.' But as events were to prove, it was the peasantry rather than big capital investments which was going to be the salvation of Dominica.

Land Tax

In 1886, the Governor, Viscount Gormanston, made plans to change the system of taxation on the island. Taxation was uneven. A house and land tax existed in Roseau, outlying villages and the Queen's Chains; elsewhere was free. Merchants, people with the most capital at the time, took out trade licences which were tax-free and many large land-owners resided outside the taxed areas and were therefore exempt. Gormanston wanted to sweep away the old methods and introduce laws that applied everywhere in the island. He wanted also to alter export duties; revise the Road Tax and make sure that income tax was paid by all who could afford to do so.

Many of the electives saw this as a threat to their interests and strongly opposed these bills. They made the excuse that not enough time had been given to consider the action and walked out of the Assembly, remaining absent for the rest of the session and the bills were passed without them. These electives, landowners and tradesmen with property and interests throughout the island, resolved to obstruct the Governor. They held meetings in various areas agitating against Viscount Gormanston and his reforms. The first of these was held in Roseau Public Garden which existed opposite the Court House. Feelings were strong, as when one member referred to Gormanston as 'a jackass without brains'. Four days later a mass meeting was held in the market place. It was a Saturday and the town was full of vendors and country folk. A platform was erected on pork barrels beneath a banner proclaiming 'WE DON'T WANT LAND TAX' and speakers included many leading politicians of the day: SR Pemberton,

ES Dawbiney, William Davies, ARC Lockhart and OD Riviere among others.

As emotions rose, the crowd was urged to march on Government House and demand the Governor to account for his action. Over one thousand people advanced on the residence, invading the grounds, damaging plants and shouting slogans against the land tax. The police guard was overpowered; (according to some sources they had been persuaded to support the action beforehand and offered little resistance). Lord Gormanston appeared on the front steps and agreed to talk with a delegation of five on condition that the demonstrators left the premises. With some trouble this was achieved and a group presented him with three resolutions expressing disapproval of the new tax measures and the method in which they had been passed; it also supported the elective's decision to walk out. They also protested about such a tax at a period of 'financial and industrial distress' and stated it would be better to reduce the expenditure on the 'feudal staff notorious of inefficiency of administration'.

The Colonial Office took the disturbances lightly and the Acts were assented to. The new laws directed a tax of $\frac{1}{2}$ percent of the value of the property as well as general income tax according to the amount of money earned. With some misgivings Dominicans accepted and settled down to the new system but were happy to see Gormanston depart soon afterwards.

This story has a final twist. The new Governor, William Haynes-Smith appeared before the assembly in May 1888 with plans to increase taxation and multiply the revenue three-fold in order to develop the island. He made no demands on the members; the final decision would be theirs; but he dealt so diplomatically with the electives that they gave him every cooperation. Fifteen measures were passed including an increase on house and land tax to 2 percent – three times as much as in 1886. To the amazement of the authorities in London, the same members who had protested so strongly then, now unanimously approved the substantial increase.

Another tax which was the cause of much bitterness was that imposed on all persons for their use of the roadways and was intended as a source of revenue for road maintenance. This was contained in The Road Act of 1856 which stipulated that citizens either had to give work on the roads for a set period each year or pay the equivalent time in tax instead. This 'Twaveau', as the tax was commonly called, was widely opposed and in the first three months 130 persons were jailed for breaches of the Act. In 1881 women were excluded from having to pay the tax or provide labour.

The La Plaine Uprising

The 1888 rise in property tax received its first major resistance five years later at La Plaine. This village on the windward coast was, in 1893, one of

The La Plaine Land Tax riot.

the poorest districts in the island. Sugar cultivation had fallen on hard times years before and was by then non-existent. The only cash products, arrowroot and cassava farine, had to be carried overland to Roseau along the precipitous track that led past Grand Fond and over the island by way of the Freshwater Lake – the road that had been used since the eighteenth century. When the people of Au Vent reached the capital, merchants bought their produce at pitifully low prices. To travel by open sea was costly and dangerous and many are the village stories of loss of life and produce along the cliffs of Boetica and Pointe Des Fous.

It was a life almost without money and because of this the villagers had developed a community system of work. Neighbours and friends would build a house or shingle a roof in return for similar assistance. All food came from the land and, because it was impossible to get products from outside, the people lived as a self-sufficient society. This was also true of other villages throughout the island.

In 1893, a certain Pierre Colaire was unable to pay the tax due on his houselot and it was ordered to be sold under a provision of the House and Land Act. On 6 April, a bailiff, John Jarvis, who had previously been active against smuggling in the region, and a Police Inspector, came from Roseau with a warrant to take possession of the property. An angry mob had assembled and the two men sought refuge in the police station before fleeing across the Tabery River.

On 13 April, Governor Haynes-Smith arrived off the windward coast in

HMS Mohawk, *the 225ft Torpedo Cruiser of 1770 tons, under Capt EH Bailey which went to Plaissance Bay, La Plaine. (From a photograph in the National Maritime Museum, Greenwich, England.)*

the Royal Navy cruiser, HMS *Mohawk*. He landed accompanied by Commander EH Bailey and walked to the La Plaine church presbytery where the people had gathered to express their grievances. Pierre Colaire was interviewed privately but refused to vacate his property and the Governor ordered his ejection.

As nine policemen and twenty-five armed sailors from the *Mohawk* left the presbytery, the sound of conch shells echoed from ridge to ridge. At this signal a mass of people moved towards the house site. No sooner had Colaire been evicted than a villager, Gregoire St Ville gave a sign, and the rioters closed in attacking the forces with stones. The troops in turn opened fire and the crowd scattered leaving four of their men dead and two women wounded.

The incident caused shock throughout the island. The electives of the Assembly at once telegraphed the Secretary of State for the colonies requesting an inquiry. They did not defend the action of the mob but vigorously denounced the use of rifles. The dispatches sent by Haynes-Smith to London raised many serious questions on the running of the colony, the relations between government and legislature and the whole subject of taxation. For years the Colonial Office had been faced with the unrest and political bickering on the island and in the last decade of the nineteenth century it made vain efforts to stop it once and for all.

16
New Men, New Energy

The Victorians

The British Empire was expanding with amazing energy during this period of the nineteenth century. It was the largest empire in the history of the world, comprising a quarter of its population. Victoria herself was a Queen-Empress of such aged majesty that some of her simpler subjects considered her a divine being. At 'Home', Great Britain had developed as a massive industrial power. Steel, iron, coal, machinery and every kind of manufactured product were pouring out of her factories. The red tint which signified British possessions was spread across the map of the world.

But Victorian writers painted a gloomy picture of Dominica. 'It is impossible,' says Anthony Trollope in 1860, 'to conceive a more depressing sight. Every house is in a state of decadence. There are no shops that can properly so be called. The people wander about, idle, chattering, listless, there is no sign of money made or of money making . . . Everything seems to speak of desolation, apathy, ruin.' All other visitors throughout the century seemed to share his view, and it was JA Froude, calling 1887, who was most bitter. Here he was ashamed to see the Union Jack flying over the island. 'England has done nothing, absolutely nothing, to introduce her own civilisation; and thus Dominica is English only in name.'

However, there were Britons who made their mark on the island. Men came out as civil servants and medical officers to develop the agriculture and welfare of the colony, and they were a noticeable change from the attorneys and planters of former years. Most noted among them was a Scotsman, Dr John Imray. He had come to Dominica in 1832 at the age of twenty-one to join his brother Dr Keith Imray who had been practising here for some time. By skill and hard work he soon became the leading physician on the island. It was a period when yellow fever, malaria and yaws were a common scourge and even then scientists had little knowledge of tropical diseases. Imray made important discoveries on the nature, causes and treatment of these ailments and was the first British practitioner to outline certain characteristics of yellow fever. As an authority in his field, the articles he presented to medical magazines attracted much attention.

Sir HAA Nicholls. Medical practitioner, agricultural researcher, botanist, politician and explorer.

Dr John Imray, who by his singular effort did much towards the well being of Dominica in health, agriculture, botanical science, education and research of the island. Sketch taken from a photo about 1875.

Besides his developments in medicine he was a famous botanist, discovering many unknown species of flora in the forests of Dominica and his name has been given to several of our rarer plants. He introduced the cultivation of Liberian coffee and the lime 'ti citron vert' which eventually brought great economic changes to the island. In politics he was a leading member of the Executive Council, and as chairman of the Board of Health, he organised the foundation of our present health service and the Roseau hospital. He died in 1880 and a marble plaque in the St George's Anglican church tells us simply the character of Dr John Imray:

'His sterling qualities, scientific research, medical skill, kindliness of disposition and patriotic love for his adopted home endeared him to the entire community and won for him universal respect.' This splendid marble memorial, as well as another large descriptive one dedicated to Charles Leatham, was tragically shattered to bits when the Anglican Church was destroyed by Hurricane David in 1979.

In 1873 Imray was joined by a young London-born physician who was to take over from him and continue to develop the health services on the island. Like Imray, Dr Henry Alfred Alford Nicholls was not only a man of professional skill but had the enquiring mind of a scientist which led him to develop the propagation and cultivation of certain tropical crops, publish a major text book on tropical agriculture and explore the interior of the island. He publicised Dominica's Boiling Lake in geographical journals and claimed to have discovered it in March 1875 accompanied by a party of hikers. This discovery was made fun of by *The Dial* newspaper which claimed that early mapmakers and local hunters knew of the Lake's existence a century before. Nicholls served for years as a nominated member of the Council. He often tried to gain election, but because of his conservative views the local politicians made certain of his defeat.

As a founder-member of the Agricultural Society he did much to promote the sale of Dominica's produce abroad. He was later knighted for his service to the colony where he died in 1926.

The Royal Commission

Reports from Dominica on the dissatisfaction and political unrest raised such serious questions that the Secretary for the Colonies appointed a Commission to make a 'diligent and full inquiry into the state of affairs existing in Our Island of Dominica.' Sir Robert Hamilton, Her Majesty's Commissioner, arrived in Dominica on 21 November 1893. His inquiry

The entrance to the Botanic Gardens from Valley Road in 1905.

was a searching one and he visited the various districts of the island to observe local conditions. He noted the shocking waste of funds, especially in the field of road construction and advised a number of changes in the government of the colony. In 1895 the status of the head of the island government was raised to an Administrator who could communicate directly with the Secretary of State, rather than go through the Governor in Antigua. Hamilton had also advised on changes in taxation especially the hated house and land tax. Dominicans received his report with satisfaction and many of the suggestions were carried out. Another royal commission visited the island in 1896 as part of an inquiry into the sugar situation in the West Indies.

The Colonial Office was then in the hands of the energetic minister, Joseph Chamberlain who looked on the Empire as an undeveloped estate into which new life should be planted by a series of wise and just measures. He was however a classic imperialist and because he did not trust the local Assembly to handle funds properly, he was only willing to give Dominica Imperial aid on condition that it was ruled by crown colony government; if the old elected-type constitution continued there would be no grant.

Speaking in the British House of Commons he urged the members to grant £30,000 to the colony, and reminded those who opposed him of the vast amount of money Britain had taken from Dominica when the island was sold in 1773–1778.

The House voted in favour of the grant, which besides aid for Dominica included £120,000 for colonial relief. When crown colony rule was secured later that year, Chamberlain fulfilled his side of the bargain. £15,000 was provided to pay off the colony's debts while the other £15,000 was to go towards opening up roads to Crown lands in the interior.

Hesketh Bell

Just before the Imperial grant was made, Dominica received its first Administrator, PA Templer. He began a vigorous plan of bridge and road construction, including the laying of a road across the island from Layou. Before work began however, a coffee planter, formerly in Ceylon, bought a large area of Crown land in the centre of the island. Here, he hoped to plant coffee on a large scale, and as this was a big investment for the island, plans for a transinsular road were changed, and in 1898 Templer started building a road inland from Canefield. But he hardly saw the beginning of his scheme, before he fell ill and had to return to England.

At this time, the newspapers were still vigorously protesting over crown colony rule and Templer's schemes, but in the following year even the most bitter writers had changed their tune. The Administrator who took over Dominica in September 1899 had the island stunned.

Henry Hesketh Bell had barely unpacked his bags before *The Guardian* newspaper began to compare his vigorous activity to that of the previous Administrator. It recorded Bell's first week in breathless detail. Every day had been filled with a busy programme of visits, interviews and inspections. By June 1900, he had visited almost every part of the island, including the Boiling Lake and the Carib quarter. Both *The Guardian* and *The Dominican* expressed delight.

Bell's early success lay in the fact that he was an excellent and shrewd diplomat. He flattered and won over the editors and politicians. He had private discussions with them outlining his intentions and ideas. With the newspapers on his side and public opinion in his favour, he was ready to put his many plans into action.

He immediately realised that much had to be done to put the colony into 'good shape'. He observed, 'Roseau contains about 7,000 inhabitants . . . With the exception of two or three main thoroughfares, all the streets are paved with cobblestones dating from the French days, while the lighting only consists of a few kerosene oil lamps. Nearly all the public buildings are in a wretched condition and devoid of paint.

'There is no public library and no poorhouse save for a ruinous building on top of a hill . . . The hospital is in fair order, but only has accommodation for fifty patients. There is no hotel worthy of the name, and ice, which has to be imported costs two-pence a pound.

Hesketh Bell in 1901.

A settler's house near Middleham in 1908. Within twenty years, the forest had taken over everything once more.

'There are three or four miles of driveable road in the neighbourhood of Roseau, but everywhere else wheeled traffic is impossible. There are not more than three carriages in the whole island and of course not a single motor car . . . There is no telephone communication with the country districts . . .

'The interior of the island is entirely untapped and only a fringe of land around the coasts is cultivated. All this shows that a great deal has to be done if the colony is to be put into good shape . . . At present Dominica is stagnating.'

By the time Hesketh Bell left Dominica in 1905, after six years of service, many of the problems he had noted on his arrival had been overcome. In 1901 the Treasury statements actually showed a surplus of £5,000, something that had been unbelievable in Dominica. In June 1902 Portsmouth was connected to Roseau by telephone, and by 1905 there were 200 miles of telephone lines throughout the island. Arrangements were made with the Royal Mail Company to supply Dominica with a small coastal steamer for service around the island and a sawmill was ordered to utilise the island's timber resources. The remains of this mill have long since rusted away near Portsmouth. In 1902 Bell built the small Victoria Library and then in 1905 the famous Scottish-American philanthropist, Andrew Carnegie, responded to Bell's application for £1,500 to build the Public Library which was designed by the Administrator himself. In the same year, Bell initiated the first electricity service.

He noted the value of views of the island on postage stamps for advertisement as well as revenue, and climbed to the masthead of a ship in the harbour to take a photograph of Roseau. This view of the capital was the first to appear on a local postage stamp. Bell was responsible for making it possible for property in the West Indies to be insured against hurricanes. He had carried out a study of hurricane activity to prove to insurance companies that it was a worthwhile venture.

In August 1905, he opened a new jetty at Roseau just below Fort Young. It was a substantial iron and wood structure and was named in honour of the Administrator – Bell's Jetty; and although it no longer exists, the area is still known by that name. For many years the site was dominated by a huge iron anchor which has been removed.

The Imperial Road and New Settlers

Bell was of the opinion that a road fit for wheeled traffic was essential if important plantations were to be established in the interior of the island, and he proposed that most of the imperial grant should be used to complete Templer's road inland. In 1901 the Colonial Office approved his plans for the remaining £12000 of the grant to be used on the road. Early in 1902

New Men, New Energy 151

The Carnegie Library in 1910 with its beautiful fountain and garden.

HMV Yare anchored off Roseau in 1912. It circled the island on a regular schedule bringing supplies and collecting produce and passengers from the isolated communities along the coast.

work was well underway under the energetic command of William Miller, Chief of the Public Works Department.

This road, which is still important today, wound up from the coast in a series of hairpin bends to a height of 1,800 feet. From here it dipped down into an area almost in the centre of the island called Bassinville, known commonly today as Bells. The sixteen miles of road opened up thousands of acres of Crown lands fit for growing coffee, vanilla, oranges, nutmegs and other products which would thrive in the wet climate of the district. As the money for this road had been given by the Imperial government, Bell christened the thin winding route 'the Imperial Road'.

To develop these Crown lands, the Administrator set out on a scheme to attract new settlers to Dominica.

'I am already convinced that the right people to develop these new lands would be the same class of young men from Home, who have been such a success in Ceylon, Burma and Malaya. This is the policy I am going to work on . . . '

He sent letters and articles to newspapers and magazines in Britain drawing attention to the advantages offered by Dominica for the investment of capital in Agriculture enterprises. He wrote a guidebook for people intending to settle in Dominica: 'Notes on Dominica and Hints to Intending Settlers.' He also worked on a scheme to bring three thousand Boer War prisoners from South Africa to settle in the interior, but this never materialised. Between 1904 and 1905, a considerable number of people arrived from Britain with a view to taking up land that was for sale. Thirty to forty families bought lots of considerable size, and estates such as Middleham, Corona, Vermont, Brantridge and Riversdale sprang up. The white population, which was then only a mere handful, rose to almost 400 by 1907.

Hesketh Bell himself purchased an estate on the road and called it Sylvania. It was run as an experimental plantation where prospective settlers could see for themselves the proper methods of cultivating tropical products. He noticed the area was suitable for rubber trees, and two varieties of rubber were planted along nine miles of the Imperial Road. His ideas for rubber production were never developed, and only one or two of his trees remain by the roadside.

For a while, the money brought by the English settlers had a marked effect on the circulation of cash in the island, and public revenue increased slowly. But, like so many schemes before and since, this one was doomed. Within a few years the English families abandoned their estates for a variety of reasons including World War I and sold out or just let razor grass and tree ferns take over their enterprises. Those few who remained, like GW Penrice, gave up any hope of profit.

But while Bell was still in Dominica prospects for the island looked hopeful. On his return from leave in England in February 1903, he found

Pupils of the Agricultural School at Morne Bruce in 1906.

Roseau decked with triumphal arches and decorations. Country people had come to town, and when Bell stepped ashore, the horses were taken away from his carriage by the crowd, and it was drawn by the people up to Government House. At the end of 1905, Bell was promoted in the colonial service to Commander-in-Chief of Uganda. He left Dominica at the height of his popularity; even the *Leeward Islands Free Press*, which had been started in 1905 and was no friend of his, had to admit his achievements. A few weeks later in England, he received a silvergilt dessert service and centre-piece of old Italian silver on which was inscribed:

'Presented to
His Excellency Henry Hesketh Bell CGM.
Acting Governor of the Leeward Islands In recognition to his invaluable services to Dominica.'

Agriculture

In the last decade of the nineteenth century, Dominica got a considerable lift in her agriculture production. Sugar was by then a minor industry, with only one estate, Canefield, exporting the commodity and not even enough being produced for local consumption. Some estates still produced rum, and peasant farmers crushed cane juice or *visou*, which got a good sale locally. Coffee continued to be exported, but in most cases estates had been turned over to cocoa and limes, which became the chief crops of the island.

The Imperial Department of Agriculture for the West Indies was established in 1898, and the local department of agriculture was developed soon afterwards. Mr Joseph Jones, also curator of the Botanical Gardens, became the first Superintendent of Agriculture. Between 1900 and 1914, the revenue from cocoa and limes rose sharply. The firm of British chocolate manufacturers, Rowntree and Company, owned three large estates in the northern district. Oranges, coconuts, vanilla and spices, cassava starch and small quantities of pineapples and other exotic fruit, had ready markets in the United States and Britain. The Royal Mail Steam Packet Company, the Canada Pacific Ocean Services and the Quebec Steamship Company maintained regular contact with Dominica.

During the period before the First World War, trade soared and by the 1914–1915 financial year, exports were valued at £237,187 and imports £205,773. For a change the island was producing more than it consumed. This prosperous condition was reflected in the running of the estates and the work of the large number of peasant farmers. The Dominica Agricultural Society which was formed in the 1880s had developed into an important body. Under the able guidance of Mr Jones, the Agricultural Department provided planters with advice on proper methods of cultivation and the Botanical Station supplied high quality seedlings.

The first steps towards establishing the Botanical Gardens were made in 1889, and in January 1891 the site to the east of Roseau was bought by the Government from Bath Estate. The first curator was Charles Murray of the Edinburgh Botanic Gardens. He was followed very soon afterwards by Henry F Green, who began planning and laying out the grounds. In 1892 Joseph Jones took over what was to become, for him, a lifetime vocation.

The Botanical Gardens' function was strictly economic and experimental in character, with ornamental plants grown to make the grounds attractive and interesting. Plants from every part of the tropical world were carefully tended while chief attention was paid to providing farmers with seedlings. In its early years and up until the Second World War, the Botanical Gardens of Dominica had a reputation of being the finest in the West Indies.

The station also ran an agricultural training school for the sons of small farmers. Admission to the school was regarded as a distinction, and boys from all parts of the island attended. The two-year course gave a thorough training in the correct and most economical methods of cultivation.

Limes

Dr Imray had introduced lime cultivation on a large scale in the 1860s. For some years the crop was propagated mainly on an experimental basis, but the industry steadily gained ground so that in 1875 lime estates were yielding far greater profits than sugar, and the owners of coffee estates were changing over to limes. But some looked on this as a bad move, claiming that lime juice was never likely to be as important an article of commerce as coffee or cocoa. They were proved wrong, for the industry continued to make steady progress, so that by 1892 the value of lime products exceeded those of cocoa and was established as one of the three main industries of the island. From then on, the crop boomed, sugar rapidly declined and became of little importance, while the cultivation of cocoa failed to keep pace.

Under Jones, the Agricultural Department developed a method of judging the quantity of limes produced; limes were measured in terms of how much fruit made a barrel of juice. In grading the crop by 'barrels', it was easy to calculate how many limes were being produced each year.

As profits increased, estates were turning their old cane mills into lime processing works. There were several lime products: an important trade in green limes existed with the United States; raw lime juice was shipped to Britain and the US; these markets also received concentrated juice from which citric acid was produced. Limes pickled in sea water were also exported along with two types of essential oil from the skin of the lime. The process was time consuming, the limes were individually hand pressed by rotating the fruit over the blunt spikes of a ecuelle. This action broke the cells of the skin and the oil was collected at the base of the funnel-shaped tool.

In their own works, the estates concentrated the juice, and many of the old stream crushers and boilers can still be seen on some estates. Citrate of lime was being produced in large quantities by Messrs L Rose and Company who, even in those years, were famous for their Lime Juice Cordial. Small farmers sold their fruit to larger producers or, using the old sugar teches, they processed their own crop.

The lime industry got a tremendous boost with the arrival of an American millionaire Andrew Green. His engineering company was making a fortune working on the locks for the Panama Canal then under construction. He purchased the ailing Canefield sugar estate and converted it to limes, introducing some of the most advanced citrate processing machinery of that time powered by steam as well as by the traditional waterwheel. Green was a generous philanthropist who concentrated his donations on health care. He put in an entire water and sewerage system as well as other buildings for Roseau hospital. Amazingly, after offering £7,000 towards building a new hospital, in 1918, it was turned down by government in 1922 with the excuse that it could not find matching funds. Such sites as the old infirmary and a quarantine station were also donated by him.

As far as agriculture was concerned these were bright years, and even after the First World War and the damages of the 1916 hurricane, Dominica was by far the largest producer of limes in the world.

17
Between Two Wars

On 3 August 1914 news reached Roseau that war had been declared in Europe. During that day, the government, acting on instructions received from the Secretary of State, converted the defence reserve into the Defence Force. Its 25 members, mostly planters, were called into Roseau along with the police force which was then about 40 strong. Captain H Peebles was put in charge of defence measures. Armed police were stationed to guard the harbour, the military storehouse and Colonial Bank. The next day Germany declared war on Russia.

As it became more certain that Britain would be involved, concern in Roseau increased. The quickest means of getting information were the news cables, and for many days crowds gathered around the Cable Office waiting for fresh news. Guards were stationed where the cable lines came ashore. Ox-carts and the few motor cars that existed were ordered to standby to take government stores to a hiding place behind Wotton Waven. On 5 August the formal declaration of war between Britain and Germany was read on the steps of the Court House, and a small brass band paraded in Roseau, followed by a crowd waving flags and shouting 'God Save the King'.

Five days later Martial Law was proclaimed in the colony. During those first few days the island was rife with rumour, and there was talk of ships being blown up in Caribbean waters. The fishermen no longer went out to catch 'ton' four or five miles off the island, as they were afraid of the German fleet. In the Roseau valley, the Defence Force was protecting the money of the Colonial Bank which was being taken to Wotton Waven where huts had been erected and a store of provisions laid in case of an emergency. If a German cruiser was sighted, the government intended to evacuate the capital, and the small steamer, *The Yare*, was commandeered as part of the local defence equipment. An article in the *Dominica Chronicle* made fun of all these defence measures, but most of the population and particularly the Government were taking it all very seriously.

The excitement and uncertainty of those first two months soon wore off, however, and on 5 October 1914 the Defence Force was disbanded and the members were only required to parade once a week. In April 1915 there was a minor sensation when a German was found among the crew of a whaling vessel at Portsmouth and was thrown into jail in Roseau. But for the rest of the war the only effects felt in Dominica were the drop in trade and increased price of imported food. There was a shortage of shipping, and the valuable green lime trade with the US was almost completely cut. In 1917 the export of cocoa was only allowed by special licence, and for a time the price of raw lime juice for the Royal Navy increased as more supplies were needed to combat disease on the battleships.

The supply of flour to Dominica was uncertain and there was a controlled price for milk and salt fish. It was only towards the end of the war that the price of cloth and other imported articles rose sharply.

Throughout the 'Great War', the loyalty of the West Indies to the Empire was impressive and Dominica was no exception. The War Office had declined from accepting a contingent of men from the colony in September 1914 on the grounds that they would be more useful in the West Indies, but as the action in Europe intensified, men from Dominica were welcome in England. By the middle of 1917 the island had sent more recruits than any other colony in the Leeward Islands, and it was observed by the Administrator that most of the men who offered themselves were labourers and the sons of small proprietors. The Legislative Council voted money towards War Funds and local charities raised funds for the Red Cross and other such bodies in Britain.

But even if Dominica was safe from the ravages of war, she was not spared by natural disasters. In 1915, 1916 and 1917 storms lashed the island. The hurricane of August 1916 was the most serious. Limes suffered considerably, with cocoa, livestock and peasant food crops badly damaged. The windward coast of the island received the worst blow; roads and bridges were swept away. On the west coast at Colihaut the village was entirely flooded and several inhabitants lost their lives by being swept to the sea with their houses and belongings. Funds raised for war purposes were diverted to assist storm damage.

Dominica came out of the war years less prosperous than she had been before but on 27 November 1918 there were parades, and masquerade was allowed on 3 December. Twenty-four men from Dominica were lost in the war, and later their names were engraved on a memorial in Roseau; one of the many that were erected throughout the British colonies in the West Indies.

A New Constitution

The removal of the right to vote, in 1898, had been a great blow to politically minded Dominicans, although many believed that it was the electives' own disorder which had led to their downfall. The elected repre-

The bust of CEA Rawle on Federation Drive, Goodwill.

Lennox and Elma Napier who at different times during the 1930s and 40s represented the North-eastern District in the Legislature. In 1940 Mrs Napier became the first woman in the Caribbean to be elected to any parliament.

sentatives at the time appeared to have no constructive platform and their tactics seemed to have been merely to obstruct. Because of this, they failed to inspire the confidence of either the British government, who questioned their competence, or the voters who became doubtful of their sincerity.

But after twenty-five years of crown colony rule, there was a noticeable change as new personalities entered the political scene. Most dynamic among these new men was a Trinidad-born lawyer CEA Rawle. The *Dominica Tribune* reflected the feelings of this new order.

'Twenty-five years ago Dominica lost her constitution and her people were deprived of one of the fundamental privileges of British citizenship – the franchise. The civil obligations of taxation and service remained however unimpaired.'

As there were no voters, controversial tax measures and laws had been made without consulting the needs of the taxpayers, and this caused even supporters of the Crown Colony system to think again and consider constitutional changes. In the years before the First World War, resentment against the system rose steadily, and soon a movement was launched to bring about some modification in Crown Colony rule. Starting in Grenada with the writings of T Albert Marryshow, it spread throughout the islands, with the noticeable exception of Antigua, which was criticised as being a 'conspicuous ally of Crown Colony rule.'

In Dominica the movement for constitutional reform met with great support, and in March 1919 the Representative Government Association was formed with an elected Assembly as its leading goal. The Legislature voted unanimously in favour of bringing elected members back into the Council, and a definite promise was given by the British government that the constitution would be altered to meet popular requirements. When Major EFL Wood, later Lord Halifax, made his official visit of enquiry into West Indian political demands, he was left with no doubt as to the views of Dominicans. He not only sensed a stronger feeling against Leeward Islands federation than anywhere else, but also heard with sympathy the demands for representative government. He received a petition of over 2,000 signatures backed by the Representative Association, the Chamber of Commerce, and the Agricultural Society.

The final Wood Report, however, was very lukewarm about the merits of representative elections. He pointed out that 70 per cent of the people were illiterate and that the mountains and scattered nature of the villages would make elections difficult. He was also concerned that if Dominica succeeded in her wish for separation from the Leeward group, the other islands would clamour for the same changes.

Despite his misgivings, the report did advocate a semi-representative form of government for Dominica. The announcement was followed by a period of uncertainty as authorities decided on the number of members which the Legislature should contain. A local commission eventually decided on four elected members and two nominees to replace the former six nominated members. 1923 ran its course and nothing was heard from London. In the first months of 1924, St Lucia, St Vincent and Trinidad received their new constitutions; Dominica looked on dejected. Then in September, the constitution approved in London, arrived. Although the four elected members would be a minority in the Council, this break in the wall of Crown Colony government 'was received with acclamation.'

In 1925 there were elections. The elected members were: AA Baron for the Northern District, H D Shillingford for the Eastern District, Sidney LV Green for the Western District, and for Roseau – CEA Rawle. A new era in Dominican politics had begun.

The traditional cattle mills were still widely used for crushing sugar cane and limes. The estate owner (centre) poses here in front of his lime factory.

The Decline of Limes

In 1920 and 1921 well over 510,000 barrels of limes were exported. Then in May 1922, withertip disease of limes appeared on an estate in the southern part of the island. From this point it spread with extraordinary speed so that by the end of September few of the main lime estates remained unaffected. (There is another theory that the disease had existed on many estates for some time beforehand, and it was only when the scare was raised that planters observed the disease on their estates.) Added to this was the outbreak of 'red root' disease affecting the base of the trees. Much of the crop for 1922 was damaged and exports fell disastrously the following years, halting progress and throwing growers into a state of alarm.

Specialists were rushed out from England and the Imperial College in Trinidad to investigate the conditions. The import of all lime plants from overseas was stopped in 1925, but by then it was far too late. Although it was thought that estates on the coast would still be able to cultivate limes by taking special precautions there was a serious stagnation in trade.

In September 1923 the local agricultural department began to experiment with ways of propagating lime plants resistant to disease; budding shoots onto the stock of common sour citrus proved successful against 'red root' but by that time there was little hope. Cheaper materials for producing citric acid were being found. Sicily's lemon industry had become a serious competitor to limes, and there was a drop in price.

The Imperial Commissioner of Agriculture for the West Indies, Sir Francis Watts, compiled a report on agricultural conditions in Dominica and made suggestions for new crops to replace limes; the cultivation of coconuts and bananas were encouraged. But the world was facing an economic crisis which started in Wall Street, New York in 1929 and shook the finance, industry and commerce of the world in the thirties. For the next twenty years, Dominican agricultural production was in a state of gloom.

Carib Problems

When Dominica had been surveyed and divided into lots in the eighteenth century, 232 acres of mountainous land around Salybia was left for the Caribs. In 1902, Hesketh Bell sent a lengthy report to the Secretary for the Colonies outlining the history of the Caribs and made certain proposals for their future. His major concern was that some 3,700 acres should be set aside for them and that they should be responsible for dividing up the reserve among themselves.

Bell was unable to find any title deed for the original 232 acres surveyed and it was probable that no such title had ever existed. Although he tried to settle the question of boundaries he achieved little or nothing with regard to the title of ownership. However, his efforts were significant, for it led to the expansion of the 'reserve' and its organisation as it exists today.

Bell suggested that the Carib 'chief' should be officially recognised and be given a token allowance of £6 annually. He was formally invested, given a silver-headed staff and an elaborate sash, on which was embroidered in gothic lettering 'The Chief of the Caribs'. These symbols of goodwill were highly prized by the isolated community of 400 pensive and reserved descendants of the conquered warriors of the island.

Then in 1930, early on the morning of 19 September, five armed policemen under the command of a Corporal, entered the 'reserve' with orders to search for smuggled goods and arrest suspected persons. When they tried to seize a quantity of rum and tobacco and take away suspects, a struggle ensued. Stones and bottles were hurled at the police, who retaliated by firing into the crowd and injuring four Caribs, two of whom died later from their wounds. The police were forced to escape from the area and arrived at Marigot beaten and battered, with neither prisoners nor seizures.

Without consulting the Executive Council, the Administrator summoned the Royal Navy frigate, HMS *Delhi*, which was cruising the Caribbean. A day later the warship appeared off the Carib quarter and made a show of force by firing star-shells into the air and giving a display of searchlights. The Caribs, unaccustomed to these signals, rushed from their houses and took refuge in the woods. Marines were landed and assisted local police in the search for the ringleaders of the disturbance.

The exact details of the incident took some time to reach Roseau, and even weeks later newspapers in the town were uncertain as to what had occurred on the windward coast. The rumour however, caused much excitement and all over the island people talked wildly about a Carib 'rising'.

In 1931 the Governor of the Leeward Islands appointed a commission of inquiry to investigate the general conditions of the Caribs and the disturbance of the previous year. As one person remarked, 'the Report smacked everybody's head a little and the Carib Chief's the hardest of all'. He was degraded from his position, his staff and sash were confiscated, and he was forbidden to call himself 'king'.

In August 1949, the Caribs wrote to the Administrator saying that since 1930 they had been 'begging for a chief' but had received no favour. After almost three years, an agreement was reached, and in June 1952 the Administrator visited the Reserve and held an investiture ceremony at which a chief was installed and presented with the staff of office and a new sash. The Carib administration later became part of the local government scheme, with a Carib Council for the entire district. But many questions remained unanswered; among them the relevance of an old Carib tradition whereby a Carib woman is not allowed to remain in the Reserve if she marries an outsider and the problem of ownership and title to the land, and even more basic: the definition of 'a Carib'.

Politics in the Thirties – The Dominica Conference

The four men who had been elected to the Legislative Council under the 1924 Constitution, were soon experiencing a growing sense of frustration. On many occasions their schemes and resolutions were defeated by the government officials in Council who voted as one body, supported by the Administrator and, when he was visiting, the Governor. With few of their motions ever approved, the electives began to question the effectiveness of their presence on the Council. Soon the unofficial nominees were supporting the elected minority, and the stage was set for new campaigns against Crown Colony rule.

In 1927 the Taxpayers Organisation was formed, followed in 1931 by the Constitutional Reform Association which more or less consisted of the same people, who saw the need for greater constitutional freedoms. The following year there was a sensational walk-out of unofficial members from the Council chamber led by Ralph E Nicholls. They tendered their resignation and created what was virtually a strike of Legislators. The move was watched with admiration by other islands.

To make up the required number of members in the Council, the Administrator quickly nominated men to take their places. Mr Norman Lockhart, owner of Geneva estate, was one of those who accepted, and soon after his nomination Geneva House was burned to a shell. It was strongly believed that the fire was a political gesture and the Administrator issued a reward of £250 to anyone who could give information on the issue. But there was silence, and relations continued to be strained between government and the local leaders.

The thirties were years of political unrest and transformation in the West Indies. The world-wide Depression had hit the sugar estates and factories in the islands. Between 1934 and 1938 workers went on strike in Trinidad, St Kitts, St Lucia, British Guiana and Jamaica. In 1937 blood was shed in Trinidad's oil belt and in Barbados fourteen rioters were killed. Because Dominica lacked factories and was a peasant based society, the colony was spared such disturbance. But in action for constitutional change, Dominica was a leader in the region.

In October 1932, the Dominica Conference, for the purpose of considering West Indian confederation and self-government was opened at the Union Club in Roseau. Seventeen delegates, comprising some of the most progressive West Indian leaders of the day, met to discuss and plan the future of the region. Their ideas were passionate and idealistic, and necessarily so, for as members of Council, most delegates had experienced the frustration and senselessness of Crown Colony rule in the twentieth century

DELEGATES TO WEST INDIAN CONFERENCE
HELD AT DOMINICA BWI 28 OCTOBER TO 4 NOVEMBER 1932
Back Row: JS Sainsbury (Barbados), HD Shillingford (Dominica), RM Anderson (St Vincent), Capt GF Ashpitel (Dominica), E Duncan (St Vincent), H Wilson (Antigua), JB Charles (Dominica), T Manchester (St Kitts), RH Lockhart (Dominica), W Wyllis, JRR Casimir (Secretaries). Front Row: Miss Josephine Roberts (Stenographer), Hon'ble CL Elder (Barbados), CEA Rawle, Chairman (Dominica), Hon'ble J Fleming (Grenada), Captain the Hon'ble AA Cipriani (Trinidad), GSE Gordon (St Lucia), WA Seaton (St Kitts), S Osborne (Montserrat).

West Indies. Now there were West Indians with the education, determination and ability to manage their own affairs and the Conference itself proved this without doubt. It was chaired by the dynamic local politician and barrister CEA Rawle. In his opening address he lay down the ideals of those West Indian pioneers.

'Let us hope that ultimately there will arise in our islands a self-governing dominion worthy to take its place in the councils of the Empire. We are going to seek to remedy the grievance we speak of, not by the method of the assassin, nor by arson, nor by other acts of violence of any kind, but by constitutional methods, relying on the righteousness of our cause and if the people of the West Indies are united, and determined, if they do not get frightened at the mere term "self government" . . . if we stand together and march together boldly demanding our rights as British Citizens, refusing to be regarded any longer as political outcasts, our cause will conquer in the end!'

Plans for the operation of a general government of the British West Indies were outlined, but there was a sharp divergence on how voting for the federal representatives should be conducted. Eventually a compromise was reached and the conference only supported full adult franchise, or the right to vote, as an 'ultimate aim' of a new West Indies Federation. It suggested that every colony should conduct its voting as each local legislature saw fit. This uneven system was obviously unfair and unworkable and it was one of the main causes of Albert Marryshow's rejection of the conference report. The 'Father of West Indian Federation' continued to distrust any federal propositions not clearly based on the universal vote.

However, the delegates were aware of the difficulties of orderly universal suffrage in the thirties and rather than attempt to adopt every measure immediately, they saw an elected majority in the legislature as their first goal. In the words of Rawle, they had been 'powerless to mould policy' and what the conference demanded first was that the islands should have internal self-government within the British Commonwealth of Nations.

In December 1932, the Closer Union Commission, appointed by the British Government, arrived in Dominica and its duty was to examine the possibilities of a federation of the islands. As a result of the Conference held here a few months earlier, the commissioners found the island in a state of political excitement. 'Dominica has always been politically minded' they reported, but were impressed with the 'spirit of earnest reasonableness' of the local political leaders.

The Commissioner shied away from federation and instead suggested a loose grouping of the Leeward and Windward Island colonies overseered by a Governor. And, largely because of the sound and fury of 1932, a new constitution was granted to Dominica in 1936.

The Legislative Council was to consist of the Governor, three ex-officio members, four nominated members and seven elected members. In this constitution the elected members were equal in number with the ex-officio and nominated members combined and, although the Governor had a casting vote, there was more possibility of getting schemes adopted. Nevertheless, it was still restricted with an independent Executive Council responsible to the Crown. But it was a welcomed step forward, and the following year elections took place. Dominica's first political manifesto was printed and issued to voters by the main political group – parties had not yet been formed. It was vivid evidence of the constructive political developments that had taken place during that decade; it outlined the group's intentions with regard to roads, agriculture, education, public health, wages and finance, and concluded:

'The day of destructive criticism is past, what we must have now, to make the New Constitution a success, is constructive thought and action. We must eliminate petty and parochial feeling and the imputing of selfish and self-interested motives, and all stand together in an earnest endeavour to prove ourselves worthy of the measure of Self Government which Dominica has won for herself.'

> Signed   Ralph E Nicholls
> Lennox P Napier
> Howell D Shillingford
> Philip A Rolle

As in all political manifestos, these were hopeful words, and although there was a change in outlook, the clashes between the electives and executives continued even if in a more restrained manner. At the end of the thirties, Dominica was separated from the Leeward Island grouping and became a colony of the Windward group on 1 January 1940.

The Society

The society which had evolved over the past one hundred years since full emancipation in 1838 still maintained a certain semblance of the rigid stratification of the previous century, although in comparison to the old sugar islands like St Kitts, Antigua and Barbados, Dominican society was considered to be quite liberal. The depressed economic situation, as well as the isolation of those planters outside of Roseau did not make for the cohesive social elite which characterised those other islands.

The remnants of the white plantocracy had effectively given up trying to run their estates. Most of their land had been let as 'gardens' to tenants or had reverted to bush. Hardly any of Hesketh Bell's English settlers remained after 1920. Descendants of the old families held onto their estates which no one yet had money to buy. There was Lockhart with Geneva, Judge Pemberton with Point Mulatre, Janet Johnson with Rosalie, Castle Bruce, Shawford and Montpelier. In the north, Ashpital held Melville Hall, Stebbings held Londonderry and Woodford Hill. Blenheim and Picard were still British-owned. Elsewhere the merchant planters of the 'mulatto gros bourg' held sway: Bellot, Rolle, Garraway, Shillingford, Riviere, Fadelle, Giraud, Potter and Green were the largest land-holding families in this group. And scattered among all these were the handful of European 'romantics' who simply came to live, as Jean Rhys put it, 'for the moon on the Caribbees'; among them Peter Dewhurst, Stephen Haweis, Holly Knapp, Paul Ninas and the Napiers.

When the economy started moving after the Second World War some large estates changed hands; Robert Douglas and Frobel Laville returned with their earnings from working in the oil refineries of Aruba and Curaçao. Douglas bought Hampstead, and Laville bought Governor, Londonderry and Hatton Garden. Trinidadian medical practitioner Dr Armour bought up Hodges and Blenheim.

The small white Roseau elite was headed by the British Administrator and included officials such as the Crown Attorney and heads of departments and professionals in the medical service. The whites usually belonged to the Dominica Club while the 'coloured' elite belonged to the Union Club. A guest book, in a hut at the gates of Government House, lay open to be signed by those wising to be invited to the 'At Home', the Administrator's social event.

In between all of this, in a class of their own, and yet at the same time related through business to all sectors, were the Syrians and Lebanese. They had migrated to the Caribbean and Dominica from the Middle East since the 1890s and were joined by others as the twentieth century progressed. Arriving first as itinerant peddlers going from village to village, they brought goods to isolated communities for the first time. They built up a trusted network among the peasantry and working class and through thrift, business acumen and social self-sufficiency they soon set up small stores. As the banana boom took off in the 1950s their traditional good customer relations paid off and business flourished. Family members branched out into motor car sales and service, manufacturing, construction and hotels. The earliest arrivals of Karam and Dib were followed by Astaphan, Nassief, Raffoul, Azar and Brohim, each in their own way making significant contributions to the society over several generations.

Like the other British West Indian islands at the time, Dominica politics was dominated by a liberal-minded middle class group of professional men and farmers. Educational and electoral divisions did not allow for the mass politics of the present day. Educational standards were still extremely low, and although a large number of peasant proprietors earned or owned enough to vote, few, if any of them, had the time and resources to be elected representatives, who up until 1947 received no salaries for their services. Political development was further aggravated by the lack of communications which made the affairs and personalities of Roseau appear more important than the country districts.

But the isolated village communities had a vital society of their own. Living self-sufficiently, depending on what they produced to provide housing, food and materials, the villages existed very much as they had in the previous century. The occasional visit of the district doctor was the only medical service they knew. As in the past, they relied heavily on the traditional home cures and in serious cases an invalid would have to be carried for miles in a hammock to the nearest hospital or motorable road.

Agricultural produce from the eastern and northern districts faced the same problems of transportation. Everything still had to be 'headed' along the mountain traces or in the case of the northern district, there was a launch service between Portsmouth and Roseau. Some other areas used canoes, but especially on the windward coast this could be dangerous.

In the village, each man helped his neighbour; from digging and clearing fields, shingling or building a house, to the final act of fellowship: making a coffin. Much work was done in return for food and friendship and the cooperative method or 'cou de main' was an important part of every community.

For entertainment there were the traditional dances and music; the vibrant folklore of *contes*, wakes, patois hymns, cantiques de Noel, and the religious festivals to which they were strongly attached. Even in Roseau, the *mulatre* elite still danced lancers and flirtations at their subscription parties until the opening of a cinema and dance halls quickly put an end to the traditional revelries.

Masquerade

Carnival, or Masquerade, as it was more popularly called in Dominica, was strongly an Afro-French festival. The observance of two days of feasting before Lent goes way back in European Roman Catholic history and was brought to the island by the French settlers. The colourful masques and dances were a feature of the French plantocracy throughout the Antilles. Samedi Gras through J'Ouvert to Mardi Gras were days when the French estate families visited each other for vast creole fêtes and the slaves would dance outside on the glacis while indoors others played music, served and entertained for tips.

With emancipation, the freed people brought the festival out onto the streets. In Roseau and Portsmouth particularly, the labourers, the porters, the 'negres bord la mer', fishermen and domestics were joined by bands from the neighbouring villages to flout and tear down the standards of the upper class. During the days before masquerade when the 'chantuelles' were rehearsing with their drummers, the people in the districts joined in the 'chanté mas' and sung the 'lavway' chorus. Those nineteenth century years of Masquerade were not days when 'the social barriers were broken down', as so many like to claim. That came later. For a long period Masquerade was a brief annual revolt of the Dominican masses against a society which, for the rest of the year, demanded their obedience. The themes of the 'chanté mas' made this clear enough. The best chanson exposed a social scandal or a social personality or a piece of injustice. There were popular districts where practices were held and it was well known that distinguished persons would bribe certain chantuelles either to keep their name out of the songs or expose a scandal of an enemy.

From J'Ouvert on Masquerade days, the matadors, the bad-johns, darkies, red-ochre, jamettes, drummers and singers would be about town. The chantuelle, now in her prime, moved backwards facing the band leading the *chanté mas* to which the band would echo the *lav-way*. In the nineteenth century the *darkies* and *red ochre* groups would form themselves into regiments on the Newtown savannah and engage in stick battles or *bois bataille* similar to the *Kalinda* of Haiti and early Trinidad. At the beginning of this century the custom died, but the bands of oiled and sooted darkie and red ochre men remained a feature of the street bands. Here the strong African influence could be seen. Many of the costumes were unaltered from

Masqueraders in traditional costume pose at the Old Roseau Market in 1912.

those used in tribal festivals of Central African kingdoms. The *sensay* outfits with cow horns were the most obvious. *Rope sensay, pai fig*, cloth and paper *sensay* were worn by the notorious *bande mauvais* who clashed in great street battles either with each other or with the police. There were sideshows and acrobats performing for spectators who sat on verandahs, and in the early years stilt men or *bois bois* danced for the crowds on their twenty-foot high stilts.

Later, a great variety of costumes developed including the *black-dress-and-corset*, the *tourists*, the *houm-baylay*, and the imported wire masks with pink painted faces and red lips. And behind the safety of the mask there came the upper sections of society; the creole elite of the twentieth century took the two days to 'run masked' and escape from their respectability. Masquerade became an official holiday (it had not been previously recognised by the government and business sector) and the *la peau cabrit* bands were given donations or hired by society groups. Merchants and government clerks donned the *sensay* and joined the *bande mauvais*, and from the twenties to the early fifties, traditional Masquerade grew and flourished.

Then, in the 1950s Carnival in Trinidad became 'respectable' due to a change in attitudes, the demand for 'clean' calypsoes and, among other things, the PNM Government's observance of Carnival as a 'national cultural heritage'. This resulted in a strange reverse to the European type festival with queens, shows and organisation. Soon Dominica followed suit, and added to this, there was a tragic fire during Masquerade of 1963 which caused the government to ban masks and *sensay* costume. But changes were already being made and they were rapid. The organisers and bandsmen looked to Trinidad for ideas, steelbands took over from the small *la peau cabrit* groups, and the Trinidad-style calypsonian replaced the *chantuelle* and her *chanté mas*. Expensively costumed bands and tidily dressed revellers took to the streets and the taunting satire and sarcasm of Masquerade was gone.

What remained most powerful were the old songs; and these popular ballads live on not only because of their lasting quality but as records of folk history. The Band Mauvais chant 'Adieu William Oh!' recounts the clash between bandsmen and the police, whose chief, William Leighton, was determined to crush the fighting group. 'Solomon roulay' was brought to Roseau by villagers of Pointe Michel, who sang of the death of Magistrate Solomon near a landslide which still bears his name. 'Hosai lamp la' exposed a saucy local scandal and 'Defay Mama Defay' recorded a disastrous fire in Roseau. Modern folk groups are collecting and reviving these melodies but traditional Masquerade is over and as the old revellers used to say on the night of the Mardi Gras, 'Bal fini, violon en sac'.

The Second World War

On the same day in September 1939 when the German army moved into Poland, all thirty members of the Defence Force went into barracks on Morne Bruce, and the governor proclaimed that the island would be defended to the last man, and to the last, and only, machine gun. A nightly blackout was ordered of all streets and windows facing the sea. Trade was for a few days altogether dislocated, and during this war the effects of the upheaval in Europe had far greater consequences on the island than World War I. A committee was appointed to consider food prices, and it showed a leaning in favour of the consumer. From all over the island, there rose the discontented cries of merchants and shopkeepers, particularly those in the country areas. Isolated village shopkeepers could not afford to sell at Roseau prices when they had to pay for the transport by land and sea and for porterage.

Conditions were made worse in early 1940, when, in order to protect food supplies in the UK, a system of strict control on the export of foodstuffs was instituted, and a limit was placed on supplies to the colonies of the Empire.

For weeks at a time Dominica had no bread and never again for many years was flour on sale except to licensed bakers. There was a lack of salt, fats, kerosene, matches, imported butter, and a variety of less essential items. But Dominicans used their resources and devised butterless cakes from grated coconut and puddings from cocoa and sweet potatoes. Cassava farine was widely used, and food was fried in local coconut oil. But fish was no longer plentiful. It was rumoured that German U-boats had orders to sink even canoes, and fishermen were reluctant to go to sea.

In 1942 German submarines made intense and successful attacks on British and allied shipping in the Caribbean and numbers of vessels were sunk at sea. Two ships were torpedoed in Port-of-Spain harbour, one in Bridgetown and another in Castries, St Lucia, where mines were also sown.

That same year sixteen bodies were washed up along the coast of the Carib Reserve and were later buried at the cemetery of St Marie at Salybia. Although it was not known at the time, these men had been part of the crew of a Spanish ship blown up by mistake by a German submarine 60 miles to the east of Dominica. Spain was officially neutral during the war, but the German U-boat captain claimed afterwards that he had taken it for a British merchant vessel in disguise.

The loss of shipping, and especially the Canadian 'Lady Boats' was very serious for the islands. But the shortage of steamship services was met to some extent in the Eastern Caribbean by the inter-island schooners, which kept up the distribution of supplies to Dominica and the other islands.

As in the previous World War, the initial excitement soon settled down and the government decided that it could no longer afford to keep the Defence Force in Barracks. Our brave boys returned to their usual jobs, and, as a local newspaper editor put it: Dominica was left at the mercy of anyone.

But during those uncertain years, there were amusing incidents. Early in the War, a strange vessel was sighted off the leeward coast. Was it one of Hitler's secret weapons? The Commanding Officer of the Defence Force, who was also Chief of Police, knew that the territorial waters of Dominica should not be violated by persons unknown. The strange craft had to be intercepted and the only vessel available was the coastal launch, *The Hope*, which in those days ploughed wearily between Portsmouth and Roseau. The Commanding Officer and a few men met the launch at Massacre, off-loaded all the passengers, and the *Hope* was commandeered in the name of the King. The strange vessel turned out to be a cattle boat on its way to Brazil, but all was not lost, the crew entertained the Defence Force, and a good time was had by all!

The most serious effects of the War were felt in the Legislature. With trade at a standstill and agriculture production low, the revenue of the colony fell sharply. It came at a time when villagers were increasing their demands for roads, bridges, and general assistance and the representatives were hard put to explain the hopelessness of the situation. Some members, notably Elma Napier in the north-eastern district, tried to develop self-help groups. In 1940, she had become the first woman in Dominica and in the West Indies to sit as a representative in the Legislature and she pioneered village Boards and cooperative ventures as a means of community growth.

By 1942, the war had intensified; the news of the fall of Singapore reached Roseau during the Masquerade and overnight the people changed the name of their song 'Hitler il mauvais' to 'Japonais yo mauvais'. Within a few weeks naked and half-eaten corpses were washed up on the windward coast, and during the height of the submarine activity shipwrecked mariners found safety on Dominica's shores.

The Free French

The United States set up naval and air bases in the Caribbean during the war, and those in Antigua and St Lucia were expected to provide protection for Dominica. But since 1940 the island had been lying defenceless between her two French neighbours whose Mother country was under German occupation. Some Dominicans feared that German forces would silently cross the channels to the north and south and take the island. In a way they were right, only that it was not the enemy who occupied Dominica, but Frenchmen fleeing from the Vichy regime.

Immediately after the fall of France there was a trickle of continental

Frenchmen who escaped to join General De Gaulle's Resistance. They crossed the channels in rowing boats, and the local authorities helped them on their way. Later the trickle became a flood and before the end of 1942 the number of refugees became unmanageable. A detachment of the South Caribbean Forces had to be summoned to Dominica to assist the local police. In their tens and their twenties and their fifties, men and a few women, landed on Dominica, until it was estimated that there were over 5,000 French citizens in Roseau alone. Many of them were unfit to join the forces, but once in Dominica the government was obliged to take care of them.

Eventually the Free French commanders recognised that the island was under great stress and sent officers of their own to supervise the refugees. Houses, small shops, and offices had been lined with bunks to provide sleeping space; anyone who could rent space for a bed made room. For a time the government was fearful of disease and epidemic.

Already the island was short of food. Now almost every cow and chicken was slaughtered and despite official price control, vegetables changed hands at outrageous prices – feeding the Frenchmen became quite a racket. Twice a day they queued at the communal kitchen, receiving, besides lodging, free food and a dollar a week pocket money. This was refunded to the Dominica government by the British Treasury who in turn was supposed to collect it from her French ally. The Dominican man-in-the-street found it hard to understand this financial arrangement, for in those days a dollar a week for doing nothing was big money. As one Roseau man remembers: 'The French could buy all the cigarettes and all the girls.'

Every day one could hear the French bugle calls and the orders, 'Un, deux, Un, deux, Un, deux', as men were marched through the streets. It was not until August 1943 that the Nazi-influenced regime in the Antilles collapsed and De Gaulle's army in Dominica was sent home again.

As in World War I, Dominicans left their island to fight for the Empire. But this time they insisted that they should be made regular soldiers and not thrust into labour battalions as had happened to so many in the First World War. Thousands of West Indians joined the armed forces in Britain and Canada, and, along with other British colonies, Dominica contributed generously to war funds.

When peace was declared, names were added to the list of fallen on the Memorial of World War I. Dominica is unique in that it has two War Memorials – one for the local forces and another smaller monument commemorating the action of the French Resistance.

18
The Church

Superimposed upon the entire political, economic and social history of Dominica, enmeshed within the warp and weave of events, is the history of Christianity on the island and, predominating, is the history of the Roman Catholic church. The first mission of Fr Raymond Breton in 1642 came well in advance of any formal French settlement. Although there were gaps in continuity for the rest of that century, his mission laid the foundations for the important role Christianity would play in the lives of future Dominicans. Permanent French settlement from 1720 determined that the island would be subject to Article 2 of Jean-Baptiste Colbert's Code Noir of 1688: 'All slaves in our islands are to be baptised and instructed in the catholic, apostolic and roman religion . . . '

Throughout the years of slavery priests belonging to a variety of religious orders – Dominicans, Franciscans, Capuchins and Jesuits among them – administered from makeshift missions at Grand Bay, Colihaut, St Joseph, Pointe Michel and Portsmouth. Permanent churches and missions along the east coast came later. Their work continued to be very much like that of Frere William Martel who was the first priest of the parish of Roseau then founded under the title of Notre Dame du Bon Port. He served there from 1730–1740 and built the first church in 1732. As the only priest in Dominica at the time he was kept extremely busy. An extract from one of his reports when stationed in Martinique gives some idea of an average Sunday.

'On Sundays and holy days, I am from 4 am either in the confessional, at the altar or in the pulpit. The first hours are reserved for hearing confessions. At 9 am I make Holy Mass, hold the sermon for the Free People, this brings me to 11 am. Then follows the instruction or the Catechism for the Creole negroes. The church is always packed. I leave at 1 pm to take luncheon. At 2 pm sharp we have vespers, etc and each time I hold a second Catechism, now for the negroes that are not yet baptised. All is usually over by 4 pm when if there is no sick call, I retire to my Hermitage.'

On working days he was out before dawn to one or other of the neighbouring estates in time to lead communal prayers which slaves recited every day before going out into the fields. To maintain themselves, the priests sometimes kept small estates such as 'Pere Massey' in the Goodwill area and at the White Friars River near Thibaut. The first English-speaking Roman Catholic priest, Fr Henry McCorry, arrived as late as 1789, taking charge as parish priest of Roseau. Communicants increased suddenly during the years 1791–1793 as French Royalist refugees, estimated at between 5,000 to 6,000, poured into Dominica escaping the effects of the French Revolution in Guadeloupe. Yet the number of resident priests were few, often reduced to a lone padre in Roseau for long periods. In 1825, Henry Coleridge was of the opinion that 'there are 2,000 Protestants in this colony, of which number the Methodists form the larger part; about 16,000 are Papists under the care of three Spanish priests.'

In the strictest sense of the law, Roman Catholics in Dominica practised their religion subject to the authority of the British, Protestant colonial government whose laws did not recognise the baptism of slaves nor the participation of Roman Catholics in the government of the colony without in effect renouncing their faith. A most significant event for Roman Catholics in Dominica therefore, was the passing, by the British parliament, of the Catholic Emancipation Act of 1829. This law had far reaching effects for Catholics in both Britain and the colonies. Here, it recognised baptised slaves as Catholics and permitted Catholics to sit in the House of Assembly. The first three Catholic men were elected to the House in 1832.

The main thrust of church expansion and organisation came in the years following the full emancipation of the enslaved population in 1838. Six years later the first school to be established on the island was started on the site of the present Bishop's House by nuns of the Order of the Sisters of St Joseph. Although the order did not remain for long, their school marks the foundation of formal education in Dominica. Since 1819, the local church had been under the jurisdiction of the Diocese of Port of Spain. As its activities here increased, it was realised that this section of the Caribbean would be better served as a separate diocese. Accordingly, the Diocese of Roseau was founded by Papal Bull of 30 April 1850 and was to comprise Dominica, the British Leeward Islands and the Danish Virgin Islands. The first Bishop of Roseau was an Irishman, Michael Monaghan, whose episcopate covered the years 1850 to 1855. The coming of bishops to direct the church in Dominica placed matters on a sounder basis, with a leader on the spot to take responsibility for the intensive evangelisation and church building which would occupy the attention of the religious well into the following century. Some of the most significant initiatives taken by the church during the latter half of the nineteenth century included its work in establishing schools in each parish, against the opposition of the British administration which, as elsewhere in the Caribbean, was attempting to control education as a matter solely for the state. Clearly the colonial

'La Belle Croix' at Grand Bay carved from stone in early eighteenth century.

The Roman Catholic Cathedral in Roseau.

government was incapable of providing even the most basic education island wide but for a time refused to assist Bishop Vesque in his efforts. Anglicanisation of education in British colonies had become a matter of policy and it was not until many years later that the government accepted that without the help of the church any expansion of educational services outside Roseau would be severely retarded. Today church-run schools in Roseau, Point Michel and Portsmouth stand as testimony to the contribution of the religious in this field.

Bishop Vesque was also responsible for bringing to Dominica the nuns of the Order of the Faithful Virgin, who arrived from Norwood, England in 1857. Among them was the Mère Marie des Neiges who had served as a nurse in the Crimean War under Florence Nightingale. The order established the Convent High School, and also what is now the St Martin's School within the year of their arrival. Finding religious orders to serve the expanding church was a serious concern of the early bishops. Since the 1850s the Redemptionist Order had come to serve in other islands of the diocese. In 1872 Bishop Poirier was successful in attracting the Order of the Sons of Mary Immaculate, popularly called the FMI, to Dominica where they are still serving after over a hundred and twenty years. This order carried the brunt of the pioneering work for the modern church in Dominica, building and holding together the isolated country parishes, constructing churches, starting schools and providing guidance and leadership to communities which seldom saw doctors or government officials from one year to the next. Alone in their far flung presbyteries and travelling the rutted tracks which served for roads, they nurtured the fledgling missions. The British government may have held sway in Roseau and, on the map at least, possessed the island, but to all intents and purposes it was the church, through the FMI, which provided leadership in the mountainous wilds of Dominica. For, to the people of these districts, Roseau and the colonial administration were as foreign as another country. The role of Fr Couturier during the Land Tax crisis at La Plaine in 1893, and his defence of the villagers against the action of the colonial government shows this clearly.

It was during this period at the end of the nineteenth century and early twentieth century that the main churches, halls and religious buildings were constructed in Roseau and the parishes. At least two buildings replaced Fr Martel's church of 1732, before work on the present Cathedral commenced in 1800. In all it took over a hundred years to complete it as we know it today, covering periods of stops and starts until 1916 when the small west steeple was completed. Made of cut volcanic stone, it was built in the style of Gothic-Romanesque revival, very popular during the mid-nineteenth century. Each section of the Cathedral has its story, each statue and altar has its date of placement and blessings, and there is much to tell: funds raised by levies on French planters; the Caribs who camped outside Roseau for three months to erect the first wooden ceiling frame; the pulpit built by convicts on Devil's Island off Cayenne; the stained glass windows, one dedicated to Christopher Columbus; and the ornate Victorian murals behind the side altars.

The possession of sizeable church lands in the centre of Roseau dates back to May 1766 when King George III, recognising the importance of the French plantocracy on this recently captured island, granted the Catholics use of ten acres in the town for 99 years for the benefit of their church. As this period of lease drew to a close, the Catholic Church appealed to the Crown for a freehold grant of these ten acres in perpetuity. This was acceded to in 1865, except for two lots on the western corner of the property which had been sub-let to people who later converted to Wesleyan Methodism, and who had made their lands available to the Wesleyan Mission. With great foresight from the Roman Catholic point of view Bishop Poirier acquired lands all over Dominica for church use. Among these was a portion of 14 acres at Salybia acquired from the Crown in 1865 in the centre of what was to become the Carib Reserve 38 years later. In 1872 the government granted the bishop the Old Artillery Officers Quarters and surrounding land on Morne Bruce as a retreat. Now it is the site of the Diocesan Pastoral Centre.

Bishop Poirier died in 1878 and was succeeded by Naughten (1879–1900) and then by Bishop Schelfhaut, a Belgian and a member of the Redemptionist Order. He was soon joined by priests of his order who took up duties at the Cathedral Parish and later at St Paul, St Joseph and St Luke, while the FMI priests continued in their work in other parishes. Together, the two orders, along with members of the Dominican secular clergy joining from the 1950s, carried the Roman Catholic faith through the twentieth century.

Evangelisation moved into print in 1907 with the publication of the *Ecclesiastical Bulletin* which was the official monthly organ of the diocese and a medium for information and instruction. In 1909 the Bishop established the *Dominica Chronicle*, a bi-weekly newspaper which, in the form of the *New Chronicle*, is still with us. When Bishop Schelfhaut died in 1921, he was succeeded by Bishop James Moris, another member of the Redemptionist Order whose pontificate lasted to his death in 1957. Moris was acutely aware of the powerful role of his church on the island and lost no opportunity in fortifying its position and extending its activities throughout the community. It was during the latter part of his period in office that his efforts to recruit local clerics bore fruit with the ordination of two priests, Bowers and Felix, who later became bishops.

In the 1930s, Moris established the St Mary's Academy with a modest beginning which eventually flourished under the Irish Christian Brothers and Dominican confreres to become the premier boys' secondary school by the end of the century. His pontificate coincided with great social and political changes on the island which was reflected in the action of the church as it extended its pastoral care increasingly into social work and community action for change. In 1937, the nuns of the Order of the Faithful Virgin, unable to provide more personnel left the island after 80 years of service and were replaced by the Missionary Canonesses of St Augustin, today called the Order of the Immaculate Heart of Mary. Among them were nuns trained in medicine and social work as well as teaching. A more detailed study could do justice to the work of Sisters Borgia, Bertine, Maria, Elsa and many others. Sister Alicia's first activity was to organise the Catholic Social Centre in Roseau. Its benefits radiated into every corner of the population. With the co-operation of lay people, parish priests and newly appointed Social Welfare Officers within the Civil Service, the activities of this centre and all its related organisations contributed to what can be regarded as a social revolution. It rode on the wave of the new spirit of the church heralded by the declarations of Vatican II in the 1950s. It contributed to areas of self-development and welfare which would have been impossible for successive governments to provide. A rough list of its projects gives some concept of the scope of its activities:

Home improvement, leadership training and strengthening of family life through the branches of the Social League of Catholic Women established all over Dominica.The Credit Union Movement; the Building and Loan Association which helped people to own their own homes at a time when bank loans for such ventures were well nigh impossible for most people to obtain; the Infant Jesus Nursing Home for children suffering from malnutrition; help for the Infirmary for the aged; creches and day nurseries in several villages and towns; public health instruction and child welfare clinics; the first pre-schools for toddlers with funds from the Dutch Van Leer Foundation; construction of community centres; the Young Christian Workers movement, co-operative activities; construction of housing particularly the Roseau Riverside Apartments; the Convent Industrial School, the first large-scale craft production concern using local materials for Dominica's famous straw mats. Less successful enterprises such as clothing manufacturing and timber production were well-intentioned attempts to provide employment and a small-scale industrial base which was locally owned and managed.

Towards the end of the century, the church, in spite of all its achievements, faced severe challenges beginning perhaps with the charged socio-

Three Roman Catholic nuns who have been pioneers in different fields: Sister Borgia, education; Sister Alicia, social welfare; Sister Bertine, vocational and handcraft training.

political atmosphere of the 1970s; the confrontational evangelisation of the US influenced fundamentalist religions and the constant search for more Dominicans to take up the vocations in the face of dwindling numbers of religious from overseas. The last three decades of the century have been both years of achievement and turbulence for the Roman Catholic Church in Dominica. Coping with greater changes than any previous bishop had witnessed was Arnold Boghaert, seventh Bishop of Roseau who served from 1957 up to his death in 1993. However, young Dominican clergy are gradually taking up places around the island, adding their own spirit of guidance and interpretation of the faith, providing a new perspective, a new style, for a new century.

The Anglican Church

The Church of England was the church of the state and arrived as part of the colonial establishment when the British took over Dominica under the terms of the Treaty of Paris in 1763. It was the duty of the Bishop of London to send out clergy to the newly ceded islands, and the first rector, Henry McLeane, was at his post on 1 July 1764.

When the town plan of Roseau was surveyed and drawn by Nathanial Minshall in 1768, a large square to the south was laid out for the Anglican Church, with a graveyard on sloping ground behind it – the present site of the Newtown Savannah. Here a large wooden church was constructed, but by the time Thomas Atwood was writing his *History of Dominica* in 1790, the building had fallen into ruin and there appeared to be little interest in its upkeep and use.

'The church is a large lofty building of wood, but it is at present much out of repair. It has a neat pulpit, reading desk and a few pews; but neither altar-piece, hangings, baptismal font, belfry nor bell. This, the only Protestant church in the island, is built on a large lot of ground, has a good church-yard of very deep and excellent black mould; but the yard is not enclosed.'

The condition deteriorated further without being checked so that when Langford Lovell wrote scathingly of the congregation in 1818 he reported that the church 'has been suffered to go to decay; and not one stone . . . is now remaining upon another . . . the people have never petitioned, as far as I can learn, either for repairing the old or constructing a new church.' When there was the occasional service it was held in the Court House. Since the scattered British population were apparently not very religiously inclined and could not attend services 'on account of the bad roads and often impassable rivers' he advocated the attendance of rectors at plantations rather than the erection of a new church which would just as likely fall back into ruin once more.

In any case the presence of rectors on the island were few and far between. Those who did not die 'a victim to the climate' left within a short time of their arrival. Some got involved in trade like the notorious John Audain who took to owning a schooner and privateering to supplement his income. Coleridge recalls him once cutting short a sermon and dashing down to the Bay Front when he observed his vessel entering the port. At the French attack on Dominica in 1805 he was wounded while handling a cannon.

While Orde was governor in 1791 he wrote in despair to the Secretary of State: 'The christenings and burials I cannot speak to, there not being a Protestant clergyman in the island nor any provision likely to be made by the present House of Assembly for any. The state of religion is indeed truly deplorable and disgraceful considering the circumstances of the colony – the marriage ceremony is performed by a Justice of the Peace.'

In 1802 an Act was passed for building a church but it was not until 1818 that a committee was appointed, which included James Garraway and others, to be responsible for constructing the new church. A new location opposite Fort Young was chosen and a handsome square stone building in the Regency style was built in 1820 within the estimated

During Hurricane David in 1979 the Anglican Church was totally destroyed as were Roman Catholic churches at Pointe Michel, La Plaine, Boetica, La Roche, Laudat, Trafalgar, Scotts Head and Pottersville which were potential hurricane shelters.

amount of £6,500. When the British population rose suddenly at the end of the nineteenth century the St George's Anglican church was extended southwards in 1900 at a cost of £2,000, changing the style of architecture at the same time.

Increasing numbers of immigrant labourers coming from the Protestant Leeward Islands to settle in the north of Dominica encouraged the construction of small churches at Portsmouth and Marigot. But the congregations gradually declined and only the St John's Church at Portsmouth survives.

When Henry Coleridge visited the recently completed Anglican church in Roseau in 1825 he observed that it was 'well situated and tolerably furnished without, but the interior is in a miserable state . . . About a hundred people, chiefly coloured, attended the morning service; they had few books . . . certainly with one or two exceptions they were entirely unacquainted with the ordinary ritual of the established religion. The Church of England indeed does not flourish in Dominica.'

During the late Victorian period things did improve. The Anglican mission in the Caribbean became more organised and better funded from England, in spite of the local legislature passing an Act in 1871 against the endowment of the church using the colony's funds. The active involvement of lay persons such as Dr Henry Nicholls and Dr John Imray helped immensely. After Imray's death, a church hall was erected, and the Imray Hall was in constant use until its destruction by Hurricane David in 1979. The church itself was also levelled by the winds destroying a marble memorial to Imray in the process, and the small congregation carried the burden of reconstruction against massive financial odds. At the same time the council was finding it difficult to secure the services of ministers for what had become one of the smallest Anglican communities in the Caribbean.

The Methodists

Methodist missionary activity in Dominica dates from January 1787 when Dr Thomas Coke 'with three other itinerant Methodist preaches, visited Dominica, and preached in the house of a Mrs Webley; but they only remained a few days on the island and did not leave any missionary behind them.' During this period Moravians, Methodists and Baptists were taking an increasingly large part in evangelisation among the slaves of the West Indies. In Britain members of these groups as well as the Quakers were pressing for laws which would ensure more humanitarian conditions for the enslaved. The first of these acts for amelioration was passed in Dominica in 1788.

But the Methodist missionaries did not approve of the teachings of the

Roman Catholics nor of the local administration's liberal attitude towards religion. In a list of instructions given to Governor John Orde in October 1783 by order of the Court of St James, he was advised to let religion be free 'provided they be contented with a quiet and peaceable enjoyment of the same, not giving scandal or offence to the government.' But Dr Coke and his party seemed appalled at the hold which the Catholics had on the island. ' . . . It was because of this permanent establishment, under a government, which tolerates every mode of religion and leaves the conscience free, that an attempt was made . . . to introduce the gospel into Dominica among men of every colour.'

Soon the Methodists had their first resident minister in Dominica – Rev McCormack. He settled in Roseau and met with much success. He hired a building in town and set it up as the first Methodist chapel. Later he found Portsmouth to be also a promising centre, but there he contracted yellow fever and died less than a year after his appointment in Dominica. In these early years there were gaps between ministers in service and if disease did not strike them down it was sometimes the conflicting philosophies of their faith and that of the planters and government officials which did them in. One minister in 1796 prayed to be exempt from military exercises on a Sunday but: 'The president, after he had heard the petition, told him that he had been informed he was a very suspicious character, who disseminated pernicious doctrines among the slaves; and instead of being exempted from military duty, he would compel him to quit the island, and gave him an order accordingly, with which order he was obliged to comply, to avoid imprisonment.'

The next missionary appeared two years later and on his arrival was warned by the governor to toe the line or else he would suffer the same fate as his predecessor. Most persevered with their fiery sermons in the chapels and the field and throughout the years before emancipation the local planters were printing and making statements decrying the Methodist ideas. Yet the numbers they attracted increased every year and in 1800 they purchased their first piece of land upon which to build a chapel.

In a report of April 1803 we read that the number of Methodists in society in Dominica is about 700. 'In the country the Negroes build little places of worship at their own expense . . . Governor Prevost gave them a grant of an acre of Crown Land, to build a chapel on, at Prince Rupert . . . One of the missionaries resided at Roseau, the other at Prince Rupert . . . we change with each other every fortnight on account of the place (Prince Rupert) being so sickly.'

After emancipation, the local Wesleyan Society organised a number of night schools and classes in Roseau, Portsmouth, Layou and at Mount Wallace, now known as Clifton. Leading Wesleyans in the community served as lay preachers and teachers. In this way The Word spread, taking its strongest hold in the main towns as well as in the villages of Marigot and Wesley. Here labourers from Antigua and the other Leeward Islands had arrived to work on the large English estates of the north coast. The latter village, formerly known by the French parish name of La Soye in which it stood, was eventually renamed Wesley, some say after a woman called Ma Wesley who lived there, others from an early reference to it as Wesleyville in honour of the founder of Methodism John Wesley.

During the nineteenth century several important Dominican families converted to Methodism particularly leading members of the 'Mulatto Ascendancy' such as Bellot, Fadelle and Falconer. Major construction work was carried out at the Bethesda chapel in Roseau culminating with the completion of the belfry in 1893. In the 1930s the Wesley High School for girls began and in 1979 the Methodist community in the north-east took the initiative in establishing the St Andrew's High School at Londonderry to serve the educational needs of children of all faiths from Calibishie to the Carib Territory.

The New Evangelists

Religion is motivated by cultural influence. Under France the prevalent religion was Roman Catholicism. Under the British, the Protestant faiths of the Church of England and Methodists were introduced. Then as Dominica increasingly came under the influence of the United States from the 1940s, it was therefore natural that the Evangelical sects, particularly those from the fundamentalist 'Bible Belt', would begin to have an impact on the population. The earliest of all were the Seventh Day Adventists with a half dozen members recorded in a census of 1901. They were gradually followed by groups such as Jehovah's Witness and Baptists. But it was the high profile, slick and upbeat 'hell-fire' tempo of the Christian Union Mission, led by American preacher William Surbrook, Sr, which gave a taste of what was to come. Starting in the late 1930s, Surbrook and his family began their mission in Roseau under the name of 'Reformed Methodists'. In the 1940s, William Surbrook Jr took over, changed the name to 'Christian Union Mission', and picked out country centres at Marigot, Castle Bruce and the Carib Territory on which to concentrate. Recorded music, radio broadcasts and outdoor sermons amplified by loudspeakers were methods of evangelisation new to Dominicans. As the ownership of radios became more common and as the impact of the US contact became stronger, there was a proliferation of religious denominations. Breaking away from the structured hierarchy of the established churches there was a mood of messianic emancipation, a freedom for everyone to participate as public readers and interpreters of the gospels. The freedom from ritual and the simple directness of the fundamentalist message attracted many away from the established churches. But census figures show that the Methodists were the least to be affected. Among the evangelicals, the Pentecostal Assembly and the Seventh Day Adventists have the largest congregations. Like others they have set up schools, day care centres and welfare programmes for their members. They do not belong to the Christian Council of Churches but have established their own Dominica Association of Evangelical Churches.

The religious fervour stimulated by these rapid changes created tensions between the faiths and divisions between the closely knit communities. In the early 1980s Prime Minister Charles called the leaders of all the religions together at the House of Assembly and appealed for toleration; that in promoting their individual faith they should not find it necessary to attack or ridicule each other.

19
Development and Welfare

The Moyne Commission

The disturbances in the West Indies during the thirties forced the British government to realise that the discontent of the labouring West Indians was no longer just a blind protest against a worsening of conditions, but the positive demand for new systems that would offer them a better life. It was decided to set up a Royal Commission under the chairmanship of Lord Moyne to investigate the social conditions in the British West Indian colonies. The Commission was in the region for some months in 1938 and 1939 and the Report which it produced was a turning point in twentieth century Dominican history. It summed up in damning detail the shocking social and economic conditions in the colonies. As the War had broken out by then, the British Government decided not to publish the full text of the Report for fear of enemy reactions. Only the Recommendations were made public. As soon as the War was over the complete Report was issued.

'Of all the British West Indian Islands,' it stated, 'Dominica presents the most striking contrast between the great poverty of a large proportion of the population, particularly in Roseau, the capital, and the beauty and fertility of the island.' The Report called for more peasant holdings, the teaching of improved agricultural methods, and better communication, particularly a road across the island. It recommended the use of rivers for hydro-electricity and a programme against malaria.

On a regional level, the Commission concluded that the West Indian colonies stood in urgent need of social services which could not be provided from their own resources. As a result the Colonial Development and Welfare Act was passed in 1940 appointing a Comptroller for Development and Welfare in the West Indies. He was given a team of technical and research officers to help him in his task and substantial sums of money were provided by the British Government to carry out schemes in the region. The permanent headquarters of the department was in Barbados until the organisation was dissolved in 1958 and the task of development and welfare was taken over by the new Federal Government.

During its eighteen years of service, the organisation built schools, hospitals, airfields, roads and reservoirs and in general was of the utmost benefit to the West Indies. In Dominica, as elsewhere in the region, it gave new hope and new materials for the building of a new society.

Linking the Island Together

From the earliest settlement of Dominica, the development of roads has been a major concern of all governments. The mountainous nature of the island had posed problems from the start; not only was cutting through the mountains expensive, but rain quickly swept away the work. The best roads were constructed by the French at great expense and effort. They were sealed with strong stone cobbles or *pavé* which lasted for centuries. Their most important road ran from Hatton Garden through the Layou valley to the Leeward coast and it was known to the English as the 'Great Road'.

In 1888 an ambitious plan was started to improve communications on the island. The main points of the scheme were to complete a chain of iron

Heavy rain, mud and limited earth-moving equipment made early road building difficult as is shown above during the cutting of a section of the Transinsular Road at D'leau Gommier in 1955.

bridges around the island; make a road fit for wheeled traffic from Roseau to Layou. It was also hoped to buy a steamer to travel around the island. £40,000 was raised for the project by a series of loans and tax measures. But soon the money drained away, and according to the Hamilton Report of 1894: 'There is little to show for an expenditure of £40,000 on the construction of roads and bridges, except some iron work for bridges which have not been built and some machinery which has not been used.'

For several years little was done. Then came the Imperial grant of 1898 and once more attempts were made to extend the road system with £15,000 provided. Under the vigorous administration of Hesketh Bell, the Imperial Road was built, but between 1914 and 1944 the only major projects were the completion of the road from Portsmouth to Pagua and building a road from Loubiere to Grand Bay.

Then in 1941 the first Comptroller of the Colonial Development and Welfare Organisation visited Dominica to see the problems for himself. Three years later £54,360 was granted to complete the Imperial Road across the island to the north-eastern district.

Work on this Transinsular Road began at Bells. Further on the Public Works set up the main camp of rough galvanised tin sheds and as it was so cold to work there, the labourers christened the place 'Norway'. From all over the island men had gathered to work on the road. They crowded into the camp asking for jobs, but there were not enough tools in the island for so many, and without bulldozers or modern earth-moving equipment, the work was slow. Within a few months it was announced that the whole British grant had run out; rain and floods helped to wash away the work that remained.

Some claimed that the workers were to blame and others talked of misspent funds and 'bobol' among the merchants and road authorities. During Masquerade in 1947, Roseau echoed with not less than three songs celebrating the scandal.

For eight more years Dominica tried for another grant, but even when it was finally received, the problems of the Transinsular Road were not over. The Governor of the Windward Islands agreed to a request for the money to be spent on diverting the road to the windward coast. But the people of the northern district protested strongly. Led by Elma Napier, then a nominated member, and Lionel Laville, representative for the district, the people registered their discontent. A monster petition, signed and marked by thousands, was prepared for the Governor. A detailed personal cable was sent to the Secretary for the Colonies, and a Question was asked by a member of the British House of Commons. A mass meeting was held in Marigot, attended by over three thousand people, at which the Governor was present. And as a result of all this, the decision was reversed and the

Narrow suspension bridges such as this one across the Rosalie river connected the mountain tracks before motorable roads were built. During heavy floods it was the only way to cross the larger streams.

A traveller on horseback, accompanied by a porter, crosses the island in 1912. This mode of transport remained necessary until the 1950s and early 60s.

Transinsular Road was rushed through. In 1956, after almost two centuries of British rule, Dominica was spanned by road.

From 1955, the Colonial Development and Welfare grants for road building increased rapidly. In the same year the road to the windward coast was begun and by 1965 the settlements along the coast were well connected. British money for roads continued to pour into Dominica during the sixties and as the 'feeder road' scheme developed to serve farmers in the hills, transportation of crops was greatly improved. Obviously this had a marked effect on the people of the rural villages. It became much easier to transport produce and the daily truck services to the capital meant that there was a greater flow of merchandise and imported goods to the country areas. But this also drew people away from the land and into the town and in general gave rise to a radical change in the life of the island.

In 1972 another important road project was completed with the opening of a highway between Roseau and Portsmouth. It is interesting to note that 180 years earlier, in 1791, the historian Thomas Atwood had written, 'Was a good open road be made from Roseau to Prince Rupert Bay, the communication between the two places would be productive of the greatest utility.'

A similar road completed at the same time, also funded by the British Government and the European Development Fund, was that from Castle Bruce to Hatton Garden passing right through the Carib Territory. The effect of this 20 ft wide highway on the isolated and reserved Carib minority has been marked. Like other areas it has enabled the rapid flow of produce out of, and imported goods into, the area, but because of the special nature of its inhabitants, tourists coming to view people rather than scenery have introduced a new element into the territory, the effects of which are yet to be fully assessed. It has encouraged the sale of Carib handicrafts, sold in traditional-style thatched or shingled huts along the roadside.

For almost the whole decade of the 1970s road maintenance was minimal. Untended drains, culverts and road surfaces resulted in an appalling deterioration of the whole network, made worse along the coasts by major erosion caused by hurricane sea surges. From 1981 the Freedom Party government embarked on the largest concerted road programme ever undertaken. Securing funds from the British, Canadian, US, Venezuelan and French governments and the ILO, the whole major-road system was overhauled; culverts replaced, new bridges constructed, realignment at certain points, improved drainage and resurfacing was carried out by foreign construction companies and the local Public Works Department.

Major roads linking each settlement were indeed a great boost to the movement of agricultural produce, but these alone could not tap the real source of production: the farmers' holdings situated up the valleys and along the ridges way above the village communities. The banana boom in the 1960s gave added urgency to the need for feeder roads into these areas.

From the mid-sixties, well over two hundred kilometres of feeder roads have been constructed. About a quarter of this has been concentrated in the north-east from Dos D'Ane to Marigot running like arteries for many kilometres along the low ridges which fan out from the heights of Diablotin. On the west coast, particularly behind Colihaut, Salisbury and in the Carlholm and Neba areas of the Layou valley, hundreds of hectares of land have been opened up. In this latter area, it has been the farmers of Dominica rather than English settlers who have made Hesketh Bell's dream of a productive hinterland come true.

Although the construction of the feeder road system has for the most part come from aid donors, it has been common for farmers in certain areas to band together with money and labour and with matching contributions from government they have linked their holdings to the main roads.

Sea and Air Ports

The open roadstead off the Roseau waterfront was for centuries the main anchorage of the island. It was by no means ideal. The land shelves steeply from the shore requiring many fathoms of anchor chain along a narrow ledge of the seabed. Swells from the south-west and no natural protection add to the hazards. At least six jetties have existed at various times on sites between the river mouth and Fort Young. Each has been wrecked in turn by hurricanes.

Construction of a deepwater wharf, now generally known as the Deepwater Harbour, began in 1974 at Woodbridge Bay, just north of the capital. Some four hectares of fill were excavated from an adjacent hillside and a reinforced concrete apron supported by steel piles driven into the sea bed forms the wharf. A combination of British, Canadian, US and Caribbean Development Bank assistance was used on its construction and for subsequent repairs necessary after severe damage by Hurricane David in 1979.

Although larger ships visit Roseau, there is a greater movement of vessels at Portsmouth, one of the best harbours in the Lesser Antilles. Schooners, sloops, small tramp steamers and yachts move in and out of that harbour daily. Several are owned and operated by Portsmouth traders, and men of the town are lured to life at sea. It is also the centre for boat construction and at least one sloop or schooner is launched annually. During the winter season the more sheltered northern corner of Prince Rupert Bay is a popular anchorage for pleasure yachts. Longhouse is the main banana export depot for the northern district and in 1982 an improved concrete jetty funded by Canada was completed for use by banana lighters tending the weekly vessels. The movement of produce and merchandise in this port is directed to and from the north: the French and Leeward Islands, the Virgins and Puerto Rico.

Smuggling at outbays along the coast has been a bugbear to authorities for centuries. Today, French liquor, drugs and car parts are the favoured items. Improved surveillance by customs officers has been a deterrent, but relieving the need to smuggle with extra customs and immigration posts has also helped. In 1982 Anse De Mai was made a legal port, thus attracting a regulated movement of small vessels between the French islands and the north-east coast. In 1984 Canada provided a floating jetty for that harbour.

The first airplane to arrive at Dominica was a seaplane which landed off the Roseau bayfront in 1925. In 1943 a single engine four-seater landed in Benjamin's Park at Portsmouth with the Governor of the Windward Islands aboard. This first airplane landing on Dominican soil was rather inauspicious, for on touching down it stuck in the mud and tipped over, fortunately injuring no one. The island's first regular air link with the outside world began at Portsmouth in the 1950s with a twice weekly service by a Grumman 'Goose' seaplane using the sheltered harbour. Later, for convenience of linking with Roseau, operations were shifted to Soufriere Bay in the south. The government 'crash launch', as it was called, ferried passengers from airplane to shore.

Since 1944, the Melville Hall Valley had been identified as the site for Dominica's airport. In such a rugged island, the wide valley bordered by a parallel line of low hills and facing directly towards the sea and into the constant trade wind was the best site available. It was however situated over 50 kilometres away from the capital at that time without any road communications in between. Construction of the airfield had to wait till 1958 after the completion of the Transinsular Road. A small airstrip with a galvanised sided shed for an air terminal, served the island until a longer strip and proper terminal were completed in 1961 using Commonwealth Development and Welfare funds. This latter was demolished in 1978 and replaced with a less functional Canadian-built terminal.

The two-hour drive to Roseau from Melville Hall became a legend for Caribbean travellers and tourist guide writers. In the mid-seventies it was planned to construct a small strip at Canefield. This was formally opened in 1981 and because of its proximity to Roseau, immediately became the preferred airport in spite of cross winds, occasional landing difficulties and its smaller size in comparison to Melville Hall.

Talk of a jet airport for Dominica has cropped up periodically over two decades. It is often motivated by the yearning for this latest national 'status symbol' rather than rational economic assessment. Foreign prospectors

Dominica's first Chief Minister, Frank A Baron.

EO Le Blanc speaks at the opening of Melville Hall air terminal 1961.

have used its allure as the standard bait for local politicians and it has featured in a score of manifestos. But the basic business of the cost of construction, maintenance and related servicing, balanced against its returns or necessity and frequency of use within forty kilometres of two of the best international airports in the Caribbean, raises questions. Improvement of existing services on the ground and improved schedules of connecting flights appear to be the most likely course in the near future. If a larger airport is constructed the ideal site would be at Woodford Hill which offers the only flight path on the island with both an approach and take-off line uninterrupted by mountains and in the direct course of the trade winds from the east.

General Services

A small electricity plant serving Roseau began operation next to the Botanic Gardens in 1905. With a few replacements and extensions it kept going until the mid-1950s when a hydropowered plant was constructed at Trafalgar. This power station tapped water from the Ti Tou Gorge and other streams high on the Laudat plateau. Large pipes shoot the water down over the Trafalgar cliffs to the turbines. In the sixties another set of turbines was installed lower down the Roseau valley at Padu and together gave a significant boost to the service. Hydropower was complemented by a standby diesel plant at Fond Cole which helps take the consumption load during peak hours. Another much smaller plant was also installed at Portsmouth.

From the commencement of operations at Trafalgar, power lines were spread south to Grand Bay via Soufriere and north along the coast to St Joseph and Salisbury. In the early seventies this line was extended to Portsmouth and in 1974 the north-east was electrified as far as Marigot with diesel stations at Blenheim and Melville Hall. For most of this period, electricity services were maintained by the Commonwealth Development Corporation (CDC), later linking with government as part shareholders and eventually, in 1983, the service became completely locally owned. Experiments towards establishing micro-hydro plants, primarily for the east coast settlements, were begun in 1982. But these were rejected in favour of developing the Laudat-Trafalgar system to serve the whole island.

Dominica's many streams provide a ready source of fresh clean water. In 1874 a dam at Riviere Douce in the Roseau valley with connecting pipes to the capital was the first supply system on the island. Basic reservoirs in streams above coastal settlements are the source of piped water to most villages. Aid schemes during the sixties gave a boost to the extension of such systems islandwide.

In 1968 a major water system was begun to serve Roseau and the south-west. Canadian funds provided for damming the Antrim River at Springfield and pipes and purification tanks were laid and built to replace the outdated systems from Riviere Claire and Riviere Douce. The provisions of standpipes and the improvement of services to homes and public conveniences is always high on the agenda of every administration and is one of the main demands of constituents. Piped water services on the island are controlled by the Central Water Authority, administered by a statutory board of citizens appointed by the government. Since the late 1970s Dominica has been exporting water by tanker under agreements with various companies. Spring water is also bottled for export.

Governor Hesketh Bell improved the Roseau telephone system in 1900, extending it to Portsmouth in 1902 and eventually it linked the entire island along its coast. But by 1950 most lines in the east were out of commission and by 1960 the remaining system, with its operators frantically plugging jack cords for every call, and with confused party lines in country areas, was near the point of collapse. During the sixties the British company, Cable and Wireless, took over the operation of telephone services from government. Forming a subsidiary, Dominica Telephones Limited, it replaced the old system with dial phones and improved its existing international service. Lines and sub-stations were spread throughout the island so that by 1978 almost every village had at least one public telephone. Events

Former Minister of Communications and Works, Henry Dyer, (second from right) talks to engineers during the surfacing of the Canefield airstrip.

in 1979, primarily Hurricane David, wiped out the service completely and a considerable reinvestment had to be made by the company for the gradual restoration of lines to pre-1978 locations.

Radio broadcasts specifically aimed at a Dominican audience were first provided by the Windward Islands Broadcasting Service, a system established with CDW funds to link the four islands with one news and entertainment service. With its base station in Grenada, WIBS provided time for the broadcast of news and notices from small sub-stations on each island. Continuity was provided throughout the day with music and other programmes from master control in Grenada. Dominica's first radio voice was that of Daphne Agar, followed by Mary Narodny, and later Francis Andre, Barnet Defoe and Jeff Charles. Initially, correspondents worked part-time, compiling news, airing programmes and operating equipment. Local WIBS stations were located at the former government offices and later at the back of the public Library, both linked to a transmitter at the Stock Farm.

In November 1971 Radio Dominica went on the airwaves, broadcasting from specially built studios on Victoria Street with its transmitter located at Hillsborough near St Joseph. The advent of this nationally owned radio service was an important step. With transistor radios available to everyone, it is a powerful agency in influencing people, and this fact did not escape the politicians. The questions of control over what was broadcast, who was employed there, whose voice was or was not permitted to be heard, and the slating of information and programming so as to make political capital, are issues which have dogged the station from its inception and which time and experience is constantly trying to correct. In general, however, the station has provided a vital link between our island people assisting in a substantial way to inform and educate the populace on a wide variety of subjects. Dominicans now know more about world events than ever before. Developments abroad have influenced their views of events around them and this increased awareness has been a noticeable contribution to social change over two decades. The introduction of video tapes and satellite television receivers and the installation of cable television in 1983 have opened a new chapter in local mass communications.

Social Services

The Social Welfare department established in 1945 soon became too limited for the wide range of services which was required of it. With a small staff and faced with poor road communications it however accomplished a great deal, working in urban and rural communities promoting better sanitation, home management, village groups, achievement days, tidy surroundings, self-help projects and other related activities. Literacy programmes were assisted by the publication and distribution of the *Social Welfare News*.

It was upon this foundation that a sizable social service system developed. Over the next forty years it grew to include, besides basic welfare projects, government divisions including Youth, Sports, Co-operatives, Culture, Local Government, Community Development and the Women's Desk.

The Youth division has stimulated the formation of youth groups islandwide, a National Youth Council and small business projects to assist with employment creation. More recently a separate foundation was set up to secure and provide funds to aid small businesses, particularly those being established by young people.

A regional youth camp was set up at Londonderry in 1969 with heavy funding from OXFAM, USAID and other agencies. It aimed at providing vocational training for youth drawn from the Commonwealth Caribbean but the institution collapsed within a few years of opening and eventually, in 1979, became the site for the St Andrew's High School.

In 1971 a National Provident Fund Scheme was introduced to provide pension savings and other workers' benefits. This was upgraded in 1976 by the Social Security Act which developed the Provident Fund Scheme to include increased benefits and new scales of employer and employee contributions. The launching of this system of national insurance was a milestone of social progress, for it instituted financial security to a workforce who had lived for centuries without any possibility of provision for guaranteed assistance in case of illness or emergency. The rearing of large families was usually the only insurance for maintenance in old age. Social Security has also encouraged the understanding of planning for the future, signalling in many ways a growing social maturity.

Because of the limited flow of cash, personal savings and commercial banking facilities only became widely used towards the middle of the twentieth century. The Colonial Bank, Barclays Bank and the Royal Bank of Canada were already established. In 1941, JB Charles and a group of other Dominican shareholders opened the Co-operative Bank which was a boon to the lower-income earner who needed only a shilling to start an account. This 'Penny Bank' as everyone called it, provided loans for small house-building and domestic requirements which had been unavailable to many people from the foreign banks. In 1978 the government established the National Commercial and Development Bank with a government appointed directorate. Dominica's French link was emphasised with the opening of Banque Française Commerciale at about the same time.

Local Government and Co-operatives

The establishment of a committee of community minded villagers at Marigot in the mid 1930s, was the start of a system of local government which grew to become one of the most successful in the Caribbean. From 1939 attempts were made to formalise the system by charging rates such as a penny per room in each house to assist with the provision of services by village boards. Pioneers of the system faced great opposition at first. Elma Napier for instance, was challenged by a hostile crowd while attempting to inaugurate a village board at Wesley in 1942. Stones were thrown and elections were made impossible at Vieille Case. The whole business of self-government and the responsibilities of providing community services was so new at the time that ill informed villagers throughout the island regarded the boards with suspicion.

Village meetings and general persuasion gradually overcame initial reluctance, and by 1945 there were village boards at Vieille Case, La Plaine, Delices, Grand Fond, Wesley, Calibishie, Giraudel, Marigot, Colihaut and Grand Bay. There was increased stimulus that same year with the establishment of the Social Welfare Department ably supervised by Lorna Grell (Robinson) and Loftus Roberts. The boards were 'charged with good government and improvement of the village.' They were given powers to make by-laws or regulations which had the force of law within the declared area. Since 1945 new legislation upgraded the local government system giving increased powers to the councils which replaced the board system. During the 1960s local government was supervised by Sylvester Joseph and rapidly became a significant political offshoot of the central party system.

Councils are elected every three years by voters in each village. The main advantages of the councils are seen in a greater interest and pride in the village. Councils are able to suggest ways and means of improvement to relevant government departments. Small projects usually overlooked by central government can be undertaken. Funds are provided to councils by government, matching those which are raised by local house and other rates. The councils have provided a useful channel for making parliamentary representatives and ministers realise district needs.

Moreover, local government through village councils affords training in democracy and an opportunity for villagers to practise the art of government and taste the responsibilities of public office. The system continues to harness the energies and goodwill of the citizens through self help and channel this towards the welfare of the community.

The growth of local government was complemented by the development of co-operatives. Among the earliest of these was the Credit Union League, spearheaded by Roman Catholic nun, Sister Alicia.

The League has grown to be one of the largest and most widely used financial agencies on the island. The respective village and district Credit Unions which make up the national League are in effect banks owned and operated by members in each community. It has significantly contributed to thrift and sound financial management among its members who make up a large proportion, if not the majority, of the population.

The co-operative movement grew with social change. Today several small businesses, craft enterprises, marine engine repair units, banana boxing plants and food processing projects are operated as co-operative ventures guided by a government co-operative division. Emerging out of the old village system of the 'cou-de-main', co-operatives play an important role in economic circulation, social development and self-employment.

A Growing Population

The greatest problem facing Dominica today is providing services and employment for its growing population. Since 1946 the population growth rate has shot up and the continuous rapid increase makes enormous demands on the island's budget – more homes, more schools, more teachers, more hospitals, more doctors. At the same time roads need to be repaired and development projects carried out and, as in most other 'Third World' countries, funds are limited. This growth rate has been high mainly as a result of the dramatic fall in the death rate, particularly during the first year of life. Infant mortality was very high in the past but has been much reduced during the last twenty years due to improved medical care and hygiene. The West Indian pattern of high illegitimacy and low percentage of marriages features prominently in Dominican society. The problems of paternal negligence and lack of the father figure has contributed to the complex nature of our modern social issues.

Already this rapid increase has begun to hit the employment sector as more young people wait for jobs that do not exist. Since more than half the population of Dominica is under the age of 15 and not yet old enough to be employed, the full impact of this problem has not yet been clearly seen by many. But, these youth will in turn become parents and more parents mean more children. Within the next few years Dominica will have to face the task of trying to house, educate, feed and employ its doubling population. Even the high emigration rate has not relieved the pressure.

The main health problem at the end of the Second World War was malnutrition. Besides Colonial Development and Welfare assistance, the United States made large gifts of skimmed milk during the fifties and the Infant Jesus Nursing Home was established in Roseau to specialise in cases of malnutrition. Like many health and social service projects in recent years, this was organised by the Roman Catholic Church.

The problems of malnutrition were closely followed by malaria and yaws; two diseases which had plagued the island for centuries. In the early 1940s Dominica had a higher incidence of yaws than any other West Indian island and it was estimated in 1940 that about 6 per cent of the population needed treatment for it. Campaigns were run by the World Health Organisation to combat these two diseases, and by 1965 they had been virtually eradicated. All severe tropical diseases are now rare: smallpox is unknown and dysentery, which was usually of a mild type, is not common. With increased foreign aid the health service has developed rapidly; more equipment, more rural health centres and better training have improved the standards of medical care as well as providing for a vital Family Planning and birth control programme.

There is still a great deal of public education required on the subject for the majority of Dominicans still fail to see the relationship between over-population and increasing burdens of unemployment, limited services and the rising costs of maintaining over-crowded households. This is, in part, a result of the fortunate position of even the poorest families when given the natural assets available. Rivers, seacoasts, forests, abandoned fruit trees and the like still afford space and support of a kind to everyone. But as the pressure of numbers mounts, even these assets, which the average citizen still considers limitless, will prove to be exhaustible.

Housing and Planning

Since 1950, housing, particularly urban housing, has been one of the major social problems of Dominica. The Moyne Commission Report noted overcrowding in slum areas of Roseau as early as 1938, and as other communities along the west coast grew in size so did the problems of living space, housing conditions and water and sewerage requirements.

The first planned housing project was the Pottersville Slum Clearance Scheme financed by a CDW grant in 1959. Forty-two houses were built at Goodwill by the newly formed Central Housing and Planning Authority. These were erected under a programme of aided self help whereby prospective owners assisted with the construction. Since then, government-organised housing schemes have been laid out at Kings Hill, Fond Cole, Bath Estate, Canefield, Point Michel and Hartford. Most of these are now suburbs of Roseau, providing for the added pressure of the drift of people to the capital from the country areas since the 1950s.

Obtaining land for such schemes has meant that several large estates with some of the flattest productive land on the island are now covered in concrete. Since 1955, governments have been obliged to purchase Goodwill, half of Canefield, Bath and Emshall estates as well as smaller portions of land for these schemes. Pre-fabricated housing programmes, both private and government run, have enabled those who already own land to construct cheaper houses.

Hurricane David in 1979 blasted almost everything that had already been achieved in terms of housing. Providing for the homeless required every assistance possible not only within Roseau but in every village in the southern half of the island. Traditional aid donors assisted, as did the Caribbean Council of Churches in the case of Scotts Head and the Seventh Day Adventist Marinatha programme which brought teams of volunteers from the US to set up pre-fabricated homes in some of the most devastated areas. But all this has not kept pace with demand. Now squatters around Roseau and other urban areas have established pockets of shanties similar to the barrios of South America. These have created greater problems of control and servicing for those involved in planning, health, social work and the basic business of laying down infrastructure. Roseau has been growing rapidly, and along with its suburbs now houses more than a quarter of the population of the entire island. Housing standards range from handsome wooden Victorian town houses, to smaller traditional vernacular, Miami-inspired suburban concrete and squatter shacks along the fringe, depressing slum ares which have become a grim symbol of the modern West Indies.

A physical planning department attempts to supervise and control the course of construction, infrastructure and the development of the island. It is vested with certain powers to ensure careful planning for present and future needs. However, as in most other countries, politicians in power, seeking quick short-term results easily overturn detailed planning decisions. One example of this clash of planning and politics has been evident on the Canefield flats, where low income housing, light industry, an airport, a sports stadium, a cultural centre, private commercial concerns and a mean-

This view of the village of St Joseph highlights some of the housing and planning needs for growing communities.

dering badly-planned highway were thrown haphazardly together on two square kilometres of land between 1968 and 1984. Refuse dumping sites, by-passes for villages, road networks and housing construction are some of the current matters of concern to the physical planning department.

As the pace of development quickens its proper operation is the most important safeguard to the social and environmental well being of the island.

Education

The members of the humanitarian movements in Britain who had worked so strongly for the freedom of the slaves of the West Indies continued to strive for the education of the newly liberated people of the islands. In 1834 funds from the Mico Charity were secured for Negro Education in the West Indies to provide elementary schools and schools for the training of native teachers. The British government particularly appreciated the work of the Mico Charity in the Catholic islands such as Dominica; the Charity was non-denominational in its teaching and the Catholics at that time were willing to attend the schools. The first allocation of £600 for education was made to Dominica in 1835.

But in Dominica there were considerable handicaps. Some planters and the Wesleyan Missionary Society had stimulated education in certain areas but generally the mountainous character of the island, the French patois and the discord among certain parties – the Wesleyans, Catholics and Assembly – caused many problems. In 1840 the Mico Charity was providing funds for 20 schools on the island which had a total average attendance of 740 pupils.

Soon after the government passed an Education Act in 1863 to operate secular schools, the scheme was faced with failure. Not only were the communities scattered but the population did not earn or use much money and few saw the advantages of education so as to make sacrifices to obtain it for their children. Most parents preferred to have their children labouring with them rather than attending school. But most important, the government realised that it was impossible and inadvisable to exclude the priests from education in a simple Catholic community such as Dominica. The Lieutenant-Governor noted in 1867 that it would be a mistake 'to do anything that would in any way withdraw children from the parental control of the priest.'

A new Education Bill was therefore passed to bring about free co-operation between the Board of Education and the Catholic priests. This provided for the establishment of schools which would be under the direction of the clergy throughout the island. Elsewhere in the West Indies education acts were passed to maintain a government hold over church schools. From this period Catholic elementary schools developed rapidly in all parts of Dominica but attendance was still low and the standard of local education remained limited well into the twentieth century. Only the occasional scholar reached any marked distinction.

Secondary education developed very late. In the 1850s the nuns of the Roseau Convent began to run classes for a limited number of girls in the town. In 1893 the Dominica Grammar School was opened with a roll of 25 boys. In 1932 the Catholic-run St Mary's Academy began operation and was followed some years later by the Wesley High School for girls. Secondary education remained for many years limited to those who lived in the Roseau area. Public transport from country districts was inadequate or non-existent and there was, and still is, the added expense of boarding a child in the capital.

In the 1960s secondary school attendance developed rapidly and soon the first rural high school was opened at Portsmouth. The existing high schools in Roseau faced the annual load of new students coming from the elementary system and in 1976 parents unable to get their children into the few places available, started the Community High School as a co-operative effort. Many of the rural pupils in Roseau came from Wesley and Marigot, mainly Methodist communities with a tradition of educational achievement. In 1979 a group supported by the Methodist Church started the St Andrew's High School which immediately opened up greater opportunities of secondary education to pupils of all denominations in the north-east. At about the same time, a Marigot teacher, Martin Roberts, opened what was to become the Foundation High School. Another high school was opened at Portsmouth by the Seventh Day Adventists. A variety of other establishments teaching typing, music and selected subjects continues to fill the demand wherever possible. LM Christians Musical Class and more recently the Kaire School of Music are among these institutions.

Meanwhile a continual effort was being made by successive governments to maintain and upgrade the primary school system. New, larger schools built by the Canadian, British, US and French governments, replaced the long wooden halls which had served as village schools for over fifty years. A local Teacher's Training College has introduced new skills to the teaching service and the traditional subjects are now complemented with social studies, agricultural science, music and handcraft courses. To provide teenage school-leavers with more than the basic primary school background, a UNESCO-sponsored Junior Secondary project has been introduced to the main village schools in each district. The Clifton Dupigny Technical College near Roseau provides a variety of technical, vocational and academic courses. The establishment of the University of the West Indies in 1948 gave new opportunities to all West Indians to further their education and an increasing number of Dominican graduates are returning annually to participate in running their country. The UWI supervised an Extra Mural Department here for several years and in 1971 opened a local University Centre in Roseau as part of this regional programme. A wide variety of other training opportunities abroad is also available through government schemes.

The momentum of educational development since the 1960s has been guided for the most part by three ministers of government who, in spite of their different political natures, maintained a continuous pattern of achievement for the island as a whole. They are WS Stevens, HL Christian and Charles Maynard who was himself once a civil servant working in education under the administration of the other two former ministers. WS Stevens, who was Minister of Education during almost the entire 1960s, noted the need 'to re-examine with the utmost care the underlying reason for educating our youth . . . He has to be educated for the contributions which he, as an individual, must make to the community in which he lives.' Today this re-examination is deepening as teachers continue to develop an education system best suited to the island's needs.

Health

The history of health care begins with the surgeons and the military hospitals for the regular troops stationed at garrisons on Morne Bruce and the Cabrits. These officers and medical buildings were aimed at keeping the men alive against the threat of yellow fever, malaria and other ill-effects of the climate. On the larger plantations, small slave hospitals provided very basic care for the sick, most being tended by old slave women using traditional herbs and home cures. For the free people, health care was subject to the availability of a doctor working privately from house to house. Since pay was minimal, such medics usually doubled up as shop keepers or estate attorneys.

Health care as we know it took over a century to develop from the time in 1839 when the foundation stone was laid of a building 'erected at the sole expense of Alexander Dalrymple Esq for the reception of the poor sick and infirm persons.' Over the next twenty years this building was expanded and in 1859 the poor were sent to a house on Morne Bruce so that the sick could be treated separately under better conditions. The site of this infirmary, as the hospital was then called, is now occupied by the ministerial buildings, between Kennedy Avenue and Hillsborough Street. It served as the main island hospital until 1956. During those ninety-seven years significant additions were made to the compound including extra wards, an operating theatre, lab, out-patients clinic and, across the street in buildings now used by the Roseau Girls' School, was the maternity ward. Health care in the latter half of the nineteenth century was dominated by doctors Imray

The Princess Margaret Hospital under construction at Goodwill in 1955.

and Nicholls and the island was fortunate to have the services of these two dedicated gentlemen. They not only investigated and helped to combat the many common diseases which afflicted the people, but equally important, they pressed for, and advised on, legislation to cover a whole range of medical and health needs. With very limited funds they did whatever they could to provide for the best services the island could then afford.

The country areas were almost totally without medical care, even for those who could afford it. As the Dominican economy gradually improved more money was available to extend services and pay for doctors and nurses, who in those days were little more than assistant maids. By the end of that century a small cottage hospital had been erected at Portsmouth, while those at Marigot and Grand Bay were opened in the late 1920s.

Gradually conditions improved. From the 1920s Midwives Ordinance became law and 77 women were registered. One of the first women to receive the new General Nursing Certificate was Mrs Francisca Dorival (née David) who later became matron of the hospital and made a valuable contribution to hospital care. In 1956 the Princess Margaret Hospital was opened at Goodwill with 240 beds. Important changes were made over the next 25 years particularly regarding the training for, and administration of, health care with emphasis on prevention and public education.

In 1980 a new programme of primary health care was begun in the South Eastern District and was soon duplicated all over the island. A new generation of nurses, both male and female, equipped with superior techniques took over much greater responsibilities than in the past. In constant contact with the people of their area, they work daily in rural clinics and households to keep disease at bay by guiding families towards better health practices.

In the 1980s the district clinics also took on a more important role, thus relieving the pressure on the central hospital. A fine example of community effort was shown in 1981, when villagers of Marigot opened a new district hospital built through the efforts of numerous people in the area. The island has also been fortunate in having a well-trained and dedicated core of Dominican doctors complemented by others from abroad serving here as part of technical aid programmes.

Sports and Culture

As new opportunities emerged for the changing society, the use of leisure time and the awareness of new and interesting pastimes encouraged a blossoming of sporting and cultural activities. Being a British island, love for the game of cricket had always been strong. In the sixties, basketball, football and tennis grew in popularity. Government officers recruited to supervise sporting activities and better communications, both locally and overseas, spurred on the formation and participation of teams. Dominican cricket teams made particular strides, with local players such as Grayson and Irving Shillingford, Norbert Phillip, Clem John, Kaleb Laurent, Augustus Gregoire, Lockhart Sebastian and others making valuable contributions to teams both regionally and in British county cricket.

Netball and rounders are popular with the ladies, the latter game being keenly contested in all the villages. Tennis, once dominated by two Roseau clubs, has now broadened its appeal. Swimming, scuba diving, hiking and athletics are all on the upswing. The laying out of playing fields in each community has also encouraged sports development.

Dominica has also enjoyed a tremendous surge of interest and participation in cultural affairs and performing arts. With the background of a vibrant folklore, modern groups have found expression through dance, song and drama. Research into creole language and folkways has increased. Small but significant steps have been taken in the plastic arts, particularly oil painting and sculpture.

In September 1978 a Cultural Department was established under the directorship of Alwyn Bully. Along with a dedicated staff, Bully, who is an accomplished dramatist, artist and writer himself, has encouraged Dominicans not only to participate in the variety of cultural activities now available to them, but on a far wider scale has encouraged a national cultural consciousness unmatched in other islands of the region.

Two other people have contributed to this vitality. Mabel 'Cissie' Caudeiron through her all-consuming passion for Dominican folklore set the pace by reviving songs and dances and encouraging the formation of groups to do the same. The other was Premier Edward Le Blanc who developed what can be called a 'cultural nationalism' in the 1960s by the promotion of National Day as an annual cultural festival. Village groups were given the opportunity to compete in a variety of folk dance, musical and artistic contests which brought the island together in a burst of spirited patriotism. The pattern of these festivities has been maintained and promoted ever since.

Emigration

Numbers of Dominicans have left their island at various periods during the last one hundred years in search of employment abroad. In the 1800s people went to work in mines in Venezuela and French Guiana and early this century Dominicans joined the vast number of West Indians who supplied labour for building the Panama Canal. Later there was a flow of workers to Aruba and Curaçao, where large oil refineries were being established.

The main exodus since the last war has been to the United Kingdom, and particularly during the three years, 1959–1962, Dominicans left in large numbers to seek employment. Census figures show that during that period, out of a population of 59,479 some 7,915 emigrated – or 13.3% of the population. Britain soon imposed immigration restrictions and the rate of departures from the Caribbean was much reduced. Canada and the United States also received many Dominicans. Students have been attracted by the North American universities and often remain to settle there. More recently the United States Virgin Islands have attracted Dominicans, but the authorities there have also had to restrict entry. The same restrictions were imposed in the neighbouring French islands where numerous Dominicans have been going in search of work. These periods of emigration have been an important feature of Dominican life as some have returned with new skills and ideas while many others continue to send back money for their families at home.

20
After God, The Land

The national motto emblazoned on Dominica's Coat of Arms declares in Creole: 'Apres Bondie c'est La Ter,' After God it is the Land. Those few words symbolise what to many Dominicans is the essential natural pattern of their lives. Despite a rise in business sector commerce and public service employment, every islander is ultimately reliant on the viability of agricultural production.

The climate and terrain of Dominica makes it suitable for an agricultural system which is based largely on tree crops whose roots bind the soil. As we have seen, coffee played an important role in the eighteenth and early

This 1930s scene of the market overflowing onto the Roseau bayfront encompasses many of Dominica's gifts: its forested volcanic hills with well-watered fertile soil; a profusion of crops for a potentially self-sufficient people and the encircling sea for fishing.

nineteenth centuries and brought great prosperity to the French planters on the west coast. This was eventually destroyed by disease. With the abolition of slavery, sugar, which had never been prosperous, fell drastically. This was followed by the reintroduction of coffee, the development of cocoa and then limes, which brought a period of wealth to the island. Disease, falling prices and the hurricanes of 1926, 1928 and the most serious in 1930 wiped out the industry. During the depressed years of the thirties agricultural production was stagnant.

Vanilla

With the decline of limes, considerable activity was shown in the cultivation of vanilla. As prices began to rise slowly in 1936, production was encouraged. From 1939 prices shot up as supplies from the Far East were cut off and in 1942 vanilla was getting almost US$12 a pound on the US market. At the time vanilla was the main source of income and was a boon to the peasant grower. Because the plants needed a great amount of personal care and each flower had to be pollinated by hand, this prevented it from becoming a large-scale estate crop. Beans were sold to local merchants or to the Vanilla Growers Association who cured and packed the product for export to North America.

The Association was headed by American Leo Narodny who arrived in 1941 to set up a distillery for citronella grass oil at his estate at L'Imprevue, and who also grew vanilla and significantly encouraged its production islandwide. Dominica's output continued to rise throughout the war reaching an all-time high in 1945 when the vanilla boom collapsed, influenced by the total destruction of 50,000 lbs of cured vanilla in the disastrous Roseau fire that same year which ruined the Association.

The devious practice of farmers selling the Association look-alike White Cedar pods as vanilla beans also had a minor effect on trade. But, as with limes, cheaper artificial methods of producing vanilla had been developed and although local production continued at a lower level for some years, by 1959 the industry had disappeared.

Bananas

Along with the development of vanilla, efforts were being made to establish a commercial banana industry in Dominica. In 1931 AC Shillingford and Co began to make shipments of Dominican bananas to the British port of Liverpool. In 1934 the United Fruit Company and the Canadian Banana Company agreed to buy bananas of the Gros Michel variety grown in Dominica. This was only on condition that a producer's association would be formed to organise the growing and marketing of the bananas. As a result, the Dominica Banana Growers Association was established and was the first in the Windward Islands.

By the end of 1934 regular fortnightly shipments began in the 'Lady Boats', and within three years exports rose sharply. Then came the war, which brought a halt to the banana trade and upset shipping in the region.

The Growers Association remained intact however and with the return to peace attempts were made to revive the industry. The Robusta and Lacatan varieties were quickly established and as they were more resistant to Panama disease they took over from Gros Michel. The problems of finding a market for the crop remained acute but then in 1949 prosperity rediscovered Dominica.

In June that year two Englishmen, PJ Foley and GB Band formed Antilles Products Ltd, with its head office in Dominica. The company announced that it would be prepared to receive bananas for shipment during the following months, and on 17 July the SS *Barena* carried the first shipment of bananas to leave the island since the war. Antilles Products agreed to purchase all bananas grown in Dominica known as Puerto Rique and commercially as Lacatan. The company was prepared to abolish the purchase of bananas on the count bunch system and pay by the weight instead. The initial price to the Association was four cents a pound. Furthermore their ships loaded bananas at Salisbury and Portsmouth as well as Roseau.

But the company was not successful and in 1954 sold out to Geest Industries Ltd which arrived with the offer of a contract with the Banana Associations of all the Windward Islands. Special agreements were made with the British Government and the industry flourished. Leafspot disease had to be controlled for successful production and great care and new materials were required to protect the fruit. Long-term contracts were signed with Geest and as the industry developed the company began to build its own specially designed 'banana boats'. 'Geest' became a word on everyone's lips along with new phrases like 'banana fortnight', 'leaf spot', 'diothene', 'nemagon' and 'The Association'. This 'green gold' as some people called it played a major part in transforming the societies of Dominica and the Windward Islands.

Money flowed into the hands of the peasants as never before. Bananas could be harvested throughout the year and for the first time provided a regular cash income; the Association and the authority of the local government protected the grower and gave new opportunities to the small cultivator. It caused a healthy minor social revolution. This could be seen at the branch meetings where small growers made decisions on marketing and policy; it could be seen in the new or repaired cottages with their tin roofings and linoleum floors and cement block walls or imported 'siding'. But it also meant that Dominica began to import much more of her foodstuffs and foreign tinned food swept into the shops.

Banana cultivation had expanded briskly since the 1950s and during the most prosperous years of the 1960s bananas accounted for just under 80 per cent of all exports. But the industry has given rise to some concern in recent years. It is thought that Dominica is depending too heavily on this crop, and there are increasing problems facing the industry.

A high incidence of banana leafspot in 1978 caused a severe strain on farmers. In many areas they had to cut down productive plants so as to rid their holdings of the disease in an effort to save the industry. Irregular field spraying was blamed for the outbreak. In 1979 farmers faced an even more drastic blow when Hurricane David reduced every banana plant on the island to shreds. Less than a year later, when production had barely recovered, Hurricane Allen hit, lashing both the fields and the farmers' confidence once more. The growers' association, with the assistance of government, has needed repeated doses of foreign aid to keep production viable, to pay for inputs and operation costs. By the eighties, the industry was deeply in debt and was seeking US aid as well as attempting to introduce new structures of administration. The reality of this forced maintenance is that, with the majority of the population almost totally dependent on this one crop for the turnover of ready cash, the banana industry has had to be kept alive at all costs.

Meanwhile the expense of fertilizers and other inputs, production handling and shipping charges have shot up. Currency exchange rates, the uncertain world market price, and more competitive banana production in Africa and Central America, among other factors have added to the questionable outlook for the future.

Coconuts

Coconut production has developed substantially in recent years with the north-eastern district being the largest area of concentrated cultivation. Until 1966, practically the whole of the island's copra production was exported to Barbados and Trinidad to be refined into oil and fat products. Then local investors led by the Nassief family formed a public company for the construction of a factory to process the island's entire crop for export. Dominica Coconut Products, under the skilful direction of Phillip Nassief, has emerged as one of Dominica's success stories. Growing dramatically from a simple production line turning out two types of soap, it gained concessions to produce international brand names for the entire Caribbean. Cooking oil in bottles and in bulk, liquid detergent and Belle, Bess, Refresh, Bomber, Palmolive and Dial soaps are among the company's products. Market limitations caused by recent inflation in purchasing countries has hit export levels from time to time.

Generally however, Dominica Coconut Products provides a fine example

The Dominica Coconut Products factory at Belfast.

of agro-industry at its best, generating substantial employment at each stage from the farm to the seaport. It leaves the island as a fully processed and packaged product rather than a raw material. It is not perishable and is not as subject to fluctuating tastes and pockets as are bananas or grapefruit.

Like other crops, coconuts were affected by Hurricane David but luckily the north-east only suffered minor damage, enabling production to be maintained even if at a lower level. A Coconut Rehabilitation Project financed by Canada gave valuable assistance with cultivation, disease prevention, and feeder road improvements. It was thanks to this project, that by 1983, three years after its commencement, copra production reached pre-David levels once more.

Citrus Fruit

The citrus industry was, until coconuts took its place, the second most important source of income to Dominica. The production of grapefruit and oranges rose in importance after the Second World War and the development of grapefruit was particularly good. Limes and lime products also expanded, and became the major source of income in the industry. There is also an important regional trade in oranges as well as small amounts of tangerines, mandarins, and lemons which are sold by local hucksters in the other islands.

The soil and climate of Dominica make citrus an ideal crop but the industry has been hampered by difficulties in shipping and marketing. The crop is mainly cultivated on large estates because of the amount of investment needed and the long period of waiting for the trees to mature. In 1951 a fruit packing plant and a processing plant was established in Roseau and in 1973 a more modern plant was constructed. The Geest 'Banana Boats' provide regular shipping links with Britain. The two most popular varieties of orange are the Washington Navel and Valencia, which contain much juice and have an excellent flavour. In 1954 the Co-operative Citrus Growers Association was founded to market, regulate and help with research and give advice to growers.

The lime industry which was once so successful in Dominica declined rapidly during the 1970s. By 1974, only 5,000 tons of limes were being produced, when 75 years earlier the annual yield totalled nearly 30,000 tons. The opening of a modern crushing factory at Bath Estate by L Rose and Company in February 1975 did little to lift production. It was in many ways badly timed, for the company had already begun to sell off its lime estates because, according to its representatives, they were no longer viable.

To build a two-million-dollar lime-juicing factory and then have it lying idle half of the year would be bad business, so it was decided to use the surplus grapefruit crop to keep the factory going for another three months of each year. But the forecast made by citrus growers of 5,000 to 6,000 tons of 'late' grapefruit was not reached. Many citrus growers, particularly those

Washing and sorting yellow limes before crushing.

A former Minister of Agriculture, Michael Douglas, participates in a Geest promotion drive for Dominica grapefruit in 1975.

in the north who had to bear hefty transport costs, found the purchasing price too low even to attempt supplying the factory. By the end of 1979 L Rose had sold all but one of its five estates. After almost a century of being in the forefront of the lime trade, during which it had become a subsidiary of the large British conglomerate Cadbury Schweppes, the company withdrew totally from the island. Government was more or less forced to take over operation of the factory, seeking investment to restore production levels and give new life to the industry. However, after amicable agreement between Roses and the government, the State only had to pay for the factory while the remaining Soufriere Estate was handed over free of costs.

Cocoa and Coffee

Like citrus, the island's soil and rainfall offers good conditions for the growth of cocoa and coffee and both have been long established in Dominica's economy. Since the last War, higher yield varieties of cocoa have been planted but the low price for peasant cocoa kept development down and because the crop was usually poorly processed it fetched a low price on the market. During the 1960s the Commonwealth Development Corporation at Melville Hall and AC Shillingford in Roseau purchased the bulk of peasants' wet cocoa for processing which caused an improvement in quality and price.

The importance of coffee in the earlier years of Dominica's history declined in this century. Bad agricultural practices, low prices and disease from the coffee leaf miner, reduced the growing of the crop on large estates. It continued mainly as a peasant crop and high world prices in the early 1950s gave a lift to production. Coffee continues as a minor export crop with most of it being sold locally.

Bay Leaf and Fruit Crops

Bay leaf and bay oil production has been a major feature of the eastern and south-eastern parts of Dominica for a long time. Many small distilleries were operated by independent growers, but recently co-operatives have been formed. The producers realised that by banding together they would be able to market their product and develop their industry on a much stronger basis.

Today, the Petite Savanne Bay Oil Producers Co-Operative is the leading exporter of this essential oil. The markets in the United States and Western Europe are however quickly saturated. Amounts required for the perfume trade are small and bay oil export has to be stopped from time to time because of gluts on the world market. Luckily it is a product which can be stored indefinitely to await upturns in price.

Old postage stamps showing aspects of agricultural production.

Agro-industrial enterprises are viewed as being the ideal investments for Dominica. Yet except for coconuts, years of studies, consultancy advisories and foreign investment efforts have been of little benefit towards the establishment of this form of production on a scale which would make a sizable impact on the economy. One small local company, PW Bellot & Co, has however maintained a regular output of hot sauces, juices and preserves made from passion-fruit, citrus, guava and paw-paw. The government produce chemistry lab, and some village co-operatives, process fruit wines, candied fruit and also package dried sorrel and banana crisps. A very small amount of sugar cane is still grown on the west coast which is processed into rum at distilleries at Belfast and Macoucherie.

Land under mango, avocado and spices continues to increase and forms a small part of agricultural exports. The production of vegetables and root crops has also developed in recent years due to the uncertain position of bananas and the increased demand for these products locally and in neighbouring islands.

A government Marketing Board has had mixed fortunes over many years in attempting to secure and maintain markets overseas for a variety of fruit and root crops. It is also involved in supporting local food outlets and retailing agricultural equipment and supplies.

The Huckster Trade

Ever since the colonisation of Dominica, women have dominated one vital area of economic activity which has survived through the centuries of disease, blight, collapse and destruction of the various monocrops: coffee, sugar, cocoa, limes and the rest. These traders or hucksters have bargained with the powerful, whether planters or merchants, marketed throughout the villages and towns, and crossed stormy sea channels to ply their trade. In this agricultural island it is a trade which has maintained a flow of commerce during slavery and freedom, the contribution of which has been grossly underestimated.

In earlier chapters, passing mention has been made of these women. The power which they commanded and the influence which they still hold cannot be effectively recorded by a study of trade statistics. Dominican hucksters, like those of St Lucia and St Vincent, are a social phenomenon within West Indian life. Following generations before them, these tough women and an increasing number of men, negotiate with farmers for quantities of fruit and food crops. These are shipped to markets in Barbados, the French, Leeward and Virgin Islands. Hucksters travel on all manner of vessels with their island produce which, besides fruit, includes baskets, handicrafts, anthurium lilies and spices. Today many fly by plane instead, so as to make the necessary arrangements before the boats arrive. On the return journey, they import a variety of merchandise often unavailable in the established shops, which they sell at street stalls and other outlets. Many of these traders have emerged as vibrant figures within the local commercial sector, establishing stores, guest houses and other enterprises in Roseau, Portsmouth and the villages. Recently a Hucksters Association was formed to organise better marketing, shipping and immigration facilities for themselves.

The Decline of Large Estates

The worldwide depression in trade and commerce during the 1930s coupled with the collapse of lime production locally was a drastic blow to Dominican agriculture and to the large estates in particular. These dominated the main river valleys along the coastal fringe. For over twenty years during the 1930s and 40s they remained idle, providing little or no employment. The critical economic climate of that period left the owners with neither money nor export markets to maintain production. Even when they tried to sell the estates there was no one with the money to buy them. Credit as we know it today was non-existent and the banks already held a number of estates to cover debts, particularly of those Roseau merchants who had used their country estates for security on commercial loans. Estates in the east such as Castle Bruce, Rosalie and Pointe Mulatre had reverted to bush and it was barely possible to maintain small acreages of cultivation on other estates where much of the land had been parcelled out to tenants, because there was basically nothing else which could be done with it.

The advent of the banana industry ended this long period of depression. Thousands of hectares of abandoned estate land was cleared and planted over with the new cash crop during the 1950s. With money now flowing, estates changed hands. The Geest banana company bought up three large estates: Woodford Hill, Picard and Brantridge. Other foreign investors purchased Rosalie and Pointe Mulatre. The Commonwealth Development Corporation bought Castle Bruce and Melville Hall. Elias Nassief bought Geneva while other estates also changed hands from their traditional owners to merchants and professionals moving into agriculture. L Rose & Co which already owned Bath, Soufriere and Emshall estates, purchased

St Aroment, and in a bid to expand lime production, bought Canefield and Wallhouse in the 1960s. Apart from Melville Hall and Woodford Hill the northern estates, previously owned by a variety of British concerns were now dominated by three local families: Hatton Garden, Governor and Londonderry by the Lavilles; Hodges, Eden and Blenheim by the Armours; and the large Hampstead estate, with boundaries virtually unchanged since 1770, by the Douglases. Shillingfords and Rolles dominated the west coast while the Bellots owned some five smaller estates covering the extreme southern section of the island. This latter family, among the oldest on the island, have owned their estates continuously from the earliest years of French settlement.

Scattered between these larger properties, were several medium-sized estates of fifty to one hundred or more acres each. Then there were the holdings of small farmers ranging from twenty to fifteen acres downwards situated mostly in the hinterland behind the main coastal villages.

In the centre of the island, and falling in some cases to within two kilometres of the coast, was a vast area of Crown Land, unsold and untouched since the days of colonisation. In the central areas, rainfall, terrain and rocky 'hard pan' beneath the thick forest made the land in many cases impossible to cultivate and, for water catchment reasons, far better left alone. But on the lower slopes, particularly in the north-east there were still large sections of Crown Land suitable for farming.

The recommendations of the Moyne Commission and other later studies proposed the organisation of settlement schemes in various parts of the island to provide more land for small farmers. Aid funds were secured and teams of government surveyors parcelled off the largest sections of Crown Lands since the surveys of John Byres in the 1770s. During the 1960s peasant landholding increased threefold and, coupled with the banana industry and construction of feeder roads, the decade began a boom period for the small farmer.

By this time, island politics were being influenced by more radical ideas introduced by a new generation of young Dominicans returning from the UWI and universities in North America. There was a surge of printed pamphlets and books as well as public meetings denouncing existing systems and advocating the need for social and economic change. Prominent among these issues was the question of land. Although the landholding pattern in Dominica was by no means as imbalanced as on other islands such as St Kitts, Antigua and Barbados, it became a most emotional issue. Statistics were often blown out of all relation to reality, but the underlying message was constant: 'Our upper-class businessmen who own and control ninety per cent of the wealth of Dominica are individually and as a class united against any change with regards to land utilisation and ownership,' wrote Rosie Douglas in his book *Chains or Change*.

The Castle Bruce Affair

Events which occurred at Castle Bruce from 10 July 1972 and which reached a turning point on 1 February 1974 with the official registering of a farm co-operative, were set against a background of this agitation. They were linked also to the traditional tone of politics at the time, where the Labour Party, which, by then, had been in government for over ten years, presented itself as a guardian of 'the little man' against 'the mulatre gros bourg' made up of large landholders and businessmen. However the new left wing elements had their own views on this claim, as outlined in an editorial in *Twavay* the organ of the Movement for a New Dominica, MND: 'Let all workers take heed of this lesson, let all workers learn of the government that says it is for the little man yet plans with the big man to choke and kill that same little man.'

The Commonwealth Development Corporation (CDC) was a statutory body set up by an Act of the British Parliament. The CDC's terms of reference were to work as a commercial organisation, investing its funds in development schemes for the promotion or expansion of economic projects that would not only help to increase the wealth of the Commonwealth territories but would also yield a reasonable return on the money invested.

CDC still operates in many parts of the world apart from the Caribbean; in East Asia, the Pacific and Africa. The wide field of economic development projects includes power and water supply, transportation, housing finance, agriculture, mining, tourism and investment in industrial projects such as factories. In Dominica CDC was involved in electric power supply, housing finance and agriculture. This latter investment was made into the purchase and operation of Castle Bruce and Melville Hall estates, producing mainly bananas, coconuts, cocoa and citrus.

In mid-1972 the CDC general manager in Dominica acting under orders from his superiors asked the newly installed manager of Castle Bruce estate to lay off 53 workers for financial reasons. The manager, Atherton Martin, who had just completed a Master's degree in Agriculture in the USA, refused to do so, arguing that as the economy of the village depended on the wages earned on the estate, a layoff of that size would create a considerable amount of hardship. In the subsequent upheaval which took place, Martin was fired, but the village rallied to his support and all estate workers refused to return to work until he was reinstated.

At several meetings with workers in the village Parish Hall, he proposed that they approach the government for a loan with which to buy the estate and then work it collectively. An elected steering committee formulated a plan for working the estate and went to various government officials to discuss their proposals.

The dispute on the east coast created a considerable stir in Roseau.

Caribbean intellectuals and related political movements in the region and North America regarded the developments with admiration and interest. Other large estate owners and the Roseau business sector were not at all enthusiastic about the events, considering them to be an ominous fortaste of 'the communist threat'.

The government at first seemed sympathetic to the workers. The parliamentary representative HL Christian attended a meeting and said that his was a socialist government and they would see in what way they could assist the workers. Some time later, the government broadcast a statement over Radio Dominica saying that they regarded the dispute as a private matter between the CDC management and labour, and advised the workers to return to work, expressing at the same time their disapproval of 'collectives' which they took care to distinguish from 'co-operatives', this latter being a system of which government strongly approved and encouraged.

In the village itself emotions ran high. There were pockets of loyalty for the British general manager and for the continued operation of the estate as under the former system. There were some outbreaks of hostility between the factions including the burning down of a house. There was an active exchange of ideas and a certain upsurge of pride at being the centre of interest, particularly when foreign film documentary teams, journalists and others descended to view this little crucible of Third World change.

By the end of the year the atmosphere was much calmer. Workers had decided to return to work because the village had been feeling the pinch of the loss of income. About 60 workers were re-hired. At the same time they decided to have one of the trade unions negotiate a settlement with CDC. Attendance at meetings dropped off considerably and the burden of organising further plans fell upon Martin and a few members of the steering committee. Eventually a co-operative was formed which received considerable overseas support.

Even before the dispute, CDC had been considering getting rid of the estates and the events of 1972 quickened negotiations. Although the corporation would not sell during, or as a result of these events, agreement was finally reached with government which in 1974 took over Castle Bruce and Melville Hall to be operated under the Land Management Authority. Melville Hall was quickly divided and sold off while parts of Castle Bruce were also purchased independently by villagers and 150 acres were set aside for the co-operative which grew out of the events of 1972.

Clearly, the idealism of the initial plan presented for Castle Bruce was reduced by a series of social, political and economic forces too powerful and established for those new ideas. Among them the traditional pattern of independent farming by villagers as opposed to new collective systems advocated: the concept of land ownership which whether for the big landowner or small subsistence crop farmer is dominated by individualism and the treasured 'title deed'.

A comment in *The Star* newspaper noted that 'More disputes, family and boundary quarrels and blows come out of land arguments in this state than over sex, religion and even money matters.'

The Castle Bruce affair is interesting because it went further than any other estate disputes and in many ways broke new ground, for as one British sociologist studying the events put it: 'There has also been a history of emotional outbursts on the part of estate workers over particular grievances when times were hard. These disputes have tended to flare up, resulting in a certain amount of violence and a good deal of hostility, and then subside, leaving the basic structure intact.'

The Geneva Affair

Mr Elias Nassief, a Lebanese merchant having long connections with Dominica, purchased Geneva Estate at Grand Bay in 1949 from Norman Lockhart. Under Lockhart's ownership there was little or no estate development and Grand Bay villagers had virtually unrestricted access, squatting all over the land covering some one thousand acres from the shore to the mountain tops.

Because of the heavy dependence by the villagers on the estate, resentment followed Nassief's attempts to evict the many squatters on their illegal holdings. The Dominica Trade Union, led by EC Loblack, made representation to the Administrator protesting the evictions. But it was proved that Nassief was acting within his rights and although the government considered buying the estate and dividing it up for small landholders, funds were unavailable. Nassief cleared up the estate, planting mostly coconuts and operating a large copra works in the old lime and sugar factory.

In the early 1970s, with the events of Castle Bruce still fresh and with heightened political activity in the area, feelings against Nassief re-surfaced. The 1974 Carnival revelries in Grand Bay were violent with clashes between police and masked persons in the banned 'sensay' costumes. Attempts were made to block the road to Roseau. In the following weeks estate livestock was stolen or killed and cultivations cut down. A ringleader nicknamed Unicef appeared in the estate yard on Monday 25 March forcing workers to flee and seizing a truck. On Tuesday he was arrested bearing a gun and ammunition but later escaped. Later that same day an incendiary was thrown into Geneva estate house but failed to ignite and telephone lines to the capital were cut. On Wednesday the road to Roseau was completely blocked by trees and one village shop was looted. Threats were made by the ringleaders to any villagers who failed to co-operate. That weekend Geneva house was stripped of most of its furniture and other items.

In an attempt to contain the violence, the Parliamentary Representative,

Stanley Fadelle, had a meeting with the main group and other villagers, but this did little to halt the tide of events.

On Tuesday 2 April, Geneva House at Grand Bay and Nassief's store in the old market square in Roseau were simultaneously burned to the ground. The proclamation of a State of Emergency in the Grand Bay area the following day did not prevent the destruction of the estate diesel fuel tanks, the burning of the copra factory and estate sheds and the stoning of the volunteer defence force, police and firemen trying to put out the blaze.

In a radio interview broadcast two days later, Premier EO Le Blanc promised government's co-operation with villagers in resolving the issues but warned that it 'would not exonerate anyone who had violated the law.' That weekend eight ringleaders were arrested but Unicef continued to evade the police. A commission of inquiry was quickly appointed to investigate the disturbances and related matters. It was obvious from the start that the root cause was to be found in certain social problems, mainly the need for land, because of the absence of other employment opportunities. In contrast to Castle Bruce, there seemed to be a serious lack of dialogue between the parties and without any balanced leadership there was an absence of organisation and direction resulting in violence as a means of expression.

In the long run government took over the estate which was added to the responsibilities of the Land Management Authority. For a time the status quo remained intact with government operating the estate through a manager, but eventually Geneva was sub-divided into agricultural and housing lots allowing for expansion of the village and a more intensive use of the estate by small farmers.

Changing the Map

By the mid 1970s the cost of cultivation and preparation of bananas for export was causing the larger estates to give up the crop. This had been the main reason for the layoffs at Castle Bruce estate. The returns, after costing inputs, transport and labour were not considered to be sufficient to the owners. In the southern half of the island these farmers concentrated on citrus and some coconuts, while in the north, coconut fields continued to spread across the coastal lowlands. Except at Rosalie and Carlholm, bananas became the preserve of the small farmer. By doing all the work himself, and with the help of his family, most of whose labour costs were not quantified, bananas provided his weekly cash income.

Those large estates not dependent on coconuts felt the strain of labour costs in relation to profits and by the end of the decade several were up for sale in sub-divisions of five or ten acre lots. Every large estate around Roseau was planned for housing development by the mid 1980s. Those estates bordering rural villages were also being sold off in portions through private negotiation or under government village extension schemes. Slowly therefore, after two centuries, during which the names and boundaries of the original sugar and coffee estates had remained almost unchanged, a new pattern was emerging upon the landholding map of Dominica.

Fishing

Fishing has been a traditional occupation for the inhabitants of all coastal villages particularly those on the west and north-east coasts and in the south at Grand Bay and Fond St Jean. Fewer people are dependent on fishing today than there were before the introduction of the banana industry. Many have turned to other pursuits and only fish occasionally. The calmer west coast is the area most popular for net fishing using seines, while the southern and north-eastern fishermen brave the channels between the French islands and go out into the Atlantic to catch mainly dorado, kingfish, tuna and flying fish.

Traditional methods, some dating from pre-Columbian times, are still widely used. The social, religious and environmental traditions which surround the whole business of fishing are closely maintained. Recent efforts at introducing new techniques and fishing craft have not been overly successful and fishermen enjoy a spirited independence born out of labouring amidst the most unpredictable elements of nature. Yet during the 1990s there has been significant government investment in improving landing places and the Fisheries Department has been working closely with fishermen and the several Fishing Co-operatives in developing the industry.

Commercial fresh-water fish farming has been attempted. Programmes for the rearing of talapia and prawns in carefully controlled ponds have been initiated with a limited response from farmers. In theory, a ready supply of water channelled from streams into the ponds would offer ideal conditions for these fish, thus promoting a cheap and relatively easy source of protein.

Timber

Since French settlement at the beginning of the eighteenth century, the island has been favoured for its timber resources. In the late nineteenth century a small Canadian company attempted to extract timber from the upper reaches of the Hodges river valley. Early in the twentieth century the Forest Timber Company was formed to extract and process timber at Portsmouth. A significant investment was made into the laying of Dominica's only railway line from the mouth of the Indian river up the valley to the rain forest near Brandy ridge. A steam-powered sawmill was set up on the coast and successful operations were maintained until the First World War.

After the Second World War, two Americans, Gus Smith and Bob Lord, arrived and set up a sawmill at Canefield to harvest timber from areas around Middleham at the end of the Imperial Road. This small enterprise was aimed mainly at supplying high quality wood for furniture and panelling, although amounts of general building timber were also produced. Operation costs, particularly the expense of extracting timber from the forest, caused the business to close and Smith and Lord diverted into operating a commission agency for vehicles and spare parts.

The next major timber investment came when Canadian and local businessmen formed Dom-Can Limited in 1967 to harvest timber on a large scale. Land at Canefield, on the present site of the airport, was cleared, and a sizeable mill was set up. Felling began in the D'leau Gommier area and a team of huge trucks transported logs down the Layou Valley to Canefield. Canadian members of the company branched out into the production of pre-fabricated houses and millions of board feet of lumber were exported or used locally. After about five years of operation however Dom-Can began to falter. Inadequate second-hand equipment was said to be part of the problem, but the more serious drain on the company was up in the forest. After the initial period of easily clearing trees near the main road, the company literally became bogged down in the muddy business of constructing tracks for the removal of timber from areas drenched by some 250 inches of rain a year. This, coupled with various managerial, accounting and equipment problems brought work to a halt and the company was liquidated.

Various attempts at seeking foreign investment for the re-establishment of the industry proved futile. Cost-assessment made the interested parties halt at the area of timber extraction, where steep ravines and the crumpled nature of the land made the expense of removing the timber virtually impossible.

In 1979, the local chapter of Rotary International sought the assistance of its fellow members in North America to set up a small mill so as to utilise trees destroyed by Hurricane David. The first mill was established between Layou Park and Pont Casee. With technical assistance and Canadian aid, operations got off to a good start. In 1982 the equipment was moved to Picard near Portsmouth. Dominica Timbers Limited was formed. Three kilns and better cutting and planning equipment were installed, and more work vehicles were acquired. Agreements were reached for tapping the forest some four miles inland at Mount Pleasant and a feeder road was built into the relatively flat area situated upon a plateau overlooking Picard.

Meanwhile at Woodford Hill, the indomitable Sister Alicia was initiating a similar scheme to extract timber from the Morne Ramier and Simpa areas on the foothills of Diablotin. With assistance from the Belgian government and other organisations, she formed a business co-operative to run a sawmill and to begin the development of pre-fabricated housing using the processed lumber. The introduction of chain-saws, complete with mechanisms for producing boards in isolated areas, has meant an increase in private timber production. Associated industries such as furniture-making, wood-carving and pre-fabricated housing units were developed. By the mid 1990s however, both these ventures had folded for essentially the same reasons as Dom-Can had done.

Resources for Tourism

Dominica cannot, and does not, attempt to boast of the usual tourist attractions common to the major tourist destinations of the Caribbean. Except for a few pleasant beaches on the north coast, the island cannot provide the miles of white sand and almost constant sunshine which are usually associated with Caribbean holidays. Until the 1950s no concerted effort was made to attract visitors to the island. A few guest houses in Roseau and one at Springfield provided a total hotel occupancy of some twenty beds.

Adventure tourism: visitors on a boat-ride up the Indian River.

The Freshwater Lake in the centre of the Trois Pitons National Park with Morne Watt in the distance.

In 1961 the Normandie beach hotel was opened at Mero, the first of its kind, in that it was constructed specifically as an hotel. Soon, with a change of ownership, it was renamed 'Castaways'. In 1964 a local public company was formed and negotiated with government for the use of Fort Young (the former police headquarters) as a twenty-room hotel. It quickly became the most successful establishment on the island and remained so until its destruction by Hurricane David in 1979. The opening of the larger Layou River Hotel in 1972 by the same company did not prove successful and became a financial burden to the parent hotel. The Armour family, through their company, Anchorage Limited, has been in the forefront of the local tourism business since the 1960s. Because of the low level of holiday visitors, most of the island's hotels depended on travelling salesmen and visiting technical aid personnel to provide their main support. Three mountain hotels, Island House, Riviere La Croix and Papillote provided a taste of natural island life for those casual visitors seeking to enjoy the river and forest vacations in which the island excels. The former two hotels were effectively wiped out by Hurricane David but the style of holiday which they offered still remains an example of the unique market which the island could corner. Papillote, virtually beneath the Trafalgar Falls, continues to utilise every natural asset including hot springs to great effect.

Tourism promotion moved from the stage of voluntary committees organised by interested individuals to an institutionalised Tourist Board charged with maintaining and supervising the industry. Under the slogan 'Nature Island of the Caribbean,' Dominica seeks to use its lush and exotic natural attractions to encourage visitors looking for a very different type of holiday.

Hiking to waterfalls, visits to historic and natural sites and 'safari tours' in open vehicles around the island are promoted. In the 1980s tourist development moved to the attractive Portsmouth area in the north-west which offers yachting and watersport facilities along the best beaches on the island.

A Delicate Balance

As an agricultural island, the livelihood of Dominica is inextricably linked to the fertility of the soil. The maintenance of an environment capable of supporting the expanding population must therefore transcend every other concern of human activity. Fertile soils, clean sources of water, unpolluted mangrove swamps, river estuaries and reefs, are vital to the quality of life of every islander. Without them, agriculture, water supplies and fishing, the basic sources of existence, are threatened. Because Dominica has been lavishly blessed with these natural assets, humans take their continuous provision for granted. Recently however, concern has increased about ensuring that water catchment areas are protected, waste disposal is controlled and the precipitous landscape of the central mountains is protected from erosion caused by deforestation. With the population of Dominica concentrated along the coast it has been possible to promote the conservation of the central range which is in fact the storehouse of water and fertile land for the villages below.

An active forestry department spearheaded by JAN Burra and Cyril Hill in the late forties was the embryo for the establishment of legislation and systems for the proper control of the ecology of the island. Forest reserves were surveyed in the northern and central mountain massifs and a system of forest guards and rangers was established. In the 1960s international and local concern over better systems for preserving the environment led to interest in organising a national parks system.

In July 1975, after almost two years of boundary studies and legal preparation, the House of Assembly passed the National Park and Protected Areas Act establishing a 35 square kilometre national park.

The Canadian Nature Federation, with the backing of the Canadian International Development Agency (CIDA) and with co-operation from Parks Canada, the National Museum of Natural Sciences and the Canadian Federal Justice Department assisted in setting up the Trois Pitons National Park. The American owner of Springfield Plantations Ltd, John Archbold, donated another larger section of forest to be attached to the park as the Archbold Preserve. A park development plan was formulated to concentrate on two elements: pedestrian access trails and environmental interpretation to explain the park to students and visitors. Six trails were completed along with picnic and rain shelters. The three most popular visitor sites are the Emerald Pool, Freshwater Lake and less accessible Boiling Lake. The two hundred hectare Cabrits headland has also been included in the Parks System.

Despite pressing economic and social problems on the island, the creation of the park represents the strong conservation commitment of the staff of the Forestry and National Parks Department, first headed by Christopher Maximea, and this young developing country as a whole. Potential returns from short-term alternate uses of the land have given way to long-term benefits and a modest nature-oriented tourism industry.

While other islands were parcelling off large areas, particularly coastland, to foreign real estate speculators, Dominica was ensuring that greater local control could be maintained over its land. An Aliens Landholding Ordinance made in 1939 was first amended in 1955 by a provision for registering licences and then in 1968 by imposing a licence fee and providing for agreements and regulations for sale of land to aliens. This was to tighten up the Act so as to prevent foreign speculators from buying land, leaving it derelict and undeveloped and selling it later for hefty profits in lots. This has helped to control land prices and has given Dominicans a fairer opportunity for ownership of their island home.

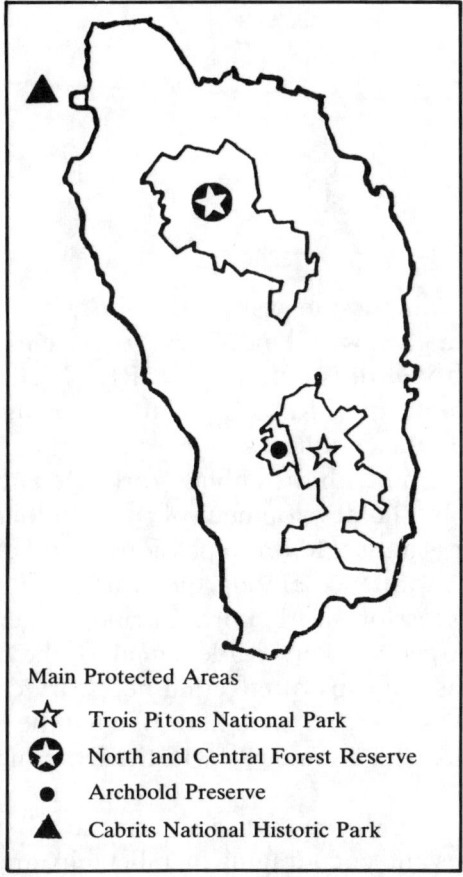

Main Protected Areas
☆ Trois Pitons National Park
★ North and Central Forest Reserve
● Archbold Preserve
▲ Cabrits National Historic Park

Map showing National Parks and forest reserves.

21
Statehood

Trade Unions

When the Moyne Commission visited Dominica in January 1939, it received evidence from groups and individuals representing a cross-section of the population. A Labour deputation, led by REA Nicholls and EC Loblack, took them into slum areas of Roseau: Balahoo Town, Fond Mico and the Pound, to show them the conditions under which the people lived. Loblack was then a master mason with the Public Works Department who had been strongly influenced by the development of trade unions and workers associations in the other islands. He was a passionate and determined man who commanded a great influence among the workers. Loblack was also encouraged by his discussions with Lord Citrine, a member of the Moyne Commission, who urged workers' leaders in all of the colonies he visited to form trade unions as a means of effecting necessary change.

Before the War was over, Loblack had solicited the help of Nicholls and Austin Winston, and on 11 January 1945 the Dominica Trade Union was formed.

The Union grew rapidly as officers went to all parts of the island establishing branches and encouraging membership, and within six months, there were 26 branches of the Union. During the same period, the Dominica Workers Association was founded and, under the leadership of the Methodist minister AE Belboda, it developed its main membership in Marigot and Portsmouth. The Teachers Union, which had been operating since the early forties, was registered in 1949.

It was not long after the formation of the DTU that Loblack succeeded Nicholls as President. The Union altered the hours of work for labourers and domestics and organised the port workers. It purchased its own property in Roseau, and the Trade Union Hall in Lagon continues to be a bastion of free political speech in Dominica. Here, a night school with government-paid teachers was established. In 1949 Loblack represented the island in Britain at the International Confederation of Free Trade Unions and took the opportunity to put Dominica's problems before the Colonial Office.

One of the most important developments during these years was the Union's activity among the tenants on estates. Soon after its formation the Union was faced with over 1,000 notices of eviction brought into its office by peasant farmers. In those days tenants could be given only two weeks to get off their land, and this was without compensation. In protest, the Union brought one of the landlords before the Courts, and pressed the government to introduce laws to protect tenant farmers. As a result, the Agricultural Small Tenancies Act was passed in March 1953.

But by this time Loblack had begun to lose his hold on the Union and there were disputes among members. This was made worse by a violent rift among port workers and was followed in 1957 by the removal of Loblack from office.

In December 1960 a former DTU executive, A Frederick Joseph, established the Dominica Banana Employees Association which grew rapidly and eventually became a general workers union; the Dominica Amalgamated Workers Union. In January 1965 there was a third rift as the port workers broke away to form the Seamen and Waterfront Workers Union, later called the Waterfront and Allied Workers Union, under the leadership of General Secretary Patrick R John and President AC Active.

As the government civil service expanded in the fifties, the employees formed their own association, the Civil Service Association, CSA. During the 1970s it grew in stature becoming one of the single most powerful forces with which governments have had to contend. The tone of this relationship was set in 1973 when key members of the CSA executive were placed under house arrest during a dispute over the transfer of an

A DTU march through Roseau in the early 1950s with banners and steelband to observe Port Workers Day.

announcer on Radio Dominica. The strength of the CSA was determined in no small measure by the astute character of its General Secretary, Charles Savarin, who, in an ironic twist of fortune, became a government senator in 1980, and in 1983, a minister of government; resulting in his resignation from the post of CSA General Secretary.

The vast mass of the working people of Dominica are self employed and most of these are farmers. There existed since the late nineteenth century an Agricultural Society made up for the most part of larger landholders, meeting to exchange ideas on cultivation methods, management, markets and prices. By the 1960s the Society was virtually defunct with only a small core group existing. With the banana industry beginning to show serious cause for concern, and with such other farm issues as feeder roads, citrus sales and limited markets affecting the livelihood of the increasing number of small farmers, a Farmers Union was formed in the early seventies. Led initially by Norrie Vidal, WS Stevens and Alvin Armantrading, the DFU held an inaugural meeting at Marigot and encouraged the formation of branches in all districts. The nature of the main issues involved determined three targets for DFU pressure: government, the Dominica Banana Growers Association and the banana purchasing company Geest. But by being a union of the self-employed, the DFU faced problems of membership and funds from the start. Membership would rise and fall depending on the urgency of each crisis. Whereas other workers' unions were supported by the regular wage deductions of their employed membership, the DFU, like the political parties, depended only on the fluctuating subscriptions and goodwill of its supporters. This problem of operational finance coupled with a lack of impetus led to the decline of the DFU.

In 1978, Atherton Martin and others revitalised the Union. A new executive was elected with Martin as General Secretary and although a younger more radical type of membership was encouraged, an effort was made to maintain the traditional farmers who formed the broad base vital to the Union's success. Soon, as the DFU increasingly became a rallying point for the left wing Dominica Liberation Movement Alliance, much of that wider base became disenchanted. The DFU however maintained a strong influence in the 'banana belt' of the north-eastern district and support surges whenever crisis looms. Martin, aware of the inherent problems of a union such as the DFU, secured outside assistance to help provide for administrative expenses and transportation and moved the union into export marketing and seed and material supply servicing while at the same time continuing its contact programmes throughout the districts.

Just as DAWU had emerged out of the executive of the DTU, so was another new union established by a breakaway member of DAWU. Rawlings Jemmot left DAWU to form the National Workers' Union in 1977. Concentrating at first on attracting agricultural estate workers, the NWU soon won workers' representation ballots in established business places. Since 1945 the combined action of these unions and the various government administrations has resulted in several significant pieces of legislation protecting the rights of workers and promoting the orderly conduct of industrial relations in Dominica. The settlement of disputes by arbitration before balanced tribunals, regulations regarding strike action and employee-union contracts are some of the major advances made over four decades. These securities of workers' rights replaced the former arbitrary treatment of the work force subject to the individual attitude of the employer.

In the face of increased Trade Union activity and legislation, the employers found it necessary to form the Dominica Employers Federation. Its main service is to advise on legal requirements, assist with the resolution of disputes and contracts and participate with unions and government in matters relating to industrial relations.

The First Political Parties

In 1894, Sir Robert Hamilton stated in his Commission Report: 'The evidence that I have taken as well as the general incidence of taxation shows that the interests of poorer classes, who form the bulk of the population, have not hitherto received the consideration they deserve and that they have to some extent at least, been subordinated to the interests of the larger proprietors, the merchants, and traders.'

With the dawn of the twentieth century and the change of constitution in 1924, the movement towards fully representative self-government quickened. The conferences, commissions, reports, and restlessness of the 1930s was heightened by the Second World War. The ferment of those war years shook the political and social patterns of the entire world. In Dominica, where interest in politics had always been strong, the emergence of new leaders and the development of trade unionism made the demand for universal adult suffrage even stronger.

Even before the war, the Moyne Commission had found that the demand for full representative government was overwhelming: 'We are satisfied that the claims so often put before us that the people should have a larger voice in the management of their affairs represents a genuine sentiment and reflects the growing political consciousness.'

These two demands: Universal suffrage and representative government were strongly supported by all Dominicans. The elected members still did not have a majority in Council and although some had the interest of the mass of the people at heart, the direct voice of the poorer classes was not heard in the Legislature.

Then, in 1951, there came a turning point in the politics of Dominica and the Windward Islands. A new constitution was granted which included the two fundamental changes for which the island had been waiting. Every Dominican over the age of 21 was entitled to vote without the qualifications that were previously needed and an elected majority was created in the Legislature. Elections were held the same year and a number of new men entered the Council. But in spite of the new system the style of politics and politicians did not change immediately, and there were still no organised political parties.

Two years later a Dominican woman returned from England to her island home. She was Phyllis Shand Allfrey. Her grandfather had been the famous Sir Henry Nicholls and her uncle had helped to establish the first trade union. In England Mrs Allfrey had been an active member of the British Labour Party, and had worked as a welfare officer during the war. On her return to Dominica she put her political experience to work and along with the pioneer trade unionist EC Loblack, she founded the first political party on the island. On 24 May 1955 the Labour Party of Dominica was inaugurated from the porch of the DTU Hall in Lagon, Roseau.

Like the trade union drive ten years before, the party spread its idealistically socialist ideas throughout the countryside. In 1957, the party was joined by an ambitious and passionate young Dominican who knew the mood of his people and his island well. This man Edward Oliver Le Blanc, soon became a leading spokesman for the party. Like other politicians in the West Indies at the time, he knew the power of an orator who identified himself with the mass of the people and soon his emotional hold over many Dominicans was remarkably strong.

In 1956 the Constitution was altered once more. It introduced a ministerial system; for the first time four unofficial members sat in the Executive Council as assistants to the Administrator. Three of them were styled Ministers and were in charge of administering government departments.

General elections were called the following year and a few new political parties quickly sprang up. CAH Dupigny formed a party modelled on the Trinidad's People National Movement, but this was short-lived. In those elections four Labour Party candidates were successful: NAN Ducreay, RP St Luce, LC Didier, and EO Le Blanc. When the results were announced, the non-Labour candidates banded together to form the Dominica United People's Party so as to command a majority in the Council. It was led by FA Baron who became the island's first Chief Minister in 1960 when further constitutional changes came into effect and the number of constituencies was increased to 11.

Federation: The Noble Failure

In the 1950s the idea of a West Indian federation was not new. Islands had, from time to time, been administered in groups and in 1871 Dominica was made a federal colony of the Leeward Islands against much local opposition. In 1876 the Barbadians rioted over proposals to include their island in a federation with the Windwards. In 1921 the Wood Report considered that federation was so unpopular it would be useless to try it. In 1932 West Indian politicians met at the Dominica Conference to discuss common problems and consider questions of federation and representation.

By 1945 there had been a considerable growth in West Indian national feeling. The work of a few respected leaders, notably Cipriani of Trinidad, Rawle of Dominica, and Marryshow of Grenada, had laid the foundations of this new movement. Slowly but steadily they had succeeded in spreading the idea that the West Indies must be united if it was to survive amid the complexities of the modern world.

The first conference on British West Indian federation was held at Montego Bay, Jamaica in 1947. Speaking for Dominica, Clifton AH Dupigny made it clear that Dominica was wholly in support of the union: 'I can assure you that the entire population of Dominica and also the Legislature of Dominica are unanimously in favour of the federation of the West Indies.'

By a majority vote the conference accepted the principle of political federation. Dominica remained a strong supporter of federation throughout the conferences and discussions which paved the way to the Union. Like the other 'small islands' it was hoped that federation would give some relief to our economic problems and add to our independence. The two large territories of Jamaica and Trinidad and Tobago began to have serious doubts as to whether they would not in fact be kept back from federating with the lesser developed members of the group. However, they agreed to participate in the planned union and Federal elections were held in 1958.

In Dominica, Edward Le Blanc and Phyllis Allfrey of the Labour Party scored a landslide victory at the polls. Together they had visited the most isolated villages on the island. Armed with illustrated and simply worded leaflets bearing their photographs they were able to gain wide support and together they won in 135 out of 138 polling stations. All other candidates lost their deposits.

The Labour Party of Dominica was allied to the West Indian Federal Labour Party which secured a small majority in the Federal House of Representatives. Mrs Allfrey was given the post of Minister of Labour and Social Affairs in the Federal Government. Le Blanc sat as a representative in the Federal parliament whose administrative headquarters and capital was in Trinidad. Veteran local politicians Austin Winston and JB Charles were made Federal Senators.

But even before the celebrations and fanfare had died down the new West Indian nation seemed doomed to failure. There was dissatisfaction about the choice of the British Governor-General and his staff, and some

232   *The Dominica Story*

people were of the opinion that Britain had simply imposed a type of old-fashioned Crown colony government on the West Indian colonies. But there were the even greater problems of unity itself.

In theory federation was, and is the obvious ideal, but the practical details were overwhelming. The questions of funds, distribution, customs duties, immigration and independent island jealousies were too strong for the ideal spirit of unity. Jamaica had continued to be suspicious of the federation and eventually, in September 1961, after Jamaicans had voted against the federal agreement, Jamaica withdrew altogether. The nine-island government struggled on for a few more months but finally crashed in May 1962 when Trinidad and Tobago also decided to pull out.

Meanwhile Le Blanc had resigned as a member of the Federal Parliament and had led his party to victory in the local general elections of 1961. He became Chief Minister and Minister of Finance in the new government which had ousted the Dominica United People's Party. After this election, the 1959 constitution was fully put into action and a Speaker and Deputy Speaker were appointed to take the place of the Administrator in presiding over Legislative Council meetings.

Unlike Le Blanc, those who remained in the Federal Parliament to the very end were not so lucky. All of the ex-ministers except for Robert

Hon. Edward O. LEBLANC
Member Dominica Leg. Co.
Delegate to WIFLP Executive
Secretary-Agent DLP

Mrs. Phyllis Shand ALLFREY
President of Dominica Labour Party
Member, British Labour Party

The two Federal candidates and their symbol the Hat.

Bradshaw of St Kitts suffered politically. Phyllis Allfrey returned to Dominica but was expelled from the Labour Party in September 1962. With Le Blanc as the central figure of the Party, its power increased rapidly and his new style of government and politics coupled with the success of bananas and increased foreign aid for welfare projects and roads made him virtually a father figure for the mass of the people.

Following the dissolution of the West Indies Federation Edward Le Blanc and other political leaders of the Windward and Leeward Islands and Barbados began to discuss plans for the formation of a Federation of the eight remaining islands, the 'Little Eight'. But after four years or more of conferences, council sessions and draft schemes this attempt at unity also came to an end. This failure meant that Dominica had no choice but to seek further constitutional changes by herself – full internal self-government. At the Windward Islands Constitutional Conference in London in April 1966, the plans for Associated Statehood were drawn up. As the name implied, Dominica would become a self-governing state in association with Britain.

On Our Own

On 1 March the following year, the Dominica Constitution Order 1967 came into operation. The celebrations and festivities of Statehood were postponed until 3 November and that day, which in 1493 changed the course of the island's history, is annually observed as National Day.

Under that constitution, the executive authority of Dominica was in the hands of the Governor who acted on the advice of a cabinet made up of the Premier and ministers of government drawn from members of the House of Assembly. The attainment of Associated Statehood was in administrative terms more significant than the later attainment of independence for it give the island total self-government. Only the 'umbilical cord' of defence and foreign affairs remained to be cut. External defence remained the responsibility of the British government while Dominica had authority over wide areas in the field of external relations subject to consultation with the United Kingdom. The House of Assembly, elected regularly by the people at general elections had the power to change the provisions of the constitution of the state subject to certain procedures, including in some cases, a two-thirds majority of the votes cast by the people at a referendum.

The island was free to end her association with Britain at any time by a two-thirds majority of the elected members in the House of Assembly and two-thirds of the votes cast at a referendum. No referendum was however necessary for the purpose of joining with an independent Commonwealth Caribbean country if that country was to be responsible for defence and major external affairs of Dominica. The United Kingdom Government on its part could end the association through debate and legislation in its own

The last British Administrator, Geoffrey Guy with HM Queen Elizabeth II on her arrival at the Roseau jetty for a one day visit in February 1966.

Premier EO Le Blanc receives the constitution of Associated Statehood from a British Government representative in March 1967.

parliament but it was agreed that a conference with island leaders would be held to discuss the political and economic implications of such a step. In the end, this latter method was used to gain full independence for Dominica in 1978.

The advent of Associated Statehood found the ruling Dominica Labour Party at the zenith of its popularity and power. The social and economic advances of the early 1960s assured the DLP a landslide victory at the general elections of 1966. Of the eleven seats in the Legislature only one was secured by the DUPP. This one, the Soufriere constituency, was won by Anthony Moise who became Leader of the Opposition and remained a member of parliament for almost twenty years. When the people of that constituency came to Roseau for market, after the 1966 election day, they were derided by supporters of the victorious party with the words of Mighty Sparrow's latest calypso: 'Ten to One is Murder!'.

The new cabinet of 1966 included Dominica's first female minister of government, Mrs Mable Moir James. The other Dominican woman politician of the day, Phyllis Allfrey, had become the Caribbean's first female minister during the Federation and, as events were soon to prove, this was just the beginning of Dominica's ascendancy of women in politics.

The reasons for Le Blanc's great popularity were clear. Although most of the roads and social programmes financed by the CDW funds had been planned, and in some cases begun, before the DLP took office, it was during the period 1961–1966 that they were completed and bore fruit. The DLP was identified with these achievements. A prize-winning patois song celebrated the road to the east coast with the words:

> *Anou haylay hooray!*   Let us shout hooray!
> *Anou haylay bwavo!*   Let us shout bravo!
> *Chimen wivay Au Vent, Au Vent,*   The road has reached La Plaine,
> *Labour ba nou chimen!*   Labour gave us the road!

But historically, there were two even more basic reasons for the success, from which everything else resulted. The first was that never before had there been such a surge of development concentrated at one time upon a people who, for generations, had lived at subsistence level at the mercy of social and political conditions over which they had had no control. The second was that the Labour Party had presented them with a form of leadership with which they could identify, speaking in a language and presented in a manner which they could understand.

The background and character of Le Blanc was the key to this. Born in the north and later working as an agricultural extension officer in the east and west of the island, he knew more than most Dominicans about the people he led and the conditions under which they lived. Above all he had a passionate belief in Dominica and things Dominican as only those who are intimate with this island can have. His skills of communication with 'the little man', in the field, at the bayside, in the street, in the rum-shop, became renowned. These associations were in many ways his greatest strength.

But there was another part of Le Blanc's character which in one way spurred him on and in another way distorted his judgement of issues and events, particularly towards the end of his leadership. This was his deep-rooted dislike of the traditional establishment, particularly the powerful Roseau-based group of farmer-merchants and professionals usually identified by the DLP as 'the mulatto gros bourg'. These feelings had been reinforced by a personal experience during his youth related to selection for further training. The reverberations of this attitude led to bitter divisiveness and recrimination within Dominican society which took years to simmer down.

Dominica was not alone in being swept by the tide of social change during the 1960s. Increased aid, trade and training, more employment and greater opportunities were affecting the other islands too, and their leaders: Bird, Bradshaw, Compton, Joshua, Gairy, Bramble, were all to enjoy long terms of leadership as a result. It was much a matter of being in the right place at the right time when the political opportunity and funds were available to initiate social welfare schemes.

In Dominica, where there had always been a deep division between Roseau and the countryside, another type of change was also taking effect.

Roseau people had always dominated island affairs from shop clerks, bank cashiers and office staff to key posts in the civil service. Within one decade this was completely overturned and although some newspaper columnists wrote scathingly about 'square pegs in round holes,' and Roseau people talked of 'the country boukeys', this movement was a significant step forward in bridging that age-old gap which divided society. It was part of Le Blanc's policy to raise rural affairs above those of the close-knit Roseau interests, and generally the DLP, under his leadership, is credited with overseeing significant material and social change throughout the island.

The change from colony to self-government was greatly assisted by the style of the last two British administrators of Dominica. His Excellency Alec Lovelace understood and sympathised with Le Blanc in much of what he was trying to achieve, and participated fully in the community activities as did his successor, Geoffrey Guy, who, before he left the island, adopted a Carib son.

Mr Guy was followed after Statehood by the first native governor, Sir Louis Cools Lartigue, who had distinguished himself in the civil service and had been the Speaker of the Legislature.

The greatest threat to power is the corrupting influence which it has on those who hold it. Soon the assured power of the DLP was attracting a circle of hangers-on seeking to benefit from the spin-offs of political patronage. Several key civil servants, members of Statutory Boards and a growing number of businessmen, including important figures in the Syrian and Lebanese sector, were increasingly using their influence to entrench the party's power and thereby secure their own. Interests of the Party took precedence over decisions of state.

With virtually no opposition voice in Dominica, the three local newspapers bore the weight of commentary on what was going on. The newspapers of that decade were *The Chronicle* edited by Stanley Boyd and published by the Roman Catholic Church, *The Herald* edited by poet and author Edward Scobie, and *The Star* published and edited by Robert and Phyllis Allfrey since 1965. The DLP government had been wary of newspaper criticism from the beginning. Mrs Allfrey was expelled from the DLP in 1962 for publishing an editorial in *The Herald* (which she then edited) which was critical of certain DLP tax levies. *The Chronicle* was apolitical almost to a fault. *The Herald* under Scobie had its independent brand of criticism headed by a weekly political scandal column 'Is it True?' The papers were by no means united, as when Scobie gave his classic description of his rival editor: 'That pale pink woman with her pale pink paper!'

But circumstances which developed in 1968 galvanised the press and gave vent to opposition feelings which had been simmering since 1966. Under the 1967 constitution the Leader of the Opposition was entitled to recommend one person to be appointed by the Governor as a nominated member of the House. Elkin Henry, a former DUPP minister, held this position after 1967. Together with barrister Eustace Francis, Mr Henry and Antony Moise formed the very short-lived National Democratic Party.

In July 1968 the government prepared a bill for presentation to the House of Assembly which was aimed at placing sweeping controls on newspapers, general publications and public statements curbing the freedom to criticise with particular reference to the Governor and ministers of government. This Seditious and Undesirable Publications Act was drafted with little or no notice to those it most affected. As news of the intended legislation spread, the three newspaper editors, Stanley Boyd, Scobie and Allfrey, joined other concerned citizens to protest against the infringement of their rights. On the night of 4 July a public meeting was held at Lagon, Roseau, which was addressed by the editors and by Henry, Francis and others, all decrying the Bill as a threat to one of their basic freedoms, the right to freedom of speech.

The following day people swarmed into and around the old Court House where the Assembly was then held, but the bill was swiftly passed through all its three stages. From then, a loosely-knit group calling themselves the Freedom Fighters stomped the country explaining what this 'shut-your-mouth bill' was all about and calling for its repeal. The issue brought together former DLP pioneers EC Loblack and Allfrey as well as a few old DUPP members and a handful of new politicians.

These meetings culminated in September with a protest march through

The demonstration against the Seditious and Undesirable Publications Act moves up Cross Street, Roseau, on its way to the government headquarters on 24 September 1968. Editor Phyllis Allfrey and Carib Chief (with staff) hold placards in front line.

Roseau and a demonstration in front of the government headquarters then situated at High Street. At the climax of this protest, a petition for repeal signed by hundreds, was presented to Le Blanc. At this point the Premier emerged on the balcony and announced forcefully to the crowd below that 'We are here to rule and rule we will.'

In immediate response, a woman pushed through the crowd, grabbed the microphone on the protestors' Land Rover and retaliated with a vibrant barrage on democracy and constitutional law. The woman was barrister Mary Eugenia Charles who from that moment flung herself unflinchingly into the political arena. The idea of forming a political party took root. In October, Moise, Henry, Francis, Miss Charles, the Allfreys, Scobie, Loblack, Loftus Roberts, Antony Agar, Star Lestrade, Martin Sorhaindo and others met to establish what became known as the Dominica Freedom Party.

From its inception the DFP had major hurdles to overcome, not the least of which was the very origins of the party itself and the nature and social background of the people who led it. The fact that its power base was in Roseau and that its leadership for the most part was of the 'mulatto gros bourg', gave Labour Party spokesmen a large, obvious and easy target for refuting every criticism made by the DFP. As leader, Miss Charles was accused of being a harsh, merciless, avaricious woman and the stern nature and landholding interests of her father, JB Charles, were constantly brought into play.

Since her return to Dominica in 1949, after attending the University of Toronto, Canada, and being called to the bar in England, Miss Charles had risen to be regarded as the leading lawyer on the island. Her astute and thorough manner of handling affairs earned her a reputation which attracted clients from amongst the largest firms and business interests on the island. And yet there was another side which the public never saw. Her contributions to education and to care of the aged through her work for the Infirmary were among those other interests of which she seldom spoke. It was to take another twelve years for Dominicans to understand and appreciate the diverse character of Mary Eugenia Charles.

But even without political detractors it was natural that the mass of the people would not leap to enfold a party associated with urban-based 'elite'. People of that class had in many ways only themselves to blame for their reputation. In most cases these people were seen to be negative and unadventurous in enterprise, warily protective of their property and businesses, watching askance the new people filling places of prestige and influence. Sometimes one's own best friends are one's greatest enemies and this was the position in which the DFP found itself.

General Elections were called for 26 October 1970. Two years of constant campaigning were slowly building up the strength of the DFP with its strongholds concentrated in the southern parishes. In September 1970 a sudden and unexpected rift split the ruling DLP when three ministers, NAN Ducreay, Mabel James and WS Stevens, along with certain party executive members, sought to expel Le Blanc from the party. Le Blanc promptly fired the three from his cabinet and appointed new ministers, a move which *The Chronicle* described under the memorable headline: 'Ouster Ousts Ousterers.'

There was a dispute over the party name and voting symbol which resulted in a court decision that the rebel members had the right to retain the name Dominica Labour Party and the symbol of the hat. Without much trouble Le Blanc immediately formed a new party called the Le Blanc Labour Party with the symbol of the shoe. As was expected, this rift made little difference to the election results, for the name of Le Blanc alone was enough to maintain the massive traditional vote for the party he led. The attitude contained in the saying 'Mwe se yon labouwe mwe ni pou vote Layba' still stood strong, for the word 'labourer' was strongly identified with Labour; in other words, the party for the labouring people. The only gain for the DFP was the Southern District constituency won by Stanley Fadelle. Antony Moise easily retained his South Western seat. Eugenia Charles lost Roseau North to newcomer Patrick John but she entered the House of Assembly in 1970 for the first time, as nominated member. Among the five ministers appointed to the new DLP cabinet was the young and, at the time rather radical barrister, Ronald Armour, who had represented the Roseau South constituency since 1966. He was also designated Deputy Premier and was seen in those days as the heir to the leadership, should Le Blanc step down. No one was aware at that time, however, of the ambitions of another young minister in that same cabinet: Patrick Roland John.

Since the official state visit of Prime Minister Forbes Burnham of Guyana for National Day 1969, it was noticeable that the DLP was developing close links with Burnham's PNC. It was following with interest the steps towards the establishment of the Co-operative Republic and the manipulation of a strong central party control of that South American nation. Because of its history, Guyana was also part of the Commonwealth Caribbean and as such Burnham began to initiate a plan which not only envisaged the creation of a close sub-regional union, but one in which Guyana was to take a foremost role.

In 1971, the leaders of Dominica, Guyana and few other Caribbean states gathered in St George's Grenada, to compile and sign an accord known to history as the Grenada Declaration. Le Blanc stated that at last there was hope for all these islands to go together as one entity. 'When I signed it I understood the full implications,' he said in an interview. 'It made provision for participation at all levels, and the appointment of a commissioner to oversee the whole phased programme. There was to be discussion at all stages in the House of Assembly.' These views were not shared by some other regional leaders and John Compton of St Lucia decried the Declaration as an agreement between sardines and a shark.

This was also the view of many Caribbean citizens and not least many Dominicans, most of whom were already resenting the growing links with Guyana. A key figure in this Dominica-Guyana menage was Leo Austin, a Guyanese school-master, later trained in law, who originally arrived here to teach at the Dominica Grammar School. After returning from legal training abroad, he was appointed Attorney General and craftily used his position over a period of years to a point where he virtually dominated the political process of the state albeit behind the scenes. By the 1970 elections Eustace Francis had shifted his allegiance to the DLP, founding *The Educator* newspaper as the party organ and becoming Speaker of the House of Assembly.

Towards the end of 1971 the Grenada Declaration issue, added to other more local concerns, caused a sharp rise of political tension. That year the DFP won the Roseau Town Council elections and entered into the petty dispute with central government over ownership of part of the land on which the new Roseau market was being built. In retaliation, government sought to get rid of the Town Council completely by dissolving it and appointing an Interim Commissioner to run the affairs of the capital instead. The Roseau Town Council (Dissolution and Interim Commissioner) Bill was to be passed on 16 December 1971. Bitter feelings against both this and the Guyana issue exploded with a massive demonstration on that day. There had been a strong appeal for withdrawal of the Bill from the four trade unions, the business sector and the Council of Churches. Public meetings were held in Roseau and Goodwill on the nights leading up to the demonstration. The number of persons attending meetings increased rapidly, from some 400 on 9 December to 3000 on 15 December. The language used became more inflammatory and decisive.

Extra police were detailed for duty around the Court House, a riot squad was prepared, and the volunteer Defence Force was embodied. But the rapidity with which the crowd assembled, the large numbers and leadership of Louis Benoit of WAWU, took the police completely by surprise. Fifteen minutes before the House was to commence its sitting, the people had burst through the main gate, poured into the Chamber, and were in possession of the Court House, the courtyard and Victoria and High Streets.

The second phase was in the chamber. The Speaker's chair and members' seats were occupied, papers torn up, glasses and chairs broken, the horseshoe table collapsed and the Sergeant-at-Arms fought to protect the silver Mace.

The third phase was the arrival of the Speaker, Eustace Francis, who forced his way to the dais; an act made more difficult when it was discovered he had a gun in his pocket. While Francis tried to reason with the crowd, DFP members were setting up a public address system outside. The main theme of the speeches were repeated calls to go and get Le Blanc if he did not come to the Court House. The Defence Force made a late and brief appearance. Few members of the House had turned up that day and with its forceful occupation, no meeting was held, no bills were passed.

When Le Blanc spoke over the radio that afternoon he played heavily on 'the irresponsibility of the Freedom Party leadership.' Appealing to the vast majority of rural listeners, he dismissed the demonstration as a Roseau affair asking them whether violence was the type of leadership they wanted for themselves. It was also announced that due only to the letter from the Council of Churches the Bill would be withdrawn.

Numerous persons involved in the demonstration, including Miss Charles, were charged for their part in the events. The cases, heard before a visiting magistrate and with a defence council made up of regional lawyers, lasted for many weeks. Several of the cases were dismissed but a number of the accused were found guilty and fined. Erskine Ward of Barbados was appointed as a one-man Commission of Enquiry to investigate the disturbances and his report recommended the retention of the Town Council and the improvement of systems for the control of demonstrations and crowds. The mood of political activity as represented by the 16 December demonstration was a foretaste of the volatile decade to follow, precipitated by a lack of consultation and dialogue between parties and an increasingly authoritarian style of government.

In July 1974, after over fifteen years in public office, during thirteen of which he had led the government, Edward Le Blanc resigned from politics. In April of that year he was already hinting at his departure in an interview with the *New Chronicle*.

'Though I accept and welcome change, I myself can't change too much, that is why people said that I was "Black Power" and this and that. . . . When we returned and got the constitution in 1967, I let it be known to my Party that I will remain for only two terms and after that they will have to get another leader. In a democracy at times the sort of pressure you get, people sometimes not being sincere and what not, you tend to react and when a leader starts reaching that position it is not good for him or the country.' Already Le Blanc was being accused of autocracy in his manner of dealing with the opposition, the unions and even with members of his own executive. The rising dissension in the country, his previously stated views on the subject, and family considerations, led to his resignation announcement on 26 July.

For over a year, Patrick John, Eustace Francis, Austin and others had been working on undermining Ronald Armour's claim to DLP leadership and eventually ensured the resignation of Armour as Deputy Premier and Minister of Finance and Development on 13 July, 1973. The path was now clear for the ascendancy of John, so that when Le Blanc resigned in 1974 he was in direct line for the Premiership.

The political assassination of Armour was completed in August with his expulsion from the DLP. 'It seems I am now a victim of trial by Radio and Newspaper,' Armour commented bitterly. He analysed the situation in a public statement: 'Every few years, as an election approaches, certain reactionary forces, impelled by motives of personal gain and attempts to wield power, have attempted to seize the Labour Party by using the non-political elements in the Executive to influence decisions to choose the weakest leader. In 1970 the Labour Party Executive did the same thing by choosing Mr Ducreay as the political leader and attempting to destroy EO Le Blanc.'

As always, in the midst of such chaos there were amusing incidents. There was a verbal skirmish in the House of Assembly over the seating of Armour, who gave reasons for his right to sit on the government side. But this was turned down. The Acting Speaker suggested he be seated with the Opposition, but Miss Charles objected to this and was supported by Premier John. Then Mr Armour asked to be 'placed somewhere'. This was done; he seated himself in the middle of the House, halfway between both sides, thereby setting a peculiar precedent for parliament. Armour founded the Progressive Labour Party in preparation for the 1975 general elections, but John's intense vilification of him continued unabated, using Armour's family business and landed interests as additional ammunition to ensure his total defeat.

Social Unrest

The offshoots of the seeds of change sown in the 1960s sprang up in the following decade in the form of increased political awareness, new ideas on political ideology and forms of government, union and party demands, cultural searching and restlessness with established systems, and social and economic aspirations often beyond the capabilities of this island state. Buffeted in the midst of all this was a political leadership, both in government and opposition, trying to mould a framework of statehood; forced to achieve within a few years, standards which more developed nations, critical of our inexperience, had taken centuries to evolve.

These problems were made no easier by our peculiar historical background, emerging from a system of the harshest exploitation of man by man, based on institutionalised divisions of race and class. Being so close to the USA and under the heavy influence of North American attitudes and events, the tide of US Civil Rights protests and Black Power demonstrations of the 1960s was being felt in the Caribbean. Indeed young West Indians, including a number of Dominican activists, were involved in those events, most notably Rosie Douglas at Sir George Williams University in Canada. It takes time for ideas or fashions to drift down to the Caribbean, and so the effects of the protests in the US were not felt here until the very end of the 1960s. The more radical movements in the region, and groups and individuals in Dominica, generally referred to as 'the Black Power boys', had their own forms of protest. These included the burning of the Canadian flag in front of the Royal Bank of Canada and regular 'Black Power meetings' at the Botanic Gardens. Caribbean leaders and the press, stressed that the position of the black man in the Caribbean was different to that of the black American. Here, they pointed out, black people held top positions and they did in fact have total power. *The Educator*, organ of the ruling DLP, went so far in its editorial of 29 May, 1974 as to accuse the MND members of being 'bogus . . . their Black Power is really Mulatto Power, a sinister plot . . . to return the mulatto to political power'.

Like other Black Power advocates in the region, they replied that groups such as their own were showing solidarity with 'our oppressed brothers in the US and Africa', claiming that there were still economic and social conditions in Dominica which caused black oppression and required change. The positive effect of that movement during those years was greater local awareness of, and pride in, the African diaspora elsewhere in the world.

There had been brief but significant periods of such concern over black struggles abroad during the earlier part of the century. In the twenties and thirties the activities and statements of Marcus Garvey and his UNIA movement were closely followed by the local newspapers, the *Tribune* and the *West Indian Times*. Articles by JR Ralph Casimir, secretary of the Dominica branch of UNIA, 1919–1922, and WW Wyllis, brought the black movement into focus for Dominican readers. The Italian occupation of Abyssinia, now Ethiopia, in 1935, and the lack of response by Britain to the plight of Selassie's kingdom, caused a rumble of ill feeling noticed by officials on the island.

But all this was minor in comparison to the 1970s wave of animosity which swept among the youth, particularly the urban youth, fanned by publications and statements made by 'graduates and intellectuals', a term used derisively by the local establishment, suspicious of these educated activists. The motives of protest were not only fed by 'Black Power' but involved a reaction to class and traditional European social and cultural influences. And here the political leaders themselves were to blame for the situation which now confronted them. These youth had grown up during a decade fed with a constant diatribe by those same politicians attacking 'the bourgeois exploiters', 'the mulatre gros bourg', 'the oppressors', 'the white aliens', and keeping open every possible wound between 'gros bourg' and 'petit bourg' for political purposes. As the 1970s wore on Dominica became a messy lacerated sore of inter-infected social and political stigmas.

A letter signed by 'Dominican Overseas' in the 8 June, 1974 issue of the *New Chronicle* asked in desperation: 'Do tell me what is happening in Dominica. Are you people striving to be another Cuba or Guyana? What is wrong with you people? You are all Black or coloured, you have your own government. Matters not whether you are near White, by all standards you are considered negro. The only thing that passes you is your behaviour and actions. The rest of the world especially the White world accepts you as to your comportment, and the way you can govern yourselves, and your people.'

But the tide was flowing so strong that by then serious incidents were following one another thick and fast. In 1972 a disturbance broke out at St Mary's Academy which blew up out of a confrontation between the principal and a student over the state of his 'Afro' hairstyle and resulted in a virtual strike of pupils. All the existing forces active in the society immediately took sides turning the affair into a national issue. Conditions at SMA deteriorated rapidly. In a discussion with a pupil delegation, a cabinet minister announced that 'no one can tell a man how to grow his hair'. Control and discipline by the Canadian order of the Christian Brothers of Ireland, who operated the school, was undermined as the white brothers became targets for racial attacks. Normal operation of the school became impossible and the brothers decided it was best to leave the island. It was thanks to the untiring efforts of a Dominican member of the order, Br Egbert Germain, that SMA was eventually able to regain its former stature and re-emerge with an even higher standard of discipline and esprit de corps.

Within a month of the SMA debacle, the Castle Bruce estate affair broke and while that was still simmering in 1973 one of the first of many major confrontations between government and civil service clamped the island into a State of Emergency, the proclamation of which was to become a common occurrence over the next ten years. Born out of the transfer of radio personality Daniel 'Papa Dee' Caudieron from Radio Dominica to a desk job in the ministry, the CSA strike was basically in defence of the principle that disciplinary action should not be taken against a public officer unless that officer has been charged and given an opportunity to defend himself with the assistance of his union. But that whole issue became lost in a cloud of emotion and politics which included the placement under house-arrest of members of the CSA executive.

By Carnival 1974 the heat had intensified further. The streets of Roseau shook to the words of the road march calypso:

> *Black man time is come!*
> *White man had his fun!*
> *Black man stronger than white man!*
> *Black man sweeter than white man!*

As the bands were winding their way back home on Mardi Gras night, a white visitor, John Jirasek, was shot dead in an isolated spot near Peebles Park. The echoes of that gunshot lingered for over five years of legal battles, appeals, protests, public meetings, political radio statements and lobby campaigns in Britain and North America, all flavoured by the heat of other issues steaming at that time. On 20 August, 1974 the trial opened at the High Court in Roseau of The Queen vs Desmond Trotter and Roy Mason, both charged with the murder of Jirasek. Mason was found not guilty; Trotter was found guilty and was sentenced to hang. The case brought out the sharp divisions in the land. Trotter, defended by lawyers Brian Alleyne and Grenadian Maurice Bishop, was seen by the establishment to represent the 'destabilising forces loose in our land' while in his defence he denied any involvement and claimed to be part of those seeking 'to eliminate all forms of oppression, exploitation and corruption inherent within our society'. His supporters accused the State of 'a frame up'.

The verdict stood through all stages of appeal, but as a result of intense campaigning (although this was not admitted to be the cause) the sentence was commuted to life imprisonment and eventually in 1979, Trotter was released.

The Dreads

Meanwhile, a minor but highly vocal section of the youth was intensifying their abuse of whites. And with Dominica having the lowest percentage of whites on any Caribbean island, most of this abuse fell upon visitors. The epithet of 'honky' was in constant use, they were jostled, sometimes spat on, cameras were occasionally smashed, cases of stone-throwing were reported and things were generally made uncomfortable for whites passing or coming into contact with 'the four corner boys'. The cultivation, use and trading of marijuana was increasing and there were more cases of praedial larceny as youth in the hills raided food crops and molested villagers in their isolated gardens. By now the 'Afro' hairstyles were being replaced by 'dread locks' to denote followers of the Jamaican Rastafarian movement.

What little tourist activity that existed fell rapidly as journalists and guidebook writers advised their readers to avoid Dominica. 'It's an island for botanists' quipped one major US magazine, 'but you'd better arrive with a Green Beret rather than a green thumb.' Taxi drivers and hotel workers waving US dollar notes demonstrated through Roseau against the incidents of tourist abuse. During Carnival 1974 violence also erupted at Grand Bay setting in motion disturbances at Geneva Estate. Deputy Premier Patrick John came on radio after the Carnival incidents to state:

'We have never known ourselves as a violent people and the new trend in our society is without doubt the handiwork of a few degenerate leaders who see themselves as the architects of a new society projecting new standards, cultures unacceptable to the majority of the Dominican people ... There is absolutely nothing to be gained by militance and violence ... More effective measures will later be introduced to stamp out the menace that threatens our progress and development.'

Many of the disaffected youth, particularly those wearing 'dread locks' were already finding out what some of those 'more effective measures' were, as police, defence force men, and civilian special constables descended upon shacks, garden plots and homes occupied by persons who were by now commonly called Dreads. Individuals and groups such as the Movement for a New Dominica complained, but the society in general, already stirred into a state of fear, turned a blind eye to the rather more excessive methods of law enforcement. Now they felt protected by the tough-sounding bravado of the Deputy Premier, increasingly taking the limelight and making radio statements to 'calm the fears of our concerned citizens'.

As a result, John was riding a wave of popularity for his firm attitude towards the Dreads but certain analysts such as the editorship of *Twavay*, organ of the MND, would not allow themselves 'to be carried away by the mass-hysteria, Logarou-hunting, Jumbie search and paranoia that Patrick R John is creating and leading'.

In July, Le Blanc resigned and John became Premier. Against a background of the Dread issue he sharpened his tactics in preparation for a general election due the following year. The mood of instability provided the DLP with a wide field of attack against any individuals or parties remotely linked to any form of opposition, who, in spite of their own differing ideologies, were conveniently lumped together as 'advocates of destabilisation'. A skilful campaign orchestrated by radio and entertainment personality Dennis Joseph promoted John as the only possible choice for the maintenance of law and order.

The growing demand for more decisive action than the already intense efforts of the police and defence force units, was met with the passage of The Prohibited and Unlawful Societies and Associations Act. 'The Dread Act' as it was called, was more successful as a psychological damper to the people's fears than it was as an effective piece of legislation. It provided an immediate dose of reassurance at a time of acute fear and as such was supported by the parliamentary DFP opposition with the understanding, according to Miss Charles, that 'it should not stay on the statute books a moment longer than necessary'. But it was going to remain there for the next seven years.

Only some individuals such as Rupert Sorhaindo and, more vocally, Brian Alleyne, dared to voice apprehension about the alarming content of the Act. In a full-page critique published in the *New Chronicle* 7 December

1974 Alleyne pointed out: '... this is the inevitable result when people (and more so with a body of people rather than a single individual) allow themselves, in fits of emotion, to be ruled by irrational fear rather than by reason, which we have the right to demand from our legislators in enacting a law which, it is unanimously agreed, drastically cuts into our fundamental rights and freedoms and, at the very least, comes perilously close to offending against the Constitution.'

The Dread Act attempted to define the words 'Association' and 'Society' and went on to state that any such body whose members do, are required to do, or fail to do a variety of things 'is hereby declared an unlawful society'. Section 3 of the Act, although aimed at the Dreads, was worded in a manner which encompassed virtually every society, association, organisation, club, limited liability company, trade union, church, political party, etc., in the State while Section 13 gave the minister responsible the right by order to extend the categories and make unlawful any society which may have fallen outside the almost all-embracing folds of Section 3. These provisions paved the way for Section 9 of the Act which read: 'No proceeding, either criminal or civil, shall be brought or maintained against any person who kills or injures any member of an association or society designated unlawful, who shall be found at any time of day or night inside a dwelling house.'

The problem of the act in relation to Dreads was made more complex by the fact that the Dreads were not really members of any association and were only called, or identified as Dreads by the way they looked, most notably the length and style of their hair. 'Where long hair is a shooting matter' screamed a headline in the liberal British newspaper *The Guardian* 'Licence to Kill' said the *Trinidad Express*. But with general elections less than four months away, the Dread Act had its intended political effect as the people found protection in the tough measures it proposed.

One afternoon in November 1974, only days after the passage of the Dread Act, a retired Canadian couple, Mr and Mrs Bright, who had settled here and built a house at Pont Casse, returned home from a shopping trip to Roseau. The Brights were brutally murdered on arrival and their house was set ablaze with their bodies inside it. In spite of wild accusations, the case has never been satisfactorily explained. With unaccustomed journalistic speed, *The Educator* printed a vivid cover story on the incident the following day and the tragedy was added to the wild spiral of unnerving events causing increased tension.

On 24 March 1975 Dominicans went to the polls. Since the general elections of 1970 the number of constituencies had been increased from 11 to 21 and this time four parties contested: the DLP, the DFP, the Progressive Labour Party and the small Caribbean Federal Party. There were ten independent candidates, and since only the DLP fielded a whole team of 21, the total number of candidates contesting amounted to 61.

With the Dread issue considered to be the State's main problem during the last months of 1974 and early 1975 this overshadowed the many other subjects covered in the various party manifestos. The DLP concentrated its attack on the Freedom Party, its main contender, with particular emphasis on its leader Eugenia Charles. A front page editorial in *The Educator* the week before elections headlined 'Danger Lady' can be classed as one of the most vicious character assassinations in Dominica's political history. With a team of mainly new, younger men promoted as a 'dynamic combination', Patrick John's DLP swept up 16 of the 21 seats, with three going to the DFP and two to independents.

Given the background against which the elections were contested, the results were no surprise. The DFP had still not yet cultivated a sufficiently strong base to swing the mass Labour voters. The party leader, as in most elections, is the key to how the electorate views the party they support and in the Caribbean, voters tend to vote along party lines as if each island is one whole constituency. Patrick John was presented as a man of action at a time of crisis and his decisive moves and virulent speeches on platform and radio, backed on the surface by a new team to give a fresh start for those who were beginning to have doubts about Le Blanc's regime, all pointed in the DLP's favour.

John's background contained the traditional pre-requisites for a popular Caribbean leader. Born of poor parents in Roseau who made sacrifices to provide his education, John later became a school teacher and trade union leader through the DTU and his formation of WAWU. He was a keen sportsman and held his first major political post as Mayor of Roseau where he got into trouble for questionable financial dealings. This did not prevent him from winning a seat in the 1970 general elections when he was appointed a minister in Le Blanc's cabinet before progressing to leadership. His close and dedicated supporters were part of that steady progress; neighbourhood friends, pupils, sportsmen, union members and many more who identified themselves with his easygoing open nature which contributed so much to his popularity. For the most part John surrounded himself with people whom he knew he could control and was wary of those who, through their superior acumen, appeared to be a threat. One of those was Michael Douglas, Minister of Agriculture, Lands, Fisheries and Co-Operatives in John's first cabinet. He was to find, like Ronald Armour before him, that their relationship was never to be a comfortable one. In this election Eugenia Charles won the Roseau Central seat and a new phase of politics began as she replaced Antony Moise as Leader of the Opposition.

With the election won, John still had the Dreads to deal with and he continued his broad offensive against all those assumed to be associated with this group. However his racial attacks upon a white Dominican appointed to the Opposition side of the House was in peculiar contrast to the climate of harmony he was claiming to be attempting to achieve.

The activities of the security forces were intensified. The Volunteer Defence Force had been embodied from August 1974 onwards and worked with the police and a unit of special constables in combing suspected areas of the island. The most violent group of Dreads totalling about a dozen were encamped in the Jacko area in the forest west of Belles, still known by the name of the eighteenth century Maroon Chief. Caves in the area called Vante Zara and huts made of forest palms were being used as shelters for this group of Dreads. The adverse conditions which had confronted the Rangers and soldiers in the 1780s bedevilled the twentieth century forces also; the rugged terrain, the darkness of the thick understorey of the rain forest, even at midday, and the constant humidity and rain.

During one clash in the forest near Belles, Defence Force member Registe was shot and killed. At the mammoth funeral service held next day at the Roseau Cathedral, Dominican priest Fr Edward Alexander spoke out on the whole pathetic state of the society but he was a lone voice. At a time when the Premier was stating that he would 'fight fire with fire' it was unpopular to talk of reconciliation.

On 13 November 1975 an act for the establishment of a full-time Defence Force was passed. Its role was to maintain the integrity of the boundaries of Dominica, to assist the police force in the maintenance of law and order during civil disturbance and to assist with relief at times of national disaster as well as to 'assist with the development of Dominica by productive means'. Patrick John assumed the rank of Colonel of the Force. The act provided for a Defence Board to be responsible for the command, discipline and administration of the Force but this did not extend to its operational use. As Colonel and Prime Minister, thereby in charge of security, John began a very personal control over the Force and the activities of its members.

By 1978 the working and organisation of the Force was cause for concern. The state of discipline was a shambles; conditions at barracks were appalling; there was sexual laxity between officers and certain members of the women's auxiliary corps which led to resentment among the lower ranks; key officers and private soldiers smoked marijuana together; few of the senior officers had any academic qualification; and storage and use of ammunition and equipment did not conform to the standards of a military force. This shocking state of affairs was exposed in the report of an enquiry conducted that year. But the political nature of the force, with officers confident that they were immune from disciplinary action, ensured that the main recommendations of the commissioner were never carried out nor was the report published during John's regime.

With the Dread scare abated by 1976, the Force's main occupation was volleyball and band practice on the barracks compound. Halfhearted attempts at agriculture and livestock-rearing were never maintained. Worse perhaps, were the deep divisions which emerged between the Defence Force and the Police. Already the enquiry had noted that there had not been any contact with the police to plan future operations and this division became worse as John increasingly favoured the Defence Force over the Police and aligned DDF officers closer to the ruling party.

The Dreads were now a minor concern, the core at Belles had cooled down, legislation had been passed against the wearing of grass skirts and other such fibrous material, a number had been jailed under the Dread Act, or for growing and being in possession of marijuana, and there was a general mood of reassurance among the population.

In late August 1975 a Commission of Enquiry had been appointed to investigate the whole Dread problem and to report on an eight-point terms of reference. An amnesty which was to end on 31 August was extended to 16 September and then to 30 September to allow the Commission to work under conditions favourable to meeting as many youth as possible. In the circumstances, interviews and meetings were conducted in a variety of places including Belles, Roseau, out-lying villages and the prison. It was found that the numbers believed to be in the hills had been greatly exaggerated and that the dissatisfied youth were of three types: the peaceful counter-culture group, the political activists and the criminal element. Although accepting the reasons for passing the Dread Act at the time, the main recommendation was that it should be revised to become a 'Terrorist Act' concentrating on terrorism generally rather than relating to societies and physical appearance. But government considered the report weak and too conciliatory and the recommendations on legislation were only carried out in the midst of another crisis in 1981.

The main Dread incident after the 1974–75 period was the offensive against one Galloway alias 'Tumba' who, along with others, kidnapped two girls from Portsmouth and held them in their camp on the slopes of Diablotin. The girls were rescued during a police raid and a search for Tumba resulted in his death.

At the end of the 1970s and in 1980 a small group of Dreads in the south of the island associated with Leroy Ettiene alias 'Pokosion' also became active. A villager was killed at Giraudel on the way to his garden and several months later another suffered the same fate at La Plaine. In March 1980 retired school teacher Maurice Laurent was murdered in his garden at Grand Bay. Only the killers of Laurent were found guilty but Pokosion continued to evade the law and even when he was eventually remanded to await trial, Hurricane David burst open the prison letting him free to continue his depredations.

The population was by now differentiating between Dreads and Rastas. Followers of the Jamaican Rastafarian movement looked to Ras Tafari Makonen, known best as Selassie of Ethiopia, as 'the elect of God, conquering Lion of Judah' and the hope of African redemption. There is no definite creed for the Rastas and for some it is a fashion rather than a lifestyle. Most smoke marijuana but for the most part maintain peace with the society and are vegetarians, avoiding shellfish and meat, particularly pork. Processed or salted food is suspect and they prefer 'I-tal,' natural grains, fruit, roots and vegetables. Some shun work while others are farmers and fine woodcarvers and craftsmen. The police and the corruption of modern society is 'Babylon' and they hope one day to find peace in 'Zion'. The spread of reggae music which helped popularise the Rastafari has influenced youth throughout the Caribbean and in the West Indian centres in Europe and North America.

Union Unrest

The 1970s were characterised by the near total breakdown of relations between government and the Public Service. Suspicions and bitter ill feeling on both sides led to a series of stiff legislative measures and cases of victimisation on one hand, and disputes and industrial action on the other. An unpopular Civil Service Act, a politically loaded Public Service Commission, and a confusing run of wage negotiations from 1974 followed by failure to meet agreed payments, were the main grievances of the Civil Service Association. But these were interspersed with a whole range of lesser issues.

After the 1973 strike and related state of emergency, the next serious confrontation was in September 1976. It began with an incident at the PMH nurses' hostel where CSA executive members were discussing with a number of nurses the negotiations for implementation of the 1974 revision of salaries and specific matters relating to the nurses. The Minister for Health and others broke into the meeting and moved to evict the CSA officers from the hostel. The seventeen nurses involved were suspended. A six-day strike began which was supported by the entire civil service and resulted in the commencement of the new rates of pay.

But a more serious strike was called the following year to press for the payment of arrears in respect of the period 1974 to 1976. The mood of this confrontation was made worse by a typical public outburst from Premier John threatening imprisonment for those who went on strike. 'We have place for them,' he stated at a convention on the Newtown Savannah. 'Even if the prison overflow we going to jail them at the Cabrits.'

This only helped to inflame the workers further and strengthen the hand of the CSA. That strike lasted for forty-seven days during which the whole island was virtually shut down. No one attended at the port or at the airport, no scheduled flights came or went, a skeleton staff maintained the hospital. For almost seven weeks the Caribbean looked on amazed that it was possible for a country to do such a thing, but by relying on their own resources, the civil service and the country as a whole sat it out. Eventually government was forced to bargain and agreed to pay the amounts of 'back pay' due to the workers as well as for the period they were out on strike.

The question of wage levels and salary arrears however overflowed into successive administrations by which time the temper of negotiations had considerably improved. In 1981 government entered into certain agreements with the International Monetary Fund to enable it to meet conditions of public sector wage increases.

Satisfactory relations ensuring a good Civil Service, have become a prerequisite of steady growth. Speaking during the 1975 Budget debate, Miss Charles quoted Sir Arthur Lewis on the subject:

'Failure to establish systems of recruitment and promotion based on merit leads to inefficiency; failure to pay competitive salaries leads to corruption and failure to delineate the respective roles of professional administrators and of party politicians leads to confused decision making. Development planning is hardly practicable until a country has established a Civil Service capable of implementing plans.'

Two Tragedies

During that decade of social and political upheaval, the island was struck by two tragedies of providence. On 21 May 1975 an overloaded truck from the village of Morne Prosper with some 35 pilgrims aboard, bound for a 'Christ is the Answer Crusade' in Roseau, got out of control on a sharp bend and shot over a precipice. Twenty-eight men, women and children were hurled to their deaths. Throughout the night servicemen and volunteers searched for victims among the trees and branches on the cliff face. On the following day two huge funerals were held in Roseau, one at the Cathedral the other at the Pentecostal church.

During the hurricane season of 1977, days of torrential rain loosened the rocky hillside above the southern village of Bagatelle, sweeping tons of soil and debris through a section of the village, smashing and covering houses and killing eight villagers. In spite of Herculean efforts by police and volunteers, some of the bodies were never found. In both cases, the populace responded generously, offering assistance to the stricken families.

This whole string of events: the demonstrations, strikes, Dreads, acts of terrorism, political intrigue and natural disasters came as a sort of 'baptism by fire' for the fledgling State. From 1976 these dramas were played out upon the road to one of Dominica's last stages in constitutional reform – the move to full independence.

22
Towards Independence

The termination of association with Britain was requested by the Government of Dominica in 1976. The first official statement advocating separate independence was made on 29 August that year by Premier John at the annual convention of the ruling DLP in a statement called The Salisbury Declaration after the village where it was made.

At the time of the 1975 elections the DLP had favoured independence in federation with other territories. However, the opposition DFP objected to the government's policy of seeking termination under Section 10 (2) of the West Indies Act to be passed by an Order in Council approved in draft by the British Parliament. The DFP leader argued that since the independence question had not been a major issue in the 1975 election campaign, the government should instead proceed under Section 10 (1) of the Act. This provided for the holding of a national referendum on independence, a two-thirds majority of which would permit the unilateral termination of association regardless of the wishes of the British government.

A session of the House of Assembly in December 1976 at which it was formally announced by the quickly sworn in Acting Governor that termination under Section 10 (2) was being requested from Britain with effect from November 1977, was boycotted by the DFP on the grounds that this was a political matter and it was improper for the Governor to be involved. It was felt at the time that the Governor, Sir Louis Cools-Lartigue, himself realised this and gave an excuse for not attending, allowing Attorney General Leo Austin to be sworn in as Acting Governor for a brief period so as to make the Address. The DFP's request for a referendum on the independence issue questioning the type of new constitution, was rejected by government on the grounds that it would leave 'a whole trail of anti-British and racial feelings and bitterness in its wake.'

Intense political activity commenced as all parties rushed to propagate their various views on the matter. Rosie Douglas, waging his own campaign, formed a series of Independence Committees and helped to flood the House with vocal supporters of the government view when it met to discuss proposals in March 1977. After volatile debate, the House approved by 16 to three a motion proposing the termination of association. A preliminary meeting was then held that same month with the British Foreign and Commonwealth Officials in London to pave the way for a full constitutional conference in May.

At this conference, held at Marlborough House, both the DLP and the DFP representatives stated that they were in agreement on the principle of seeking independence, although the conference failed to resolve a number of serious differences between them on the details of the proposed constitution and on the method and timing of its introduction. The main point of contention was over the proposal by the DFP that Dominica should move to full republican status with a President as head of state rather than the British monarch. The government eventually accepted this but there were differing opinions on how the President should be chosen. The size and type of parliament was also a cause for dissent. The government had originally wanted two chambers one of which would be an upper house composed of senators. The DFP objected and finally a single chamber was adopted with nominated 'senators' being members of that one House of Assembly. Perhaps the DFP's most crucial demand related to the conduct of elections and

Delegates at the Constitutional Conference at Marlborough House, London, May 1977. From L to R: Dr Claudius Thomas, Eastern Caribbean High Commissioner; Vernon Shaw, Cabinet Secretary; Victor Riviere, Minister of Finance; Leo Austin, Attorney General; Richard Posnett, FCO adviser; Premier Patrick John; Michael Douglas, Minister of Communications and Works; Evans Luard MP, British Under-Secretary of State FCO; FCO official; EO Le Blanc; Eustace Francis; Arden Shillingford, future Dominica High Commissioner in UK; Lennox Honychurch; M Eugenia Charles, Leader of the Opposition; Antony Moise.

their proposal for a politically balanced Electoral Commission was eventually adopted. The requirements for citizenship and other more general sections of the proposed constitution also received lengthy consideration. It was accordingly stated by Mr Evan Luard, the Under Secretary of State for Foreign and Commonwealth Affairs, who chaired the conference, that inter-party discussions should be resumed in Dominica and that a further process of consultation might be necessary if these failed to produce broad agreement.

Because of the inconclusive outcome of the constitutional conference as well as internal problems, the government put back its target date for independence from November 1977 to 'early 1978'. The Assembly again voted in favour of termination of association in October by 16 votes to five. Copies of a paper summarising the government's constitutional proposals were circulated and intensive use was made of the radio. Without recourse to the radio, the DFP embarked on 'Independence Seminars.' Using charts and distributing their 'Think it Over' booklet, the DFP went from village to village discussing the constitution and independence generally. This activity was heightened by heated parliamentary debate on a motion of no confidence in the Government moved by Leader of the Opposition Miss Charles in October 1977. The debated lasted for six weeks ending just before Christmas, airing every shred of bitterness between the two main parties.

By early 1978 some progress had been made however in resolving the areas of difference relating to the Independence Constitution. Mr Richard Posnett, dependent territories adviser for the British government, visited Dominica in May 'to discuss the remaining issues and to form an assessment of the state of public opinion.' Mr Posnett's report published in July 1978 concluded that while further progress in narrowing the constitutional differences between the two parties seemed unlikely, the constitution proposed by the DLP government was a good one, containing substantial safeguards. Mr Posnett recalled the agreement by both parties on the principle of independence in May 1977 adding: 'There is no doubt in my mind that in this they correctly reflected the views and aspirations of their people. I met no more than one or two people who were opposed to independence as such.'

On 12 July a resolution requesting and consenting to the order for termination was passed by the Dominica Assembly. On 21 July it was debated in the British House of Commons. Mr Luard stated that the British government accepted the main finding of Mr Posnett's report that 'the majority of the people did want independence and there was no major movement against it, though there might be doubts on particular points.' Mr Luard added that given the majority votes in the Dominica House of Assembly in favour of termination of association, he was satisfied that termination under Section 10 (2) procedure had the consent and support of the people of Dominica. Mr Luard said moreover that in view of Britain's minimal duties in connection with its responsibility for Dominica's defence and external affairs, 'it can truthfully be said that termination of association will amount to very little more than the formalisation of the status quo.' On 24 July it was debated in the House of Lords and the formal Order was made on the following day.

Under the constitution 'the executive authority of Dominica' was vested in the President, but in the exercise of most of his executive functions the President is required to 'act in accordance with the advice of the Cabinet or a minister acting under the general authority of Cabinet.' In the appointment of a Prime Minister the President is required to choose 'an elected member of the House who appears to command the support of the majority of the elected members of the House', other cabinet ministers being appointed by him on the advice of the Prime Minister. Ministers are required to be members of the House of Assembly, and it is laid down that not more than three appointed senators could hold ministerial office.

The Constitution makes provision for the protection of fundamental rights and freedoms and provides for the appointment of a Parliamentary Commissioner or ombudsman to investigate allegations of administrativ· injustice. Among the various statutory commissions provided for in the

Dignitaries attending an Independence Day Rally at the Botanic Gardens, 3 November 1978. L to R: Interim President, Sir Louis Cools-Lartigue; Lord Napier; HRH Princess Margaret; Lady-in-waiting; Mrs Desiree John; Prime Minister Patrick John; Ted Rowlands MP, British Foreign and Commonwealth Affairs.

constitution was the Public Service Commission and an Electoral Commission, a balanced appointed board as proposed by the DFP which would oversee the conduct of elections.

The Independence Constitution took effect on 3 November 1978, the 485th anniversary of the sighting of Dominica by Christopher Columbus. The Queen of the United Kingdom was represented by her sister Princess Margaret at the formal ceremony marking the transfer of the Constitution and the raising of the new flag based on a design by artist Alwyn Bully of seven colours upon a forest green background.

Dominica was the only former British territory in the Caribbean to move immediately to full republican status. In an attempt to avoid further complications over the similarity of names with the Spanish speaking Dominican Republic, the island assumed the formal nomenclature of The Commonwealth of Dominica.

Colonel John, who became the island's first Prime Minister, stated in his speech at the ceremony that his Government would respect citizens' rights to 'life, liberty and pursuit of happiness', that an independent Dominica would adopt a non-aligned foreign policy of support for 'the Third World in its struggle for social and economic justice', and that it was the government's intention to have neither 'a state-owned economy nor a capitalist monopoly'.

The longstanding disagreements between the DLP and the Opposition were emphasised when Miss Charles delivered her speech at the ceremony held before thousands at the Windsor Park in Roseau. Likening Dominica to a traveller setting out upon a journey carrying a few basic supplies inherited from its colonial past, she accused the Government of 'not yet having learned its lesson of democracy from the mother country' and of attempting to rig elections and to curtail the freedom of speech.

Under a transitional provision of the Constitution, the last Governor, Sir Louis Cools-Lartigue, became interim President pending discussions between John and Miss Charles on the nomination of a new President. The DFP nominee John Bully was however rejected by the government, necessitating a contested election in the House of Assembly in December which was won by the DLP's nominee Fred E Degazon. He was formerly in the regional colonial civil service and had been Speaker of the Dominica House of Assembly in which capacity his conduct had dismayed the listening public. President Degazon was sworn in on 22 December. His period of office on the island was however only to last for five months. Early one morning the following June, during a national crisis, he fled Dominica and sat out eight more months of his Presidency as an exile in England, finally resigning the post in February 1980.

The DLP's post-independence economic policy was defined by Colonel John in 1977 as 'New Socialism' based on three main sectors, public,

Patrick John parading in his Colonel's outfit takes the salute next to Governor Sir Louis Cools-Lartigue at a rally.

Prime Ministers Oliver Seraphin and Tom Adams of Barbados.

private and co-operative, providing scope for mixed ownership between these sectors. He added that 'under new socialism we shall ensure that natural resources are locally owned and controlled and therefore exploited for the benefit of the nation as a whole.'

In reality Dominicans were soon to learn of deals which handed over vast tracts of land with sweeping powers of control to foreign corporations. The island's economic position at independence showed that it would be obliged to depend heavily on external aid funds to finance its economic development for the foreseeable future. There was a persistent serious shortfall in the government's revenues as against its expenditure to meet the basic expenses of running the country. One of the main arguments in favour of independence was that it would open up greater avenues of international aid. In the words of one local journalist 'enabling us to become better beggars with more people to beg from.'

After Independence a new section of society developed, similar to the enclaves which dot the capitals of all Third World states: The Foreign Experts. Ironically the number of expatriates involved in the running of the country after independence rose out of all proportion to those few colonial officials who had served here before. House rents rose also as consultants, advisers, technocrats, contractors and writers of reports replaced one another in the more desirable residences of Goodwill, Canefield and Belfast. These helpful international transients accounted for the marked rise in the white population as reflected in the census of 1981.

Independence itself could not change the scale or style of 'small island politics' based on personalities and minor issues which were blown up into major affairs of State. By 1978 there had developed a sort of 'elective dictatorship' whereby the House of Assembly became largely in the hands of the government Cabinet machine so that the government controlled the parliament and not the parliament the government. More and more, debate where it was not actually stifled was becoming a ritual interrupted by abuse and catcalls. Politics had become a matter of which shops got business, who you spoke to, who got land or low cost houses, who could evade certain taxes under certain regulations, which newspaper got advertisements, who got jobs, who was promoted or whose truck got hired. In an island where jobs were limited and opportunities scarce, people bent to such a system. Even the Governor and for a time the President had been reduced to a tool in the hands of the Cabinet for in most cases his position as head of state often permits the holder of this mainly ceremonial office little independence or choice. However there is great scope for the President to use his supposedly apolitical position to heal social and political wounds, encourage dialogue and become a harmonious link between the different groups and forces in society.

The style of government, the method of the political party system and the whole economic process was giving rise to the demand by vocal left-wing elements for a totally new order based roughly on Marxist socialism. This internal movement was assisted by international events most notably the activities of Cuba and, after March 1979, the events in Grenada.

The Movement for a New Dominica, MND, which began in the early seventies, later consolidated itself into a full-fledged political party, The Dominica Liberation Movement Alliance linking smaller groups such as L'eshelle of Grand Bay into one national organisation. University graduates, Dr William 'Para' Riviere, Atherton Martin, Ron Green and Bernard Wiltshire were among those who spearheaded the Alliance, appealing to persons disillusioned with the whole system of 'old politics'. 'One of the fundamental reasons for our existence is that the existing "system" does not operate to the benefit of the broad masses of people in the country.' In the same statement, published in *Twavay* in March 1974, while still operating as the MND they decried the existing parties: 'It is this kind of politics we call "old politics" – old farcical politics! These political parties only have interest in the masses of the people when election time is around and afterwards completely forget them . . . In an organisation like ours, we must be first and foremost servants of the people . . . This can only be done if we immerse ourselves among the people, listening attentively to their complaints and reasoning out with them in dialogue the best way possible of overcoming these obstacles. We must not go to them armed with solutions to all their problems but merely as a guide.'

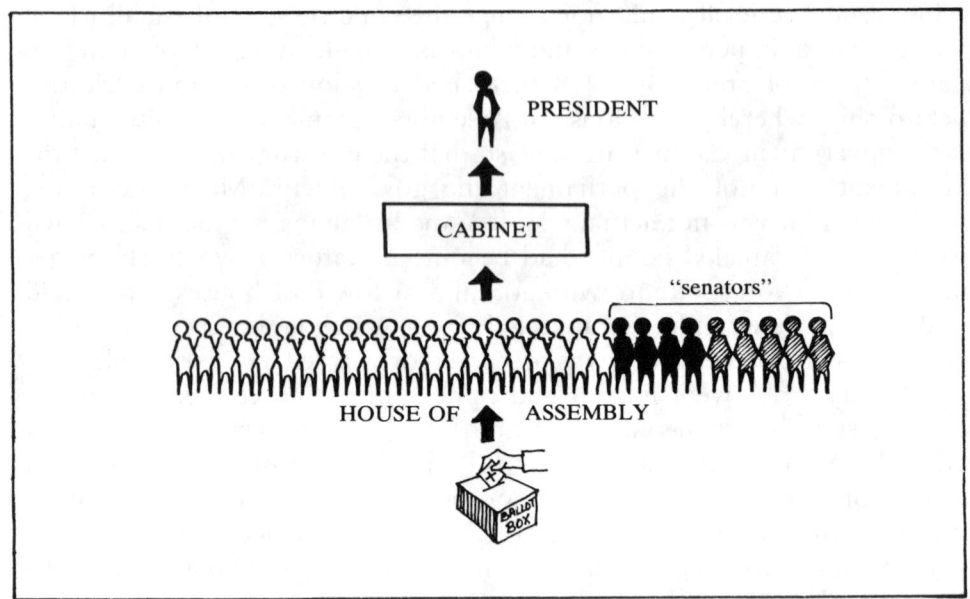

Diagram of the parliamentary system of the Independence Constitution of 1978.

Dominicans were not as unaware of the notion of socialism as some other Eastern Caribbean islands. When the DLP was formed in 1955 by Phyllis Allfrey it was made clear that the party would be guided by what she called 'Tropical Socialism'. Patrick John unveiled his 'New Socialism'. The socialist orientation of the DLMA claimed that it was not just a repeat of those types of social reformism but a non-capitalist alternative which would be developed in stages. Yet as time wore on, the DLMA leadership realised that even they had to work on bridging the gap between the international Marxist text book solutions and the small island realities of trade, free enterprise and the general desire for electoral democracy.

The development of a left-wing movement similar to those groups existing in St Vincent and Antigua, added a new dimension to post-Independence politics of Dominica. It was another strand in the complex web of forces which encompassed the young nation at the dawn of that decisive year – 1979.

23
A Stormy Path

Within months of independence the pressures on the DLP government were severe. Not only had its conduct and methods of administration created cause for public concern, but the whole internal party machinery had broken down as a small section of the Cabinet, notably John and Leo Austin, were dictating affairs of the DLP and the state.

The tragedy of the DLP was that its early promise had been allowed to fade. More attention had been given to reaping the fruits of government than to nurturing the roots of the party planted throughout the country villages during the 1950s and 1960s. The final destruction of the party started almost from the day Patrick John took over leadership in 1974. John exploited its popularity rather than nurtured it. Party branches became inactive and ceased to exist. The executive tended only to meet if there was a crisis. As a product of Roseau, John increasingly surrounded himself with a clique of town-based friends and business speculators seeking crumbs from the table of power and giving self-interested advice which only drove the leadership and the party further down the road of self-destruction. John's use of a string of titles including Colonel, Comrade and Doctor of Metaphysics was a topic of derision.

The DLP's ideological leanings were also very puzzling to foreign observers who did not understand the tendency to skip from one position to the other depending on the mood of the moment. Some uncertainty surrounded the John government's policy towards the left wing of Caribbean politics, represented notably by Cuba and Guyana. On the one hand the DLP had supported the activities of the Dominica-Cuba Friendship Association led by Rosie Douglas and was continuing to strengthen its relations with the Guyanese ruling party of Forbes Burnham, leading to allegations that it was the DLP's aim to introduce Guyanese-style socialism to Dominica. On the other hand, however, in January 1978, John had dismissed two Cabinet Ministers, Michael Douglas (Rosie's brother) and Ferdinand Parillon, accusing them of communist tendencies and had spoken of a communist plot to take over the island after independence.

The Douglas brothers will probably go down in history as interesting phenomena of Dominican politics during the late twentieth century. Both have been political mavericks who between them have formed or been members of at least ten political parties, associations or political movements between 1974 and 1984. Their political base at Portsmouth provided them with the independence to re-emerge from every crisis during that decade.

John's supporters cite his achievements as those of leading the island to independence in 1978, destroying what one foreign pro-John newspaper described as 'a potentially explosive force – the black power, Red-controlled Dread terrorist movement,' and encouraging relations with the United States, France, West Germany, Venezuela and several other 'friendly nations'. Under his administration Dominica assumed membership of a number of international organisations including the United Nations and IMF.

Even before independence, his constant visits abroad were causing criticism not so much for the number of trips but the costs incurred by the large entourage of other ministers and of officials which he carried along with him. By 1979, some of the people who were consulted during such visits, and the deals agreed upon, contributed to local unrest and became international news resulting in a series of disclosures which hastened the government's decline.

The Free Port Fiasco

Early on in John's premiership he began to associate with a Barbadian called Sydney Burnett-Alleyne, a self-declared international mercenary and gun runner. Along with Leo Austin, they hatched a plan which they estimated would turn Dominica into a boom centre for commerce and tourism. The money for this development would be obtained by Alleyne and others from various undetermined business sources and channelled through Alleyne's newly-formed Mercantile Bank with offices in Bridgetown, Barbados. The Bank would provide the money to a development corporation set up by Austin. Alleyne needed to show his prospective clients his development area, so over 400 acres of the best agricultural and beach land around Woodford Hill was compulsorily acquired. Here, the corporation was to build a jet airport, hotels and near Portsmouth, an oil refinery.

Much smaller deals of this kind had been mooted since the 1960s when an American resident, Bruce Robinson, formed the Sunday Island Port Authority (SIPA) with plans to cut the Cabrits headland off from the rest of the island by means of a canal and set up a Bahamas-style free port, dock and jet airport. The required investment was not forthcoming and it was followed by another similar effort called Valhalla.

The Alleyne free port scheme of 1975 made little headway and created only a slight stir. There were articles in the Bajan papers, a few heated exchanges in the Dominica and Barbados Houses of Assembly and a bit of embarrassment to the then Prime Minister of Barbados Errol Barrow. But

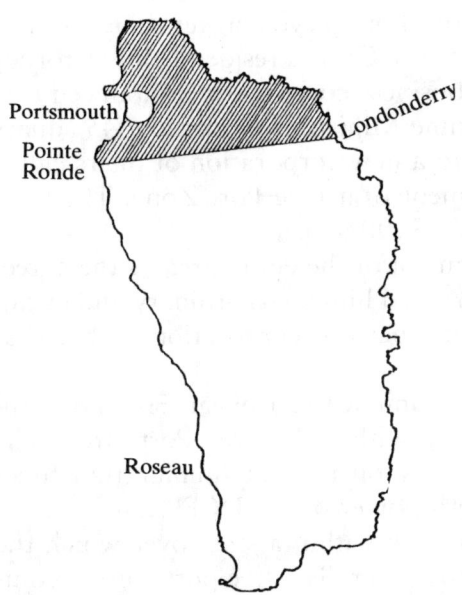

The shaded area on the map shows the 45 square miles of the island handed over to Don Pierson's Caribbean Southern Corporation by the DLP regime.

Don Pierson, President of Caribbean Southern Inc with the corporation's symbol composed of a corruption of the National Coat of Arms.

having found a foothold in Dominica, Sydney Burnett-Alleyne began to use his ties with John and Austin to embark on his own personal adventures and thereby got John into a lot of trouble. Alleyne made an abortive attempt to sail to Barbados with arms. He was intercepted off Martinique and imprisoned. Later Austin was to get Dominica involved with a company known as Planet Earth Development and Finance, soon renamed the Federal Bank of Dominica with a one-room office in Cheshire, UK. In September 1978, after serving time in a Martinique jail, Alleyne was contacting a Major John Banks in England and commissioned him to draw up invasion plans for Barbados, where Alleyne's arch enemy Tom Adams had become Prime Minister. According to Alleyne, the take off point for this invasion was to be Dominica. The British Special Branch had information of meetings between Major Banks and John in London in December 1978 and the signing of another development plan agreement between Alleyne and John followed by a celebration party thrown by Major Banks.

John has strongly denied his involvement with any plan to assist or provide cover for the invasion of Barbados, but Alleyne declared on British television that 'My life is dedicated to this. We will topple Tom Adams.' Alleyne however continued to involve John, Austin and Finance Minister Vic Riviere with a series of dubious individuals who all hoped to benefit from the bizarre plans intended for Dominica.

Meanwhile John and Austin had moved on to even bigger things. In late February 1979, Don Pierson and his son Grey, President and Attorney respectively of an undisclosed Texan business corporation announced that they had signed an agreement with Prime Minister John leasing 45 square miles of Dominica's northern district to a new corporation of theirs called Caribbean Southern for the establishment of a Free Port Zone. The lease would last 99 years at a charge of only $100 a year.

Pierson would have virtually full control of the entire area as the agreement, secretly signed on 9 February, granted him 'extraordinary and exclusive rights and powers to authorise any person, corporation or business entity to operate'.

The agreement stated further: 'The Dominica Caribbean Free Port Authority shall be responsible for security within the Free Port Area. The Commonwealth of Dominica shall be responsible for immigration functions within the area subject to the veto-power of the DCFPA.'

This was in effect the creation of a state within a state over which the people of Dominica would have had no power. The free port zone encompassed 40% of the cultivated agricultural land of Dominica and over one third of the island's population. Coming as it did just three months after the attainment of independence this sellout to foreign interests made a mockery of the speeches, functions and flag raisings which Dominicans had witnessed on 3 November the previous year. It was a blatant example of the fragility of these small island states.

In spite of the Piersons' PR campaign and in the face of Patrick John's repeated speeches on how good the free port would be for Dominica, the people united in their condemnation of the project. After public meetings by the Farmers Union, Freedom Party and other political groups a giant rally was planned in Roseau to protest against the deal. On 4 May, three days before the march was expected to take place, John wrote Pierson cancelling the deal. Just days after strongly defending the scheme John stated: 'From the reactions of the landowners, farmers, legislators, leaders of the people and the churches both in the area and throughout Dominica as a whole, it is now quite clear that you will not be able to obtain the lands since the people in the north, by their public protests and appeals to me, have shown that they do not wish a free port in the area and will not lend their lands to the Free Port Authority.'

It was some days later that a copy of a letter from Leo Austin to the Minister Commercial of the South African embassy in London became public. It was dated 6 February and copied to Burnett-Alleyne. It stated that 'On behalf of the Government of The Commonwealth of Dominica, I hereby express agreement of my Government to enter into building relations with your Government . . . to enable those priority Projects as herein listed or from time to time to be carried out immediately.'

Those projects which were agreed upon were described in the letter as 'the promotion, stockpiling, a re-sale and refining of crude oil and petrochemical products to meet the needs and exigencies of our respective countries.' It was significant that the date given by Austin for the commencement of the Dominica deal with the South Africans was 9 February, the same day as the signing and the commencement of the free port agreement. A South African Government statement issued on 15 August 1979 confirmed that the South African embassy had dealt with 'persons professing to be the accredited representatives of the authorities of Dominica' whom it had referred to 'private sector concerns.'

The 29 May Crisis

The cancellation of the free port did little to relieve John of pressure from the public. He now faced renewed warnings from the Dominica Civil Service Association of its refusal to make further concessions in its negotiations for wages and salary increases. The civil servants intended to strike as from 1 June in demand for what government estimated would be EC$16 million or four times the pay-out in 1977 following a 47 day strike. Now the civil servants warned of 'the longest ever strike'.

On top of this there was an islandwide protest against two controversial Bills to be tabled in the House of Assembly on 29 May. The Industrial Relations (Amendment) Act was aimed at severely limiting the right to strike among civil servants and workers in essential services. It sought to prevent persons from giving financial assistance to striking unions and workers. It was to establish a permanent tribunal which the unions were against.

There was also an amendment to the Libel and Slander Act making it mandatory for newspaper editors to disclose the identities of anonymous writers who published articles critical of a person in his professional or official capacity. This was aimed at protecting Leo Austin who had been facing widespread criticism in the local press over his foreign deals and his handling of official duties while at the same time working for private clients dealing with the government.

After two weeks of intense campaigning by opposition forces, some 10,000 demonstrators appeared around the House of Assembly at Government Headquarters on the morning of 29 May.

The peaceful demonstration began with police wandering easily through the crowd. Opposition members were cheered as they entered, government members were jeered and jostled. The Defence Force arrived, tear gas was fired, people scattered. In anger people hiding in the back alleys, their faces covered with damp cloths, threw stones at the army and the cement and glass building which towered above the surrounding slums.

Then the Defence Force opened fire. There were no rubber bullets, the shots were not fired in the air. Standing in the centre of the car-park the gunmen sprayed the square with their lethal ammunition. One youth, Phillip Timothy, fell dead, shot through the hip, and was carried into government headquarters. Ten others suffered bullet wounds, four of them, including a 13-year-old boy, were critically injured.

Amidst shouts, cries, gunfire and the sound of stones smashing against the building, the House commenced its sitting. The mood was made more dramatically sombre by the dark clouds and heavy rain. News filtered into the Assembly that a youth lay dead downstairs and that several others had been shot.

The Opposition Leader, Eugenia Charles protested against the meeting of the House under such conditions but the Prime Minister was adamant, the Bills must be passed, whatever happens, he declared. The opposition walked out and the revolt against the government began. All trade unions and businesses immediately went on strike and resolved to close the whole island down until the government resigned.

The Caribbean listened to each new development like the enraptured audience of a radio soap opera series. Every day another startling development took place. The first minister to resign was Oliver Seraphin who had been absent from the 29 May sitting of the House due to ill health. In his statement, Seraphin confirmed the relations with South Africa and Sydney Burnett-Alleyne and decried the continued association with Austin. He continued, in his resignation letter to John: 'I paid the political penalties by being maligned, for my so-called boldness, in bringing to the attention of

A section of the thousands of demonstrators gathered around Government Headquarters on 29 May 1979.

Cabinet the alarming developments of which most Cabinet colleagues were ignorant. You then, it is reported, openly expressed a desire to eliminate me politically . . . ' Shortly afterwards, Seraphin, Francis and others announced the formation of The Democratic Labour Party of Dominica.

The President, Fred Degazon, and his wife fled the island at dawn on 11 June for England without informing anyone. The retired Governor Sir Louis Cools-Lartigue agreed, at John's request, to become Acting President only to resign less than 24 hours later after being pressured to do so by his family and by stone-throwing incidents and looting around his family's house and cake shop.

Civilian guards assisted the police in security patrols. Road blocks made of boulders, old cars, trees and even boats were set up to monitor the movement of traffic across the island. There were some thirty road blocks in the north alone. The coasts were watched. Suspicious sightings were reported to The Committee for National Salvation members, mobilising patrols. Shops of staunch Patrick John supporters were looted in anger after it was suspected that his supporters had set the Court House and Registry building on fire on 16 June. Still Patrick John broke the silence of strike-bound DBS radio to make angry speeches and to repeat the words 'I shall not resign'. Every verbal attack launched against opposition members only angered his listeners further. The withdrawal of Leo Austin from office had no effect. Tempers rose, more ministers resigned.

After clearing the streets with tear gas and gunfire, the DDF squad, surrounded by stones thrown by protestors, reassembles on Kennedy Avenue to stand guard on Government Headquarters while the government members of the Assembly continue their meeting in the chamber above.

In the midst of these developments a spirit of unity gripped the people of Dominica. It was such a mood that brought about the formation of the Committee for National Salvation (CNS). The Left, the moderates, the church, the business sector, the farmers, the unions all joined in this organisation of 28 which for some 20 days acted as the *de facto* parliament of Dominica.

There were moments when tempers flared among Committee members. The debate on constitutional or non-constitutional solutions saw the most argument. Emotional Left wing elements accused the Opposition Freedom Party of a 'sellout' when Eugenia Charles agreed to link with the remnants of the battered Labour Party to form a constitutional Assembly under the Prime Ministership of Oliver Seraphin.

In the last days of the crisis, Dominicans got a crash course in constitutional law as laymen stood on street corners debating clauses and provi-

The Committee for National Salvation (CNS) a broad-based organisation representing every sector of the Dominican community. The Committee was set up to bring a speedy end to the political crisis. Seated left to right: Sheridan Gregoire (DEF); Pamela Liburd, Bernie Didier (Social League); AF Joseph (DAWU); Louis Benoit (WAWU); Pierre Charles (Youth Council); Percival Marie (CSA). Standing left to right: Norris Charles (DAWU); Julius Sampson (DAIC); Charles Maynard (Church Council); Norman Rolle (DEF); Lloyd Pascal (Youth Council); Rosie Douglas (NDAP); Bernard Nicholas (partially hidden – DTU); Fr Huysmans (Church Council); Eugenia Charles (Freedom Party); Milton Eloi (NWU); Mike Douglas (LM); Brian Alleyne (Freedom Party); Charles Savarin (CSA); Curtis Augustus (WAWU); Athie Martin and Alvin Armantrading (Farmers Union); Julius Timothy (DAIC); Rawlings Jemmot (NWU); Bernard Wiltshire (DLMA).

sions allowing for the swearing in of a new Acting President or the lack of an official Leader of the Opposition. Due to the astute chairmanship of CSA Union leader Charles Savarin, the Committee was able to ride out its more stormy moments and find a solution acceptable to all sides except, understandably, to the few remaining DLP members of the Assembly who had not resigned.

At 1.10 pm on 21 June, the resident Judge Winszey Bruno, acting on the advice of the Chief Justice, then in Antigua, swore in barrister-at-law Jenner Armour as Acting President. At 1.15 pm Armour swore in Oliver Seraphin as the new Prime Minister of Dominica. Minutes later Patrick John was officially informed that since he now failed to command the majority of members in the Dominica House of Assembly, his appointment as Prime Minister was thereby revoked. It was hailed as a 'constitutional coup'. *Caribbean Contact*, the monthly newspaper of the Caribbean Council of Churches headlined it a 'palace coup' but the Caribbean media generally welcomed the outcome as a victory for the people of Dominica.

Basically, Dominica was then governed by a multi-party coalition, intended as an interim government. Due to rather unique provisions in the constitution of 1978, the parliament of the Commonwealth of Dominica comprises one chamber in which there are twenty-one elected members and nine nominated members who are called 'senators'.

The twelve elected members who supported Seraphin as Prime Minister included Democratic Labour Party, Freedom Party members as well as independents. All of the nine former 'senators' resigned in order to vacate their seats in favour of persons chosen by the CNS. Three of these new senators were made ministers: Atherton Martin, Brian Alleyne and Charles Maynard.

The question of Leader of the Opposition is a confusing one to those who have not carefully followed the developments in Dominica. Now that the majority of elected members supported the interim government, the persons who still followed Patrick John were the largest group in opposition to the government in the House. However, Patrick John could not become Leader of the Opposition because the constitution provides that he, having won his seat in 1975 as a member of the party which won the largest number of seats in the House, could not qualify to be the official Leader of the Opposition. This provision is aimed at preventing the type of shift which occurred in St Vincent where Ivy Joshua, a member of the majority party became Leader of the Opposition so as effectively to deny the position to Son Mitchell. The Dominica Constitution provides that when such a vacancy exists, the President can act without a Leader of the Opposition.

Eugenia Charles preferred to sit as a backbencher, stating that if she took an administrative position in any government she would wish to do so only when the people had, by their votes, brought her party to power.

Hurricane David

The interim Government was barely two months old when one of the three most destructive hurricanes ever known to hit Dominica lashed its shores, stripped trees from its mountains and tore the fragile homes of its people apart. Only twice previously had such severe hurricanes struck the island. In the 1806 hurricane 131 people died mainly as a result of the Roseau river shifting its course and flooding the capital, and in the 'Great Hurricane' of 10 September 1834, widely acknowledged as the worst of all, over 200 lives were lost.

At first expected to hit Barbados, the hurricane, code-named David, shot across the southern section of Dominica on 29 August. There was little local radio warning and no operational systems for disaster preparedness. With swirling 150 mile-an-hour winds, David pounded Dominica for six hours from about 9.00 am. Thirty-seven people were killed and an estimated 5,000 injured, some requiring amputation of limbs. Three-quarters of the 75,000 population were left homeless with many others temporarily so, sleeping under rough cover in the open or huddled into the homes of more fortunate friends for weeks and months after the storm.

The Dominican economy was almost totally destroyed resulting in disastrous social and economic after effects. Roads and bridges were blocked and swept away. There was no electric power or piped water. The only contact with the outside world was Fred White's battery operated ham radio until other links were restored. The Commander of the Royal Navy frigate HMS *Fife* which arrived through mountainous waves to give relief next day, likened the scene to a bombed-out battlefield. Volunteers from the *Fife* began basic repairs to the hospital, worked on cleaning streets and restoring the radio and essential services. Its helicopter pilots working under dangerous conditions ferried the dead and wounded from isolated areas.

The plight of the Dominicans got swift attention from the region and the wider world. First medical personnel and supplies, then generating equipment, water purification apparatus, food, clothing and tents arrived mostly from the United States, Britain and Canada. Appeal and relief committees, such as the UK National Appeal for Dominica were formed by concerned West Indians and friends abroad. Caribbean countries, particularly Barbados, St Lucia and Antigua allowed temporary residence for scores of Dominicans who fled the island or who sent their children away until conditions improved. Heavy rains caused by the close passage of Hurricane Frederick on 4 September tore away what had already been loosened by the winds six days before.

The authorities grappled with restoring the island to some sort of normalcy. A food ration system was initiated. Foreign forces; contingents

Destruction on Bath Road, Roseau, 30 August 1979. Men from HMS Fife *begin clearing the street and citizens carry water.*

Victoria Street and Newtown the morning after Hurricane David showing the hillsides stripped of trees.

of the French Army, US Cee Bees and Royal Engineers set up camps here and assisted with relief efforts.

By November Prime Minister Seraphin estimated the pledges of assistance were at over US$37 million and that there was the probability of more in the long term. In addition to Canadian, American and British aid, there was assistance from the IMF, International Red Cross, the Non-Aligned Movement, the Organisations of American States, the EEC and Caribbean Community States among others.

As was to be expected, the distribution of relief to the thousands who needed it posed problems of control. There were accusations of gross irregularity and hoarding of materials particularly in the case of galvanised roofing sent by the US. After the initial tension of the first six months wore off, there was more intense manipulation of these supplies. A rift developed between USAID and Seraphin's DDLP after he ordered the Defence Force to remove hundreds of sheets of galvanise from USAID storerooms and distribute it for party political purposes.

Slowly the agricultural sector tried to recover. Farmers cleared the total devastation of their banana fields. Coconuts in the south were almost completely blown down but there was minor damage in the north except for the Concorde Valley, the alignment of which had funnelled winds from

Thousands of rough shacks, such as these at Morne Prosper, were made by destitute families out of the broken remains of their homes.

the south. The citrus trees appeared to have survived the hurricane best, owing to their small stature and robust nature. Roads along the coast were severely eroded and a major sea defence programme commenced. For months the island echoed with the sounds of chain saw, hammering and electric generators as the people attempted to rehabilitate themselves.

General Elections

The Committee for National Salvation had collapsed by the end of 1979. 'It was blown away by the winds of David,' said Oliver Seraphin. It was suggested by press reports that Mr Seraphin wanted to prolong the period before holding general elections to give his newly formed Dem-Lab time to consolidate itself and preside over the major reconstruction programmes funded by the international agencies. Already he was getting rid of the non Dem-Lab sections of his precarious coalition government. In October 1979 he dismissed Minister of Agriculture, Senator Atherton Martin for 'making public statements and pursuing ideological paths that have served to embarrass me and affect my image as head of the interim government.' In December, Ferdinand Parillon resigned from his post in protest against alleged interference in his responsibilities by Michael Douglas who had already taken on the duties of Agriculture as well as Finance, Trade and Industry.

In January 1980 letters of dismissal and resignation between Seraphin, and Brian Alleyne and Charles Maynard, crossed each other stating reasons for their parting.

During February 1980 pressure on government to call elections was intensified as unions, associations and church groups made demands to this effect. That same month, Acting President Jenner Armour resigned and announced his intention to contest the next general elections. Mr Aurelius Marie, a former magistrate, was then appointed President as the agreed nominee of all parties in the House of Assembly. This appointment had been made possible by the resignation in February also of President Degazon who had been in England since June 1979.

The Barbados Government had given valuable assistance with the preparation of new voters' lists and when elections were eventually called for 20 July 1980, there was general satisfaction that the voters' register was fair and correct.

The state of the parties facing that election showed varied fortunes. The DLP contested with no real chance of success. The party was deserted by those members who had any public credibility left after June 1979. According to the *Caribbean Quarterly* of the UWI: 'It had been reduced to a hotch-potch of political hangers-on and people with very tarnished public images.'

The Dem-Lab had never really been able to get itself together in time. Its leadership was made up of the more lucky survivors of the DLP collapse. A few post-David scandals including an agreement to sell Dominican passports to exiled Iranians at US$10,000 apiece did not improve its political fortunes. To quote *Caribbean Quarterly* again:

'In a sense Seraphin was thrown as a lamb to the slaughter when he was made Interim Prime Minister. He was given a government of rightists, centrists and leftists. The possibility of achieving the kind of balance which would have been necessary to make such a government function was virtually nil, given the inexperience and limited ability of Seraphin.' The Dem-Lab's colourful array of expensive campaign gimmicks, which included a huge helium-filled balloon, had no effect upon a hurricane-battered population who looked for a complete change. In the end Dem-Lab and the DLP ended up competing against each other for the same votes.

In spite of their repeated disapproval of the electoral system of Westminster-style politics, the Dominica Liberation Movement Alliance contested the elections for the first time in 1980. The mass of the people were generally sceptical of the DLMA's leftist ideology but they did not reject it outright either, for although the Alliance failed to win any seats, the small percentage of votes gained provided a foundation for future campaigning.

The Dominica Freedom Party had been working tirelessly since its second defeat in 1975. Eugenia Charles had attracted and given guidance and encouragement to a core of youth who complemented her expertise with their energy, assisting her with five years of ceaseless organisation and meetings, expanding the DFP base throughout the rural communities. In 1977 the Young Freedom Movement was founded and developed a network of village branches. Their task was made much easier as a result of the excesses carried on by the John administration. Miss Charles had stayed clear of association with the interim government, taking no risk of tarnishing the DFP's chances as a result of that government's performance.

On 20 July there was a 79.9% turnout among the electorate of 38,452. The atmosphere of the election campaign was described by *Caribbean Insight* as one of 'mutual animosity, with character assassination and blatant lies being bandied about.' The DFP took 17 seats with 52.34% of the votes. Neither the DLP nor the Alliance secured any seats and Dem-Lab won two, with the remaining seats going to two independent candidates, Conrad Cyrus and former Acting President Jenner B Armour. Both former Prime Ministers lost their seats.

Miss Charles became the Caribbean's first female Prime Minister and immediately set about repairing the internal and external damage which had been inflicted on Dominica by political mismanagement and natural disaster. She stated, after her formal appointment on 23 July, that the DFP was a 'liberal, democratic and anti-communist' party and that her government would pursue a non-aligned foreign policy seeking foreign investment in order to promote industrial development since the agricultural sector could not provide sufficient new jobs to overcome the country's serious unemployment problem.

Miss Charles assumed the portfolios of Finance, Foreign Affairs and Development and appointed five other ministers. Among them were two former members of the interim government, Brian Alleyne and Senator Charles Maynard. The immense task which faced this Cabinet involved not just the material rehabilitation and expansion of infrastructure and services but the restoration of confidence, discipline, pride, and an overall sense of national purpose among all Dominicans. These intangible psychological pre-requisites of development were at a depressingly low ebb in 1980.

Externally, foreign affairs was in a shambles. John's scandalous deals and associations had plunged the name of Dominica into disrepute and in spite of a whirl of post-David goodwill visits abroad, Seraphin lacked the time or diplomatic strength required to overcome this. International publicity over his government's sale of citizenship did not help either. Within months after the election Miss Charles had galvanised the Caribbean into taking a new opinion of Dominica and Dominicans and was steadily cementing international friendships so that by the middle of the 1980s Dominica and its Prime Minister Eugenia Charles had secured a position of high esteem within the councils of world affairs.

A Freedom Party motorcade during the 1980 general elections.

Kidnap and Subversion

Internally however, the DFP government was presiding over a society still racked by critical political divisions. The most bitter detractor was Patrick John, surrounded by a group of dedicated supporters including senior officers and persons from the lower ranks of the Defence Force who considered that their opportunities had been torn from them by a series of unfair events. After ten years of political skirmishing, Eugenia Charles was his arch enemy and he had vowed during the 1975 election campaign that if Dominicans ever made the mistake of electing her to power, he would ensure that 'every time she take one step forward, I will make sure she have to make two steps back.' And from 1980, this was the policy he pursued.

Miss Charles sought immediately to consolidate her position with the security forces by inspecting the Police and Defence Force the day after she was sworn in to office and to meet their members to outline areas of operation. The mood of the Defence Force was disinterested if not hostile. Soon she initiated measures designed to end party political bias within the DDF and to remove other undesirable elements from the Force, and a number of officers were sent on compulsory leave, apparently in connection with the trading of arms for drugs. The decision to carry out a weapons' inventory prompted demonstrations by soldiers who presented a list of

Prime Minister Eugenia Charles inspecting a detachment of the Defence Force on 24 July 1980, the day after taking office. She was already aware of the animosity among senior officers against her.

various grievances and demands of government. Anti-government sentiment within the DDF was supported by the Alliance, but more so by John who accused the Government of 'disarming' the Force in preparation for the declaration of a one-party state. During one lunch period when the rest of government headquarters was unoccupied, a group of Defence Force men entered the building and attempted to force their way into the Prime Minister's Office knowing that she was alone inside. In December 1980 Miss Charles ordered the transfer of all DDF weapons and ammunition to the police armoury where a full inventory was to be carried out. This was precipitated by indications that members of the Force were in regular contact with a group of Dreads encamped at Beline in the valley behind Giraudel. They were seen to be making frequent visits to the house of the late Eustace Francis at Gomier in the same area. Francis had died suddenly two months after the general elections and his house was being overseered by a junior member of the Defence Force.

One night during the same period, the Giraudel village co-operative shop was broken into and much of its stock stolen. These goods were transported in a vehicle to Francis' house and then were partly transferred by the Dreads to their camp at Beline. The President of the Co-operative which ran the shop was Giraudel farmer Ted Honychurch who was also a member of the village council, a former executive member of the Farmers Union, and father of Government's Press Secretary at the time, Lennox Honychurch. He reported the incident to the police and attempted to assist them with investigations.

Unstable conditions at Gomier and Giraudel had intensified during the month of January and there was a constant, and at times unexplained, movement of people and vehicles during the nights, to and from Francis' house and along the tracks behind Mr Honychurch's estate into the valley. Once when a police van was sighted, Mr Honychurch's former overseer was surrounded by armed men and interrogated about police movements.

Realising that the situation was far more complex than at first imagined, the police took time to act. At the same time they were noting the flurry of meetings being held between dissident DDF personnel and senior DLP supporters, but it was becoming almost impossible to relate the jig-saw puzzle of events and information into one clear pattern.

The police special squad decided to act on 12 February 1981 and moved in on the Gomier area at dawn. In the armed clash which followed, two Dread youth were killed and police recovered some of the stolen items as well as Defence Force uniforms before withdrawing to Roseau.

That afternoon, eight Dreads dressed in new green army fatigues, bearing 303 rifles and SLR machine guns surrounded Mr Honychurch's home. They killed his pet parrot and dog, seized him, his wife, cook and gardener and set the family's wooden bungalow ablaze. Had they planned to destroy a part of Dominica's heritage, they could not have made a better choice for the house was packed with a mass of historical material and articrafts as well as Mrs Honychurch's copious notes and drawings on the flora and herbal medicines of the Caribbean.

The kidnappers, under the leadership of Pokosion (Leroy Ettiene), marched their captives cross-country down into the valley at Beline. They accused Mr Honychurch of conniving with police, thus assisting with the deaths of their brethren that morning, and through his son, of plotting with Miss Charles against them. After several hours in the forest, they released his wife, the cook and gardener with a letter written by Mr Honychurch from their dictation to be delivered to the Attorney General Ronan David. It demanded a number of things to be done within three days in return for his release. These included the freeing from prison of two Dreads sentenced for the murder of teacher Maurice Laurent in 1980, and an inquiry into the squad raid of that morning and 'an end to police brutality'.

In a broadcast announcing a state of emergency on 13 February however, Miss Charles said that government 'cannot accept the requests made by the terrorists' and would discuss the kidnappers' demands only after they had released their hostage and surrendered their weapons. 'We know also that disgruntled politicians, completely rejected by the electors, are assisting the terrorists in an attempt to destabilise the country,' Miss Charles said.

The opposition parties reacted by issuing 'statements of concern' but accused Miss Charles of inflexibility. Mr John, who had made far more virulent broadcasts during his Dread offensives of 1974–75, criticised the

Edward 'Ted' Honychurch, 1923–1981.

terms of the Prime Minister's statement as likely to 'produce division and unnecessary retaliation'. With certain DDF personnel linked to the Dreads at Giraudel, and also seen to be acting in concert with the leadership of the DLP, it was likely that the issuers of that statement were not unaware of the situation surrounding the kidnap and the prevailing conditions at Gomier and Beline.

There had been a hope which lingered until May, that Mr Honychurch would have been released. But in early June one of the Dreads involved in the kidnap, Eric Joseph, admitted to killing Mr Honychuch during the night of 12 February, stating that he had shot him in a ravine after he had fatally stabbed one of his captors in an escape attempt. Honychurch's body was burnt next day and the Dreads moved on eastward through the forest. Joseph reported on the relations and meetings between Defence Force personnel and his group of Dreads at Beline prior to the events of 12 February.

Eric Joseph had been found seriously injured at the roadside near Boetica shortly after the incident and was taken to hospital. Other members of the group were later involved in setting up an armed road block at Belles, where they stopped cars and threatened passengers. Three of these Dreads were killed in a police raid. The leader, Pokosion, continued to evade capture and later organised the abduction and murder of another farmer, Eden Bellot, in the heights of Morne Prosper. One of the SLR machine guns traded for marijuana by the DDF was subsequently handed back to the police by other Dreads from Belles.

Other incidents at that time included the murder of police officer Lugay who had been active against the terrorists and who was lured up to Fond Colé where he was shot dead. The finding of the corpse of a Mahaut youth some time later, led to accusations of police reprisals.

Coup and Invasion Attempts

On 7 March 1981, while the Honychurch kidnap was still unsolved, Miss Charles announced that the security forces had discovered a plot to overthrow her Government on 14 March during Carnival celebrations, in connection with which the arrests had taken place, under emergency powers, of Patrick John, Defence Force senior officers Newton and Reid and a DLP executive member and a former Director of Broadcasting as well as Cpl Howell Piper of the DDF. These arrests had been precipitated by an intriguing series of events, beginning with the detention of Reid and another DDF member after French officials reported an attempt by them to buy drums of acid in the French islands. While in the cell at Police Headquarters in Roseau on 6 March, Reid had tried to send a letter to an alleged accomplice which was intercepted by police. The contents gave clues to the even broader involvement of mercenaries from the United States.

Because of the state of the Defence Force since the 1980 elections and in the light of the key role allotted to the DDF in executing the planned coup, the government also announced the disbanding of the Force. Legislation to formalise this was passed in the Assembly in mid-April after a debate in which government cited severe criticisms of DDF personnel in the reports of two enquiries carried out in 1978 and 1980.

The bizarre story which emerged out of the events between March and June 1981 pointed to the launching of a coup attempt involving the Defence Force and other local recruits including a group of Dreads, notably those led by Leroy Ettiene, and American and Canadian mercenaries. Among the mercenaries were members of the racist Klu Klux Klan and neo-Nazi groups aided by US$10,000 in donations from an unidentified underworld leader who wanted to use the island as a base for drug-trafficking and international fraud.

That invasion threat ended on 27 April when United States Federal agents, operating on tips from a charter boat owner and the Ontario provincial police, arrested two Canadians and eight Americans near New

The ten handcuffed mercenaries walk into a Louisiana jail shortly after being apprehended by the FBI while embarking for Dominica. Michael Perdue at top of picture.

A US Federal agent shows some of the weapons and ammunition taken from the mercenaries intended for use in the Dominica coup.

Orleans as they prepared to set sail for Dominica with ammunition, arms landing craft and supplies.

Code-named Operation Red Dog, the invasion was designed, according to US leader of the group Michael Perdue, to oust Prime Minister Charles and to install Patrick John. He would have acted as ruler and in turn have named mercenaries and their backers to important posts. But unknown to the plotters, the matter had been leaked to the Ontario police who passed the word to superiors and American investigators. The boat owner, Michael Howell, meanwhile, had alerted agents of the United States Bureau of Alcohol, Tax and Firearms that he had been detained by men who said they worked for the CIA.

The authorities installed an agent on Mr Howell's ship and recorded meetings by the plotters. Dominica was alerted through the US State Department and already the Roseau police were tracking the local turn of events. On the night of 27 April the mercenaries met at a Louisiana marina with undercover Federal agents, who convinced them to put their semi-automatic assault rifles, shotguns and explosives in one truck while they rode in another. Instead of being driven to the boat however, the mercenaries were driven to an open area where they emerged from the vehicle in the glare of floodlights and 100 Federal and State lawmen.

The ten men arrested appeared in a Louisiana court and nine were sentenced to imprisonment for different terms on various charges related to the invasion attempt. Perdue gave evidence of meetings with DDF personnel and others in Dominica at which agreements were reached on plans to stage the coup.

In a mopping-up operation in Dominica, a Canadian, Mary Ann McGuire, was arrested and found guilty of being involved in the local preparation for the invasion arrival. Two others who arrived hoping to rescue her from prison were deported. She had been found out when a clerk became suspicious of the dramatic words of a cable she sent: 'Alexander is Dead' meaning that the plot had been uncovered.

Meanwhile other Dominicans had been arrested for their alleged role in the coup attempt. Government called a tribunal within two weeks of their detention to consider the validity of their arrest. In October 1981, the nine men were committed for trial before a magistrate in Roseau. Four accused, John, Reid, Joseph and David were kept in custody, but the magistrate ordered five other detainees to be released for want of sufficient evidence against them.

On 19 December that year, there was another coup attempt. It commenced at about 3 am when armed and masked men tried to seize the prison and control the police headquarters and armoury in a simultaneous operation. Led by Major Newton, it was aimed at releasing Patrick John and his co-defendants from imprisonment before their trial which was scheduled to open in the following month. It was to have involved raiding the armoury and eradicating the government.

One policeman was killed and several others injured during the engagement while ex-DDF corporal Howell Piper was shot dead at the prison. The Commissioner of Police, Oliver Phillip, was among those seriously injured during the action at police headquarters. Later that day police shot WTO Benjamin, identified as one of the attackers. Involvement of French citizens in the smuggling of weapons was uncovered and the French authorities, reportedly acting on direct instructions from Paris, rendered immediate material assistance to the security forces.

Of the seven ex-Defence Forcers who were arrested and tried in June 1983 for the murder of the police Constable Alexander, six were found guilty and sentenced to hang, while one was found not guilty and released. Ironically at John's trial a year earlier, Judge Mitchell found no case for the defendants to answer and so the ex-Prime Minister and the other accused were released. The State however appealed against the decision, and the Court of Appeal found in favour of the State in regard of John, Reid and David and ordered a new trial to take place.

Steering a Course

The unsettling detractions during the first three years of DFP government were not allowed to halt the development projects and the reorganisation of certain key areas of administration, foreign affairs and investment programmes. Miss Charles had always noted that her government would require to embark on a two-pronged policy upon taking office: repairing neglected infrastructure and systems while at the same time initiating new projects.

By 1983 her intense campaign of negotiations abroad had resulted in a substantial flow of financial and technical assistance and increased opportunities for the training of Dominicans in skills necessary for key areas of the public and private sectors.

Health, education and social programmes spreading training and general services throughout the rural areas had been boosted by significant contributions from UNESCO, WHO and the Pan American Health Organisation as well as government to government assistance direct from national aid agencies.

The Prime Minister's initial disappointment with the private sector and other non-governmental institutions, which she felt were not bearing their full load of participation in development, was based on her belief that parliament alone was not the beginning and end of the democratic system. She had advocated that the principles of self-reliance and self-government must pervade every branch and activity of island life. Free and responsible

US President Reagan and Prime Minister Eugenia Charles brief the US and international press on the Grenada crisis.

professional or community institutions were just as important as local and central self-government, Miss Charles believed.

Very gradually a change in political ideas was being noticed. The population were realising that leadership now demanded a high degree of professionalism not only in dealing with local circumstances but also with the highly competitive field of aid negotiations, investment seeking and foreign affairs. A significant contributor to this new mood of stability was the man who was elected in 1983 by the House of Assembly to be Head of State. Up to then each term of the Presidency had been short-lived. The first President Fred Degazon had fled the country. Jenner Armour was then selected as Acting President to end a constitutional crisis. Aurelius Marie assumed office when Armour chose to resign to contest the 1980 general elections. So the election of Clarence Seignoret, a former Cabinet Secretary, to the post, was really the first settled Presidential appointment that the island had enjoyed in four years of independence. From 1983 to 1993 Seignoret won the respect of all Dominicans for his disciplined yet easy style, the concern he took to educate the country on matters of protocol and his support for the cultural traditions of Dominica and defence of its natural environment. Knighted by Queen Elizabeth II when she visited the island in 1985, Sir Clarence was awarded the Order of Merit by the state on the completion of his two terms as President in 1993.

Miss Charles' detractors have accused her of an abrasive attitude towards resolving matters of state but the situation facing Dominica when she took office in 1980 could not have been tackled by excessive 'sweet-talk' and a faint heart. It required strength and perseverance which Miss Charles had learned the hard way during over ten years in Opposition. For this reason she tends to be impatient with those people who do not share her capacity for strenuous resolve. This factor has sometimes caused pressures to surface among certain senior civil servants, statutory boards and even members of her own Cabinet, evident in her dismissal of Minister Henry Dyer in 1983.

Her fervent belief in the methods of democratic government as laid down in the constitution which she herself had helped so much to compose, has brought her into conflict with political parties which she felt were attempting to undermine that system of government. Her aversion to communism has been the cause of some of the bitterest attacks upon her government as well as the source of her most powerful support. This was seen even before September 1981 when Government came into conflict with the Alliance group over accepting a party-to-party offer from the ruling Communist Party of Cuba to provide scholarships for Dominicans. The Charles Government has expressed its opposition to the establishment of diplomatic relations with Cuba 'until it is proved that Cuba's role in the Caribbean is not to destablise some of the countries which are opposed to her ideology'.

Miss Charles' leadership role in the Caribbean was dramatically highlighted in October 1983, when as Chairman of the Organisation of East Caribbean States, founded in 1981, she worked with other Caribbean leaders in spearheading the invitation to the United States for intervention in Grenada. Her role in this affair dominated the international media and led to greater recognition of Dominica and the region as a whole.

The Grenada intervention was immediately precipitated by the murder of Prime Minister Maurice Bishop and other members of his cabinet as well as over 100 civilians following a leadership struggle within that island's Revolutionary Government. Fellow members of the OECS were alarmed at this escalation of tension within their area and the assassination of a fellow-member of the Organisation's council at a time when relations between the Grenadian leader and other member states were improving rapidly. Besides this, however, was the growing concern which all other OECS governments had harboured about the build-up of arms and Cuban/Soviet backed military personnel on the island. The OECS leaders were also alarmed at the ruthless brutality exhibited by the new strong men towards the Grenadian people during their first few days in power. This was totally inconsistent with the OECS ideals for the modern Caribbean and they were aware that the citizenry of Grenada were powerless to defend themselves against this onslaught. Then there was the matter of internal security within each island state. The subversive activities of small groups of political dissidents and their associations with the military government in St Georges were known to be linked with Libya and North Korea.

Miss Charles' involvement in the massive armed intervention which followed at the end of October unleashed a mixed barrage of condemnation, primarily from international forums, and widespread support from Grenadians and the Caribbean people in general. Dominicans welcomed her back from Washington with an emotional motorcade all the way from Melville Hall and through Roseau. In November, the Prime Minister defended the OECS action before the Commonwealth heads of government in New Delhi, India. The Grenada affair also heralded in a period of greater co-operation between OECS members in defence, coast-guard services and security.

Involvement in the US Caribbean Basin Initiative (CBI) and other similar partnership programmes has emphasised Dominica's growing ties with the US. Trade and socio-cultural links between these two countries date back to even before the establishment of that giant North American union in 1776. Emigration northwards, air transport and mass media communication advances have strengthened that bond which has had an ever-increasing influence on the lifestyle and attitudes of our island people.

24
Inventing a Nation

The high point for Dominica under the Freedom Party government was 1988. In ten hectic years since Independence, the island had resurrected from the damage of hurricanes and coup attempts and strengthened its economy. Tourism figures were rising, the price of bananas was good and a feeling of unaccustomed confidence was in the air. The mood was further strengthened by visits of heads of government of each of the CARICOM states and of thousands of Dominicans who returned home from Britain, North America and elsewhere to celebrate 'Reunion '88'. The year-long open house was aimed at encouraging Dominicans overseas to see the improvements and to consider returning permanently to settle and invest in their island. It was also intended to send a message to the rest of the Caribbean that Dominica was back on its feet. In the midst of the celebration the situation did indeed look and feel upbeat but in reality the year was a short plateau rather than a rung on the ladder.

Looking back on that period five years later Prime Minister Charles commented bitterly that the years since then had not been very kind. 'When we celebrated our tenth anniversary as a nation in 1988, we were on the brink of an economic breakthrough. The wealth of our country had increased and all communities had an equitable share. Public confidence was high and the prospects for the future looked good. But,' she lamented, 'there have been many unfavourable changes.'

She noted that even though we are not among the poorest of the world, the level of our dependency makes us vulnerable to changes in the external environment. The main impact came from changes in international trade and aid which she listed as: The establishment of the European Single Market, a threat to the banana trade of the island. The future effects of the North American Free Trade Agreement NAFTA. The fall of communism and the developments in Eastern Europe leading to international focus on those new emerging democracies thus redirecting foreign aid away from the Caribbean. The new CARICOM arrangement for a common external tariff affecting the duties on imports was one change coming from within the region.

The list itself says much about the fragile base on which the economy existed and by the same token, the mainspring of the Freedom Party's success in 1980s. Dominica was more dependent on bananas than any other member of the Windward Islands. High prices during the mid 1980s gave farmers no inclination to take up the call to diversify into other crops which appeared to have less returns. When prices began to fall due to changes in Europe there was no safety net in place to soften the economic collapse. At the same time rising debt related to loan arrangements made with the IMF and World Bank in the 1980s were causing concern. Loans had been taken out for projects which it was hoped would have stimulated productivity and generated the income necessary to enable repayment to proceed smoothly over the long term. These were associated with structural adjustment programmes which typically consist of a package of economic reforms, based on the philosophy of 'earn more' – primarily from increasing productivity with exports – and 'spend less' usually by cutting government expenditure particularly by tightening up on the civil service. The government found itself caught in a situation where it was unable to regulate the activities of foreign earnings while under pressure to reduce government expenditure.

The change in US attitude after the fall of communism in Eastern Europe was another blow to the Prime Minister and her government. After having played along with the United States and the two Republican Party presidents during the 1980s, the government had reaped financial benefits for its determined support of the US intervention in Grenada. In April 1987 Miss Charles received the James Monroe Memorial Award from President Reagan in recognition of her role in the Grenada affair. The award, said Reagan, was based on Monroe's philosophy of 'protecting the New World from the depredations of foreign imperial powers'. It was with a hint of a feeling of betrayal that Miss Charles told the nation in November 1993, 'The United States in particular, seems to have withdrawn from its close relationship with our region and aid flows from that country have virtually dried up.'

During the heady days of the 1980s journalists and political commentators in Dominica and the region had warned that the relationship should be tempered with caution. Experience elsewhere in Latin America had shown that US goodwill, particularly towards a tiny friend, was subject to the changing mood of its political interests. Additionally there was an awareness that a careful balance had to be maintained to ensure that friendship was not taken for an open licence by Washington to take arbitrary decisions affecting Dominica's affairs.

In the event Miss Charles made the most of what she could get out of the US while the going was good. The threat of communism was the tool that she had used so adeptly on the US State Department and USAID to get more money for projects in Dominica. Evidence of hurricane damage and coup attempts were all grist to the mill. Her political argument was that if the US did not help, the DFP government would not be able to provide the high visibility projects which would keep it elected. And if the DFP lost, weak 'communist-influenced groups' would take over and there would be a resurgence of instability on the doorstep of the United States. Paranoia over the communist threat was even directed at the leaders of non-governmental organisations, former supporters of the MND Alliance, who were attempting to promote small scale development projects through community action. The government's main suspicions were directed at members of the Small Projects Assistance Team (SPAT), Oxfam and, ironically, the US Save the Children Federation. The latter was effectively closed down and sent packing by government pressure. Other factors influencing this behaviour was the desire of government to control and dispose of the funds itself and the fear that project leaders would gain some political foothold in the communities as a result of their aid programmes.

As the threat of communist hegemony faded, the DFP attempted to shift the line of argument replacing the threat of communism with the threatening impact of the international drug trade. US military helicopters and manpower were already assisting the local Special Service Unit (SSU) arm of the police in destroying pockets of marijuana in the hills. In 1991 the captain and 11 crew members of a Colombian cargo ship were arrested and charged with smuggling 3,051 lbs of cocaine valued at some US$93 million or almost the equivalent of the annual state budget. The ship was seized and sold and the drugs were publicly burnt in a huge trench at Copt Hall. After long drawn out legal proceedings the Colombians were deported in March 1993. Miss Charles was presented with a plaque by the US in recognition of her prompt action and in receiving it did not fail to underline the threat that drug smuggling posed to internal security.

The spectre of Dominica turning into another Haiti was also increasingly being used in speeches by government ministers in the 1990s. Foreign Affairs Minister Brian Alleyne conjured up the picture of 'several little Haitis' when he spoke before the United Nations General Assembly in 1993. In 1994 the London *Times* quoted Eugenia Charles as saying, 'If bananas go down, Haiti will be like apple pie compared to us.' The shock factor seemed always necessary to ensure that the donor countries were not allowed to forget Dominica.

Whatever her tactics, Miss Charles did not miss an opportunity to try to get something for the island whenever the chance arose. Heads of State seemed to warm to her outspoken frankness. In spite of the small size of the country she governed, the Prime Minister had made quite a name for herself. Paramount among the honorary degrees and national honours which she received was the knighthood granted to her by Queen

Elizabeth II while attending the Commonwealth Heads of Government Conference in Harare, Zimbabwe in 1991.

The political upheavals and the social and physical dislocation caused by Hurricane David in 1979 meant that the Charles administration was the first government since Independence to effectively attempt to chart a course for the country. Many aspects of governance were being instituted for the first time particularly in foreign affairs and international aid and relations. In seeking solutions the people as a whole were inventing a nation. Behind the economic improvements was a record of good financial housekeeping for which the government was universally praised by the World Bank and donor countries. But Dominicans, who, according to one calypsonian were 'feeling the heat' of these strict financial measures, soon seemed less enthusiastic.

Much of the DFP's apparent success in the 1980s was due to very large doses of foreign aid for road building and other infrastructural projects. The millions of dollars which poured in helped with employment and internal circulation of cash. It was hoped that all this would jump-start the economy, but the battery itself was too weak. If one subtracts the unprecedented amounts of foreign aid, and cuts the $1.6 million which came into the country every week in 1988 from banana exports, then one is left with virtually nothing with which to run a country. Not even the much vaunted tourist industry would have much impact. Finding a way out of this cycle of dependency, which has been our fate since the Treaty of Paris in 1763, is the challenge of future governments. The new colonialism is based on market forces controlled by the trade agreements of powerful metropolitan states coupled with their control of communications technology beamed into almost every home.

In 1983 when the first cable television service, run by Marpin TV, began operation in Dominica, the Prime Minister was impatient with those who raised concern about the effects of its adverse influence. In one travel magazine she was quoted as saying it would be good for Dominicans. 'They can see the starving children of Ethiopia and realise how lucky they are here.' But the impact of eight TV channels beamed by satellite from the United States 24 hours a day into the households of some three-quarters of the island's population became noticeable. When she addressed the nation on National Day in November 1993, the Prime Minister made it one of the main themes of her message. What she saw happening around her had obviously altered her opinion.

'Domestically, changes are taking place rapidly in the quality of family life, social behaviour, attitudes to each other, community spirit and enterprise, the unselfish giving in voluntary service, among many others. These changes have been brought about, to a large extent, by rapid and intense communications systems of modern technology, mainly through the television media. Fashionable though these changes may be, they are all wrong.

And we must admit that, and we can all endeavour to do something about them. We need at this period of our independence to recapture our own independence of thought and action.'

But the opportunity for that had already been lost. The neo-colonialism of metropolitan-controlled communications technology is directly opposed to 'independence of thought and action'. The very power of small island leaders to influence the societies which they lead has been undermined. Their power to direct a course for their communities to create development best suited to the realities of their island state is being severely challenged. The attentions and expectations of their people are focused elsewhere, as they reject the reality outside their own windows. Added to this social flux in the 1990s was the emergence of a new élite; 'the banana children' as one sociologist put it. This group had been born during the banana boom in the 1950s. They had benefited from the educational reforms under the Le Blanc era in the 1960s and 70s. By the 1980s they had risen to positions of influence in the commercial sector and public service 'bureaucratic bourgeoise'. Many of them rapidly bought out the old businesses and lands of the declining 'mulatto gros bourg' (most of whose children had emigrated to the US and Canada). By the 1990s this new élite had become power brokers in politics, law, business and on statutory boards. In spite of the struggling economy, status was exhibited in lavish houses, highly bred guard dogs and expensive vehicles. On the other end of the scale, also reflecting the US lifestyle which many now yearned for, were the growing urban slums. Here, in dress, drugs and disillusionment is a growing, tragic imitation of the ghettos of Chicago and Miami and the back alleys of Kingston, Jamaica.

Politics and General Elections

Against the backdrop of the mighty economic and political changes on the world stage in the 1980s, the personality-driven micro-politics of Dominica rambled along. In February 1985 the Dominica Labour Party which had been split into two factions for some time, (the DLP and Dem-Lab), reunited as the Labour Party of Dominica after months of talks between leaders Oliver Seraphine and Michael Douglas. Douglas took over as leader of the reunited party giving it some coherence after five years of chaos. In June, Douglas accused the DFP of receiving election funding from the CIA. He was repeating an allegation made in a book on the CIA, *Viel* which had just been published in the US written by Bob Woodward who had exposed the Watergate scandal in the 1970s. Miss Charles denied the charges, but author Janet Higbie in a biography of the Prime Minister published in 1993 indicated that if granted, it was likely the funds, amounting to US $100,000, would have gone to the DFP election campaign. The DFP certainly did distribute a generous amount of promotional material, manifestos and campaign gimmicks in the weeks before the poll. At the elections held on 1 July the DFP won 15 of the 21 seats in the House of Assembly. The Labour Party of Dominica won five, including Patrick John who won the St Joseph seat. Rosie Douglas, campaigning under his own United Dominica Labour Party, won his seat at Paix Bouche. Once again Charles Savarin, former CSA general secretary, lost the contest for the Portsmouth seat and shortly afterwards was appointed Dominica's ambassador to the European Community based in Brussels where he served for seven years. Patrick John held his seat for less than a year on account of being found guilty of attempting to overthrow the government of Dominica in 1981 and being sentenced to 12 years imprisonment at a retrial of the case. In the by-election held for the St Joseph seat on 5 May 1986, Wilmut Shillingford of the DFP won over the DLP's Rosie Mills.

On 5 July 1988, 20 years to the day since the Freedom Fighters began their protest action against the ruling Labour Party, another new political party was founded. The Dominica United Workers Party was launched by

Leader of the Opposition, Edison James, addressing farmers on 10 May 1993. One of the several protest demonstrations held on the subject of falling banana prices.

a six-member steering committee chaired by Edison James. He was a former manager of the Dominica Banana Marketing Corporation, who was elected leader of the party at an inaugural meeting in October.

In local government, the DFP appeared to be no less manipulative than the DLP before it. In a bid to control the Portsmouth Town Council in August 1987 it overrode the elected majority of councillors and through the nomination system ensured the appointment of one of its supporters as Mayor. In November the following year, the Prime Minister announced a one year postponement of the Roseau Town Council elections which had fallen due. This postponement was attacked by both the DLP and the UWP.

In the House of Assembly, Crispin Sorhaindo, a former Vice-President of the Caribbean Development Bank, was elected Speaker of the House of Assembly on 19 January 1989. In 1993 he was chosen as the new President of Dominica on the retirement of Sir Clarence Seignoret. Marie Davis Pierre who had served as Speaker since 1980 and as Clerk of the House since 1967 had dedicated herself to maintaining the order of parliament in both capacities through twenty-two of the most turbulent years the chamber had ever known.

In September 1989 Prime Minister Charles broke her leg during a visit to Taiwan when she slipped and fell in her hotel room. The injury took a long time to heal and for several months after her return to Dominica she governed the country from her home at Wallhouse at Loubiere.

Political activity heated up in the first five months of 1990 as all the parties went on the campaign trail in preparation for the general elections. For the first time television was used as an election tool. The DFP scraped home to its third consecutive victory in the elections of 28 May with its majority reduced from 13 seats to only one. The DFP won 11 out of the 21 Assembly seats while the UWP, contesting for the first time, gained six seats to become the official opposition. The DLP won four seats, the same number as in the outgoing parliament. The maverick Dominica Progressive Party was not a serious contender, the public meetings of its leader 'Pappy Baptiste' being more a subject of mirth than political analysis.

A record low turn out of 66.6% suggested that many traditional DFP and DLP supporters stayed away. By percentage of the electorate, figures showed that the DFP would govern with an overall minority vote of 49.4%. The UWP got 26.9% and the DLP 23.5%. The remaining 0.2% were spoilt ballots. It was significant that the six constituencies won by the UWP encompassed the most productive banana farming areas of the island, indicating the farmers' concern and growing apprehension about their future. Despite all the publicity and promotional hype emanating from the Ministry of Agriculture over the previous five years it appeared that the farmers in the field had not been impressed. Several seats were won by very narrow majorities ranging from 16 to 40 votes.

The hierarchy of the Freedom Party were visibly stunned by the result. It was a hollow victory and celebrations were muted. However Miss Charles said that her policies would not change. 'I am looking forward to the next five years in office,' she said. 'I'm going to do what I want to do now; I don't care what they think, because I am not going to stand again.' She later created a political furore by announcing at a victory celebration rally at Point Michel that the party should not be blamed if 'our eyes fall on those 11 constituencies who voted us into office.'

All 11 successful DFP candidates were given government posts in an enlarged Cabinet. The Prime Minister appointed former teacher and long time DFP loyalist Rupert Sorhaindo as Senator and Minister for Education. Some months later Maynard Joseph was quietly invested with responsibility for Agriculture and Charles Maynard was left with Trade and Tourism.

This term was to be marked by hurdles on all fronts beginning with wage negotiations with the police and civil service, a subject which had made the last years of the previous Labour Party government so bitter. At the annual 3 November Independence Day parade there was a boycott by police and cancellation of the parade after public workers had staged a one-day strike over pay increases. The banana crisis overshadowed everything as economic reports began to bury the 1980s' optimism with a regular issue of adverse statistics on almost everything except tourism arrival figures.

But in early 1992 the island momentarily held its breath in shock when Michael Douglas made the announcement that he was terminally ill with an inoperable cancer of the pancreas. He died on 30 April, one week after his 52nd birthday. He had been first elected to the House of Assembly in 1975 on a DLP ticket for the Portsmouth constituency and served as Minister of Agriculture and later as Minister of Communications and Works. He had been fired from the government by Patrick John and as a member of the CNS joined the interim government in 1979 as Minister of Finance. He was Leader of the Opposition from 1985 to 1990. The DLP representative for Grand Bay Pierre Charles took over as deputy leader of the party until election for a new leader was held on 29 November 1992. Roosevelt 'Rosie' Douglas was elected to replace his brother as head of the party. He had won the by-election for the vacant seat in July. At first Rosie appeared to bring a new vibrancy to the DLP but his preoccupation with his international agenda was out of touch with the domestic concerns of the electorate. His quixotic offer to mediate in the Anglo-Irish peace effort in late 1993 was ridiculed both by the DFP and the UWP and he was accused of links with terrorism. This probably contributed to the loss of a DLP seat to the UWP in a by-election in the Salybia constituency on 20 December 1993.

The Cold War anti-Cuban stance taken by Eugenia Charles and the DFP mainly to fall in line with the wishes of the US during the 1980s softened in March 1993 when Cuba's Ambassador to the United Caribbean Alvaro Cabasas met External Affairs Minister Brian Alleyne. Discussions centred on the possible expansion of trade relations and establishment of diplomatic relations. In fact Dominica had been informally trading with Cuba for some time beforehand while both governments turned a blind eye. Dominica Coconut Products, with the help of contacts through Rosie Douglas and Dominican Cuban resident Claxton Thomas, had engineered a trade arrangement for sale of soap products to Cuba via Jamaica in spite of the Dominica government's official anti-Cuban position. In July 1994, Dominica joined with 25 other Caribbean countries, including Cuba, to establish the Association of Caribbean States ACS.

In August 1993 the Freedom Party elected Brian Alleyne as leader-designate to take over the helm when Eugenia Charles resigned. This she had announced she would do at the end of the 1990–1995 term. He was voted in by party delegates over three other contenders: Charles Savarin, who had ended his stint in Brussels, Alleyne Carbon and Charles Maynard.

Tying up the Coup Cases

Legal proceedings related to those involved in the attempted *coup d'état* in 1981 lingered into the 1990s. In April 1985 six former military personnel convicted for the murder of police officer Alexander in 1981 had their appeal against their conviction dismissed by the Court of Appeal. In February of 1986, the government recommended that the death sentences on five of the six former soldiers convicted of murder during the attack on the police station, should be commuted to life imprisonment. The exception was Frederick Newton whose sentence remained and who was hanged at the Stock Farm prison on 8 August 1986.

Meanwhile in October 1985, Patrick John was convicted and imprisoned for conspiring to overthrow the government in 1981. John and former defence force captain Malcome Reid were jailed for 12 years each and salesman Julien David was sentenced to five years. The trial was the second on the same charges, since a retrial was ordered after the government successfully appealed against the acquittal in 1982. Judge Satrohan Singh told John before passing sentence, 'You could not take the idea of not being Prime Minister.' John, he added, was prepared to sell Dominica to foreigners 'to satisfy his lust for power'.

Julien David was released from prison in February 1988. Then on 29 May 1990, the day after the general election, John and others were released. It was no coincidence that the DFP had chosen the same day of the month as the big demonstration in 1979 which had precipitated John's downfall. There were indications that the DFP government, expecting to win with a landslide, had intended that John's release would come while victory celebrations were in full swing thus giving him a salutary lesson of their popularity on the 11th anniversary of his defiant behaviour. Ironically however the streets of Roseau were silent, even mournful, on 29 May 1990.

John was released having served less than four years of his 12 year sentence. Fifteen other prisoners were also released on the same day including Malcome Reid, former captain in the disbanded Defence Force, who was jailed along with John.

Still in prison was the man whose actions on 12 February 1981 along with others had lit the fuse which eventually blew the whole cycle of events into the open. Eric Joseph had appeared in the High Court in 1983, was found guilty of murdering Ted Honychurch, and was sentenced to hang. For five more years his lawyers lingered through all the various levels of appeal until in 1988 the Privy Council, like the West Indies Supreme Court before it, rejected the appeal and upheld the original sentence in the High Court. From 1988 under Attorney General Brian Alleyne, and then after 1990 under Jenner Armour (whose law firm had originally defended the accused) the government dragged its feet. Then in November 1993, twelve years after the crime was committed, a Privy Council ruling on a case of long delayed execution in Jamaica, ensured that the death sentence was commuted to life imprisonment. The delay by the government appeared to clash with the speedy execution of Newton for a crime of equal severity. All that the Prime Minister said on the subject was , 'I will never be able to tell you the reasons for the delay in carrying out the sentence. There are many and I am not in a position to disclose these to anyone.' The curtains were thus drawn on the last act of a saga which had given the government its baptism by fire in 1981.

Concrete, Current and 'Colas'

The end of the 1980s also saw the completion of major infrastructural projects which were expected to provide the physical framework upon which economic expansion could take place. Private sector investment in this area was led by the British multi-national corporation Cable and Wireless which during the decade carried out a total modernisation of the island's entire telephone network installing digital technology, making Dominica the first country in the world to go entirely digital. This massive project, made more challenging because of the island's mountainous terrain, cost some EC $33 million and was funded entirely by the company's own resources. In July 1987 telephone connection with the east coast was opened again after eight years. The lessons of Hurricane David were not lost on the company and wherever feasible lines were buried. Long distances across the island were linked by microwave transmitters so that a chain of dishes and 'passive reflectors' perched on prominent mountain peaks connected the whole island without use of telephone lines except within village units. The introduction of fax, mobile telephones, beepers and other services backed by excellent international connections, placed the best technology within the reach of every home. By the mid 1990s, in a population of 75,000, there were 20,000 subscribers. In October 1985 Cable and Wireless renewed its contract with government for a monopoly on the country's telecommunications service for another twenty years.

That same year the Dominica Electricity Corporation (DOMLEC) signed a contract with a US company for the installation of 22 miles of electric transmission lines as part of government's rural electrification programme which involved wiring up 25 villages and hamlets on the east coast for the first time. Giant poles and lengths of cable were dragged over some of the most inhospitable areas of cliff and forest. Lines were slung over deep valleys, gorges and ravines until the entire circumference of the island was tied into the grid. Meanwhile at Laudat, Trafalgar and in the Freshwater Lake area work was progressing on the enlargement of the hydro-electric production capacity in order to serve the increased numbers of households and businesses connected. There was also the idea, that by providing cheaper electricity than most other Caribbean states there would be an added incentive for foreign investment in manufacturing and industry. As it turned out, unexpected problems with the terrain, particularly on the Trafalgar cliffs, conflict with certain contractors and initial maintenance expenses due to landslides, coupled with an economic downturn and lack of expected foreign investment, put a damper on the original optimism about the scheme. Even at an increased cost however, the project did increase the supply of electricity available although there was still a significant need for back-up power provided by generators at Fond Colé using imported diesel. At the end of 1990 the new electric station was opened at Laudat with the usual fanfare and ministerial addresses. With the completion and opening of the Trafalgar power station a year later, the entire project, costing an officially declared figure of EC $63 million was complete. But a legal dispute with the French company Nord France over the laying of pipes, lingered on for years adding a costly burden in fees and settlements.

Airport and seaport services were improved. In 1986 a French aid loan of EC $3 million was provided for the construction of an airport terminal at Canefield. More French funds in 1993 were obtained to construct a cruise ship berth along the Roseau bay front. In 1990 work began on port expansion and development projects at the deepwater harbour at Woodbridge Bay including an extended pier and container park. In the north at the Cabrits a new cruise ship berth and tourism reception centre was constructed on the site of the old garrison dockyard. Both projects were financed by the government itself at a cost of EC$28 million.

In August 1993 a major extension to the Roseau waterfront was opened. As well as providing a vital sea defence along the severely undermined bay front, the sixty foot wide infill allowed for increased parking and better flow of traffic. A new general post office replaced that department's cramped quarters in the old market house dating from 1810. The entire project was financed by the British government whose Overseas Development Minister Linda Chalker stated that Dominica 'exemplified the example of steady policies of prudence and self-reliance'. In 1993 British aid to the island since political Independence had amounted to 21.5 million pounds sterling.

Agriculture

The massive injections of money and effort ploughed into the agricultural sector during the 1980s had not borne the desired fruit by the 1990s. Millions of dollars went to various projects aimed at crop diversification. The Canadian financed coconut rehabilitation project was extended and it constructed several new feeder roads facilitating the transportation of crops from isolated farms. A coffee project sought to revitalise the stands of coffee while a similar cocoa rehabilitation scheme funded by the Canadians absorbed EC $9 million in grant aid. Similar smaller projects promoted passion fruit, avocado and other three crops. Meanwhile in May 1991 the Citrus Growers Association, founded in the 1950s, which had spearheaded the marketing of Dominica's second most important crop, was dissolved. Only 14 of the association's 400 members were still able to sell their produce. DAI, a government-supported corporation attempted to utilise the disbanded L Rose & Co grapefruit juicing plant at Bath Estate, but heavy losses on export orders caused its collapse.

Still it was the banana industry which caused Dominica its greatest anxiety. As Prime Minister Charles pointed out, 'It has provided the engine for growth in income and employment. To be more basic, it has facilitated the education of our people, expanded the rural housing stock, improved standards of living throughout the countryside, and created a dynamic rural sector which is democratic, enterprising and forward-looking.' But in summarising the position at the end of 1993 she detailed the stark facts of the threat to society and domestic economy.

'The establishment of the European single market has put our trade in bananas in jeopardy as the preferred position which we formerly enjoyed in the United Kingdom market is being gradually eroded and the forces of competition (and a very unequal competition it is) have lowered the price and the incomes we get from our banana exports. Internally, in our search for solutions to the many problems that now beset the industry, disruptive conflicts threaten to sever the bonds of unity that previously held us to a common purpose and a unified strategy.'

Locally, money and technical assistance had been poured into the industry. In July 1984 operations had been restructured with the establishment of the Dominica Banana Marketing Corporation to take over banana marketing and management of the industry from the DBGA under a new scheme with support funding and technical assistance from USAID and the British Overseas Development Ministry. In September 1986, government wrote off all the debts of the DBMC but by the end of the decade its debts had multiplied once more. 1988 had been one of the best years, earnings were good and the DBMC aimed at a production target of 74,000 tonnes of fruit that year. The eventual output totalled 70,357 tonnes compared with 63,874 tonnes in 1987 with gross earnings increasing from EC$86 million to EC$99.5 million. But even then, according to the DBMC Chairman the quality of the fruit left much to be desired. Exports in 1989 dropped to 46,000 tonnes because of damage due to the close passage of Hurricane Hugo. Income never again reached the 1988 figures. For most of her last term in office Eugenia Charles put all her energy into trying to negotiate more favourable terms for the industry in the face of increasing pressure from the powerful US-backed Latin American producers. She lobbied tirelessly in Europe, but the physical and economic realities of small farmer production at home and the overwhelming forces at work in international trading circles, particularly in relation to the European Community and the General Agreement on Tariffs and Trade GATT, appeared insurmountable.

'Trying Something'

Economic growth in 1988 was greater than financial institutions had predicted but by the time of the annual budget of July 1991 capital spending was being cut as aid funds from foreign donors for big projects declined. In March 1992 the General Statistical Office announced that real GDP growth in 1991 had been 2.1% compared with 6.6% in 1990. Officials of the department said the drop in the growth rate had resulted from the decline in banana production and the weakening of the manufacturing and construction sectors. By the beginning of 1992 the external public sector debt including the debt to the IMF was US$83.9 million compared with US$63 million the year before. The population had declined as young people emigrated in search of employment elsewhere. The census of May 1992 registered a population of 71,794, a fall of 3.8% on the 1981 figure of 74,625. The population of Roseau was 20,755 or 28.9% of the total.

In the face of these sobering economic and demographic figures a period of desperation hit the government as it sought schemes which they hoped would conjure up some speedy investment of foreign capital. Yet they had to avoid being accused of the recklessness for which they had criticised the Labour Party in its quest for foreign investment in the 1970s. Suspicions had been nurtured by the unfulfilled deals under the John regime. Sharp operators are always on the lookout for desperate gullible governments. As experience all over the Caribbean had shown, there was often the need to have the courage to refuse certain temptations dangled by smooth-talking businessmen from North America, Germany or wherever seeking to hoodwink local politicians with offers of jet airports, casinos, condominium complexes, free port zones and fenced-off tourism enclaves in return for slavish concessions and brief political kudos. It was found necessary carefully to assess investment so as to separate the genuine entrepreneurs from the 'carpet baggers'. Already the DFP government had been stung by such cases as that of a German who persuaded it to part with ten acres of prime land at the Cabrits on easy terms based on visions of a marina and condominium construction. Another got them hooked on the idea of spa development using the island's hot springs. Paid handsomely for a report on the subject he also encouraged them to select a German company for an EEC funded contract to supply material for tourism promotion. Not much more than an issue of brochures and posters turned up, out of the extensive package originally agreed upon and paid for. Talk of a much publicised Italian-funded spa resort in the Soufriere Valley rose and faded. Lesser adventurers came and went wasting civil servants' time and effort. But as one minister commented, 'We have to try something.'

It was reported at the end of December 1990 that government had concluded the outline of a 50-year agreement with Guiness Management Ltd, registered in the Cayman Islands, for development of a tourist resort, industrial park, commercial centre and residential area on an 880-acre site at Point Ronde on the north-west coast. After complicated land transfer arrangements it was purchased by Windward Estates/Guiness Ltd for EC$1.8 million. The formal agreement was signed in May 1991 and Managing Director Byron Ellison said, 'Work is expected to start within three months'. It was clear to several independent observers that Ellison and his small group were merely speculators. The UWP were quick to point out that rather than bringing in capital, the company had actually borrowed the purchase money from the local branch of the Royal Bank of Canada. In September 1993 the government terminated the agreement with Guiness Ltd announcing that the company had failed to find the necessary capital for the scheme.

While all these efforts were being made to attract foreign tourism-related investment, numerous local entrepreneurs were busy building up the industry on their own, making significant contributions to the tourism product. There was a marked increase in complimentary articles by travel writers in international magazines intrigued by the lush 'unspoilt' nature of Dominica. The island's exciting scuba diving sites complete with submarine boiling springs and volcanic pinnacles encrusted with coral outcrops, attracted an increasing number of scuba divers. Dominican operators pioneered that sector. Small hotels, almost all locally owned, ensured the desired interlinking of the industry with farmers, craftsmen, transport sector, restaurants and tour guides. While other Caribbean destinations suffered the economic side effects of 'all inclusive' resorts and international chain hotels, more money per visitor was staying in the island than elsewhere. As numbers of arrivals rose, local investment in the industry responded favourably. The delicate balance which had been destroyed by over-rapid growth elsewhere was being avoided in Dominica. It would be important for the sake of the whole society that the balance should be maintained. But by 1995, increasing crime and drug-related assaults were causing concern in the industry.

In October 1988 the Industrial Development Corporation IDC merged with the reconstituted Tourism Division into a new entity called the National Development Corporation NDC. Under the ministerial portfolio of Charles Maynard the activities of the corporation, particularly in tourism, was given maximum publicity and a high profile in national affairs. The world-wide interest in 'eco-tourism' was an important factor and Dominica attempted to make a niche for itself in this market. The National Park Service played an increasingly vital role in tourism through the establishment and maintenance of national parks, information and interpretation as well as its earlier focus on forest management and wildlife conservation. Meanwhile cruise ship calls also increased rapidly as combined action by the Ministry of Tourism and local shipping agents provided attractive shore excursions and improved facilities at Roseau and Portsmouth. The tourism industry proved that regulated growth coupled with local ownership, management and involvement at all levels, provided the stability for sustainable development.

The powerful leverage which foreign concerns could have over government decision-making was exemplified in January 1993 by a threat that the American owned Ross University School of Medicine based in Portsmouth, might be closing down operations and leaving Dominica. Ross was owing sizeable sums accumulated over many years through failure to pay dues to the state under the agreement of its establishment in Dominica. Government, in need of money, pressed for payment. Ross declared that as a result it would have to leave the island. The people of Portsmouth whose shopkeepers, bus drivers and landlords depended on the medical students for their business, became agitated. Their parliamentary representative Rosie Douglas protested. Even Attorney General Jenner Armour, who owned property at Portsmouth, threatened to resign. Government backed down and the Prime Minister devised a settlement with Ross whereby the value of the land occupied by the school at Picard became part of an exchange whereby no money changed hands. The land would belong to government after 16 years, Ross was saved from having to hand over any funds, and the continued economic benefits from student rentals and purchases in Portsmouth was assured.

Government, through the Agricultural and Industrial Development (AID) Bank and the NDC had invested in the construction of numerous factory sheds at Canefield industrial estate since 1980. The project was based on the now increasingly outmoded theory of development economics, that enclave industries in poor countries would be the spring board to a more permanent manufacturing sector while providing employment. This effort hardly lived up to expectations. As a study by Dominican Cecilia Green bluntly put it, 'Dominica has generally had poor luck with enclave industries.'

The study notes that: 'The employment generating capacity of these enterprises in the short term cannot be denied. Neither however can other salient aspects – their fickleness; their totally self-serving motivations; the price the nation and workers have to pay for the dubious advantage of temporary, low paying, hazardous and mind numbing employment.'

Another report on Dominica and the world economy goes further, by suggesting that such enclaves contribute to long term poverty by encouraging people from the countryside into Roseau for jobs that do not exist, disengaging them from the island's source of production in agriculture thus creating an unemployed urban lumpen proletariat which adds to the social burden of the state. As it turned out, few of the small number of the foreign 'finishing-touch' industries which came ever stayed very long in Dominica. Significantly, by the mid 1990s, most of the sheds were occupied by Dominican-owned and operated small businesses.

The Caribbean Basin Initiative was another disappointment for Dominica. The CBI, officially the Caribbean Basin Economic Recovery Act (CBERA) announced by President Reagan in February 1982, became law on 5 August 1983 and has been in effect since January 1984. But the detailed list of restrictions and commitments imposed on what could or could not be exported to the US by the islands made it little more than political window dressing in the aftermath of the Grenada crisis.

Professor Pontojas-Garcia who identifies the underlying model for the CBI as being Puerto Rico's Operation Bootstrap, summarised its pitfalls. 'It seems clear that the political and economic conditions established by the CBI are mainly intended to stimulate US investments in the region and only marginally to result in expansion of locally owned productive activities.'

Growing disillusionment with the CBI among participating countries prompted the US government to introduce a number of additional measures starting in November 1985. Among the most important of these was the

Puerto Rico Investment Programme allowing Puerto Rico to finance 'twin plants' in other islands under section 936 of the Internal Revenue Code. One of Dominica's only benefits from this was the setting up of the ABC cardboard container-making plant at Belfast. Ironically it was producing boxes in direct competition to the regionally owned WINERA container plant based at St Lucia.

New Citizens: The Chinese Dominicans

Shortly after taking office in 1980 the DFP government joined some 23 countries in the world in choosing to recognise and have diplomatic relations with the Republic of China on Taiwan rather than the government of mainland China. The prospects of aid from Taiwan was one of the main factors influencing this decision. A resident diplomat arrived shortly afterwards and gifts in money and kind soon followed. In 1985 a loan of EC$2.6 million was given to finance purchases of equipment for fishing. Chinese technicians in fishing and farming began work on technical assistance programmes at various parts of the island. Visits by Chinese sports and cultural groups became regular occurrences. As ties were increasingly strengthened during the latter half of the 1980s influential citizens and politicians were invited on free trips to Taiwan. On their return, ministers of government, rather like explorers who had seen the promised land, eulogised the society they had seen. Speeches were peppered with references to Chinese discipline and hard work, of big buildings and busy cities. They argued that the Taiwanese presence would influence Dominicans' 'need for a new work ethic' and change 'the laid-back attitude by training and example'. It was inferred that the introduction of Chinese from Taiwan and Hong Kong into Dominica would not only provide foreign capital and employment but would 'improve the mentality of Dominicans'.

On 31 May 1991 parliament approved a government proposal to offer economic citizenship to Taiwanese and other persons from countries of the Pacific rim, more specifically Hong Kong. It was argued that similar programmes had been initiated elsewhere to attract foreign investment. Dominica passports would be granted to those persons and their families who deposited US$35,000 in an escrow account which would be considered to be an 'investment' in Dominica, thus classing the 'economic citizen' as an 'investor'. The vast majority of these economic citizens had no interest in Dominica but desired a passport which would enable them to travel more easily than a Taiwanese one. By March 1992 economic citizenship had been granted to 34 Taiwanese and to their 58 dependants. By June the following year some 466 Taiwanese and their dependants had been granted citizenship with total deposits announced to be US$5.8 million. Dominicans who described what was going on as 'a sale of passports' were rebuffed by government ministers with the argument that they were simply giving investors a stake in their investment.

The programme of economic citizenship and Taiwanese settlement was spearheaded by Grace Tung, a Taiwanese business woman who the government had appointed as Dominica's consul general to Taiwan and later also to Hong Kong. She had an interest in encouraging people to take up economic citizenship and approved lists of applicants for government acceptance. She was also president of a company which purchased the ailing Layou River Hotel and surrounding lands from Dominican shareholders prominent among whom was the Prime Minister herself. Indeed all shareholders were relieved to be rid of the financial albatross which had been hanging around their necks for twenty years. In April 1992 a ground breaking ceremony conducted according to Buddhist rites took place at Layou River Hotel and Grace Tung unveiled her plans for a 250 room 'Shangri La Hotel', 700 seat conference centre, hillside villas and Chinese health spa 'to be started within a few months'. After over two years had passed and no building had commenced, there was a start on 'revised plans'. Meanwhile a Chinese laundry, restaurant and jewellery assembly and retail workshop became the first tangible investments to begin operation.

Charge d'Affaires of The Republic of China on Taiwan, Mark Hsia (centre), accompanied by police while trying to talk to demonstractors at the start of a protest march against 'economic citizenship'.

As the economic citizenship scheme hit the headlines a group calling themselves 'the concerned citizens', led by former interim Agriculture Minister Atherton Martin, barrister Alix Boyd Knight and conservationist Mona George Dill raised public doubts about the entire scheme in an effort 'to alert Dominicans to this unhappy marriage'. The UWP who had voted in favour of the concept of economic citizenship in May 1991 were now strongly opposed to the details of its implementation. On 29 May a year later the party organised a demonstration around Government Headquarters which drew some 400 people protesting against 'the sale of citizenship'. Already Taiwanese in Dominica had begun to complain of incidents of harassment and abuse. In December 1992 it was disclosed that Taiwanese Chargé d'Affaires Mark Hsia was advising prospective applicants for citizenship on the resentment in Dominica over the programme. He said he had no choice but 'to tell them the true situation'.

At the same time government, concerned at the tide of opposition to the scheme, began reviewing the citizenship policy which in turn led to some concern from Grace Tung as to the status of current and future economic citizens. The Dominica Association of Industry and Commerce (DAIC), although supporting the concept, called for a minimum deposit of US$100,000 per applicant. Visits were made to Taiwan and Hong Kong by Ministers Jenner Armour and Charles Maynard in the hope of returning with some positive investment commitments so that they could bolster Dominicans' confidence in the scheme. In April 1992 Armour had, with great publicity, lauded Miss Tung as 'Amazing Grace'. Another twist was added when Kenny Alleyne, brother of Foreign Minister Brian Alleyne left his post as manager of the National Development Corporation and became an employee of Miss Tung. As Dominica became more deeply embroiled in the quagmire of economic citizenship it became obvious that a careful division had to be maintained to ensure that the sovereignty of government and its continued ability to control the situation was not compromised in the face of possible increasing Chinese demands backed by access to funds and business pressure in relation to their ultimate influence on political power.

Our history has shown us that attempts at introducing 'new men and new energy' in an effort to 'develop' Dominica has been tried many times before: the large land sale of the 1760s and introduction of British investors; American Loyalist pioneers in the 1780s; Bell's attempt to bring over South African Boers and his brief success with another wave of British settlers in the early twentieth century; failed schemes for a Swedish residential colony at Point Mulatre in the 1950s; a similar idea at Mero for Americans and English pioneered by the Marquis of Bristol at his Emerald Hillside Estate; others who were expected to come with the Sunday Island Port Authority or Don Pierson's Free Port Zone encompassing the north coast. All these attempts arose and fell or never got off the ground. In each case, it has been some other people from some other place who have been presented as the ones who will deliver the holy grail. One day perhaps it will be realised that the future lies right here within the people of Dominica themselves.

In defending her government's record towards the end of her fifteen-year term as Prime Minister, Dame Eugenia summed up her case:

> 'If we reflect well, if we remove all our biases, if we provide a fair examination, we will conclude that it is not only in the area of infrastructural development and improvements that we have excelled in advancing this country forward way into the modern age, but in the building of people's confidence in themselves, in establishing a creditable image abroad, in earning the respect of our donor friends and in the provision of adequate health, education, recreational, financial institutions and community services, to expand the necessary environment for our people to excel in whatever endeavour of life they have chosen.'

After all the attempted schemes and dreams there seemed, in the end, to be a realisation of where the future lay:

> 'We have tried many times. Success is not easy for Dominica . . . [but] undoubtedly there is a bright and growing point in the private sector that we must give our attention. That is the small business enterprise . . . It is our determination to provide a special incentive scheme for small businesses. That will include the provision of equity and technical assistance to enable good project ideas to flourish in production and marketing. We would like to expand and improve agro-industry for special markets, and to link in agriculture with our tourism promotion and development.'

Subject as the island is to the turmoil and buffeting of world affairs and an erratic international economy, such self reliance appears to be the most realistic option for a micro state in a troubled world. Standing on this threshold of time we can look back and take stock of where we have come from and what we are. An island of natural splendour upon which man has been a passing visitor in many forms; as Igneri and Kalinago/Carib seafarer, European settler and African inheritor, rising and falling through their own periods of domination. The French influence is everywhere in our Afro-Creole culture; most noticeable in our language; while the British left their greatest mark on our system of government. And the story is still unfolding. The concept of an independent nation state may soon be found to be impractical. New systems and regional relationships will be devised.

As a self-governing people we alone are responsible for the choices we make. Peddling our birthright in return for some brief political kudos and the modern equivalent of flattery and trinkets has wasted enough in time and dashed hopes. The game of accusing the ex-colonial power or former political factors for every malaise becomes senseless with the passage of time. It is not enough simply to be against something, one must be for something. Our problems demand new ideas, new plans, new ways of looking at the basic needs of our life.

This new challenge means a great number of things; it means a new inner strength both for each Dominican and the society as a whole. It means in brief a more positive citizenship. This story is woven of the threads of events, political changes and personalities which have brought us to the present day and which have created what we are. We, now, shall have to create what will be.

After God the Land.

Bibliography

CHAPTER 1   An Island of Fire

Dutton, R, Bailey, W et al *Caribbean Landscapes* Collins, 1983.

Multer, Weiss & Nicholson *Antigua, Reefs, Rocks & Highlands of History* LISA Antigua, 1986.

Lambert, D *The Cambridge Guide to the Earth* Cambridge University Press, 1988.

Beard, JS *The Natural Vegetation of the Windward and Leeward Islands* Oxford Forestry Memoirs. #21, 1949.

Bond, J *Birds of the West Indies* Collins, 1960.

Howard, RA *The Vegetation of the Antilles* ed A Graham. Elserier Press, Amsterdam, 1973.

Linhart, YB *Local Biogeography of Plants on a Caribbean Atoll* Journal of Biogeography, 1981.

MacArthur, R & Wilson, E *The Theory of Island Biogeography* Princeton University Press, 1967.

Malfait, B & Dinkelman, M *Circum-Caribbean Tectonic and Igneous Activity* Bulletin of the Geological Society of America 83, 1972.

Mattson, PH *Plate Tectonics in the Caribbean Nature* London, 1972.

Grisebach, A *Flora of the British West Indies Islands* London, 1864.

Vail, PR & Hardenbol, J *Sea Level Changes during the Tertiary* Oceanus v 22, 1979.

National Parks Service, Dominica Miscellaneous Pamphlets and booklets by James, A, Honychurch, P and Zamore M on Dominica Flora and Fauna.

Sigurdsen, H *Studies on Volcanism in Dominica* University of Rhode Island College of Oceanography, 1978.

Hodge, WH *The Vegetation of Dominica* 1943.

CHAPTER 2   The First Settlers

Rouse, I *The Entry of Man Into the West Indies* Yale University Publications in Anthropology 61, 1960.

The Tainos Yale University Press, 1992.

Rogers, DJ *Some Botanical and Ethnological Considerations of Manihot Esculenta* Economic Botany 19, 1965.

Meggers, B & Evans, C *Lowland South America and the Antilles*. Ancient Native Americans, WH Freeman & Co, 1978.

Fewkes, J *Relations of Aboriginal Culture and Environment in the Lesser Antilles*. Bulletin of American Geographical Society 46(9), 1914.

Goodwin, RC *The Prehistoric Cultural Ecology of St Kitts*, PhD diss. Arizona State University. Tempe, 1978.

Mézin, L *Archéologie Martinique*. Musée Départemental d'archéologie. Fort de France, 1991.

Petitjean-Roget, H *Les Population Amérindiennes Aspects de la Préhistoire Antillaise,* Historical Antillais #1, 1981.

Allaire, L *L'archéologie des Antilles* Grand Atlas de l'Archéologie Universalis. Paris, 1985.
Collected Papers *Proceedings of the Annual Congress for Caribbean Archaeology*, 1976–1989.
Nicholson, DV *The Importance of Sea Levels in Caribbean Archaeology*. Antigua Archaelogical Society, 1976.
Honychurch, L Fieldwork notes with H Petitjean-Roget on archaeological site, Soufriere, Dominica, 1976.
Nicholson, DV *The Archaeology of Antigua and Barbuda*. Museum of Antigua & Barbuda, 1992.
Alegria, R *History of the Indians of Puerto Rico*. Colección de Estudios Puertorriquenos, San Juan, 1983.
Olsen, F *On the Trail of the Arawaks*. University of Oklahoma Press, 1974.

CHAPTER 3   The Kalinago
Myers, RA *Island Carib Cannibalism*. New West Indian Guide, Utrecht 58, 1984.
Alegria, R *On the Historicity of Carib Migrations in the Lesser Antilles*. American Antiquity 45 (2), 1980.
Breton, R *Dictionaire Caraïbe-Français*. Auxerre, 1665.
Bullen, R *The Archaeology of Grenada*. Contributions of the Florida State Museum, Social Sciences, no 11, Gainsville, 1964.
Cruxent, JM *Early Man in the West Indies*. Scientific American, 221 (5), 1969.
Glazier, S *Impressions of Aboriginal Technology: The Case of the Caribbean Canoe*. Proceedings of the 13th Caribbean Archaeology Congress, 1991.
Gonzalez, NL *Sojourners of the Caribbean: Ethnologenisis and Ethnohistory of the Garifuna*. Urbana: University of Illinois Press, 1988.
Nicholson, DV *Pre-Columbian Seafaring Capabilities in the Lesser Antilles*. Antigua Arch Society, 1976.
Cohen, JM *The Four Voyages of Columbus*. Ed & trans Penguin, 1969.
Gullick, CJ *Island Carib Traditions about their Arrival in the Lesser Antilles*. Congress on Pre-Columbian Cultures of Lesser Antilles #8, 1980.
Taylor, D *The Island Caribs of Dominica*. American Anthropologist, 1935.
The Caribs of Dominica. Smithsonian Institution Bureau of American Ethnology, Bulletin #119, 1938.
Notes on Star Lore of the Caribees. American Anthropologist, 1946.
Tales and Legends of the Dominica Caribs. Journal of American Folklore, 1952.
Languages of the West Indies. John Hopkins UP, 1977.
Hodge, WH & Taylor, D *The Ethnobotany of the Island Caribs of Dominica*. Webbia Vol 7 n 2.

CHAPTER 4   Columbus and Spain
Keen, B Trans & ed, *The Life of the Admiral Christopher Columbus by his son Ferdinand*. Rutgers University Press, 1992.
Morison, SE *Christopher Columbus, Mariner*. Meridian, 1983.
Walker, DR *Columbus and the Golden World of the Island Arawaks*. Ian Randle, Pub. Jamaica, 1992.
Cardona Bonet, WA *Shipwrecks in Puerto Rico's History Vol 1 (1502–1650)*. San Juan, Puerto Rico, 1989.
Verin, PM *Carib Culture in Colonial Times*. Paper delivered at Congress for Study of Pre-Columbian Cultures in Lesser Antilles #2, 1968.
Midas, A *Caribs and Frenchmen: the Struggle for the Islands*. The Caribbean 14(2), Port-of-Spain, 1960.

Arens, W *The Man-eating Myth*, Oxford UP, 1979.
Harris M *Cannibals and Kings. The Origin of Cultures*, Fontana/Collins, 1978.
Boromé, J *Spain and Dominica 1493–1647* in Aspects of Dominican History, Government Printery, 1972.
López de Haro, Bishop of Puerto Rico c 1644 *Memorial to the King*. (ms) British Museum, Add ms 36326.
Whitehead, NL *Lords of the Tiger Spirit A History of the Caribs in Colonial Venezuela and Guyana 1498–1820*. Foris Pub Holland, Caribbean Series #10, 1988
Sauer, C *The Early Spanish Main*. Berkley. Univ of California Press, 1966.
Hume P & Whitehead N *Wilde Majesty* Oxford University Press, 1992.
Hakluyt, R *The Principal Navigations*. 12 vols Glasgow, Maclehose, 1903–5.
Warburton, E *Memoirs of Prince Rupert*. London, 1849.

CHAPTER 5 Land of Two Nations

Labat, JB *Nouveau Voyage aux Isles de l'Amerique*. The Hague, 1724.
The Memoirs of, 1693–1705. Frank Cass, 1970.
Moreau, J–P *Un Flibustier Français dans la mer des Antilles en 1618–1620*. Edition Pierre Moreau, Paris, 1988.
Montbrun, C *Les Petites Antilles Avant Christophe Colomb*. Editions Karthala, 1980.
Moreau, J–P *Les Petites Antilles de Christophe Colomb à Richelieu (1493–1635)*. Editions Karthala, 1992.
Watts, D *The West Indies, Patterns of Development, Culture and Environmental Change since 1492*. Cambridge University Press, 1987.

Andrews, KR (ed) *English Privateering Voyages to the West Indies 1588–1595*. Hakluyt Society, 1959.
Crouse, NM *French Pioneers in the West Indies 1624–1664*. New York, Colombia University Press, 1940.
Davies, J *The History of the Caribby Islands*. London (translation of C de Rochefort, 1658), 1666.
De Rochefort, C *Histoire naturelle et morale des Isles Antilles de L'Amerique*. Paris, 1658.
Du Tertre, J–B *Histoire générale des Antilles*. 4 vols Paris, 1667–71.
Haring, CH *The Buccaneers in the West Indies in the 17th century*. Archon Books. Connecticut, 1966.
Anon *Antigua and the Antiguans*. London, 1844.
Warner, A *Sir Thomas Warner: Pioneer of the West Indies: A Chronicle of his Family*. London, 1973.
Allfrey, R *Indian Warner*, Dominica Herald. Nov 10, 1962.
Beckles, H *Kalinago Resistance to European Colonisation of the Caribbean*. Caribbean Quarterly Vol 38 #2 & 3, 1992.
Dunn, R *Sugar and Slaves*. WW Norton & Co US, 1973.

CHAPTER 6 France Moves In

Burns, Sir A *History of the British West Indies*. London, 1954.
Crouse, NM *The French Struggle for the West Indies 1665–1713*. New York Colombia University Press, 1943.
Roberts, WA *The French in the West Indies*. Cooper Square Pub New York, 1971.
Boromé, J *The French and Dominica 1699–1763* in Aspects of Dominican History. Government Printery, 1972.
Higham, CS *The Development of the*

Leeward Islands under the Restoration 1660–1688. Cambridge, 1921.
Williamson, JA *The Caribbean Islands under the Proprietary Patents.* Oxford University Press, 1926.
Proesmans, R *Unpublished ms* Bishop's House, Roseau, 1970.

CHAPTER 7   The British in Dominica

Atwood, T. *The History of the Island of Dominica.* Johnson. London, 1791.
Byres, J *Map of Commissioners for Sale of Land of the Ceded Island of Dominica.* London, 1778.
Aytoun, J *Memoirs of a Redcoat in the Caribbean.* Cambridgeshire Regiment, 1982.
Anon *Some Observations on our new West India Colonies.* London, 1764.
Edwards, B *The History, Civil and Commercial, of the British Colonies in the West Indies,* London, 1793, 1801, 1826.
Jefferys, T *Map of the Island of Dominica.* London, 1768.
Smelser, M *The Campaign for the Sugar Islands 1759.* Institute of Early American History & Culture, University of North Carolina Press, 1955.
Maps *War Office, Colonial Office, at the Public Records Office, Kew.* Numbers 3381–3391 all of Dominica. Plans of Towns, Fortifications, Estates, 1765–1832.
Hotblack, K *Chatham's Colonial Policy.* London, 1917.
Hayter, T *The Papers of William Viscount Barrington 1755–1778.* Army Records Society, 1988.

CHAPTER 8   The Plantation

Lowndes, J *The Coffee Planter,* London, 1801.
Lewis, MT *Journal of a West India Proprietor.* London, 1834.
Goveia, EV *Slave Society in the British Leeward Islands at the end of the 18th century.* Yale University Press, 1965.
Parry, JH & Sherlock, PM *A Short History of the West Indies.* Macmillan, 1971.
Augier, Gordon, Hall, Reckford *The Making of the West Indies.* Longmans, 1964.
Brunias, A *Paintings and Prints depicting Society and Scenes in Dominica,* c 1770–1796.
Caudeiron, MA *From Livre to Doullette.* In Dies Dominica, Government Printery, 1965.
Patterson, O *The Sociology of Slavery.* London, 1971.

CHAPTER 9   The French Return

Boromé, J *Dominica During French Occupation 1178–1784,* in Aspects of Dominica History. Government Printery, Roseau, 1972.
Goodridge, CA *Dominica – The French Connection.* Aspects of Dominica History. Government Printery, Roseau, 1972.
Priestly, HI *France Overseas through the Old Regime.* New York, 1939.
Southey, T *A Chronological History of the West Indies.* 2 vols London, 1827.
Pares, R *Yankees and Creoles.* Oxford University Press, 1956.
Davis, ND *One Hundred Years Ago or the Battle of Dominica.* Demerara, 1882.
Mair, J *Eyewitness Account of the Action of 12 April.* MS Jamaica Archives, 1782.
St Johnson, Sir R *French Invasions of Dominica.* Private Pub, 1933.

CHAPTER 10   The Fighting Maroons

Roberts, LA *The Negres Marron of*

Dominica. Notes. Roseau Public Library.
Price, R Ed *Maroon Societies: Rebel Slave Communities in the Americas.* Anchor Books, 1973.
Davis, DB *The Problem of Slavery in Western Culture.* Pelican Books, 1970.
Robinson, C *The Fighting Maroons of Jamaica.* Kingston. Collins & Sangster Press, 1969.
Craton, M *Testing the Chains: Resistance to Slavery in the British West Indies.* Ithaca. NY, 1982.
Colonial Office Files, Public Records Office, Kew. CO 71–10 Orde dispatches 1786 Feb–July. CO 72–2 Instructions for Orde. Oct 1783.

CHAPTER 11   Revolution and Ransom

Colonial Office Files, Public Records Office, Kew. CO 71–19 Orde to Grenville. Dispatches 1791. CO 71–20. Orde to Grenville. Dispatches 1791. CO 71–25. Orde to Grenville. Dispatches 1793.
Orde, Sir J Papers. National Maritime Museum, 1786–1805.
James, CLR *The Black Jacobins.* Vintage. NY, 1963.
Hamilton, H Governor. *Account of French Invasion.* Royal Commonwealth Society Library, 1794–1796.
Buckley, RN *Slaves in Redcoats. West India Regiments 1795–1815.* Yale University Press, 1979.
Johnstone, AC *Defence of Hon AC Johnstone.* Evidence at his trial, varied commentaries; letters relating. London, 1805.

CHAPTER 12   The Last Maroon War

Colonial Office Files, Public Records Office, Kew. CO 71–51. Account and returns of Runaway Slaves, 1814–1815.
Anon *Account of the effects of the Anglo-American War of 1812 and Hurricane of 1813.* Roseau Public Library, 1818.
Dominica Chronicle 1825 bound volume. Dupigny. Roseau.
Coleridge, HN *Six Months in the West Indies in 1825.* London, John Murray, 1832.

CHAPTER 13   Peace and Freedom

Dary, J *The West Indies, before and since Slave Emancipation.* London, 1854.
Gurney, JJ *A Winter in the West Indies.* New York, 1824.
Hall, D *Absentee Proprietorship in the West Indies, to about 1850.* Jamaica Historical Review, 10, 1959.
Green, WA *British Slave Emancipation: The Sugar Colonies and the Great Experiment 1830–1865.* Oxford. Clarendon Press, 1976.
Murray, DJ *The West Indies and the Development of Colonial Government 1810–1834.* Oxford. Clarendon Press, 1965.
Riviere, WE *Labour Shortage in the West Indies after Emancipation.* Journal of Caribbean History, 4, 1972.
Ragatz, LJ *The Fall of the Planter Class in the British Caribbean 1763–1833.* Octagon Books NY, 1963.
Sewell, WG *The Ordeal Of Free Labour in the British West Indies.* New York, 1862.
Sturge, J & Harvey, T *The West Indies in 1837.* London, 1838.
Williams, E *From Columbus to Castro.* 1970.

CHAPTER 14   The Years of Change

Boromé, J *How Crown Colony Government came to Dominica.* Aspects of Dominica History. Government Printery, Roseau, 1972.

Boromé, J *Charles Gordon Falconer.* Caribbean Quarterly 6, 1959.

Newspapers, Dominica: *Chronicle*, 1813–1827. *Colonist*, 1825–1868. *Dominican*, 1839–1907. *New Dominican*, 1871–1873. *The People*, 1877–1880. *Dial*, 1882–1893.

Colonial Annual Reports Blue Book. Royal Commonwealth Society Library. Cambridge.

CHAPTER 15   An Unsettled Society

Imray, J & Nicholls, HAA MS *Notes and Memoirs on Events 1840–1893.* Private & Papers of Allfrey Collection Roseau.

Churchill, JS *Reports in Colonial Annual Reports. Blue Books.* Royal Commonwealth Society Library. Cambridge, 1882–1887.

Haynes Smith to Ripon *Copies of Extracts from the Correspondence on the Subject of the Late Fatal Disturbances in the Island of Dominica.* CO 152/186 & House of Lords Sessional Paper 280, 1893.

Beachey, RW *The West Indies Sugar Industry in the Late 19th Century.* Oxford Press. Blackwells, 1957.

CHAPTER 16   New Men, New Energy

Froude, JA *The English in the West Indies or the Bow of Ulysses.* London. Longmans Green & Co, 1888.

Henderson, J *The West Indies.* London, 1906.

Bell, H *Notes on Dominica and Hints to Intending Settlers*, 1903.

Bell, H *Glimpses of a Governor's Life.* Sampson Low. London, 1946.

Report on the Caribs of Dominica. Colonial Reports: Misc #21 (HMSO: London 1902), 1902.

Treves, Sir F *The Cradle of the Deep.* Smith, Elder & Co. London, 1910.

Aspinal, Sir A *A Wayfarer in the West Indies.* London, 1927.

Hamilton, Sir R *Report of the Royal Commission to Inquire into the Condition and Affairs of the Island of Dominica* (C 7477), 1894.

Report of the West India Royal Commission 1897. Colonial Office.

Naftel, CO *Report on Agricultural Capabilities in Dominica.* Colonial Reports. Misc #9, 1898.

Trollope, A *The West Indies and the Spanish Main.* London, 1860.

Ober, FA *Camps in the Caribbees*: David Douglas. Edinburgh, 1880.

Rhys, J – *Smile Please.* Andre Deutch, 1978.

Fadelle, FS 1902 – *Dominica a Fertile Isle.* Roseau, 1902.

The Boiling Lake of Dominica. Roseau, 1904.

Nicholls, Sir HA *Report on the Layou Flats.* Roseau, 1883.

CHAPTER 17   Between Two Wars

Agar, EA *Diary of Experiences relating to the Great War in Dominica.* MSS, 1914–1918.

Wood, Hon EFL *Report on Visit to West Indies and British Guiana.* Parliamentary Papers (Cmd. 1679), 1922.

Napier, E *Call Back Yesterday.* Bim Magazine. Barbados, 1965.

Rhys, J *The Day they Burnt the Books.* Short story in collection. Penguin Books, 1971.

Proceedings of *The West Indian Conference* held at Roseau, Dominica. (Castries 1932).

Stanley Rae, J & Armitage-Smith *Conditions in the Carib Reserve, and the Disturbances of 19 September 1930.* (HMSO London), 1932.

Waugh, A *The Sugar Islands*. London, 1958.
Moyne *Report of Commission of Inquiry*. Visited 1938–39 (HMSO London), 1945.
Davis-Pierre, M *The House of Assembly of Dominica, Procedure and Working Methods*. Government Printery, 1975.
Watts, Sir F *Report on Agricultural Conditions in Dominica*. Imperial College of Agriculture. Trinidad, 1925.
Stockdale, Sir F *Development and Welfare in the West Indies*. Report. London, 1940–42.
Gullick, CJ *Myths of a Minority*. Van Gorcum, 1985.

CHAPTER 18 The Church
Roberts, LA *The Contribution of the Roman Catholic Church to the Development of Dominica*. Roseau, 1972.
Coke, T *A History of the West Indies, Containing the Natural, Civil and Ecclesiastical History of Each Island*. 3 vols. Liverpool, 1808–1811.
Pemberton, SR *History of the Church of England in Dominica*. MS, 1876.
Oliver, VR *The Monumental Inscriptions of the British West Indies*. Dorchester, 1927.
Moris, J, Bishop of Roseau *Account of the History of the Roman Catholic Church in Dominica, Parish by Parish*. MS Bishop's House, Roseau, 1922–1957.
Proesmans, R *Unpublished Papers on Religious History*. Bishop's House, Roseau.

CHAPTERS 19–24
Information on these five final chapters are from the author's own notes, observations, participation in events, experiences and interviews with the people involved. Local newspapers covering this period:
The Herald, 1961–1972
The Dominica Star, 1965–1982
The Dominica Chronicle/New Chronicle 1909–1994
The Educator, 1974–1977

GENERAL REFERENCES
Caribbean Insight, Newsletter. London 1985–1994.
Gordon, LK *The Growth of the Modern West Indies*. New York, 1968.
Main Currents in Caribbean Thought. Heinemann. Kingston. Port-of-Spain, 1983.
Beckles, H & Shepherd, V *Caribbean Freedom*. IRP Kingston and J Currey, London, 1993.
Benitez-Rojo, A *The Repeating Island. The Caribbean and the Postmodern Perspective*. Duke University Press, 1992.
Trouillot, MR *Peasants and Capital. Dominica and the World Economy*. J Hopkins University Press, 1986.
Douglas, R *Chains or Change*. Toronto, 1969.
Burra, JAN *Report on Land Administration in Dominica*. Government Report, 1953.
Clyde, DF *Two Centuries of Health Care in Dominica*. Private Pub, 1980.
Fermor, PL *The Traveller's Tree: A Journey through the Caribbean Islands*. London. Murray, 1950.
Green, C *The World Market Factory. A Study of Enclave Industrialization in the Eastern Caribbean*. CARIPIDA, 1988.
Higbie, J *Eugenia, The Caribbean's Iron Lady*. Macmillan, 1992.
Lowenthal, D *West Indian Societies*. Oxford University Press, 1972.

SOURCE LOCATIONS

Archives of Dominica and Documentation Centre, Kennedy Avenue, Roseau: containing Colonial Reports, Court Records, Newspaper files. Government correspondence, local publications from 1765.

Public Records Office, Kew, London.
Rhodes House Library, Oxford University.
Balfour Library, Pitt Rivers Museum, Oxford.
Tylor Library, Oxford.
Royal Commonwealth Society Library, UK.
Bishop's House, Roseau: Moris and Proesman's Papers.
Napier Archives, reports, articles, letters 1930–1965
Allfrey Papers, Roseau.
Roseau Public Library.

Index

Afranchis 54
Agricultural School 153
Agricultural Society 228
agriculture 51, 153–5, 161, 297–8
  of Kalinago 23–4
  peasant 139–41
agro-industries 207–13
aid: foreign 289
Ainslie, George Robert 118
air ports 190–2, 296
Alleyne, Brian 294
Alleyne, Sydney Burnett- 262–3, 266
Allfrey, Phyllis Shand 230–4 passim, 236–7
America: war against Britain 1812 119–20
  War of Independence 83–4
American loyalists: in Dominica 91–3
Anglican church 179–81
  St George's 181
animals: introduction of 9
apprenticeship 123–4
  industrial 125
Arawakan-speaking people 11, 16–17, 25–6
artefacts 14
  Igneri 18
  Ortoiroid 15
  pre-Colombian 16
Assembly 69, 233, 259
  coloured majority in 127
Austin, Leo 253–4, 261–6 passim
avocados 213

'banana children' 290
bananas 189, 207–9, 214, 219, 287, 297–8
  crisis 293
  disease 209
banking 195
Batalie estate: land dispute 137–8
Battle of the Saintes 88–90
bay leaf and oil 212
Bell, H. Hesketh 148–50, 152–3, 187, 193
Bellaire dancing 77
'Belle Croix' 56
Bellot, J. 134
Black Power 242–4
Boiling Lake cauldron 5, 147, 224
Bois Cotlette estate house 72
Botanic Gardens, Roseau 147, 154

Breton, Fr Raymond 41–3, 173
bride-capture: by Kalingo 21–2
British: in Dominica 40–8 passim, 61–71, 100
  recapture of Dominica 88–90
Brown Privilege Bill 123, 127
Bully, Alwyn 204, 257

Cabrits 112, 115, 224
Canefield airstrip 193, 296
cannibalism 22, 38
canoes 18
  Kalinago 24–5
Caribbean Southern Corporation 263, 264
Caribs ix, 11, 20–2, 48, 189
  and cannibalism 22
  flute dance 27
  problems with 161–2
  see also Island Carib; Kalinago
Carnegie Library 150, 151
Castle Bruce estate 124, 216–18, 244
Catholic Social Centre 177–8
cattle mills 160
Caudeiron, Mabel 'Cissie' 205
CBI, Caribbean Basin Initiative 285, 301–2
CDC, Commonwealth Development Corporation 216–17
census: disturbances over 135
Charles, Dame Eugenia 238, 241–2, 248, 254–5, 257, 266, 268–9, 274–6, 278–9, 281–5, 286–94 passim, 305
charm makers: Kalinago 28–9
churches 173–84
Ciboney 11, 15
citrus fruits 210–12, 219
climate 5–9 passim, 206
clothes 80–2
  national dress 82
CNS, Committee for National Salvation 268, 273
Cochrane Johnstone, Andrew 111–14
cocoa 137, 154, 157, 207, 212, 297
coconuts 209–10, 219, 297
'Code Noir' 1685 53–4, 101, 173
coffee 72–3, 119, 154, 206–7, 212, 297
  disease 74, 126
  processing 73, 76

Colihaut 106, 135
  revolt 1795 108–10
Columbus, Christopher 20–1, 30–2
conservation 223–5
constitutions 157–9, 229–30, 233
  Conference, London 1977 254
  Independence 1978 255–6, 257, 260
Cools-Lartigue, Sir Louis 256–7, 267
co-operatives 196–7, 216, 217
coup attempts 279–82, 294
Court House 69–70
Crown Colony Rule 128–34 passim, 159
cruise ship berths 296
cudgelling match 80, 92
culture 204–5

dancing 77, 79, 80, 167
Davies, W. 133–4, 142
Dawbiney, E.S. 142
de Beaumont, Fr Phillipe 43
defence 67–8, 87, 156–7, 170–1
  Force 249–50, 276–7, 279
Degazon, Fred 257, 267
DeGrasse, Admiral 88–9
demonstrations 237–8, 240, 265–7
disasters 252
Dominica 1–3, 9
  Conference 1932 162–5
    delegates to 163
  depression in 120–1, 145
  grants to 148
  name of 26, 32
  nationalities in 36–7
  as neutral territory 46–7, 55
  as no-man's land 47
  as refreshment point 34–5, 38, 113
  self-reliance 305–6
  in Victorian period 145–55
Douglas Bay 68
Dreads, the 245–51, 277–80
drug smuggling 288
Duchilleau, Marquis 85, 87, 94

ecology 13–15
economy 257–8, 289, 298
  and hurricanes 270
education 166–7, 200–2
  Act 1863 200
  and churches 174–5, 177, 183, 200–2
  secondary 201
electricity 150, 192, 296
emigration 205, 298
employment 205
environment: degradation of 4–5, 47–8
erosion: of landscape 4–5
estates: decline of 214–15
evangelists, new 183–4
expatriates 258–9

Fadelle, Joseph 129
Falconer, Charles 128, 130–2, 136–7

Federation, West Indian 230–3
fishing 25, 220
  commercial fresh-water farming 220
  Kalinago 25
FMI 176–7
forest reserves 225
forests: types of 7–10 passim
Fort Young 112, 114
free coloureds 54, 80–2, 100–2
Free French 171–2
free ports 64–5
  scheme 262–5
French: attacks by 84–6, 114–15
  in Dominica 40–60 passim, 85, 87–8, 94, 100, 173
  invasion 1795 106–8
  revolution, and subversion 102–6

games 79–80
gaol 88, 93, 103, 104, 131
Garraway, James 129
general elections 273–4, 292
Geneva estate 74, 214, 218–19
Gormanston, Viscount 141
government: local 195–6, 292
  post-independence 259–60
  pressures on 261–2
  under British 68–71
  under French 54–5
Grand Bay 219
  Jesuits at 56–8
  revolts 103, 135
great houses 78
Grenada 284–5, 287
  Declaration 1971 239–40

Hamilton, George 104–5, 107
Haynes-Smith, William 142–4
health 197–8, 202–4
  primary care 204
Honychurch, Ted 277–9
housing 198–9
huckster trade 213–14
Hugues, Victor 105–6, 110
hurricanes 57, 87, 92, 119–21, 252, 298
  1916 155, 157
  David 1976 194, 198–9, 210, 223, 270–3, 289

Igneri 17–19, 21–2, 26
Imray, Dr John 145–6, 154, 181, 202
independence 253–60
  Day 1978 256
Indian immigration 125
indigenous people 11, 14–15
industry: enclave 301
infrastructure: 1980s projects 295–7
invasion attempts 280–1
Island Carib 20–1, 25–6
Itassie 41, 43

Jacko steps 97
John, Patrick 241–2, 246, 248–9, 253–4, 256–7, 261–2, 264–5, 269, 276–7, 278–9, 281, 294–5

Kalinagos 20–9, 38, 42, 48
  culture 23–4, 29
  legends 27–9
  population, decline of 47
  raids by 44–7 *passim*
  and Spanish 33–6 *passim*
Karifuna group 24
kidnaps 276–9

labour crisis 124–5
La Grange, General 114–15
La guerre negre 136
land: church 176–7
  coastal strip 64, 126, 137–8, 215
  division and sale 62–4, 215–20
  sale, to former slaves 125–6
  tax 141–2
  value 64
landscape ix, 93, 106, 206
language 12–13
  Kalinago 25–6
La Plaine uprising 1893 142–4
La Vallette, Fr 49, 56–8
Leatham, Charles 129
Lebanese 166
Le Blanc, Edward 205, 219, 230–3, 235–6, 239, 241
Leeward Island Federation 132
Le Grand, Commander 50, 51
Lesser Antilles 2–3, 13
limes 140, 154–5, 157, 207, 214
  decline of 160, 211–12
Loblack, E.C. 226–7, 230
Lockhart, A.R. 134, 142

maces 70
malaria 197
malnutrition 197
managers: plantation 75, 78
mango 213
Mariegalante 40
Maroons ix, 71, 88, 93–4
  chiefs 94–7 *passim*, 116
  pacification of 117
  wars 91–9, 116–19
Martel, Fr Guillaume 55, 173
martial law 135, 156
Masquerade 167–9
Maxwell, Charles 122
Melville Hall 191, 192, 217
Methodists 181–3
militia: system, local 70–1
  treatment of 71
missionaries 41–4
Morne Micotrin 4, 6
Mornes Negres Marron 95
Motard, Norbert 109

Moyne Commission 1938 185, 215, 226, 229
mulattos 54, 100–2, 127, 167
  Ascendancy 127–8
  gros-bourg 235, 238, 290
music 79

Napier, Elma 158, 171, 187, 196
Nassief, Elias 214, 218–19
National Day 233
National Parks 224, 225
NDC, National Development Corporation 300
newspapers 70, 127, 129, 177, 236
Nicholls, Sir (Dr) H.A.A. 146–7, 181, 203, 230

Orde, John 91, 94, 98, 102–4
Ortoiroid peoples 15–16, 17

Pagua rock 29
Paulinaire, Jean Louis 103
pegall (conta) 27
Pharcelle, Maroon chief 94, 98, 104, 106
Pierson, Don 263–4
place names 50, 64–6
  changes to 65–6
planning 199–200
plantations 5, 54, 72–82, 100
  problems on 119–20
  society 75–8
  see also estates
plant life 5–10
plantocracy, white 165–6
political parties 229–30, 259–60
population 129, 298
  growth of 54–5, 197
ports 189–90
Portsmouth 41, 64, 125, 188, 190, 223
  1765 town plan 63
  defences at 68
postal service: stamps 150, 213
pre-history 12, 14
Presidents 283–4
Prevost, George 115
Prince Rupert Bay 64, 85, 188, 190
  defences at 68, 113
  hurricane at 120–1
  trading at 37

radio communication 194
Rastas 251
Rawle, C.E.A. 158–9, 163–4, 231
religious: life 55, 62
  riots 136, 138–9
  toleration 184
Riviere, D.O. 134, 142
roads 96, 98–9
  construction 148, 150, 186–9
  feeder system 188–9
  Imperial (Transinsular) 150, 152, 186–7
  tax 142
Rodney, Admiral Sir George 88–90

Rollo, Lord Andrew 58–60
Roman Catholic church 173–9
Rosalie 67
  in first Maroon war 95
Roseau 41, 50, 52, 83, 106, 149, 188, 199
  British attack on 58–9
  cathedral 176
  Deepwater Harbour 190, 296–7
  defences at 68
  depopulation 120
  destruction by fire 87, 115
  as free port 83
  French attack on 85
  market 206
  martial law 1795 105
  settler's house 52
  Town Council buildings 67
Royal Commission 1893 147–8
rum manufacture 76
runaways: see Maroons

St Eustatius 83, 90
St Joseph 199
Saladoid 18
Scotts Head: French capture of 84–5
seed dispersal 5, 7, 9
Seignoret, Sir Clarence 283–4, 292
Seraphin, Oliver 258, 268, 272–4
settlement 14
  pre-Colombian 16
  schemes 215
settlers 11–19, 61–2, 152
  house, Middleham 149
shanties 199
shifting cultivation 126
slaves 33, 51, 53–4
  abolition of trade 117, 122–3
  French 'Code Noir' 53–4
  French, refugees 126
  house 78
  laws for 69, 98
  plantation 78
  risings by 71, 103
smuggling 190
  see also drug smuggling
social: services 194–5
  unrest 242–4
society 165–9
  see also plantation society
songs 169
Sorhaindo, Crispin 292
Spanish impact: in West Indies 32–3
spices 213
sports 204
Stapleton, Sir William 45, 46
state of emergency 244, 251
strikes 251–2, 265, 266
sugar 51, 73–6 passim

  decline 140–1
  plantation 73–5
surnames: origins of 55
Syrians 166

Tainos 17, 20, 22
  genocide of 33
Taiwan Chinese 302–4
tarrish 3
telephones 150, 193–4, 295–6
television, cable 289–90
Templer, P.A. 148
timber 51, 220–2, 224
  co-operative sawmill 222
Toucari 68
tourism 245, 296, 299–300
  adventure 222
  resources for 222–3
towns 64–6
trade unions 226–9
  unrest 251
trading 154
  and American War of Independence 83
  and Free Ports Act 64–5
  by Kalinago 37
  during world wars 157
Trois Pitons National Park 222, 224
Twaveau 142

urban slums 290
US: friendship with 287
  influence of 290

vanilla 207
Vielle Case 41
villages 126
  councils 196
  self-sufficiency of 167
volcanoes 4

wages: field labour 141
Warner, Indian 44–5
Warner, Phillip 44, 45
wars: First World War 156–7
  Second World War 170–2
  Seven Years 58–9
  see also under Maroons
water supply 192–3
Welfare Act 1940 185
West India Regiments 110–11
  Eighth, revolt by 111–14
Willoughby, Lord Francis 44
wood cutting 49

yaws 197

zemis 19, 23
  'three-pointer' 19